Finanzbuchhaltung 4 **Lösungen**

Franz Gianini
Anton Riniker

Finanzbuchhaltung 4

**Ergänzende Bereiche
der Finanzbuchhaltung**

**Geldflussrechnung,
Planungsrechnung,
Konzernrechnung und
Analyse des Jahresabschlusses**

Lösungen

VERLAG:SKV

8. Auflage 2014   ISBN 978-3-286-32348-3

© Verlag SKV AG, Zürich
www.verlagskv.ch

Alle Rechte vorbehalten.
Ohne Genehmigung des Verlages ist es nicht gestattet, das Buch oder Teile daraus in irgendeiner Form zu reproduzieren.

Umschlag: Brandl & Schärer AG

Inhaltsverzeichnis

2 Geldflussrechnung — 9

2.1	Buchungstatsachen und Fonds Flüssige Mittel	9
2.2	Buchungstatsachen und Cashflow	10
2.3	Liquiditätsfonds	10
2.4	Geldfluss aus dem Geschäftsbereich	11
2.5	Geldfluss aus dem Investitionsbereich	12
2.6	Geldfluss aus dem Finanzierungsbereich	12
2.7	Cashflow	13
2.8	Direkte und indirekte Berechnung des Cashflows	13
2.9	Geldflussrechnung der Maestrini AG	14
2.10	Geldflussrechnung des Einzelunternehmens Berini	15
2.11	Geldflussrechnung der Monte Baro AG	16
2.12	Geldflussrechnung der Bellina AG	17
2.13	Geldflussrechnung der Colletta AG	18
2.14	Summarische Geldflussrechnung der Comaris AG	20
2.15	Geldflussrechnung der Panda AG	20
2.16	Walter Meier Holding (WMH) während Jahren ohne Free Cashflow	21
2.17	Jahresrechnung der Musti AG	22
2.18	Jahresrechnung der Huber AG	23
2.19	Geldflussrechnung der Gerber AG	24
2.20	Geldflussrechnung der Bader AG	26
2.21	Geldflussrechnung der Mara AG	27
2.22	Geldflussrechnung der Diener AG	28
2.23	Geldflussrechnung der Kauf AG	30
2.24	Geldflussrechnung der Trevalli SA	31
2.25	Geldflussrechnung der Turbinenbräu AG	33

3 Planungsrechnung — 35

3.1	Planerfolgsrechnung	35
3.2	Planbilanz	36
3.3	Planerfolgsrechnung, Planbilanz und Finanzplan	36
3.4	Planungsrechnungen Domaso SA	38
3.5	Planungsrechnungen Favogno SA	41
3.6	Planungsrechnungen Piazzalunga SA	42
3.7	Planungsrechnungen Breva SA	44
3.8	Mehrjahrespläne der Plano SA	47
3.9	Planungsrechnung der Sesselbahn AG	48
3.10	Comi AG	50

4 Konzernrechnung — 51

4.1	Konsolidierungspflicht	51
4.2	Konsolidierung einer 100%igen Tochtergesellschaft	52
4.3	Konsolidierung Carmen AG und Tamara AG	53
4.4	Konsolidierung mit Minderheitsanteilen	55
4.5	Konsolidierung Miri AG und Franga AG	56
4.6	Konsolidierung Mela SA und Filu SA	58
4.7	Konsolidierung Moderna SA und Oldi SA	60
4.8	Modern Holding	62
4.9	Konzerngeldflussrechnung der Cormi Gruppe	63
4.10	Konzerngeldflussrechnung der Marmic Gruppe	64
4.11	Quotenkonsolidierung	65
4.12	Vergleich zwischen Voll-, Quotenkonsolidierung und Equity-Methode	66
4.13	Wahl der Konsolidierungsmethode und Goodwill	67
4.14	Stichtagsmethode	70
4.15	Stille Reserven in den Vorräten und Sachanlagen sowie latente Steuern	71
4.16	Eigenkapitalnachweis der MH-Gruppe	72
4.17	Eigenkapitalnachweis des Vulcano-Konzerns	72

5 Analyse des Jahresabschlusses — 73

5.1	Analyse der Bilancio SA	73
5.2	Analyse der Erfo SA	73
5.3	Analyse der Bilerfa SA	74
5.4	Stille Reserven auf den Forderungen aus L+L	75
5.5	Betriebsergebnis und stille Reserven	76
5.6	Stille Reserven auf dem Warenlager	77
5.7	Kennzahlen und stille Reserven	78
5.8	Auswirkungen der stillen Reserven auf Kennzahlen	79
5.9	Voraus- bzw. Anzahlungen, Rechnungsabgrenzungen und Bilanzkennzahlen	80
5.10	Analyse der Lagerverhältnisse	81
5.11	Aktivitätskennzahlen (Vorräte und Forderungen aus L+L)	81
5.12	Branchenkennzahlen	81
5.13	Bereinigung der publizierten Jahresrechnung der Handel AG	82
5.14	Leverage-Effekt	83
5.15	Zusammenhang von verschiedenen Kennzahlen	84
5.16	Analyse der Forderungen aus L+L, Verbindlichkeiten aus L+L und Lagerverhältnisse	84
5.17	Finanzierungsarten und Leverage-Effekt	85
5.18	Gesamtkapitalrentabilität und Eigenkapitalrentabilität	87

5.19	Analyse zweier Aktiengesellschaften	88
5.20	Cashflow-Kennzahlen mit kumulierten Geldflussrechnungen	92
5.21	Analyse der Mittelflussrechnung der Gang AG	93
5.22	Verschuldungsfaktor	93
5.23	Verschuldungsfaktor und Cashflow	94
5.24	Analyse der Giazh AG	95
5.25	Kennzahlensystem (Du Pont-Schema)	97
5.26	Aktienbewertung der Marcomis Holding	98
5.27	Aktienbewertung und Aktienanalyse der Duo-Gruppe	99
5.28	Analyse des Konzernabschlusses Schindler 2000	100
5.29	Analyse des Geschäftsberichtes Straumann 2001	103
5.30	Analyse des Geschäftsberichtes Tritech 2002	104

2 Geldflussrechnung

2.1 Buchungstatsachen und Fonds Flüssige Mittel

		Flüssige Mittel (Kasse, Post, Bank)		
		+	0	−
1	Barverkauf einer Maschine	×		
2	Krediteinkauf von Waren		×	
3	Die Generalversammlung beschliesst am 20.2. eine Dividende (= Dividendengutschrift bzw. -zuweisung).		×	
4	Die beschlossene Dividende wird eine Woche später durch die Bank überwiesen (= Dividendenausschüttung).			×
5	Bankbelastung für an der Börse getätigten Wertschriftenkauf			×
6	Zahlung einer bereits gebuchten Lieferantenrechnung durch die Post			×
7	Umwandlung eines (langfristigen) Darlehens in eine Hypothek		×	
8	Kreditverkäufe von Waren		×	
9	Anzahlung eines Kunden auf das Bankkonto	×		
10	Kundenüberweisung auf das Postkonto	×		

2.2 Buchungstatsachen und Cashflow

	Buchungstatsache	(Operativer) Cashflow +	0	−
1	Abschreibung von Mobilien		×	
2	Warenbezug gegen Rechnung		×	
3	Zahlung einer Lieferantenrechnung durch die Post			×
4	Baraktienkapitalerhöhung		×	
5	Verminderung der WB Forderungen aus L+L		×	
6	Warenlieferung an Kunden gegen Rechnung		×	
7	Lohnzahlung durch die Post			×
8	Amortisation (Tilgung) der Hypothek		×	
9	Die Bank setzt eine Kreditlimite aus.		×	
10	Kundenüberweisung auf das Postkonto	×		

2.3 Liquiditätsfonds

Der Fonds Nettoumlaufvermögen beinhaltet auch Positionen, die nicht Zahlungsmittel sind. Eine Abnahme der Flüssigen Mittel bei gleichzeitiger Erhöhung der Forderungen aus L+L oder Vorräte oder Abnahme der Verbindlichkeiten aus L+L führen lediglich zu einer Verschiebung innerhalb des Fonds Nettoumlaufvermögen. Die Liquidität erscheint gleich «gut» wie vorher. Die Veränderung im Fonds wird so aber nicht als Liquiditätsanspannung betrachtet.
Ein Teil der Vorräte ist zudem häufig langfristig gebunden (eiserner Bestand, Pflichtlager) und kann nicht verflüssigt werden.

2.4 Geldfluss aus dem Geschäftsbereich

	1	2	3	4	5	6
Warenertrag	560	840	740	1 200	560	700
+/− Δ Forderungen aus L+L	− 15	+ 20	− 10	+ 30	+ 15	+ 38
Warenaufwand	−392	−700	−800	− 900	−392	−260
+/− Δ Warenvorrat	+ 15	− 30	+ 20	− 10	− 15	+ 4
+/− Δ Verbindlichkeiten aus L+L	− 12	− 5	+ 9	− 50	+ 12	0
Geldfluss aus Geschäftsbereich	+156	+125	− 41	+ 270	+180	+482

Erläuterungen anhand des Unternehmens 1

Warenertrag	560		
− Zunahme Forderungen aus L+L	− 15	+ 545	(= Kundenzahlungen)
Warenaufwand	−392		
+ Abnahme Warenvorrat	+ 15		
− Abnahme Verbindlichkeiten aus L+L	− 12	− 389	(= Lieferantenzahlungen)
Geldzufluss aus Geschäftsbereich		+156	

	Forderungen aus L+L		Warenertrag	
Anfangsbestand	40			
Kreditverkäufe	560			560
Kundenzahlungen		545		
Schlussbestand, Saldo		55	560	
	600	600	560	560

Nur die Kundenzahlungen von 545 sind liquiditätswirksam.

	Warenvorrat		Warenaufwand		Verbindlichkeiten aus L+L	
Anfangsbestand	70					45
Krediteinkäufe			377			377
Lieferantenzahlungen					389	
Bestandesabnahme		15	15			
Schlussbestand, Saldo		55		392	33	
	70	70	392	392	422	422

Nur die Lieferantenzahlungen von 389 sind liquiditätswirksam.

2.5 Geldfluss aus dem Investitionsbereich

	Mobilien		WB Mobilien		Immobilien		Abschreibung	
Anfangsbestand	150			60	1 050			
Abschreibung Mobilien				15			15	
Abschreibung Immob.						30	30	
Mobilienkauf	60							
Schlussbestand, Saldo		210	75			1 020		45
	210	210	75	75	1 050	1 050	45	45

Geldabfluss aus dem Investitionsbereich 60 (= Mobilienkauf)

2.6 Geldfluss aus dem Finanzierungsbereich

	Dividende		Obligationen-anleihe		Hypothekar-schuld	
Anfangsbestand		30		100		50
Dividendenauszahlung	30					
Rückzahlung Obl.-Anleihe			20			
Erhöhung Hypothek						5
Dividendengutschrift		40				
Schlussbestand	40		80		55	
	70	70	100	100	55	55

	AK		Gesetzliche Kapitalreserve		Gesetzliche Gewinnreserve		Gewinnvortrag	
Anfangsbestand		1 000		100		80		1
AK-Erhöhung		200						
Agio				50				
Jahresgewinn								46
Zuweisung an gesetzl. Gewinnreserve						5	5	
Dividendengutschrift							40	
Schlussbestand	1 200		150		85		2	
	1 200	1 200	150	150	85	85	47	47

Finanzierungsbereich

Dividendenauszahlung	− 30
Rückzahlung Obligationenanleihe	− 20
Erhöhung Hypothekarschuld	+ 5
Aktienkapitalerhöhung	+200
Agio auf Kapitalerhöhung	+ 50
Nettogeldzufluss	+205

2.7 Cashflow

Direkte Methode		Indirekte Methode	
Kundenzahlungen (2 000 − 50)	1 950	Jahresgewinn	100
Lieferantenzahlungen (1 300 + 35 − 30)	−1 305	Abschreibungen	+ 70
Zahlungen ans Personal	− 400	Zunahme Forderungen aus L+L	− 50
Zahlungen für übrigen Betriebsaufwand (100 − 10)	− 90	Zunahme WB Forderungen aus L+L	+ 10
		Abnahme Vorräte	+ 35
Zahlungen für Zinsen (30 − 5)	− 25	Abnahme Verbindlichkeiten aus L+L	− 40
		Zunahme Passive Rechnungsabgrenzung	+ 5
Innenfinanzierung (Cashflow)	+ 130	Innenfinanzierung (Cashflow)	+130

2.8 Direkte und indirekte Berechnung des Cashflows

Direkte Methode		Indirekte Methode	
Kundenzahlungen (5 000 + 50)	5 050	Unternehmensgewinn	250
Lieferantenzahlungen (2 250 + 75 + 100)	−2 425	Abschreibungen	+625
Zahlungen ans Personal (1 500 + 9)	−1 509	Aufwertung Beteiligung	−150
Zahlungen für diversen Aufwand	− 850	Abnahme Forderungen aus L+L	+ 50
Dividenden- und Zinseinnahmen	+ 175	Zunahme Materialvorräte	− 75
Zinsausgaben	− 25	Zunahme HF und FF	−250
Steuerausgaben	− 75	Abnahme Verbindlichkeiten aus L+L	−100
		Zunahme Aktive Rechnungsabgrenzung	− 9
Cashflow	+ 341	Cashflow	+341

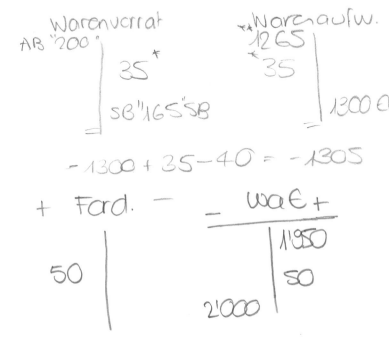

2.9 Geldflussrechnung der Maestrini AG

		Fonds Flüssige Mittel	
		Zunahme	Abnahme
Geschäftsbereich			
Jahresgewinn	54		
Abschreibungen	+ 45		
Zunahme Forderungen aus L+L	− 45		
Zunahme WB Forderungen aus L+L	+ 3		
Abnahme Vorräte	+ 45		
Abnahme Verbindlichkeiten aus L+L	− 36		
Zunahme Passive Rechnungsabgrenzung	+ 3		
Innenfinanzierung (Cashflow)	69	69	
Investitionsbereich			
Kauf von Mobilien	− 60		
Nettogeldabfluss	− 60		60
Finanzierungsbereich			
Zunahme Bankschuld	6		
Aktienkapitalerhöhung	150		
Rückzahlung Hypothek	− 30		
Dividendenausschüttung (Vorjahr)	− 15		
Nettogeldzufluss	111	111	
Veränderung Fonds Flüssige Mittel			
Anfangsbestand	75		
Endbestand	195		
Zunahme Flüssige Mittel	120		120
		180	180

Die Dividendenzuweisung (Gewinnvortrag / Dividende 30) ist nicht liquiditätswirksam.
Nur die Dividendenausschüttung (Dividende / Flüssige Mittel 15) ist liquiditätswirksam.

2.10 Geldflussrechnung des Einzelunternehmens Berini

		Fonds Flüssige Mittel	
		Zunahme	Abnahme
Geschäftsbereich			
Jahresgewinn	370		
Abschreibungen (290 + 20)	+310		
Abnahme Forderungen aus L+L	+ 40		
Zunahme Vorräte	– 50		
Abnahme Verbindlichkeiten aus L+L	– 20		
Innenfinanzierung (Cashflow)	650	650	
Investitionsbereich			
Kauf Maschinen und Einrichtungen (1 300 – 290 – 1 600)	–590		
Nettogeldabfluss	–590		590
Finanzierungsbereich			
Rückzahlung Hypothek	– 50		
Nettogeldabfluss	– 50		50
Veränderung Fonds Flüssige Mittel			
Anfangsbestand	80		
Endbestand	90		
Zunahme Flüssige Mittel	10		10
		650	650

2.11 Geldflussrechnung der Monte Baro AG

		Fonds Flüssige Mittel	
		Zunahme	Abnahme
Geschäftsbereich			
Jahresgewinn	237		
Abschreibungen	+ 53		
Abnahme Forderungen aus L+L	+ 80		
Zunahme WB Forderungen aus L+L	+ 10		
Zunahme Aktive Rechnungsabgrenzung	− 25		
Zunahme Vorräte	− 60		
Abnahme Verbindlichkeiten aus L+L	−112		
Innenfinanzierung (Cashflow)	183	183	
Investitionsbereich			
Verkauf Mobilien	+ 12		
Kauf Maschinen	− 70		
Verkauf Gebäude	+ 80		
Kauf Gebäude	−295		
Nettogeldabfluss	−273		273
Finanzierungsbereich			
Dividendenausschüttung (Vorjahr)	− 30		
Aufnahme Hypothek	+150		
Nettogeldzufluss	+120	120	
Veränderung Fonds Flüssige Mittel			
Anfangsbestand	250		
Endbestand	280		
Zunahme Flüssige Mittel	30		30
		303	303

2.12 Geldflussrechnung der Bellina AG

		Fonds Flüssige Mittel	
		Zunahme	Abnahme
Geschäftsbereich			
Jahresgewinn	48		
Abschreibungen	+ 9		
Rückstellungsaufwand	+ 3		
Zunahme Forderungen aus L+L	−20		
Zunahme Warenvorrat	−30		
Zunahme Verbindlichkeiten aus L+L	+15		
Innenfinanzierung (Cashflow)	25	25	
Investitionsbereich			
Kauf Mobilien	−12		
Kauf Fahrzeuge	−14		
Verkauf Fahrzeuge	+ 3		
Kauf Immobilien	−40		
Nettogeldabfluss	−63		63
Finanzierungsbereich			
Aufnahme Hypothek	+22		
Aktienkapitalerhöhung mit Agio	+45		
Dividendenausschüttung (Vorjahr)	−30		
Nettogeldzufluss	+37	37	
Veränderung Fonds Flüssige Mittel			
Anfangsbestand	10		
Endbestand	9		
Abnahme Flüssige Mittel	− 1	1	
		63	63

2.13 Geldflussrechnung der Colletta AG

A Cashflow

Direkte Methode			Indirekte Methode		
Kundenzahlungen		3 000	Jahresgewinn		121
Lieferantenzahlungen		−1 875	Abschreibungen		+230
Beteiligungseinnahmen (Dividende)	+	28	Rückstellungsaufwand	+	15
Zahlungen ans Personal	−	400	Aufwertung der Beteiligung	−	30
Zahlungen übriger Betriebsaufwand	−	643	Gewinn aus Fahrzeugverkauf	−	3
			Zunahme Forderungen aus L+L	−	50
			Zunahme Vorräte		−200
			Zunahme Verbindlichkeiten aus L+L	+	25
			Zunahme übrige kurzfr. Verbindlichkeiten	+	2
Innenfinanzierung (Cashflow)	+	110	Innenfinanzierung (Cashflow)		+110

B **Geldflussrechnung 20_2**

		Fonds Flüssige Mittel	
		Zunahme	Abnahme
Geschäftsbereich			
Innenfinanzierung (Cashflow)	110	110	
Investitionsbereich			
Kauf Mobilien	− 10		
Kauf Fahrzeuge	− 90		
Verkauf Fahrzeuge	+ 53		
Kauf Liegenschaft	−120		
Nettogeldabfluss	−167		167
Finanzierungsbereich			
Zunahme Bankschulden	+ 22		
Aufnahme Hypothek	+ 50		
Rückzahlung Darlehen	− 15		
Aktienkapitalerhöhung	+ 50		
Dividendenausschüttung	−100		
Nettogeldzufluss	+ 7	7	
Veränderung Fonds Flüssige Mittel			
Anfangsbestand	100		
Endbestand	50		
Abnahme Flüssige Mittel	− 50	50	
		167	167

C Beteiligungen gehören zum Anlagevermögen und dürfen höchstens zum Anschaffungswert ausgewiesen werden (OR 960d und 960a).

D Der Anhang enthält nur die Nettoauflösung von stillen Reserven (= Gesamtbetrag aufgelöste stille Reserven minus Gesamtbetrag gebildete stille Reserven), wenn dadurch das erwirtschaftete Ergebnis wesentlich günstiger dargestellt wird (OR 959c/1, Ziff. 3).

Beispiele zur Wesentlichkeit
- Der tatsächliche Jahresgewinn wird um mehr als 10–20 % günstiger ausgewiesen.
- Aus einem Jahresverlust wird wegen der Nettoauflösung ein Jahresgewinn.

2.14 Summarische Geldflussrechnung der Comaris AG

Die zutreffenden Aussagen sind: 2, 4, 6, 9 und 10

Erklärungen für die falschen Aussagen:

1. Der Cashflow (Geldfluss aus Geschäftsbereich) beträgt +81, ist positiv.
3. Die Bankkonten sind nur ein Teil der flüssigen Mittel.
5. Der Cashflow von 319 ist grösser als der Geldabfluss aus dem Investitionsbereich 279.
7. Der Cashloss vermindert die flüssigen Mittel.
8. Die Veränderung der Flüssigen Mittel ist nicht identisch mit dem Nettoumlaufvermögen.

2.15 Geldflussrechnung der Panda AG

A 1 Geldflussrechung 20_5

		Fonds Flüssige Mittel	
		Zunahme	Abnahme
Geschäftsbereich			
Kundenzahlungen	940		
Lieferantenzahlungen	−580		
Zahlungen ans Personal	−120		
Mietzinszahlungen	− 40		
Zinszahlungen	− 19		
Zahlungen übrigen Betriebsaufwand	− 70		
Cashflow	111	111	
Investitionsbereich			
Käufe Mobilien und Maschinen	−130		
Verkauf Fahrzeug	+ 40		
Nettogeldabfluss	− 90		90
Finanzierungsbereich			
Erhöhung Aktienkapital	+ 60		
Dividendenauszahlung	− 25		
Rückzahlung Darlehen	− 30		
Nettogeldzufluss	+ 5	5	
Veränderung Fonds Flüssige Mittel			
Anfangsbestand	50		
Endbestand	76		
Zunahme Flüssige Mittel	+ 26		26
		116	116

A 2

Schlussbilanz vom 31.12.20_5

Umlaufvermögen			Kurzfristiges Fremdkapital	
Flüssige Mittel		76	Verbindlichkeiten aus L+L	101
Forderungen aus L+L		84	Passive Rechnungsabgrenzung	7
Aktive Rechnungsabgrenzung		22	Langfristiges Fremdkapital	
Vorräte		59	Darlehen	155
Anlagevermögen			Rückstellungen	31
Sachlagen	474		Eigenkapital	
WB Sachanlagen	–142	332	Aktienkapital	180
			Reserven, Gewinnvortrag	99
		573		573

B **Cashflow indirekt**

Jahresgewinn	32
Abschreibungen	+ 30
Bildung Rückstellungen	+ 8
Abnahme Forderungen aus L+L	+ 20
Abnahme Vorräte	+ 15
Zunahme Aktive Rechnungsabgrenzung	– 5
Zunahme Verbindlichkeiten aus L+L	+ 15
Abnahme Passive Rechnungsabgrenzung	– 4
Cashflow	111

2.16 Walter Meier Holding (WMH) während Jahren ohne Free Cashflow

A Free Cashflow

B
1. Aufnahme von Fremdkapital zur Beschaffung von flüssigen Mitteln
2. Die Zinsbelastung (Fremdkapitalzinsen) steigt und dies führt zu einem Geldabfluss (Finanzaufwand / Flüssige Mittel) und verringert den Cashflow.
3. Aufnahme von zusätzlichem Fremdkapital, um die Zinsen zahlen zu können!

C
1. Zinsen   Fr. 81 Mio.
2. Neuverschuldung mit Fremdkapital   Fr. 76 Mio.
3. Negativer Free Cashflow   Fr. 93 Mio.

D Die Interpretation der Kennzahl ist Sache der Geschäftsführung (und auch der kreditgebenden Banken). Gegen Ausklammerungen («unter Berücksichtigung» und «wenn und aber») ist keine Kennzahl gefeit!

2.17 Jahresrechnung der Musti AG

A Erfolgsrechnung 20_7

Warenaufwand	800	Warenertrag	1 110
Personalaufwand	180	Jahresverlust	15
Diverser Aufwand	125		
Abschreibung Mobilien	12		
Abschreibung Immobilien	8		
	1 125		1 125

B Schlussbilanz nach Erfolgsverbuchung vom 31.12.20_7

Umlaufvermögen		Kurzfristiges Fremdkapital	
Liquide Mittel	6	Verbindlichkeiten aus L+L	50
Forderungen aus L+L	40	Langfristiges Fremdkapital	
Warenvorrat	150	Darlehen	10
Anlagevermögen		Hypotheken	380
Mobilien	217	Eigenkapital	
Immobilien	772	Aktienkapital	440
		Reserven (Sammelposten)	305
	1 185		1 185

C Geldflussrechnung 20_7

		Fonds Flüssige Mittel	
		Zunahme	Abnahme
Geschäftsbereich			
Jahresverlust	−15		
Abschreibungen	20		
Zunahme Forderungen aus L+L	−10		
Cashloss	−5		5
Investitionsbereich			
Kauf EDV-Anlage	−15		
Verkauf Mobilien	6		
Kauf Liegenschaft	−80		
Nettogeldabfluss	−89		89
Finanzierungsbereich			
Erhöhung Aktienkapital	40		
Erhöhung Hypothek	80		
Rückzahlung Darlehen	−20		
Dividendenauszahlung	−10		
Nettogeldzufluss	90	90	
Veränderung Fonds Flüssige Mittel			
Abnahme Flüssige Mittel	−4	4	
		94	94

2.18 Jahresrechnung der Huber AG

A

Erfolgsrechnung 20_8

Warenaufwand	1 400	Warenertrag	2 600
Personalaufwand	900		
Diverser Betriebsaufwand	190		
Rückstellungsaufwand	15		
Abschreibung	60		
Jahresgewinn	35		
	2 600		2 600

B

Geldflussrechnung 20_8

		Fonds Flüssige Mittel	
		Zunahme	Abnahme
Geschäftsbereich			
Jahresgewinn	35		
Abschreibungen	60		
Rückstellungsaufwand	15		
Zunahme Forderungen aus L+L	– 40		
Abnahme Lager	80		
Zunahme Verbindlichkeiten aus L+L	20		
Cashflow	170	170	
Investitionsbereich			
Verkauf Fahrzeug	20		
Kauf Mobilien	– 50		
Kauf Land	– 90		
Nettogeldabfluss	–120		120
Finanzierungsbereich			
Erhöhung Aktienkapital	60		
Agio aus Aktienkapitalerhöhung	30		
Rückzahlung Hypothek	– 10		
Dividendenauszahlung	–100		
Nettogeldabfluss	– 20		20
Veränderung Fonds Flüssige Mittel			
Zunahme Flüssige Mittel	30		30
		170	170

2.19 Geldflussrechnung der Gerber AG

A Geldflussrechnung 20_9

		Fonds Flüssige Mittel	
		Zunahme	Abnahme
Geschäftsbereich			
Kundenzahlungen	2 000		
Lieferantenzahlungen	− 990		
Zahlungen ans Personal	− 450		
Mietzinszahlungen	− 250		
Zinszahlungen	− 110		
Zahlungen übriger Betriebsaufwand	− 380		
Cashloss (Cashdrain)	− 180		180
Investitionsbereich			
Verkauf Maschine	+ 32		
Kauf Mobilien	− 60		
Kauf Liegenschaft	− 350		
Nettogeldabfluss	− 378		378
Finanzierungsbereich			
Erhöhung Aktienkapital	+ 200		
Agioeinzahlung	+ 100		
Dividendenauszahlung	− 50		
Aufnahme Hypothek	+ 150		
Rückzahlung Darlehen	− 80		
Nettogeldzufluss	+ 320	320	
Veränderung Fonds Flüssige Mittel			
Abnahme Flüssige Mittel	− 238	238	
		558	558

B Erfolgsrechnung 20_9

Produkteertrag	1 900
Zunahme Halb- und Fertigfabrikate	+ 180
Betriebsleistung	2 080
Materialaufwand	− 860
Personalaufwand	− 450
Mietaufwand	− 250
Rückstellungsaufwand	− 40
Übriger Betriebsaufwand	− 380
EBITDA	100
Abschreibungen	− 160
EBIT	− 60
Zinsaufwand	− 140
EBT vor ausserordentlichem Aufwand und Ertrag	− 200
Ausserordentlicher Gewinn aus Maschinenverkauf	+ 10
Jahresverlust	− 190

C Cashflow indirekt

Jahresverlust	− 190
Abschreibungen	+ 160
Rückstellungsaufwand	+ 40
Ausserordentlicher Gewinn aus Maschinenverkauf	− 10
Abnahme Forderungen aus L+L	+ 100
Zunahme Materialvorräte	− 90
Zunahme Halb- und Fertigfabrikatevorrat	− 180
Abnahme Verbindlichkeiten aus L+L	− 40
Zunahme Passive Rechnungsabgrenzung	+ 30
Cashloss (Cashdrain)	− 180

2.20 Geldflussrechnung der Bader AG

A Geldflussrechnung 20_0

		Fonds Flüssige Mittel Zunahme	Fonds Flüssige Mittel Abnahme
Geschäftsbereich			
Jahresgewinn	2 100		
Abschreibungen	+1 400		
Zunahme Rückstellungen	+ 175		
Zunahme Forderungen aus L+L	− 700		
Zunahme Warenvorrat	−1 400		
Zunahme Verbindlichkeiten aus L+L	+ 350		
Cashflow	1 925	1 925	
Investitionsbereich			
Verkauf Fahrzeug	+ 350		
Kauf Mobilien, Fahrzeug	−1 050		
Kauf Immobilien	−1 050		
Nettogeldabfluss	−1 750		1 750
Finanzierungsbereich			
Aktienkapitalerhöhung	1 050		
Agio auf Aktienkapitalerhöhung	+ 350		
Dividendenausschüttung	−1 750		
Amortisation Hypothek	− 175		
Nettogeldabfluss	− 525		525
Veränderung Fonds Flüssige Mittel			
Abnahme Flüssige Mittel	− 350	350	
		2 275	2 275

B Cashflow direkt

Kundenzahlungen	44 800
Lieferantenzahlungen	−25 550
Lohnzahlungen	−14 000
Zahlungen übriger Aufwand	− 3 325
Cashflow	1 925

2.21 Geldflussrechnung der Mara AG

A Geldflussrechnung 20_1

		Fonds Flüssige Mittel	
		Zunahme	Abnahme
Geschäftsbereich			
Jahresgewinn	3 150		
Abschreibungen Sachanlagen	+1 350		
Zunahme Rückstellungen	+ 450		
Zunahme Forderungen aus L+L	−1 350		
Zunahme Warenvorrat	−1 350		
Zunahme Verbindlichkeiten aus L+L	+ 900		
Verlust aus Fahrzeugverkauf	+ 135		
Ausserordentlicher Finanzertrag	− 90		
Cashflow	3 195	3 195	
Investitionsbereich			
Kauf Mobilien und Fahrzeuge	−2 250		
Verkauf Fahrzeug	+ 315		
Kauf Liegenschaft	−2 250		
Nettogeldabfluss	−4 185		4 185
Finanzierungsbereich			
Aktienkapitalerhöhung	2 250		
Agio auf Aktienkapitalerhöhung	+ 450		
Dividendenausschüttung	−2 700		
Erhöhung Hypothek	+ 900		
Rückzahlung Obligationenanleihe	− 360		
Nettogeldzufluss	+ 540	540	
Veränderung Fonds Flüssige Mittel			
Abnahme Flüssige Mittel	− 450	450	
		4 185	4 185

B **Cashflow direkt**

Kundenzahlungen	84 150
Lieferantenzahlungen	−45 450
Lohnzahlungen	−27 000
Zahlungen übriger Betriebsaufwand	− 8 505
Cashflow	3 195

2.22 Geldflussrechnung der Diener AG

A Geldflussrechnung 20_2

		Fonds Flüssige Mittel	
		Zunahme	Abnahme
Geschäftsbereich			
Kundenzahlungen	4 965		
Lieferantenzahlungen	−2 210		
Zahlungen ans Personal	−1 810		
Zinszahlungen	− 35		
Zahlungen übriger Betriebsaufwand	− 615		
Cashflow	295	295	
Investitionsbereich			
Verkauf Fahrzeug	+ 50		
Kauf Mobilien	− 15		
Zahlungen für Renovation Liegenschaft	− 80		
Nettogeldabfluss	− 45		45
Finanzierungsbereich			
Erhöhung Aktienkapital	+ 100		
Agiozahlung	+ 100		
Dividendenauszahlung	− 375		
Amortisation Hypothek	− 140		
Nettogeldabfluss	− 315		315
Veränderung Fonds Flüssige Mittel			
Anfangsbestand	120		
Endbestand	55		
Abnahme Flüssige Mittel	− 65	65	
		360	360

B **Cashflow indirekt**

Jahresgewinn	370
Abschreibungen mobile Sachanlagen	+130
Abschreibungen Immobilien	+ 30
Bildung Rückstellungen	+ 25
Ausserordentlicher Gewinn aus Fahrzeugverkauf	− 10
Zunahme Forderungen aus L+L	− 35
Zunahme Vorräte	−100
Zunahme Aktive Rechnungsabgrenzung	− 10
Abnahme Verbindlichkeiten aus L+L	−110
Zunahme Passive Rechnungsabgrenzung	+ 5
Cashflow	295

C

Cashflow	295
Nettogeldabfluss im Investitionsbereich	− 45
Free Cashflow	250

Der Geldabfluss für Nettoinvestitionen konnte mit dem Cashflow (Geldzufluss aus dem Geschäftsbereich) finanziert werden. Langfristig muss mit dem Cashflow der Geldabfluss für Nettoinvestitionen bezahlt werden können, da sonst eine Finanzierungslücke besteht, die entweder mit Fremdkapital oder Eigenkapital gedeckt werden muss.

Da die Geldflussrechnung sich nur auf ein Jahr bezieht und Investitionen nicht unbedingt gleichmässig über die Jahre verteilt anfallen, ist es sinnvoll, eine kumulierte Geldflussrechnung aus mehreren Jahren zu erstellen, um dann den Free Cashflow zu berechnen.

D Der Cashflow verändert sich nicht, da die Abschreibungen liquiditätsunwirksam sind.
Wenn die Abschreibungen erhöht werden, verkleinert sich der Jahresgewinn um den gleichen Betrag; d. h. auch bei der indirekten Cashflow-Berechnung verändert sich die Höhe des Cashflows nicht.

2.23 Geldflussrechnung der Kauf AG

A Geldflussrechnung 20_3

		Fonds Flüssige Mittel	
		Zunahme	Abnahme
Geschäftsbereich			
Kundenzahlungen	4 050		
Lieferantenzahlungen	−2 470		
Lohnzahlungen	− 900		
Zahlungen übriger barer Aufwand	− 700		
Einnahmen Obligationenzinsen	+ 5		
Einnahmen Dividenden	+ 6		
Verlust auf Wertschriften	− 30		
Nettogeldabfluss (Cashloss)	− 39		39
Investitionsbereich			
Kauf Mobilien	− 110		
Kauf Beteiligungen	− 12		
Landverkauf	+ 215		
Nettogeldzufluss	+ 93	93	
Finanzierungsbereich			
Erhöhung Aktienkapital	+ 40		
Rückzahlung Darlehen	− 108		
Dividendenausschüttung	− 66		
Nettogeldabfluss	− 134		134
Veränderung Fonds Flüssige Mittel			
Anfangsbestand	140		
Endbestand	60		
Abnahme Flüssige Mittel	− 80	80	
		173	173

B Cashflow indirekt

Unternehmensgewinn	114
Abschreibungen Mobilien	+ 80
Bildung Rückstellungen	+ 20
Gewinn aus Landverkauf	− 25
Gewinn Beteiligungen	− 8
Zunahme Forderungen aus L + L	− 50
Zunahme Vorräte	−210
Zunahme Verbindlichkeiten aus L + L	+ 40
Nettogeldabfluss (Cashloss)	− 39

2.24 Geldflussrechnung der Trevalli SA

A Geldflussrechnung 20_4

		Fonds Flüssige Mittel	
		Zunahme	Abnahme
Geschäftsbereich			
Kundenzahlungen	68 110		
Lieferantenzahlungen	−35 700		
Lohnzahlungen	−17 570		
Zahlungen übriger Betriebsaufwand	−15 242		
Zinszahlungen	− 490		
Zinseinnahmen auf Wertschriften	+ 18		
Verlust Wertschriften	− 36		
Nettogeldabfluss (Cashloss)	− 910		910
Investitionsbereich			
Maschinenkäufe	− 1 330		
Maschinenverkäufe	+ 350		
Verkauf Grundstück	+ 1 190		
Zahlungen für Renovation Immobilien	− 350		
Nettogeldabfluss	− 140		140
Finanzierungsbereich			
AK-Erhöhung	+ 1 750		
Agio aus AK-Erhöhung	+ 1 750		
Dividendenauszahlung	− 1 050		
Rückzahlung Darlehen	− 700		
Rückzahlung Hypotheken	− 700		
Nettogeldzufluss	+ 1 050	1 050	
Veränderung Fonds Flüssige Mittel			
Anfangsbestand	700		
Endbestand	700		
Keine Veränderung Flüssige Mittel	0		
		1 050	1 050

B Cashflow indirekt

Jahresgewinn		1 575
Abschreibungen bewegliche Sachanlagen	+	700
Abschreibungen Beteiligungen	+	70
A. o. Verlust Maschinenverkauf	+	70
A. o. Gewinn aus Immobilienverkauf	–	490
Zunahme Forderungen aus L+L	–	1 715
Zunahme Vorräte	–	1 400
Zunahme Aktive Rechnungsabgrenzung	–	70
Zunahme Verbindlichkeiten aus L+L	+	700
Abnahme Vorauszahlungen	–	175
Abnahme Passive Rechnungsabgrenzung	–	175
Nettogeldabfluss (Cashloss)	–	910

2.25 Geldflussrechnung der Turbinenbräu AG

		Fonds Flüssige Mittel	
		Zunahme	Abnahme
Geschäftsbereich			
Jahresgewinn	65 891		
Abschreibung und Amortisation	+206 390		
Zunahme langfristige Rückstellungen	+ 2 989		
Cashflow auf NUV-Basis	+275 270		
Veränderung operatives NUV	−141 497		
Cashflow	133 773	133 773	
Investitionsbereich			
Erwerb Finanzanlagen	−248 428		
Investition in Brauereianlagen	−102 139		
Nettogeldabfluss	−350 567		350 567
Finanzierungsbereich			
Aufnahme Aktionärsdarlehen	+198 000		
Rückzahlung Bankdarlehen	− 30 000		
Nettogeldzufluss	+168 000	168 000	
Veränderung Fonds Flüssige Mittel			
Anfangsbestand	116 939		
Endbestand	68 145		
Abnahme Flüssige Mittel	− 48 794	48 794	
		350 567	350 567

Veränderung operatives Nettoumlaufvermögen

Abnahme Forderungen aus L+L	+ 5 720
Abnahme andere kurzfristige Forderungen	+ 2 519
Zunahme Vorräte	− 28 296
Abnahme Verbindlichkeiten aus L+L	−121 440
Zunahme operatives Nettoumlaufvermögen	−141 497

Erklärung zu den Brauereianlagen

Die in der Ausgangslage genannte Investition in Brauereianlagen von Fr. 102 139.– kann mit den folgenden Konten auch hergeleitet werden.

Baukonto		Brauereianlagen		Goodwill		Abschreibung und Amortisation	
100 936		740 096		1 485			
	60 561	60 561			748	748	
		102 139	205 642			205 642	
			697 154		737		206 390
100 936	100 936	902 796	902 796	1 485	1 485	206 390	206 390

3 Planungsrechnung

3.1 Planerfolgsrechnung

Mehrstufige Planerfolgsrechnung 20_1

Bruttoerlös	2 408 247	
Erlösminderungen	− 72 247	
Nettoerlös		2 336 000
Bruttoeinkaufswert	1 361 940	
Bezugsspesen	+ 42 122	
Bruttoeinstandswert der eingekauften Waren	1 404 062	
Rücksendungen	− 14 462	
Nettoeinstandswert der eingekauften Waren	1 389 600	
Bestandeszunahme	− 7 200	
Warenaufwand ohne Abschreibungen	1 382 400	
Abschreibung auf dem Warenlager	+ 19 200	
Warenaufwand mit Abschreibungen		−1 401 600
Bruttogewinn		934 400
Vertriebsaufwand	233 600	
Verwaltungsaufwand	116 800	
Übriger Betriebsaufwand	374 000	
Gemeinaufwand		− 724 400
Betriebsgewinn		210 000
Immobilienaufwand		− 23 120
Jahresgewinn vor Steuern		186 880
Steueraufwand		− 93 440
Jahresgewinn		93 440

3.2 Planbilanz

Planbilanz (nach Gewinnverwendung) vom 31.12.20_2

Umlaufvermögen		**Kurzfristiges Fremdkapital**	
Flüssige Mittel	45	Verbindlichkeiten aus L+L	240
Forderungen aus L+L	240	Dividende	120
Warenvorräte	390	**Langfristiges Fremdkapital**	
Anlagevermögen		Hypotheken	225
Mobile Sachanlagen	270	Rückstellungen	45
Immobilien	840	**Eigenkapital**	
		Aktienkapital	810
		Reserven, Gewinnvortrag	345
	1 785		1 785

3.3 Planerfolgsrechnung, Planbilanz und Finanzplan

A Planerfolgsrechnung 20_3

	Aufwand	Ertrag
Warenertrag		2 700
Warenaufwand	1 800	
Personalaufwand	450	
Übriger Betriebsaufwand	150	
Abschreibungen	120	
Finanzaufwand	90	
Jahresgewinn	90	
	2 700	2 700

B Planbilanz vor Gewinnverwendung vom 31.12.20_3

	Aktiven	Passiven
Flüssige Mittel	60	
Forderungen aus L+L	270	
Warenvorräte	150	
Betriebsanlagen	2 580	
Verbindlichkeiten aus L+L		306
Bankkontokorrent		240
Hypotheken		1 116
Aktienkapital		900
Reserven, Gewinnvortrag		498
	3 060	3 060

C Finanzplan als Plangeldflussrechnung 20_3

		Fonds Flüssige Mittel	
		Zunahme	Abnahme
Geschäftsbereich			
Jahresgewinn	90		
Abschreibungen	+120		
Zunahme Forderungen aus L+L	− 60		
Abnahme Warenvorräte	+ 30		
Zunahme Verbindlichkeiten aus L+L	+156		
Innenfinanzierung (Cashflow)	+336	336	
Investitionsbereich			
Kauf Betriebsanlagen	−300		
Nettogeldabfluss	−300		300
Finanzierungsbereich			
Gewinnausschüttung (Dividende)	− 72		
Amortisation Hypotheken	− 24		
Erhöhung Bankkredit	+ 60		
Nettogeldabfluss	− 36		36
Veränderung Fonds Flüssige Mittel			
Anfangsbestand	60		
Endbestand	60		
Keine Veränderung Flüssige Mittel	0		
		336	336

3.4 Planungsrechnungen Domaso SA

Die Buchungen sind nicht verlangt, erleichtern Ihnen aber mit den Erläuterungen, den Lösungsweg nachzuvollziehen.

1 a Forderungen aus L+L / Verkaufserlös 2 700

b Bei einem Bruttogewinnsatz von 33⅓% beträgt der Verkaufserlös 133⅓%.
Der gesamte Warenaufwand (Einstand der verkauften Waren) ist 2 025.
Ermittlung des Endbestandes Waren:

Anfangsbestand (AB)		360		
– Januar		– 40,5	(keine Einkäufe; 90% des Vorjahres)	
			20_3 Verkaufserlös 60	100%
			20_4 Verkaufserlös 54	90%
			20_4 Einstandswert 40,5	90%
– Februar		– 20		
usw.			Eingänge und Ausgänge sind gleich gross.	
+ Dezember		+ 40,5	Einkauf für Januar 20_5	
Schlussbestand (SB)		340	Lagerabnahme von 20	

Warenaufwand / Verbindlichkeiten aus L+L 2 005
Warenaufwand / Warenvorräte 20

c Es dauert 45 Tage, bis die Kunden zahlen.

Verkäufe: November	396 : 2	= 198
Verkäufe: Dezember		= 270
Offene Kundenrechnungen (SB)		= 468

Forderungen aus L+L

AB	525	2 757	Zahlungen von Kunden
Verkäufe auf Kredit	2 700	468	SB
	3 225	3 225	

Flüssige Mittel / Forderungen aus L+L 2 757,5

d **Verbindlichkeiten aus L+L**

Zahlungen an Lieferanten	2 024,5	60	AB
SB	40,5	2 005	Einstand der eingekauften Waren, Krediteinkäufe (siehe auch 1 b)
	2 065	2 065	

	Verbindlichkeiten aus L+L	/ Flüssige Mittel	2 024,5
2	Betriebsanlagen	/ Flüssige Mittel	40
	Abschreibungen	/ Betriebsanlagen	4
3	Personalaufwand	/ Flüssige Mittel	304
4	Finanzaufwand	/ Flüssige Mittel	66
5	1. Quartal 50; 2. Quartal 50; 3. und 4. Quartal zusammen 95 = 195		
	Übriger Betriebsaufwand	/ Flüssige Mittel	195
6	Abschreibungen	/ Betriebsanlagen	70
7	Reserven, Gewinnvortrag	/ Flüssige Mittel	60
8	Bankkontokorrent	/ Flüssige Mittel	77,5

A	**Planerfolgsrechnung 20_4**	Aufwand	Ertrag
Verkaufserlös		2 700
Warenaufwand	2 025
Personalaufwand	304
Übriger Betriebsaufwand	195
Abschreibungen	74
Finanzaufwand	66
Jahresgewinn	36
	2 700	2 700

B	**Planbilanz vor Gewinnverwendung vom 31.12.20_4**	Aktiven	Passiven
Flüssige Mittel	20
Forderungen aus L+L	468
Warenvorräte	340
Betriebsanlagen	1 566
Verbindlichkeiten aus L+L		40,5
Bankkontokorrent		2,5
Hypothek		1 100
Aktienkapital		1 000
Reserven, Gewinnvortrag		251
	2 394	2 394

C Finanzplan als Plangeldflussrechnung 20_4

		Fonds Flüssige Mittel	
		Zunahme	Abnahme
Geschäftsbereich			
Jahresgewinn	36		
Abschreibungen	+ 74		
Abnahme Forderungen aus L+L	+ 57		
Abnahme Warenvorräte	+ 20		
Abnahme Verbindlichkeiten aus L+L	– 19,5		
Innenfinanzierung (Cashflow)	+167,5	167,5	
Investitionsbereich			
Kauf Betriebsanlagen	– 40		
Nettogeldabfluss	– 40		40,0
Finanzierungsbereich			
Gewinnausschüttung (Dividende)	– 60		
Rückzahlung Bankkredit	– 77,5		
Nettogeldabfluss	–137,5		137,5
Veränderung Fonds Flüssige Mittel			
Anfangsbestand	30		
Endbestand	20		
Abnahme Flüssige Mittel	– 10	10,0	
		177,5	177,5

3.5 Planungsrechnungen Favogno SA

Die Buchungen sind nicht verlangt, erleichtern Ihnen aber, den Lösungsweg nachzuvollziehen.

1	Flüssige Mittel	/ Verkaufserlös		730
	Forderungen aus L+L	/ Verkaufserlös		6 574
2	Warenaufwand	/ Warenvorräte		1 110
	Warenaufwand	/ Verbindlichkeiten aus L+L		3 237
3	Personalaufwand	/ Flüssige Mittel		958
4	Verwaltungsaufwand	/ Flüssige Mittel		1 180
	Verwaltungsaufwand	/ Flüssige Mittel		40
5	Übriger Betriebsaufwand	/ Flüssige Mittel		244
6	Abschreibungen	/ Immobilien		70
	Abschreibungen	/ Maschinen, Mobilien		62
7	Finanzaufwand	/ Flüssige Mittel		178
8	Flüssige Mittel	/ Forderungen aus L+L		6 939
9	siehe Nr. 2, bereits gebucht			
10	Wertschriften	/ Flüssige Mittel		175
	Flüssige Mittel	/ Übrige Erträge (Sammelposten)		14
11	Flüssige Mittel	/ Maschinen, Mobilien		28
	Maschinen, Mobilien	/ Übrige Erträge (Sammelposten)		6
	Maschinen, Mobilien	/ Flüssige Mittel		180
12	Immobilien	/ Flüssige Mittel		470
13	Verbindlichkeiten aus L+L	/ Flüssige Mittel		3 363
	Bankkontokorrent	/ Flüssige Mittel		868
14	Erfolgsrechnung	/ Gewinnvortrag		245
	Gewinnvortrag	/ Offene Reserven		50
	Gewinnvortrag	/ Übrige kurzfristige Verbindlichkeiten		160
	Gewinnvortrag	/ Übrige kurzfristige Verbindlichkeiten		35

A Planerfolgsrechnung 20_2	Aufwand	Ertrag
Verkaufserlös		7 304
Übrige Erträge		20
Warenaufwand	4 347	
Personalaufwand	958	
Verwaltungsaufwand	1 220	
Übriger Betriebsaufwand	244	
Abschreibungen	132	
Finanzaufwand	178	
Jahresgewinn	245	
	7 324	7 324

B Planbilanz nach Gewinnverwendung vom 31.12.20_2	Aktiven	Passiven
Flüssige Mittel	213	
Wertschriften	210	
Forderungen aus L+L	1 930	
Warenvorräte	1 826	
Maschinen, Mobilien	621	
Immobilien	1 800	
Verbindlichkeiten aus L+L		800
Übrige kurzfristige Verbindlichkeiten		215
Bankkontokorrent		1 200
Hypothek		890
Aktienkapital		2 000
Offene Reserven		298
Stille Reserven		1 167
Gewinnvortrag		30
	6 600	6 600

3.6 Planungsrechnungen Piazzalunga SA

A Plangeldfluss aus Geschäftsbereich 20_5	
Zahlungen von Kunden	10 180
Zahlungen an Lieferanten	– 2 240
Zahlungen ans Personal	– 2 320
Zahlungen für Zinsen	– 76
Zahlungen für übrigen Fabrikationsaufwand	– 1 690
Zahlungen für Werbeaufwand	– 400
Zahlungen für Verwaltungsaufwand	– 1 420
Plan-Geldzufluss aus Geschäftstätigkeit (Plan Cashflow)	2 034

```
  Forderungen          Nettoverkaufserlös
   aus L+L
    940  |               8 480 |
  8 480  |               1 600 |
  1 600  | 10 180              | 10 080
         |    840        10 080|
 ─────── ────────        ───── ──────
 11 020  | 11 020        10 080| 10 080


 Verbindlichkeiten
    aus L+L             Materialaufwand        Materialvorrat
         |   360              |                   630 |
         | 2 320         2 320|                       |
  2 240  |                140 |                   140 |
    440  |                    | 2 460                 |   490
 ─────── ────────        ─────────────         ───────────────
  2 680  |  2 680         2 460| 2 460            630 |   630
```

B   Finanzplan als Plangeldflussrechnung 20_5

		Fonds Flüssige Mittel	
		Zunahme	Abnahme
Geschäftsbereich			
Jahresgewinn	1 024		
Abschreibungen	+ 690		
Abnahme Forderungen aus L+L	+ 100		
Abnahme Materialvorräte	+ 140		
Zunahme Verbindlichkeiten aus L+L	+ 80		
Innenfinanzierung (Cashflow)	+2 034	2 034	
Investitionsbereich			
Erweiterungsinvestition (INVEST)	–2 400		
Ersatzinvestitionen	–1 000		
Wertschriftenverkauf	+1 000		
Nettogeldabfluss	–2 400		2 400
Finanzierungsbereich			
Gewinnausschüttung (Dividende)	– 240		
Aufnahme Bankkredit (Residualgrösse)①	+ 336		
Nettogeldzufluss	+ 96	96	
Veränderung Fonds Flüssige Mittel			
Anfangsbestand	400		
Endbestand	130		
Abnahme Flüssige Mittel	– 270	270	
		2 400	2 400

① Differenzrechnung

3.7 Planungsrechnungen Breva SA

Die Buchungen sind nicht verlangt, erleichtern Ihnen aber mit den Erläuterungen, den Lösungsweg nachzuvollziehen.

1	a	Sachanlagen	/ Kurzfristige Schulden	12	
		Kurzfristige Schulden	/ Hypotheken	8	
	b	Forderungen	/ Sachanlagen	2	
		Sachanlagen	/ A. o. Ertrag	0,4	
		Flüssige Mittel	/ Forderungen	1	
		Kurzfristige Schulden	/ Flüssige Mittel	1	
2	a	Forderungen	/ Verkaufserlöse	76	
	b	keine Buchung			
3	a	Einzelmaterialaufwand	/ Materialbestand	2	25 % von 76 = 19
		Einzelmaterialaufwand	/ Kurzfristige Schulden	17	
	b	Einzellohnaufwand	/ Flüssige Mittel	19	25 % von 76 = 19
	c	Abschreibungen	/ Sachanlagen	3,3	10 % von (22,5 + 12 – 2 + 0,4)
	d	Übriger Fertigungsaufwand	/ Flüssige Mittel	19,6	12 + 10 % von 76
	e	Verw.- u. Vertriebsaufwand	/ Flüssige Mittel	12,6	8,8 + 5 % von 76
4		Kurzfristige Schulden	/ Flüssige Mittel	0,5	
		Steueraufwand	/ Kurzfristige Schulden	0,4	Steuerrückstellung
5	a	Flüssige Mittel	/ Forderungen	76,4	
	b	Kurzfristige Schulden	/ Flüssige Mittel	16,9	

```
         Forderungen                       Kurzfristige Schulden
        (Sammelposten)                        (Sammelposten)

   AB    8,0                                              2,1   AB   (1,6 + 0,5)
   1b    2,0    1,0   1b              1a    8,0   12,0    1a
   2a   76,0   76,4   5a              1b    1,0
 (7,6 + 1,0)    8,6   SB                          17,0    3a
                                       4    0,5    0,4    4a
                                      5b   16,9
                                      SB    5,1          (3,0 + 1,7 + 0,4)
         ─────────────                       ─────────────
         86,0   86,0                        31,5   31,5
```

6	Reserven, Gewinnvortrag	/ Flüssige Mittel	2	
7	Flüssige Mittel	/ Finanzertrag	0,5	
8, 9	Bankkontokorrent	/ Flüssige Mittel	6,5	

Aus der Bankschuld wird ein Bankguthaben von 2,5.
Der Schlussbestand der Flüssigen Mittel (ohne Bankkontokorrent-Guthaben) beträgt nach dieser Buchung 1,8.

A

Planerfolgsrechnung 20_9

Einzelmaterialaufwand	19,0	Verkaufserlöse	76,0
Einzellohnaufwand	19,0	Finanzertrag	0,5
Übriger Fertigungsaufwand	19,6	Ausserordentlicher Ertrag	0,4
Verwaltungs- und Vertriebsaufwand	12,6		
Abschreibungen auf Sachanlagen	3,3		
Steueraufwand	0,4		
Jahresgewinn	3,0		
	76,9		76,9

B

Planbilanz vor Gewinnverwendung vom 31.12.20_9

Umlaufvermögen		**Kurzfristiges Fremdkapital**	
Flüssige Mittel	1,8	Kurzfristige Schulden (Sammelposten)	5,1
Bankkontokorrent	2,5		
Forderungen (Sammelposten)	8,6	**Langfristiges Fremdkapital**	
Materialbestand	3,0	Hypotheken	24,0
Erzeugnisse in Arbeit	2,0	**Eigenkapital**	
Fertige Erzeugnisse	7,0	Aktienkapital	10,0
Anlagevermögen		Reserven, Gewinnvortrag	20,4
Finanzanlagen	5,0		
Sachanlagen	29,6		
	59,5		59,5

C Finanzplan als Plangeldflussrechnung 20_9

		Fonds Flüssige Mittel	
		Zunahme	Abnahme
Geschäftsbereich			
Jahresgewinn	3,0		
Abschreibungen	+ 3,3		
Ausserordentlicher Ertrag	− 0,4		
Zunahme Forderungen	− 0,6		
Abnahme Materialbestand	+ 2,0		
Zunahme kurzfristige Schulden	+ 3,0		
Innenfinanzierung (Cashflow)	+10,3	10,3	
Investitionsbereich			
Rationalisierungsinvestition	−12,0		
Verkauf Sachanlagen	+ 2,0		
Nettogeldabfluss	−10,0		10,0
Finanzierungsbereich			
Gewinnausschüttung (Dividende)	− 2,0		
Rückzahlung Bankkredit	− 4,0		
Erhöhung Hypothek	+ 8,0		
Nettogeldzufluss	+ 2,0	2,0	
Veränderung Fonds Flüssige Mittel			
Anfangsbestand	2,0		
Endbestand (inkl. Bankkontokorrent-Guthaben)	4,3		
Zunahme Flüssige Mittel	2,3		2,3
		12,3	12,3

3.8 Mehrjahrespläne der Plano SA

A Bilanzen (nach Gewinnverwendung)

	Ist 20_0	Planung 20_1	Planung 20_2	Planung 20_3
Aktiven				
Flüssige Mittel	140	120	100	110
Forderungen aus L+L	160	180	200	220
Vorräte	140	160	180	200
Anlagevermögen	200	300	340	360
	640	760	820	890
Passiven				
Verbindlichkeiten aus L+L	140	160	180	200
Übriges Fremdkapital	180	200	225	230
Eigenkapital	320	400	415	460
	640	760	820	890

B

		20_1	20_2	20_3
1	Rentabilität des EK = Erfolg · 100 : ⌀ EK	7,2 %	7,4 %	7,8 %
2	Rentabilität des GK = (Erfolg + FK-Zinsen) · 100 : ⌀ GK	5,1 %	5,3 %	5,6 %
3	Umschlagshäufigkeit der Forderungen aus L+L	4,12-mal		
	⌀ Kreditfrist	87–88 Tage		
4	Umschlagshäufigkeit der Verbindlichkeiten aus L+L	4,47-mal		
	⌀ Kreditfrist	80–81 Tage		
5	Umschlagshäufigkeit des Lagers	4,33-mal		
	⌀ Lagerdauer	83–84 Tage		

C

		20_1	20_2	20_3
1	Fremdkapitalzinsen (= Finanzaufwand)	10	12	14
	⌀ Fremdkapital	190	212,5	227,5
	Zinssatz	5,26 %	5,65 %	6,15 %

2 Da die Rentabilität des Gesamtkapitals (siehe Ergebnisse **B** 2) in allen drei Jahren kleiner ist als der Fremdkapitalzinssatz (siehe Ergebnisse **C** 1), wird sich der erhöhte Einsatz von Fremdkapital, zulasten des Eigenkapitals (= Verminderung der Eigenkapitalquote), negativ auf die Rentabilität des Eigenkapitals auswirken (Negativer Leverage-Effekt).[1]

---

1 Siehe auch Kapitel 5, Analyse des Jahresabschlusses, 55 Analyse der Bilanz, Analyse der Passiven (Kapitalstruktur).

3.9 Planungsrechnung der Sesselbahn AG

A **Planerfolgsrechnung 20_1/20_2**

Jahresgewinn 20_0/20_1		82
Zusätzlicher Ertrag:		
Mehrumsatz aus Investition	+620	
Gewinn Verkauf altes Pistenfahrzeug	+ 90	+710
Zusätzlicher Aufwand:		
Zusatzabschreibung Sesselbahn (inkl. Abbruch)	–350	
Abschreibung Pistenfahrzeug	– 50	
Rückstellung Pistenerweiterung	–100	
Hypothekarzins	– 20	
Zusatzkosten Energie	– 20	
Zusatzkosten Personal	– 80	
Zusatzkosten Werbung	– 50	–670
Planjahresgewinn 20_1/20_2		122

B Finanzplan als Plangeldflussrechnung 20_1/20_2

		Fonds Flüssige Mittel	
		Zunahme	Abnahme
Geschäftsbereich			
Jahresgewinn	122		
Abschreibungen bisher	1 502		
Rückstellungen bisher	212		
Abschreibung Sesselbahn	350		
Abschreibung Pistenfahrzeug	50		
Zunahme Rückstellung Pistenerweiterung	100		
Gewinn Verkauf Pistenfahrzeuge	– 90		
Zunahme Forderungen aus L+L	– 31		
Abnahme Verbindlichkeiten aus L+L	– 84		
Cashflow	2 131	2 131	
Investitionsbereich			
Sesselbahn (Rest)	–2 000		
Abbruch alte Bahn	– 500		
Verkauf Pistenfahrzeug	90		
Kauf neues Pistenfahrzeug	– 400		
Investition Gebäude	–2 000		
Nettogeldabfluss	–4 810		4 810
Finanzierungsbereich			
Aufnahme Hypothek	400		
Aufnahme Bankkredit (Residualgrösse) [1]	227		
Nettogeldzufluss	627	627	
Veränderung Fonds Flüssige Mittel			
Anfangsbestand	4 052		
Endbestand	2 000		
Abnahme Flüssige Mittel	–2 052	2 052	
		4 810	4 810

[1] Differenzrechnung

3.10 Comi AG

Finanzplan als Plangeldflussrechnung 20_1

		Fonds Flüssige Mittel	
		Zunahme	Abnahme
Geschäftsbereich			
Jahresgewinn ①	2 218		
Abschreibungen ②	+1 120		
A.o. Ertrag aus Verkauf AV	− 100		
Abnahme Forderungen aus L+L ③	+ 200		
Abnahme Vorräte	+ 280		
Zunahme Verbindlichkeiten aus L+L	+ 160		
Cashflow	+3 878	3 878	
Investitionsbereich			
Restzahlung Maschinen	−4 800		
Ersatzinvestitionen	−2 800		
Wertschriftenverkauf	+2 000		
Verkauf Maschinen	+ 800		
Nettogeldabfluss	−4 800		4 800
Finanzierungsbereich			
Gewinnausschüttung	− 480		
Aufnahme Bankkredit (Differenzrechnung) ④	+ 862		
Nettogeldzufluss	+ 382	382	
Veränderung Fonds Flüssige Mittel			
Anfangsbestand	800		
Endbestand	260		
Abnahme Flüssige Mittel	− 540	540	
		4 800	4 800

① 1 368 + 3 200 − 600 − 560 − 720 − 440 − 200 = 2 048 + 70 + 100 = 2 218
② 400 + 720 = 1 120
③ 16 960 + 3 200 = 20 160 : 12 Monate = 1 680
 AB 1 880 − SB 1 680 = Abnahme 200
④ Residualgrösse

4 Konzernrechnung

4.1 Konsolidierungspflicht

1. ☒ OR 963/1
2. ☒ OR 963/2 Ziffer 1
3. ☐ OR 963/1
   Eine Kollektivgesellschaft ist eine Personengesellschaft und keine juristische Person.
4. ☒ OR 963a/1 Ziffer 1
5. ☐ OR 963a/1 Ziffer 1
6. ☐ OR 963a/2 Ziffer 2
   Die Aktionäre müssen mindestens 20% des Grundkapitals vertreten.
7. ☒ OR 963b/1 Ziffer 2
8. ☒ OR 963b/1 Ziffer 1
9. ☒ OR 963b/4 Ziffer 1
10. ☐ OR 963b/1 Ziffer 1
    Das Rechnungslegungsrecht verlangt nur die Anwendung eines anerkannten Standards. Die Schweizer Börse lässt Swiss GAAP FER nur im Domestic Standard zu – nicht aber im Main Standard.

4.2 Konsolidierung einer 100%igen Tochtergesellschaft

A

Aktiven	Delta AG	Eta AG	Summen	Elimination	Konzern
Flüssige Mittel	500	0	500		500
Forderungen	0	200	200		200
Vorräte	0	500	500		500
Darlehen Eta	300	0	300	−300	0
Beteiligung Eta	200	0	200	−200	0
Übriges Anlagevermögen	0	1 000	1 000		1 000
	1 000	1 700	2 700	−500	2 200

Passiven	Delta AG	Eta AG	Summen	Elimination	Konzern
Darlehen Delta	0	300	300	−300	0
Übriges Fremdkapital	500	1 200	1 700		1 700
Aktienkapital	500	200	700	−200	500
	1 000	1 700	2 700	−500	2 200

B

Darlehen Delta	/ Darlehen Eta	300
Aktienkapital	/ Beteiligung Eta	200

C

	Delta AG	Eta AG	Konzern
Fremdfinanzierungsgrad	50 %	88 %	77 %
Eigenfinanzierungsgrad	50 %	12 %	23 %

Durch die Konsolidierung wird der Eigenfinanzierungsgrad in der Konzernbilanz (gegenüber dem Einzelabschluss der Delta AG [= Muttergesellschaft]) normalerweise verschlechtert (hier von 50 % auf 23 %).

4.3 Konsolidierung Carmen AG und Tamara AG

A

	Carmen AG		Tamara AG		Korrekturen		Summen-saldobilanz		Konzernbilanz		Konzern-erfolgsrechnung	
	Soll	Haben	Soll	Haben	Soll	Haben	Soll	Haben	Aktiven	Passiven	Aufwand	Ertrag
Flüssige Mittel	300		180				480		480			
Forderungen	2 700		2 100			250, 100	4 450		4 450			
Warenvorrat	5 000		3 800			40	8 760		8 760			
Mobilien	10 000		7 400				17 400		17 400			
Beteiligung	8 000					8 000	–					
Goodwill	–	–	–	–	180		180		180			
Kurzfr. Verbindlichkeiten		2 320		1 230	100			3 450		3 450		
Banken		800		1 200				2 000		2 000		
Darlehen		11 000		2 900	250			13 650		13 650		
Gewinnvortrag		40		20	20			40		40		
Reserven		5 000		1 800	1 800			5 000		5 000		
Aktienkapital		7 000		6 000	6 000			7 000		7 000		
Warenertrag		24 300		17 200	800			40 700				40 700
Sonstige Erträge		40		60	3			97				97
Warenaufwand	16 200		12 900		40	800	28 340				28 340	
Übriger Aufwand	8 300		4 030			3	12 327				12 327	
Konzernerfolg	–	–	–	–						130	130	
	50 500	50 500	30 410	30 410	9 193	9 193	71 937	71 937	31 270	31 270	40 797	40 797

B	1		Aktienkapital	/ Beteiligung	6 000
			Reserven	/ Beteiligung	1 800
			Gewinnvortrag	/ Beteiligung	20
			Goodwill	/ Beteiligung	180
	2	a	Warenertrag	/ Warenaufwand	800
			Warenaufwand	/ Warenvorrat	40
		b	Kurzfristige Verbindlichkeiten	/ Forderungen	100
		c	Darlehen	/ Forderungen	250
			Sonstige Erträge	/ Übriger Aufwand	3

C	1	Bezahlter Goodwill oder vorhandene, vor der Konsolidierung nicht aufgelöste stille Reserven
	2	Liquiditätsgrad 2 = (Flüssige Mittel + Forderungen) : Kurzfristiges Fremdkapital · 100 %
		Carmen AG = 3 000 : 3 120 · 100 % = 96,2 %
		Tamara AG = 2 030 : 2 430 · 100 % = 83,5 % ~~93,83 %~~
		Konzern = 4 930 : 5 450 · 100 % = 90,5 %

4.4 Konsolidierung mit Minderheitsanteilen

A

Aktiven	Mu AG	To AG	Summenbilanz	Eliminationen	Konzernbilanz
Flüssige Mittel	10	10	20		20
Forderungen aus L+L	200	400	600		600
Forderung To AG	100	0	100	–100	0
Vorräte	400	400	800		800
Beteiligung To AG	200	0	200	–120– 36–44	0
Maschinen	150	200	350		350
Immobilien	500	0	500		500
Goodwill				+ 44	44
	1 560	1 010	2 570	–256	2 314

Passiven	Mu AG	To AG	Summenbilanz	Eliminationen	Konzernbilanz
Verbindlichkeiten aus L+L	200	400	600		600
Bank	100	250	350		350
Verbindlichkeiten Mu AG	0	100	100	–100	0
Rückstellung	50	0	50		50
Hypotheken	350	0	350		350
Aktienkapital	500	200	700	–80–120	500
Reserven	360	60	420	–24–36	360
Minderheitsanteile				+80+24	104
	1 560	1 010	2 570	–256	2 314

B

Verbindlichkeiten Mu AG	/ Forderung To AG	100
Aktienkapital	/ Beteiligung	120
Reserven	/ Beteiligung	36
Goodwill	/ Beteiligung	44
Aktienkapital	/ Minderheitsanteile	80
Reserven	/ Minderheitsanteile	24

4.5 Konsolidierung Miri AG und Franga AG

A

	Miri AG		Franga AG		Korrekturen		Konzern-schlussbilanz		Konzern-erfolgsrechnung	
	Soll	Haben	Soll	Haben	Soll	Haben	Aktiven	Passiven	Aufwand	Ertrag
Flüssige Mittel	500		800				1 300			
Forderungen	1 900		1 000			600	2 300			
Warenvorräte	2 500		800			100	3 200			
Beteiligung Franga AG	4 000					4 000	0			
Darlehen Franga AG	1 500					1 500	0			
Sachanlagen	9 000		4 000				13 000			
Goodwill					1 200		1 200			
Kurzfristige Verbindlichkeiten		3 500		1 400	600			4 300		
Darlehen Miri AG				1 500	1 500			0		
Aktienkapital		12 000		2 000	2 000			12 000		
Reserven		2 200		1 500	1 500			2 200		
Minderheitsanteile (Bilanz)						700		700		
Gewinn Holding (Bilanz)								1 760		
Gewinn Minderheiten (Bilanz)								40		
Warenertrag		14 400		8 200	3 000					19 600
Warenaufwand	10 000		6 200		100	3 000			13 300	
Personalaufwand	1 900		1 400						3 300	
Übriger Betriebsaufwand	900		310						1 210	
Finanzertrag		100			90					10
Finanzaufwand			90			90				
Gewinn Holding (ER)									1 760	
Gewinn Minderheiten (ER)									40	
	32 200	32 200	14 600	14 600	9 990	9 990	21 000	21 000	19 610	19 610

B 1

Aktienkapital	/ Minderheitsanteile (Bilanz)	400
Reserven	/ Minderheitsanteile (Bilanz)	300
Aktienkapital	/ Beteiligung	1 600
Reserven	/ Beteiligung	1 200
Goodwill	/ Beteiligung	1 200

2

Darlehen Miri AG	/ Darlehen Franga AG	1 500
Finanzertrag	/ Finanzaufwand	90

3

Kurzfristige Verbindlichkeiten	/ Forderungen	600
Warenertrag	/ Warenaufwand	3 000
Warenaufwand	/ Warenvorräte	100

4.6 Konsolidierung Mela SA und Filu SA

A

	Mela SA Aktiven	Mela SA Passiven	Filu SA Aktiven	Filu SA Passiven	Korrekturen Soll	Korrekturen Haben	Konzern Aktiven	Konzern Passiven
Flüssige Mittel	2 000		1 100				3 100	
Forderungen aus L+L	3 500		400				3 900	
Konzernforderungen	900		0			900	0	
Vorräte	2 000		1 800			20	3 780	
Beteiligung Filu SA	800		0			600 +150 + 50	0	
Goodwill					50		50	
Kurzfristige Verbindlichkeiten		4 000		1 200				5 200
Konzernverbindlichkeiten		0		900	900			0
Aktienkapital		3 000		800	200 + 600			3 000
Reserven		1 900		200	50 + 150	60		1 960
Jahresgewinn		300		200	50 + 20 + 60			370
Minderheitsanteile					200 + 50 + 50			300
	9 200	9 200	3 300	3 300	2 080	2 080	10 830	10 830

	Mela SA Aufwand	Mela SA Ertrag	Filu SA Aufwand	Filu SA Ertrag	Korrekturen Soll	Korrekturen Haben	Konzern Aufwand	Konzern Ertrag
Warenertrag		16 190		4 650	1 000			19 840
Zinsertrag		150		0	50			100
Beteiligungsertrag		60		0	60			0
Warenaufwand	15 000		4 000		20	1 000	18 020	
Übriger Betriebsaufwand	1 000		400				1 400	
Zinsaufwand	100		50			50	100	
Jahresgewinn	300		200		50 + 20 + 60		370	
Gewinn Minderheitsanteile					50		50	
	16 400	16 400	4 650	4 650	1 180	1 180	19 940	19 940

B

	1	Aktienkapital	/ Minderheitsanteile (Bilanz)	200
		Reserven	/ Minderheitsanteile (Bilanz)	50
		Aktienkapital	/ Beteiligung	600
		Reserven	/ Beteiligung	150
		Goodwill	/ Beteiligung	50
	2	Gewinn Minderheiten (ER)	/ Jahresgewinn Filu SA (ER)	50
		Jahresgewinn Filu SA (Bilanz)	/ Minderheitsanteile (Bilanz)	50
	3 a	Konzernverbindlichkeiten	/ Konzernforderungen	900
	b	Zinsertrag	/ Zinsaufwand	50
	c	Warenertrag	/ Warenaufwand	1 000
	4	Warenaufwand	/ Jahresgewinn (ER)	20
		Jahresgewinn (Bilanz)	/ Vorräte	20
	5	Beteiligungsertrag	/ Jahresgewinn (ER)	60
		Jahresgewinn (Bilanz)	/ Reserven	60

4.7 Konsolidierung Moderna SA und Oldi SA

A

	Moderna SA		Oldi SA		Korrekturen		Konzern	
	Aktiven	Passiven	Aktiven	Passiven	Soll	Haben	Aktiven	Passiven
Flüssige Mittel	24		30				54	
Forderungen	34		40			12	62	
Vorräte	38		24				62	
Beteiligung Oldi SA	120		0			48 + 24 + 48	0	
Übriges Anlagevermögen	60		80			40	100	
Goodwill					48		48	
Kurzfristiges Fremdkapital		38		24	12			50
Langfristiges Fremdkapital		70		50	40			80
Aktienkapital		100		60	12 + 48			100
Reserven		60		30	6 + 24	6		66
Jahresgewinn		8		10	2 + 6			10
Minderheitsanteile						12 + 6 + 2		20
	276	276	174	174	198	198	326	326

	Aufwand	Ertrag	Aufwand	Ertrag	Soll	Haben	Aufwand	Ertrag
Warenertrag		150		240				390
Beteiligungsertrag		6			6			0
Übriger Ertrag		48		34	2 + 18			62
Warenaufwand	80		130		(80 + 20)	(80 + 20)	210	
Übriger Betriebsaufwand	100		110			18	192	
Finanzaufwand	16		24			2	38	
Jahresgewinn	8		10			2 + 6	10	
Gewinn Minderheitsanteile						2	2	
	204	204	274	274	128	128	452	452

B	1	Aktienkapital	/ Minderheitsanteile (Bilanz)	12
		Reserven	/ Minderheitsanteile (Bilanz)	6
		Aktienkapital	/ Beteiligung	48
		Reserven	/ Beteiligung	24
		Goodwill	/ Beteiligung	48
	2	Gewinn Minderheiten (ER)	/ Jahresgewinn (ER)	2
		Gewinn (Bilanz)	/ Minderheitsanteile (Bilanz)	2
	3	Beteiligungsertrag	/ Jahresgewinn (ER)	6
		Jahresgewinn (Bilanz)	/ Reserven	6
	4	Langfristiges Fremdkapital	/ Übriges Anlagevermögen	40
		Übriger Ertrag	/ Finanzaufwand	2
	5	Kurzfristiges Fremdkapital	/ Forderungen	12
	6	Warenaufwand	/ Warenaufwand	80 [1]
		Warenaufwand	/ Warenaufwand	20 [1]
	7	Übriger Ertrag	/ Übriger Betriebsaufwand	18
C		Warenertrag	/ Warenaufwand	25
		Warenaufwand	/ Vorräte	5

[1] oder keine Buchung

4.8 Modern Holding

	Tatbestand	Geschäftsbereich	Investitionsbereich	Finanzierungsbereich	Kein Bereich oder liquiditätsunwirksam
1	Kauf von Sachanlagen		x, A		
2	Emission einer Anleihe			x, E	
3	Dividendenzahlung an Holding-Aktionäre			x, A	
4	Aktienkapitalerhöhung mit Agio			x, E	
5a	Verkauf einer assoziierten Gesellschaft – Verkaufswert		x, E		
5b	Gewinn	x, U			
6	Umwandlung PS-Kapital in Aktienkapital				x
7	Eine konsolidierte Tochter zahlt der Holding eine Dividende.				x
8	Produktion auf Lager	x, U			
9	Bildung einer Steuerrückstellung	x, U			
10	Abschreibung des Goodwills	x, U			
11	Zunahme der Forderungen aus L+L	x, U			
12	Abnahme Vorräte	x, U			
13	Kauf von Wertschriften		x, A		
14	Erfassung von (Buch-)Gewinnen aus Anwendung der Equity-Methode	x, U			
15	Erhöhung des Aktienkapitals einer 100%igen Tochtergesellschaft				x
16	Dividendenauszahlung einer Tochtergesellschaft an einen Minderheitsaktionär			x, A	
17	Erhöhung WB Forderungen aus L+L	x, U			
18	Bedingte Kapitalerhöhung				x
19	Rückzahlung eines Teils des Aktiennennwerts an die Holding-Aktionäre			x, A	
20	Erhöhung der Verbindlichkeiten aus L+L	x, U			

Geldfluss aus Geschäftsbereich = Konzerngewinn – 5b – 8 + 9 + 10 – 11 + 12 – 14 + 17 + 20

4.9 Konzerngeldflussrechnung der Cormi Gruppe

A   3026 + 40 = 3 066

B
1. Falsch; siehe Investitionsbereich
2. Falsch; im Gegenteil, Kauf von 301
3. Richtig; nicht liquiditätswirksamer Aufwand
4. Falsch; Käufe von 1 192 sind kleiner als der Geldzufluss aus Geschäftstätigkeit von 2 097
5. Falsch; keine Angaben im Finanzierungsbereich

C   Forderungen aus L+L
Schlechtes Zahlungsverhalten, längere Zahlungskonditionen, grosse Auslieferungen vor dem Abschluss
Vorräte
Produktion auf Halde, Absatzprobleme, Vergrösserung des Betriebes bzw. Umsatzes

D   Passivtausch ohne Liquiditätsveränderung

Wandelanleihe   / Aktienkapital

E   Kasse, Post- und Bankguthaben auf Sicht, Call-Gelder, Terminguthaben bei Post und Bank mit einer Restlaufzeit von weniger als 90 Tagen

F   Dividende in % des Konzerngewinnes; 259 · 100 : 1 495 = 17,3 %
Eine höhere Auszahlung wäre vermutlich möglich gewesen (siehe Bestand Flüssige Mittel).
(Korrekt müsste die Dividende in Prozent vom Vorjahresgewinn gerechnet werden, ist aber nicht bekannt.)

4.10 Konzerngeldflussrechnung der Marmic Gruppe

A Dividende in % des Konzerngewinnes (Payout Ratio);
4,0 · 100 : 7,2 = 55,6 %
Nein, da der operative Cashflow von 1,3 negativ ist, d. h. ein Nettogeldabfluss aus Geschäftstätigkeit (= Cashloss) stattfand.

B
- Zunahme der Forderungen aus L + L von 33,9 gegenüber einer Abnahme von 2,7 im Vorjahr.
- Zunahme der Vorräte von 10,9 gegenüber einer Zunahme von nur 0,7 im Vorjahr.
- Die Verbindlichkeiten aus L + L haben zwar um 12,7 zugenommen, was einer Liquiditätsverbesserung gleichkommt. Trotzdem hat sich der operative Cashflow von +5,2 auf –1,3 stark verschlechtert.

C Mögliche Gründe:
- Geschäftsausweitung
- Produktion auf Halde
- Absatzprobleme

D
- Aufnahme einer Anleihe 40,0
- Verkauf von Sachanlagen 7,3
- Kapitalerhöhung 10,7 im Vorjahr
- Aufnahme von (kurz- oder langfristigen) Bankkrediten 7,3 bzw. 14,6 im Vorjahr

Einerseits: Fristenkonforme Finanzierung mit langfristigem Kapital; 40 + 10,7
Andererseits: Zunahme der Fremdfinanzierung und somit der eingegangenen Risiken

E

Verkaufspreis	– Gewinn / + Verlust	= Buchwert
20_4: 7,3	– 2,3	= 5,0
20_3: 1,4	+ 0,4	= 1,8

F Mögliche Gründe:
- Ausweitung des Geschäftsvolumens
- Hoher Bestand am Jahresende
- Kunden zahlen nicht pünktlich
- Verlängerung der Zahlungsfristen
- Konjunkturlage; den Kunden fehlt die Liquidität

G
- Agio 10,7 – 5 = 5,7
- Gesetzliche Kapitalreserve

4.11 Quotenkonsolidierung

	Bilanzen		80%	Bereinigung		Konzern
	MAG	BAG	BAG	Soll	Haben	
Aktiven						
Flüssige Mittel	4 945	160	128			5 073
Wertschriften	7 750	0	0			7 750
Forderungen	7 280	180	144			7 424
Vorräte	10 200	600	480			10 680
Darlehen	1 195	0	0			1 195
Beteiligungen	17 850	300	240		1 602	16 488
Sachanlagen	12 500	1 550	1 240			13 740
Immaterielle Anlagen	280	0	0			280
Goodwill	0	0	0	130	26	104
	62 000	2 790	2 232			62 734
Passiven						
Kurzfristige Verbindlichkeiten	6 000	765	612			6 612
Obligationenanleihe	10 000	0	0			10 000
Hypotheken	7 600	0	0			7 600
Rückstellungen	2 080	10	8			2 088
Aktienkapital	20 000	1 000	800	800		20 000
Kapitalreserve (Agio)	10 000	700	560	560		10 000
Gewinnreserven	3 220	0	0			3 220
Neubewertungsreserve	0	140	112	112		
Jahresgewinn	3 100	175	140	26		3 214
	62 000	2 790	2 232	1 628	1 628	62 734

Berechnung Goodwill

	100%	80%	
Kaufpreis			1 602
Eigenkapital BAG	1 000	800	
Kapitalreserve	700	560	
Neubewertungsreserve	140	112	
	1 840	1 472	1 472
Bezahlter Goodwill			130
Jahresabschreibung Goodwill			26

4.12 Vergleich zwischen Voll-, Quotenkonsolidierung und Equity-Methode

	Voll-konsolidierung	Quoten-konsolidierung	Equity-Methode
Aktiven			
Forderungen aus L+L	2 520	2 240	1 820
Vorräte	2 300	1 980	1 500
Darlehen an T	0	80	200
Beteiligung an T	0	0	870
Sachanlagen	4 500	4 300	4 000
	9 320	8 600	8 390
Passiven			
Verbindlichkeiten aus L+L	1 750	1 650	1 500
Darlehen	2 100	2 060	2 000
Aktienkapital	2 000	2 000	2 000
Gewinnreserven	2 300	2 300	2 300
Jahresgewinn	590	590	590
Gewinn Minderheitsanteile	60	0	0
Kapital Minderheitsanteile	520	0	0
	9 320	8 600	8 390
Aufwand			
Warenaufwand	9 500	9 100	8 500
Übriger Aufwand	2 850	2 510	2 000
Gewinn Holding	590	590	590
Gewinn Minderheitsanteile	60	0	0
	13 000	12 200	11 090
Ertrag			
Warenertrag	11 800	11 080	10 000
Übriger Ertrag	1 200	1 120	1 000
Ertrag aus Equity-Methode			90
	13 000	12 200	11 090

4.13 Wahl der Konsolidierungsmethode und Goodwill

A

Schlussbilanz	Voll-konsolidierung; Goodwill mit EK verrechnen	Voll-konsolidierung; Goodwill aktivieren und abschreiben	Quoten-konsolidierung; Goodwill mit EK verrechnen	Equity-Methode; Goodwill mit EK verrechnen
Aktiven				
Umlaufvermögen	320	320	250	180
Sachanlagen	160	160	80	0
Beteiligung BAG				100
Goodwill		184 ①		
	480	664	330	280
Passiven				
Fremdkapital	200	200	150	100
Eigenkapital Holding-Aktionäre	180	364	180	180
Kapital Minderheitsanteile	100	100	0	0
	480	664	330	280
Erfolgsrechnung				
Nettoerlös	900	900	700	500
Abschreibung Sachanlagen	– 30	– 30	– 15	0
Abschreibung Goodwill		– 46		
Übriger Aufwand	–810	–810	–635	–460
Ertrag aus Equity-Methode	0	0	0	10
Gewinn Minderheitsanteile	– 10	– 10	0	0
Gewinn Holding-Aktionäre	50	4	50	50

① Berechnung Goodwill
  Anschaffungskosten der 50%-Beteiligung der BAG   320
    Eigenkapital BAG am 31.12.20_3   200
    – Jahresgewinn 20_3   – 20
    Eigenkapital BAG am 1.1.20_3   180
  – 50%-Anteil   – 90
    Goodwill im Erwerbszeitpunkt   230
  – Jahresabschreibung Goodwill (230 : 5)   – 46
    Noch nicht amortisierter Goodwill am 31.12.20_3   184

B		Voll-konsolidierung; Goodwill mit EK verrechnen	Voll-konsolidierung; Goodwill aktivieren und abschreiben	Quoten-konsolidierung; Goodwill mit EK verrechnen	Equity-Methode; Goodwill mit EK verrechnen
1	Eigenkapitalrendite	28 %	1,1 %	28 %	28 %
2	Eigenkapitalquote	58 %	70 %	55 %	64 %
3	Cashflow	80	80	65	50
4	Umsatzrendite	6 %	0,5 %	7 %	10 %

C
- Alle Methoden zeigen den gleichen Jahresgewinn und das gleiche Eigenkapital für die Holding-Aktionäre, wenn der Goodwill im Erwerbszeitpunkt mit dem Eigenkapital verrechnet wird. Dadurch ist die Eigenkapitalrendite bei der ersten, dritten und vierten Methode gleich gross.

  Bei Aktivierung des Goodwills ist das Eigenkapital grösser und der Jahresgewinn kleiner wegen der Goodwill-Abschreibung.
- Die Vollkonsolidierung zeigt am meisten Umsatz (Nettoerlös), d. h. auch den ganzen Umsatz der Tochtergesellschaft.
- Bei der Goodwillaktivierung steigt das Eigenkapital, und der Jahresgewinn der Holding-Aktionäre sinkt wegen der Amortisation des Goodwills. Die Eigenkapitalrendite verschlechtert sich dadurch. Auch die Umsatzrendite ist schlechter.
- Die Quotenkonsolidierung ist ein Mittelweg zwischen Equity-Methode und Vollkonsolidierung. Sie zeigt mehr Umsatz und Cashflow als die Equity-Methode.
- Bei der Equity-Methode erscheint das Fremdkapital der BAG nicht in der Konzernbilanz. Dadurch ist die Eigenkapitalquote am höchsten mit 64 %. Die Umsatzrendite ist auch am höchsten, weil nur der Umsatz der Muttergesellschaft erscheint, jedoch der anteilige Gewinn der Tochtergesellschaft als Ertrag aus der Equity-Methode übernommen wird.
- Aus Sicht der Konzernleitung ist die direkte Verrechnung des Goodwills mit dem Eigenkapital vorteilhaft, da keine Goodwill-Amortisationen den Jahreserfolg schmälern. Das Eigenkapital wird dadurch allerdings kleiner, somit nimmt die Eigenkapitalquote ab.

D Die Wahl der Konsolidierungsmethode ist abhängig von der Höhe der Beteiligung (Stimmrechtsanteile). Für die Ermittlung der Minderheitsanteile ist die wertmässige (kapitalmässige) Beteiligung relevant.

Beteiligung (Stimmrechte)	Konsolidierungsmethode und Besonderheiten
100 %	– Vollkonsolidierung ohne Minderheiten – keine Minderheitsanteile
> 50 %–100 %	– Vollkonsolidierung mit Minderheiten – Ausweis der Minderheiten (Nicht beherrschende Anteile) in Bilanz und Erfolgsrechnung
genau 50 %	– Quotenkonsolidierung bei Jointventures – Anteilmässige Erfassung von 　– Aktiven und Fremdkapital 　– Aufwand und Ertrag – keine Minderheitsanteile
20 %–50 %	– Equity-Methode für assoziierte Unternehmen – Keine Konsolidierung – Bewertung und Ausweis der Beteiligung zu ihrem anteiligen Eigenkapital bzw. Substanzwert
unter 20 %	– Keine Konsolidierung

4.14 Stichtagsmethode

Bilanz der TAG im Erwerbszeitpunkt vom 1.1.20_1 in EUR und in CHF

	EUR	Kurs	CHF		EUR	Kurs	CHF
Flüssige Mittel	100	1.26	126	Kurzfristiges Fremdkapital	300	1.26	378
Forderungen	200	1.26	252	Langfristiges Fremdkapital	200	1.26	252
Vorräte	300	1.26	378	Aktienkapital	400	1.26	504
Sachanlagen	400	1.26	504	Kapitalreserven	100	1.26	126
	1 000		1 260		1 000		1 260

Erfolgsrechnung der TAG 20_1 in EUR und in CHF

	EUR	Kurs	CHF
Warenertrag	10 000	1.24	12 400
Warenaufwand	6 000	1.24	7 440
Übriger Aufwand	3 600	1.24	4 464
Jahresgewinn	400		496

Schlussbilanz der TAG vom 31.12.20_1 in EUR und in CHF

	EUR	Kurs	CHF		EUR	Kurs	CHF
Flüssige Mittel	150	1.20	180	Kurzfristiges Fremdkapital	250	1.20	300
Forderungen	300	1.20	360	Langfristiges Fremdkapital	150	1.20	180
Vorräte	400	1.20	480	Aktienkapital	400	1.26	504
Sachanlagen	450	1.20	540	Kapitalreserve	100	1.26	126
				Jahresgewinn	400	1.24	496
				Umrechnungsdifferenz	–	–	– 46
	1 300		1 560		1 300		1 560

Die ausgewiesene Umrechnungsdifferenz setzt sich wie folgt zusammen:

Fremdwährungsdifferenz auf dem Nettovermögen (Eigenkapital) am 1.1.20_1	–30	(500 EUR · [1.20 – 1.26])
Fremdwährungsdifferenz beim Jahresgewinn	–16	(400 EUR · [1.20 – 1.24])
Umrechnungsdifferenz zum Ausgleich in der Schlussbilanz	–46	

4.15 Stille Reserven in den Vorräten und Sachanlagen sowie latente Steuern

Warenvorräte	Einzelabschluss (66⅔%)	Konzern-abschluss (100%)	Stille Reserven brutto (33⅓%)	Steuerrück-stellung für latente Steuern (30% von den Stillen Reserven)	Stille Reserven netto
31.12.20_4	12	18	6	1,8	4,2
31.12.20_5	16	24	8	2,4	5,6
Veränderung	+ 4	+ 6	+2	+0,6	+1,4

Konsolidierungsbuchungen

Warenvorräte	/ Gewinnreserven	6,0
Warenvorräte	/ Warenaufwand	2,0
Gewinnreserven	/ Steuerrückstellung für latente Steuern	1,8
Latenter Steueraufwand	/ Steuerrückstellung für latente Steuern	0,6

Sachanlagen	Einzelabschluss (60%)	Konzern-abschluss (100%)	Stille Reserven brutto (40%)	Steuerrück-stellung für latente Steuern (30% von den Stillen Reserven)	Stille Reserven netto
31.12.20_4	7,2	12	4,8	1,44	3,36
31.12.20_5	5,4	9	3,6	1,08	2,52
Veränderung	−1,8	− 3	−1,2	−0,36	−0,84

Konsolidierungsbuchungen

Sachanlagen	/ Gewinnreserven	4,80
Abschreibung	/ Sachanlagen	1,20
Gewinnreserven	/ Steuerrückstellung für latente Steuern	1,44
Steuerrückstellung für latente Steuern	/ Latenter Steuerertrag	0,36

4.16 Eigenkapitalnachweis der MH-Gruppe

	Aktien-kapital	Kapital-reserve	Gewinn-reserven	Umrech-nungs-differenz	Eigen-kapital (ohne Minder-heiten)	Minder-heitsanteile	Eigen-kapital (total)
Bestand 1.1.20_6	6000	1520	3710	− 560	10670	430	11100
Konzerngewinn			1170		1170	30	1200
Dividenden			− 815		− 815	− 5	− 820
Kapitalerhöhung	200	200			400		400
Umrechnungsdiff.				− 205	− 205	− 5	− 210
Bestand 31.12.20_6	6200	1720	4065	− 765	11220	450	11670

4.17 Eigenkapitalnachweis des Vulcano-Konzerns

	Aktien-kapital	Kapital-reserve	Gewinn-reserven	Umrech-nungs-differenz	Eigen-kapital (ohne Minder-heiten)	Minder-heitsanteile	Eigen-kapital (total)
Bestand 1.1.20_1	101,3	66,0	129,9	−6,0	291,2	34,5	325,7
Kapitalerhöhung	16,0	11,5			27,5		27,5
Konzerngewinn			17,5		17,5	2,1	19,6
Dividenden			− 5,9		− 5,9	− 1,5	− 7,4
Währungsverluste				−1,2	− 1,2	− 0,3	− 1,5
Kauf Minderheits-anteile						− 7,0	− 7,0
Goodwill beim Kauf			− 2,9		− 2,9		− 2,9
Bestand 31.12.20_1	117,3	77,5	138,6	−7,2	326,2	27,8	354,0

5 Analyse des Jahresabschlusses

5.1 Analyse der Bilancio SA

1   2 900 · 100 : 4 000 =   72,5 %
2   1 100 · 100 : 4 000 =   27,5 %
3   1 500 · 100 : 4 000 =   37,5 %
4   2 500 · 100 : 4 000 =   62,5 %
5   1 030 · 100 : 2 500 =   41,2 %   (Der Gewinnvortrag ist ein Teil der Gewinnreserven.)
6   120 · 100 :   450 =   26,7 %
7   490 · 100 :   450 = 108,9 %
8   1 100 · 100 :   450 = 244,4 %
9   2 500 · 100 : 2 900 =   86,2 %
10 3 550 · 100 : 2 900 = 122,4 %

5.2 Analyse der Erfo SA

1   2 800 − 100   = 2 700
2   3 500 · 100 : 2 800 = 125 %
3   700 · 100 : 6 300 = 11,1 %
4   4 200 · 100 : 2 800 = 150 %
5   4 200 · 100 : 7 000 = 60 %
6   700 · 100 : 7 000 = 10 %
7   7 000 : 700   = 10-mal
      360 : 10   = 36 Tage
8   2 700 : 300   = 9-mal
      360 :   9   = 40 Tage
9   2 800 : 350   = 8-mal
      360 :   8   = 45 Tage

5.3 Analyse der Bilerfa SA

[A] Erfolgsrechnung

Warenertrag		560
Warenaufwand		–392
Bruttogewinn		168
Personalaufwand	110	
Sonstiger Betriebsaufwand	20	–130
Betriebsgewinn vor Abschreibungen (EBITDA)		38
Abschreibungen		– 15
Betriebsgewinn vor Finanzerfolg (EBIT)		23
Finanzaufwand		– 5
Jahresgewinn		18

[B] Bilanz

Aktiven					Passiven				
Umlaufvermögen					**Kurzfristiges Fremdkapital**				
Kasse			5		Verbindlichkeiten aus L+L			33	
Post			60	65	Bankschuld			11	
Forderungen aus L+L		55			Dividende			10	
WB Forderungen aus L+L		– 5	50	50	Passive Rechnungsabgrenzung			3	57
Warenvorrat			55	170	**Langfristiges Fremdkapital**				
Anlagevermögen					Hypothek			200	257
Mobilien		70			**Eigenkapital**				
WB Mobilien		–25	45		Aktienkapital			270	
Immobilien			340	385 385	Gesetzliche Kapitalreserve			10	
					Gesetzliche Gewinnreserve			10	
					Freiwillige Gewinnreserven			6	
					Gewinnvortrag		2	28	298
				555					555

C
1. 385 · 100 : 555 = 69,3 %
2. 257 · 100 : 555 = 46,3 %
3. 18 · 100 : 298 = 6,0 % (Der Gewinnvortrag ist ein Teil der Gewinnreserven.)
4. 115 · 100 : 57 = 201,8 %
5. 170 − 57,0 = 113
6. 498 · 100 : 385 = 129,3 %
7. 150 · 100 : 392 = 38,2 %
8. 402 : 33,0 = 12,2-mal
   360 : 12,2 = 29–30 Tage
9. 392 : 55,0 = 7,1-mal
   360 : 7,1 = 50–51 Tage
10. 18 · 100 : 298 = 6 %

5.4 Stille Reserven auf den Forderungen aus L+L

A

WB Forderungen aus L+L	Extern	Intern	Stille Reserven
Anfangsbestand	17 500.−	10 000.−	7 500.−
Endbestand	14 500.−	12 000.−	2 500.−
Veränderung	− 3 000.−	+ 2 000.−	−5 000.−

B WB Forderungen aus L+L   / Forderungsverluste   3 000.−

C 20 000.− − 5 000.− = Fr. 15 000.−

5.5 Betriebsergebnis und stille Reserven

A

Buchwert Maschinen am 31.12.20_4	260 000.–
Abschreibungen 20_4	70 000.–
Buchwert Maschinen am 31.12.20_3	330 000.–
Bestand stille Reserven	20 000.–
Effektiver Restwert am 31.12.20_3	350 000.– 70 %
Anschaffungswert Anfang 20_1	500 000.– 100 %

B

Betriebswirtschaftlich notwendige Wertberichtigung	21 700.–
Ausgewiesene externe Wertberichtigung	15 000.–
Fehlende Wertberichtigung	6 700.–

Der ausgewiesene Betrag von Fr. 15 000.– ist zu tief. Er müsste um (mindestens) Fr. 6 700.– erhöht werden (OR 960a/3).

C

Ausgewiesener Jahresgewinn 120 000.–

WB Forderungen aus L+L	Extern	Intern	Stille Reserven
31.12.20_3			7 000.–
31.12.20_4	15 000.–	21 700.–	– 6 700.–
Veränderung			–13 700.–

Auflösung von stillen Reserven – 13 700.–

Halbfabrikate	Extern	Intern	Stille Reserven
31.12.20_3			12 000.–
31.12.20_4	20 000.–	40 000.–	20 000.–
Veränderung			+ 8 000.–

Bildung von stillen Reserven + 8 000.–

Fertigfabrikate	Extern	Intern	Stille Reserven
31.12.20_3			25 000.–
31.12.20_4	80 000.–	110 000.–	30 000.–
Veränderung			+ 5 000.–

Bildung von stillen Reserven + 5 000.–

Maschinen	Extern	Intern	Stille Reserven
31.12.20_3	330 000.–[1]	350 000.–[1]	20 000.–
31.12.20_4	260 000.–[1]	300 000.–[2]	40 000.–
Veränderung	– 70 000.–	– 50 000.–	+20 000.–

Bildung von stillen Reserven + 20 000.–
Effektiver Jahresgewinn 139 300.–

[1] Siehe **A**
[2] 500 000.– – (4 · 50 000.–)

D Nein, denn es wurden mehr stille Reserven gebildet als aufgelöst.
Im Anhang ist nur eine Nettoauflösung der stillen Reserven zu erwähnen, sofern das Ergebnis wesentlich günstiger dargestellt wird (OR 959c/1, Ziff. 3).

Beispiele zur Wesentlichkeit
- Der tatsächliche Jahresgewinn wird um mehr als 10–20 % günstiger ausgewiesen.
- Aus einem Jahresverlust wird wegen der Nettoauflösung ein Jahresgewinn.

5.6 Stille Reserven auf dem Warenlager

A

		20_1	20_2	20_3
1	Ausgewiesener Warenaufwand	700	980	580
2	Tatsächlicher Warenaufwand	700 – 100 = 600	980 + 40 = 1 020	580 – 60 = 520
3	Ausgewiesener Bruttogewinn	1 150 – 700 = 450	1 800 – 980 = 820	1 040 – 580 = 460
4	Tatsächlicher Bruttogewinn	1 150 – 600 = 550	1 800 – 1 020 = 780	1 040 – 520 = 520

B

1   Ausgewiesener Jahresverlust   –50
    Bildung stille Reserven   +60
    Tatsächlicher Jahresgewinn   +10

2

	Ausgewiesener Warenvorrat		Tatsächlicher Warenvorrat		Stille Reserven	
31.12.20_2	²⁄₃	120	³⁄₃	180	⅓	60
31.12.20_3	90 %	324	100 %	360	10 %	– 36
Veränderung		+204		+180		– 24

Tatsächlicher Jahresgewinn   +10
Auflösung stille Reserven   +24
Ausgewiesener Jahresgewinn   +34

3   Die Manipulation der stillen Reserven hat nur Einfluss auf den ausgewiesenen Jahresgewinn!

4   Warenvorrat / Wareneinkauf   204
    Da die Bestandeszunahme mit 204 (extern) statt 180 (intern) gebucht wird, wurden 24 stille Reserven aufgelöst.

5.7 Kennzahlen und stille Reserven

A

Schlussbilanz (nach Gewinnverwendung) vom 31.12.20_1

Umlaufvermögen			Kurzfristiges Fremdkapital	
Flüssige Mittel		40	Verbindlichkeiten aus L+L	65
Forderungen aus L+L	86		Dividenden	5
WB Forderungen aus L+L	− 6	80	Langfristiges Fremdkapital	
Warenvorrat		130	Darlehen	50
Anlagevermögen			Eigenkapital	
Mobilien		80	Aktienkapital	200
Fahrzeuge		90	Gesetzliche Gewinnreserve	29
			Stille Reserven	71
		420		420

Erfolgsrechnung 20_1

Warenaufwand	960	Warenertrag	1 200
Personalaufwand	105		
Raumaufwand	27		
Übriger Betriebsaufwand	45		
Finanzaufwand	3		
Ausserordentlicher Aufwand	24		
Jahresgewinn	36		
	1 200		1 200

B

1   170 · 100 : 420 =   40,5 %
2   120 · 100 : 420 =   28,6 %
3   100 · 100 : 300 =   33,3 %   (Stille Reserven sind wie Gewinnreserven zu behandeln.)
4   120 · 100 :   70 = 171,4 %
5   350 · 100 : 170 = 205,9 %
6   960 : 120   = 8-mal
7   451 :   81   = 5,6-mal
8   36 · 100 : 295 =   12,2 %

5.8 Auswirkungen der stillen Reserven auf Kennzahlen

A

Sachanlagen	/ Stille Reserven	500
Sachanlagen	/ Abschreibungen	100
Langfristige Rückstellungen	/ Stille Reserven	200
Langfristige Rückstellungen	/ Übriger Aufwand oder Rückstellungsaufwand	50

Die Position stille Reserven gibt es nur für die interne Rechnung und zeigt alle in den Vorjahren gebildeten stillen Reserven (= Bestand stille Reserven) von 700.

B

Nr.	Grössen/Kennzahl	Zunahme	Abnahme	Kein Einfluss
1	Bruttogewinn			×
2	EBITDA	×		
3	EBIT	×		
4	Jahresgewinn	×		
5	Flüssige Mittel			×
6	Liquiditätsgrad 2			×
7	Intensität des Umlaufvermögens		×	
8	Fremdfinanzierungsgrad		×	
9	Kapitalumschlag		×	
10	Bruttogewinnsatz			×
11	Gemeinkostensatz		×	
12	EBIT-Marge	×		
13	Durchschnittliche Kreditfrist bei den Forderungen aus L+L			×
14	Durchschnittliche Kreditfrist bei den Verbindlichkeiten aus L+L			×
15	Durchschnittliche Warenlagerdauer			×
16	Operativer Cashflow [1]			×
17	Effektivverschuldung [1]		×	
18	Verschuldungsfaktor [1]		×	
19	Gewinnrendite [2]	×		
20	Kurs/Gewinn-Verhältnis [2]		×	

[1] Siehe auch Kapitel 2 Geldflussrechnung und Abschnitt 59 Analyse der Geldflussrechnung.
[2] Siehe Abschnitt 511 Aktienbewertung und Analyse von kotierten Gesellschaften.

5.9 Voraus- bzw. Anzahlungen, Rechnungsabgrenzungen und Bilanzkennzahlen

1	Liquiditätsgrad 1	=	$\dfrac{100 \cdot 100}{500 + 35^{①}}$	= 18,7 %
	Liquiditätsgrad 2	=	$\dfrac{100 + (400 + 40^{①}) \cdot 100}{535}$	= 100,9 %
	Liquiditätsgrad 3	=	$\dfrac{100 + 440 + (350 + 90^{②} - 50^{③}) \cdot 100}{535}$	= 173,8 %
2	Intensität des AV	=	$\dfrac{(1\,350 + 160^{④}) \cdot 100}{2\,500}$	= 60,4 %
3	Fremdfinanzierungsgrad	=	$\dfrac{1\,350^{⑤} \cdot 100}{2\,500}$	= 54 %
4	Anlagedeckungsgrad 2	=	$\dfrac{(760 + 250 + 900) \cdot 100}{1\,350 + 160^{④}}$	= 126,5 %

Erläuterungen

① Bei den Abgrenzungsposten stellt sich die Frage, ob es sich um Geldleistungen oder andere nicht geldwirksame Leistungen handelt. Für die Liquiditätsgrade sind nur die Geldleistungen zu berücksichtigen (Geldschulden 35 und Geldguthaben 40).

② Die an Warenlieferanten geleistete Vorauszahlung von 90 ist ein Warenguthaben; darum wird diese Forderung bei den Vorräten addiert.

③ Die von den Kunden geleistete Anzahlung von 50 ist eine Warenschuld; darum wird diese Verpflichtung bei den Vorräten subtrahiert.

④ Die an Maschinenlieferanten geleistete Vorauszahlung von 160 ist eine Forderung, die eine Maschinenlieferung beinhaltet; darum wird diese Forderung bei den Sachanlagen addiert.

⑤ Für den Fremdfinanzierungsgrad werden die Anzahlungen von Kunden allerdings als Fremdkapital (Verpflichtung) berücksichtigt.

Häufig werden in der Finanzanalyse die beschriebenen Unterscheidungen jedoch nicht vorgenommen.

5.10 Analyse der Lagerverhältnisse

Nr.	Warenvorrat			Einstandswert der		Waren-ertrag	Brutto-gewinn-satz	Lager-umschlag	Lager-dauer (Tage)
	1.1.	31.12.	Durch-schnitt	einge-kauften Waren	ver-kauften Waren				
1	720	540	**630**	3600	**3780**	5670	**50 %**	6	**60**
2	**280**	140	210	700	**840**	**1120**	33⅓ %	**4**	**90**
3	250	300	**275**	**1425**	1375	**1925**	40 %	5	**72**
4	**200**	**280**	240	2480	**2400**	4000	**66⅔ %**	10	**36**
5	540	660	**600**	**3720**	**3600**	**5400**	50 %	6	**60**

5.11 Aktivitätskennzahlen (Vorräte und Forderungen aus L+L)

1 2187 : 405 = 5,4-mal
   360 : 5,4 = 66–67 Tage
2 1350 : 300 = 4,5-mal
   360 : 4,5 = 80 Tage
3 2187 – 30 = 2157

5.12 Branchenkennzahlen

1 a: Flüssige Mittel 225, Forderungen aus L+L 375, Warenbestand 750, Mobilien 150; ∑ 1500
   p: Verbindlichkeiten aus L+L 600, AK 600, Reserven 300; ∑ 1500
2 1. Stufe: Warenertrag 3375 – Warenaufwand 2250 = Bruttogewinn 1125
   2. Stufe: Bruttogewinn 1125 – Gemeinaufwand 1080 = Betriebsgewinn 45

5.13 Bereinigung der publizierten Jahresrechnung der Handel AG

A

Schlussbilanz	Extern 31.12.20_1	Extern 31.12.20_2	Intern 31.12.20_1	Intern 31.12.20_2
Aktiven				
Flüssige Mittel	60	50	60	50
Forderungen aus L+L	80	70	80	70
Vorräte	200	210	300	315
Sachanlagen	1 300	1 400	1 600	1 800
	1 640	1 730	2 040	2 235
Passiven				
Verbindlichkeiten aus L+L	390	400	390	400
Langfristiges Fremdkapital	840	900	750	800
Aktienkapital	100	100	100	100
Reserven (Sammelposten)	310	330	800	935
	1 640	1 730	2 040	2 235

Erfolgsrechnung	Extern 20_2	Intern 20_2
Warenertrag	6 300	6 300
Warenaufwand	−4 350 ①	−4 345 ①
Bruttogewinn	**1 950**	**1 955**
Personalaufwand	−1 100	−1 100
Raumaufwand	− 150	− 150
Übriger Betriebsaufwand	− 380	− 370
EBITDA	**320**	**335**
Abschreibung	− 250	− 150
EBIT	**70**	**185**
Finanzaufwand	− 50	− 50
Jahresgewinn	**20**	**135**

①	Extern	Intern
Wareneinkauf (Einstandswert der eingekauften Waren)	4 360	4 360
Vorratszunahme	− 10	− 15
Warenaufwand (Einstandswert der verkauften Waren)	4 350	4 345

[B]

1	Intensität des Anlagevermögens	1 800 : 2 235 · 100	=	80,5 %
2	Eigenkapitalquote	1 035 : 2 235 · 100	=	46,3 %
3	Finanzierungsverhältnis	1 200 : 1 035 · 100	=	115,9 %
4	Umsatzrendite auf EBIT-Basis	185 : 6 300 · 100	=	2,9 %
5	Durchschnittliche Kreditfrist bei den Forderungen aus L + L	360 : {630 : ([80 + 70] : 2)}	≈	43 Tage
6	Durchschnittliche Kreditfrist bei den Verbindlichkeiten aus L + L	360 : {4 360 : ([390 + 400] : 2)}	≈	33 Tage
7	Durchschnittliche Lagerdauer	360 : {4 345 : ([300 + 315] : 2)}	≈	25 Tage
8	Rentabilität des Eigenkapitals	135 : ([900 + 1 035] : 2) · 100	=	14,0 %
9	Rentabilität des Gesamtkapitals	185 : ([2 040 + 2 235] : 2) · 100	=	8,7 %

5.14 Leverage-Effekt

[A]

	A		B		C	
Gesamtkapitalrendite (%)	8	4	8	4	8	4
Gewinn vor FK-Zinsen	80	40	80	40	80	40
5 % FK-Zinsen	10	10	20	20	30	30
Gewinn nach FK-Zinsen	70	30	60	20	50	10
[B] Eigenkapitalrendite (%)	10	4,29	12	4	16,67	3,33
[C] Fremdfinanzierungsgrad (%)	30		50		70	

[D] Die Eigenkapitalrendite wird umso grösser, je höher der Fremdfinanzierungsgrad ist, sofern die Fremdkapitalzinssätze kleiner sind als die Gesamtkapitalrendite (= Leverage-Effekt).

5.15 Zusammenhang von verschiedenen Kennzahlen

A

Bilanz			
Umlaufvermögen	90	Kurzfristiges Fremdkapital	60
Anlagevermögen	60	Langfristiges Fremdkapital	30
		Aktienkapital	45
		Gewinnreserven	15
	150		150

B

1	Umsatz	: Gesamtkapital		=	4 %
2	NUV	: Kurzfristiges Fremdkapital	· 100	=	150 %
3	EBIT	: Umsatz	· 100	=	5 %
4	Dividende	: Aktienkapital	· 100	=	20 %
5	Jahresgewinn	: Eigenkapital	· 100	=	40 %

C

Jahresgewinn	: Eigenkapital	· 100		
24,6	: 60	· 100	=	41 %

D Ist die Gesamtkapitalrentabilität höher als der Zinssatz für Fremdkapital, so ist die Eigenkapitalrentabilität umso höher, je grösser der Fremdkapitalanteil ist.

5.16 Analyse der Forderungen aus L+L, Verbindlichkeiten aus L+L und Lagerverhältnisse

1	720 000.–	: 84 000.–	=	8,6-mal
2	360	: 8,6	=	41–42 Tage
3	41–42	– 30	=	11–12 Tage
4	720 000.–	: 12	=	60 000.–
	84 000.–	– 60 000.–	=	24 000.–
5	1 000 000.–	: 250 · 100	=	400 000.–
6	400 000.–	+ 50 000.–	=	450 000.–
7	360	: 40	=	9-mal
	450 000.–	: 9	=	50 000.–

5.17 Finanzierungsarten und Leverage-Effekt

A

MAG

1) $\dfrac{10 \cdot 100}{100} = 10\%$

2) $\dfrac{10 \cdot 100}{600} = 1{,}7\%$

3) $\dfrac{(10 - 2{,}4) \cdot 100}{70} = \mathbf{10{,}9\%}$

4) $\dfrac{7{,}6 \cdot 100}{600} = 1{,}3\%$

TAG

1) $\dfrac{10 \cdot 100}{100} = 10\%$

2) $\dfrac{10 \cdot 100}{600} = 1{,}7\%$

3) $\dfrac{(10 - 5{,}6) \cdot 100}{30} = \mathbf{14{,}7\%}$

4) $\dfrac{4{,}4 \cdot 100}{600} = 0{,}7\%$

B

MAG

1) $\dfrac{10 \cdot 100}{100} = 10\%$

2) $\dfrac{10 \cdot 100}{600} = 1{,}7\%$

3) $\dfrac{(10 - 3{,}6) \cdot 100}{70} = \mathbf{9{,}1\%}$

4) $\dfrac{6{,}4 \cdot 100}{600} = 1{,}1\%$

TAG

1) $\dfrac{10 \cdot 100}{100} = 10\%$

2) $\dfrac{10 \cdot 100}{600} = 1{,}7\%$

3) $\dfrac{(10 - 8{,}4) \cdot 100}{30} = \mathbf{5{,}3\%}$

4) $\dfrac{1{,}6 \cdot 100}{600} = 0{,}3\%$

C 1

	MAG	TAG
Eigenfinanzierungsgrad	70 %	30 %
Fremdkapitalzinssatz	8 %	8 %
Gesamtkapitalrentabilität	10 %	10 %
Eigenkapitalrentabilität	**A** 10,9 %	**A** 14,7 %
Eigenfinanzierungsgrad	70 %	30 %
Fremdkapitalzinssatz	12 %	12 %
Gesamtkapitalrentabilität	10 %	10 %
Eigenkapitalrentabilität	**B** 9,1 %	**B** 5,3 %

2 Zu **A**: Gesamtkapitalrentabilität (10 %) > Fremdkapitalzinssatz (8 %)

Die MAG hat einen Eigenfinanzierungsgrad von 70 % und erreicht eine Eigenkapitalrentabilität von 10,9 %. Die TAG hingegen erzielt mit einer kleineren Eigenkapitalquote von 30 % eine wesentlich höhere Eigenkapitalrentabilität von 14,7 %.

Zu **B**: Gesamtkapitalrentabilität (10 %) < Fremdkapitalzinssatz (12 %)

Die MAG hat einen Eigenfinanzierungsgrad von 70 % und erzielt eine Eigenkapitalrentabilität von 9,1 %. Die TAG hingegen erreicht mit einer kleineren Eigenkapitalquote von 30 %, d.h. mit einem hohen Fremdfinanzierungsgrad von 70 %, nur eine Eigenkapitalrentabilität von 5,3 %.

Zusatzinformationen

Ganz allgemein besteht folgender Zusammenhang (Leverage-Formel):

$R_{EK} = R_{GK} + [(FK / EK) \cdot (R_{GK} - P_{FK})]$

R_{EK} = Eigenkapitalrentabilität
R_{GK} = Gesamtkapitalrentabilität
FK / EK = Finanzierungsverhältnis
P_{FK} = Fremdkapitalzinssatz

Zu **A**
MAG
$R_{EK} = 10 + [(30 / 70) \cdot (10 - 8)] =$ **10,9 %**

TAG
$R_{EK} = 10 + [(70 / 30) \cdot (10 - 8)] =$ **14,7 %**

Zu **B**
MAG
$R_{EK} = 10 + [(30 / 70) \cdot (10 - 12)] =$ **9,1 %**

TAG
$R_{EK} = 10 + [(70 / 30) \cdot (10 - 12)] =$ **5,3 %**

3 Bei gegebener Gesamtkapitalrentabilität und einem tieferen Fremdkapitalzinssatz als die Gesamtkapitalrentabilität wird die Eigenkapitalrentabilität umso höher, je weniger Eigenkapital eingesetzt wird, d. h. je höher der Fremdfinanzierungsgrad ist.

D 1 Eigenkapitalanteil senken (z. B. Auszahlung von Reserven) und Fremdkapitalanteil erhöhen (z. B. Aufnahme eines Darlehens, Emission einer Obligationenanleihe).

2 $R_{EK} = 10 + [(50 / 50) \cdot (10 - 8)] =$ **12 %**
Die Eigenkapitalrentabilität ist von 10,9 % auf 12 % gestiegen.

E 1 Eigenkapitalanteil erhöhen (z. B. Aktienkapitalerhöhung) und Fremdkapitalanteil senken (z. B. Amortisation einer Hypothek, Rückzahlung einer Bankschuld).

2 $R_{EK} = 10 + [(50 / 50) \cdot (10 - 12)] =$ **8 %**
Die Eigenkapitalrentabilität ist von 5,3 % auf 8 % gestiegen.

5.18 Gesamtkapitalrentabilität und Eigenkapitalrentabilität

A

Fremdkapital	300 000.–	60 %	100 %	
Eigenkapital	200 000.–	40 %		100 %
Gesamtkapital	500 000.–	100 %		
EBIT (Gewinn vor Zinsen und Steuern)	**43 000.–**			
– Zinsaufwand	– 27 000.–		9 %	
EBT (Gewinn nach Zinsen vor Steuern)	16 000.–	100 %		
– Steuern	– 4 000.–	25 %		
Jahresgewinn	12 000.–	75 %		6 %

B
1 43 000.– : 500 000 · 100 = 8,6 %
2 39 000.– : 500 000 · 100 = 7,8 %

C

Fremdkapital	350 000.–	70 %	100 %	
Eigenkapital	150 000.–	30 %		100 %
Gesamtkapital	500 000.–	100 %		
EBIT (Gewinn vor Zinsen und Steuern)	43 000.–			
– Zinsaufwand	– 31 500.–		9 %	
EBT (Gewinn nach Zinsen vor Steuern)	11 500.–	100 %		
– Steuern	– 2 875.–	25 %		
Jahresgewinn	8 625.–	75 %		**5,75 %**

5.19 Analyse zweier Aktiengesellschaften

A

	CGR AG		GBZ AG	
1	**Liquiditätsgrad 2**			
	(30 + 70) · 100 : 380	26,3 %	(50 + 70) · 100 : 400	30 %

– Der häufig genannte Richtwert von 100 % wird stark unterschritten.

2	**Eigenfinanzierungsgrad**			
	(10 + 10) · 100 : 990	2,0 %	(10 + 420) · 100 : 1 730	24,9 %

– Der Eigenfinanzierungsgrad ist bei der CGR AG bescheiden.
– Bei der GBZ AG trägt das hohe Zuwachskapital zum wesentlich höheren Eigenfinanzierungsgrad bei (siehe auch Selbstfinanzierungsgrad).

3	**Selbstfinanzierungsgrad**			
	10 · 100 : 20	50 %	420 · 100 : 430	97,7 %

– Beide Gesellschaften haben einen sehr hohen Selbstfinanzierungsgrad. Bei der GBZ besteht das Eigenkapital praktisch nur aus Gewinnreserven.
– Die Selbstfinanzierung führt dazu, dass die Liquidität erhalten bleibt und auf diesem Teil des Eigenkapitals keine Zinszahlung wie beim Fremdkapital erfolgt.
– Ein hoher Selbstfinanzierungsgrad bedeutet nicht, dass ein gesundes Finanzierungsverhältnis besteht. Beispielsweise beträgt bei der CGR AG der Selbstfinanzierungsgrad 50 %, während der Fremdfinanzierungsgrad 98 % beträgt.

4	**Intensität des Anlagevermögens**			
	680 · 100 : 990	68,7 %	1 400 · 100 : 1 730	80,9 %

– Für Handelsbetriebe ist die Intensität des Anlagevermögens relativ hoch.
– Es ist möglich, dass beide Gesellschaften (im Besonderen aber die GBZ AG) Liegenschaften besitzen.

B

	Anlagedeckungsgrad 1			
	20 · 100 : 680	2,9 %	430 · 100 : 1 400	30,7 %
	Anlagedeckungsgrad 2			
	(20 + 590) · 100 : 680	89,7 %	(430 + 900) · 100 : 1 400	95 %

– Die goldene Bilanzregel wird mit dem Anlagedeckungsgrad 2 (oder B) überprüft. Bei der CGR AG wird sie nicht, bei der GBZ AG knapp eingehalten (Richtwert 100 %).

C CGR AG

		Fonds Flüssige Mittel	
		Zunahme	Abnahme
Geschäftsbereich			
Jahresverlust	−30		
Abschreibungen	+60		
Rückstellungsaufwand	+ 0		
Zunahme Forderungen aus L+L	−10		
Zunahme Vorräte	−20		
Zunahme Verbindlichkeiten aus L+L	+10		
Zunahme übriges kurzfristiges Fremdkapital	+10		
Innenfinanzierung (Cashflow)	+20	20	
Investitionsbereich			
Kauf von Anlagevermögen	−90		
Nettogeldabfluss	−90		90
Finanzierungsbereich			
Zunahme kurzfristige Bankschuld	+20		
Zunahme langfristiges Fremdkapital	+30		
Nettogeldzufluss	+50	50	
Veränderung Fonds Flüssige Mittel			
Anfangsbestand	50		
Endbestand	30		
Abnahme Flüssige Mittel	−20	20	
		90	90

GBZ AG

		Fonds Flüssige Mittel	
		Zunahme	Abnahme
Geschäftsbereich			
Jahresgewinn	+ 20		
Abschreibungen	+250		
Rückstellungsaufwand	+ 30		
Abnahme Forderungen aus L+L	+ 10		
Zunahme Vorräte	− 10		
Abnahme Verbindlichkeiten aus L+L	− 20		
Zunahme übriges kurzfristiges Fremdkapital	+ 5		
Innenfinanzierung (Cashflow)	+285	285	
Investitionsbereich			
Kauf von Anlagevermögen	−350		
Nettogeldabfluss	−350		350
Finanzierungsbereich			
Zunahme kurzfristige Bankschuld	+ 25		
Zunahme langfristiges Fremdkapital	+ 30		
Nettogeldzufluss	+ 55	55	
Veränderung Fonds Flüssige Mittel			
Anfangsbestand	60		
Endbestand	50		
Abnahme Flüssige Mittel	− 10	10	
		350	350

D

		CGR AG		GBZ AG	
1	Umsatzrentabilität				
		–30 · 100 : 2 010	– 1,5 %	20 · 100 : 6 300	0,3 %
2	Bruttogewinnquote				
		560 · 100 : 2 010	27,9 %	1 950 · 100 : 6 300	31,0 %
3	Cashflow-Marge				
		20 · 100 : 2 010	1,0 %	285 · 100 : 6 300	4,5 %
4	Reinvestment-Faktor (Investitionsgrad)				
		90 · 100 : 20	450 %	350 · 100 : 285	122,8 %
5	Verschuldungsfaktor				
		(380 + 590 – 30 – 70) : 20	43,5	(400 + 900 – 50 – 70) : 285	4,1

- Die GBZ AG schneidet bei fast allen umsatzbezogenen Analysen besser ab.
- Die Umsatzrentabilität ist bei der CGR AG negativ und bei der GBZ AG sehr klein.
- Die Cashflow-Marge ist vor allem bei der CGR AG bescheiden.
- Der Reinvestment-Faktor ist bei beiden Gesellschaften grösser als 100 %. Die getätigten Investitionen können somit nicht mit dem Geldfluss aus Geschäftstätigkeit (Cashflow) finanziert werden. Der Free Cashflow ist in beiden Fällen negativ.
- Der Cashflow von 20 müsste bei der CGR AG 43,5-mal erarbeitet werden, um die Effektivverschuldung zu tilgen. Bei der GBZ AG hingegen müsste er lediglich 4,1-mal erarbeitet werden.
- Diese Kennzahlen sind – wie die anderen Kennzahlen auch – nur aussagekräftig, wenn sie für mehrere Perioden ermittelt werden.

E

		CGR AG		GBZ AG	
1	Lagerumschlag				
		1 450 : [(190 + 210) : 2]	7,25 ×	4 350 : [(200 + 210) : 2]	21,22 ×
2	Durchschnittliche Lagerdauer				
		360 : 7,25	≈ 50 Tage	360 : 21,22	≈ 17 Tage

- Der Lagerumschlag ist bei der GBZ AG deutlich höher.
- Die Lagerdauer der CGR AG ist relativ hoch und hat Kostennachteile (z. B. Finanzierungs-, Raum-, Personal-, Abschreibungskosten).
- Hat die GBZ AG das bessere Lagerbewirtschaftungssystem?

F Der Warenaufwand ist um die Bestandesänderung zu korrigieren.

Umschlagshäufigkeit der Verbindlichkeiten aus L+L

| 1 470 : [(140 + 150) : 2] | 10,14 × | 4 360 : [(380 + 360) : 2] | 11,78 × |

Durchschnittliche Kreditfrist bei den Verbindlichkeiten aus L+L

| 360 : 10,14 | ≈ 36 Tage | 360 : 11,78 | ≈ 31 Tage |

– Beide zahlen die Lieferantenrechnung nach rund 30 Tagen.
– Für die um 5 Tage kürzere Kreditfrist bei der GBZ AG beträgt der Zinsverlust bei einem Zinssatz von 5 % auf dem durchschnittlichen Bestand der Verbindlichkeiten aus L+L:
[(380 + 360) : 2] : 100 · 5 : 360 · 5 = Fr. 256 944.–.

G 1 Rentabilität des Eigenkapitals

| – 30 · 100 : [(50 + 20) : 2] | –85,7 % | 20 · 100 : [(410 + 430) : 2] | 4,8 % |

2 Rentabilität des Gesamtkapitals

| (– 30 + 20) · 100 : [(950 + 990) : 2] | – 1,0 % | (20 + 50) · 100 : [(1 640 + 1 730) : 2] | 4,2 % |

– Die Rentabilität des Eigenkapitals und des Gesamtkapitals der CGR AG ist negativ. Gerade bei negativen Renditen ist ein Vergleich mit früheren Perioden wichtig.
– Die beiden Rentabilitätsgrössen der GBZ AG sind zwar positiv, aber eher bescheiden.

5.20 Cashflow-Kennzahlen mit kumulierten Geldflussrechnungen

1	Cashflow-Marge (Cashflow to Sales)	$\dfrac{616 \cdot 100}{11\,100}$	5,55 %
2	Operationsindex	$\dfrac{616 \cdot 100}{257}$	239,69 %
3	Reinvestment-Faktor	$\dfrac{586 \cdot 100}{616}$	95,13 %
4	Free Cashflow-Quote	$\dfrac{30 \cdot 100}{616}$	4,87 %

5.21 Analyse der Mittelflussrechnung der Gang AG

1	(257 – 65 – 50) : 23	=	6,2-mal
2	(20 · 100) : 15	=	133,3 %
3	(23 · 100) : 560	=	4,1 %
4	(3 · 100) : 23	=	13 %
5	Anfangsbestand 36 + 70 – 45 – 2	=	59
	Endbestand 50 + 55 – 33 – 3	=	69
	Zunahme		10
6	(20 · 100) : 23	=	87,0 %

5.22 Verschuldungsfaktor

[A]

	20_1	20_2	20_3
Effektivverschuldung	410	540	600
Cashflow	130	115	90
Verschuldungsfaktor	3,15	4,70	6,67

[B] Der Verschuldungsfaktor hat sich verschlechtert. Die Sicherheit für die Gläubiger hat eher abgenommen. Der Cashflow aus dem Jahr 20_3 müsste rund 7 Jahre lang erarbeitet werden, um die Effektivverschuldung abzutragen.
Die Aussagekraft des Verschuldungsfaktors als Sicherheitskennzahl ist vor allem im Zeitreihenvergleich aussagekräftig: Einerseits nimmt die Effektivverschuldung zu und andererseits nimmt der Cashflow ab, was sich doppelt ungünstig auf den Verschuldungsfaktor auswirkt.
Das Fremdkapital hat im Betrachtungszeitraum um 150 (+21,4 %) zugenommen, in der gleichen Zeit hat sich der Verschuldungsfaktor mehr als verdoppelt (+111,7 %).

5.23 Verschuldungsfaktor und Cashflow

A 1

	Extern 31.12.20_1	Bestand Stille Reserven	Intern 31.12.20_1
Fremdkapital	1 000	50	950
Flüssige Mittel	– 100	0	–100
Forderungen aus L + L	– 300	30	–330
Effektivverschuldung	600	80	520

2

	Extern 20_1	Veränderung Stille Reserven	Intern 20_1
Jahresgewinn	140	+10/–4	146
Abschreibung	50	+4	54
Aufwand für langfristige Rückstellungen	10	0	10
Cashflow	200	+10	210

Überleitung bzw. die Korrekturbuchungen von den externen zu den internen Zahlen:
- Forderungen aus L + L   / Forderungsverlust   10
- Abschreibungen   / Sachanlagen   4

Durch die beiden Korrekturbuchungen wird der externe Jahresgewinn von 140 um insgesamt 6 (+10 / –4) erhöht.
Der in der externen Jahresrechnung zu hoch erfasste Forderungsverlust hatte zu einem kleineren externen Jahresgewinn geführt. Darum muss der zu hohe Forderungsverlust von 10 für die interne Rechnung zum externen Jahresgewinn addiert werden.
Die in der externen Jahresrechnung erfasste Abschreibung war um 4 zu klein. Dies hatte zu einem zu hohen externen Jahresgewinn geführt. Darum muss der Betrag von 4 für die interne Rechnung vom externen Jahresgewinn subtrahiert werden.
Der Cashflow (wie in dieser Aufgabe definiert) wird nur durch die Korrekturbuchung der Veränderung der stillen Reserven in den Forderungen aus L + L beeinflusst. Die Abschreibungen sind unabhängig von der Höhe der liquiditätsunwirksamen Vorgänge.

3   520 : 210 = 2,48 (rund 2,5 Jahre)

B 1   Kein Einfluss
2   Abnahme
3   Abnahme

5.24 Analyse der Giazh AG

A

Erfolgsrechnung 20_1

Warenaufwand	610	Warenertrag	1 000
Bruttogewinn	390		
	1 000		1 000
Personalaufwand	150	Bruttogewinn	390
Sonstiger Betriebsaufwand	115		
Abschreibungen	70		
Fremdkapitalzinsen	15		
Jahresgewinn	40		
	390		390

Eröffnungs- und Schlussbilanz 20_1

	1.1.	31.12.		1.1.	31.12.
Flüssige Mittel	50	60	Verbindlichkeiten aus L+L	90	110
Forderungen aus L+L	80	120	Darlehen	250	210
Vorräte	130	140	Aktienkapital	100	100
Sachanlagen	230	190	Gewinnreserven	50	90
	490	510		490	510

Geldflussrechnung 20_1

		Fonds Flüssige Mittel	
		Zunahme	Abnahme
Geschäftsbereich			
Reingewinn	40		
Abschreibungen	+70		
Zunahme Forderungen aus L+L	–40		
Zunahme Vorräte	–10		
Zunahme Verbindlichkeiten aus L+L	+20		
Nettogeldzufluss	+80	80	
Investitionsbereich			
Kauf Sachanlagen	–30		
Nettogeldabfluss	–30		30
Finanzierungsbereich			
Rückzahlung Darlehen	–40		
Nettogeldabfluss	–40		40
Veränderung Fonds Flüssige Mittel			
Zunahme Flüssige Mittel	+10		10
		80	80

B	1	Bruttogewinnsatz	390 · 100 : 610 =	63,9 %
	2	Handelsmarge	390 · 100 : 1 000 =	39,0 %
	3	Deckungsbeitragsmarge	390 · 100 : 1 000 =	39,0 %
	4	Gemeinkostensatz	350 · 100 : 610 =	57,4 %
	5	Reingewinnsatz	40 · 100 : 960 =	4,2 %
	6	Umsatzrentabilität	40 · 100 : 1 000 =	4,0 %
C	1	⌀ Kreditfrist bei den Forderungen aus L+L	360 : (1 000 : ⌀ 100) =	36 Tage
	2	⌀ Kreditfrist bei den Verbindlichkeiten aus L+L	360 : (620 : ⌀ 100) =	58 Tage
	3	⌀ Lagerdauer	360 : (610 : ⌀ 135) =	80 Tage
D	1	Rentabilität des Eigenkapitals	40 · 100 : ⌀ 170 =	23,5 %
		Rentabilität des Gesamtkapitals	(40 + 15) · 100 : ⌀ 500 =	11,0 %
E		Operativer Cashflow	40 + 70 − 40 − 10 + 20 =	80
F		Verschuldungsfaktor	(320 − 60 − 120) : 80 =	1,75 Jahre
G		Free Cashflow	80 − 30 =	50
H	1	Intensität des Anlagevermögens	190 · 100 : 510 =	37,3 %
	2	Intensität des Umlaufvermögens	320 · 100 : 510 =	62,8 %
	3	Eigenfinanzierungsgrad (Eigenkapitalquote)	190 · 100 : 510 =	37,3 %
	4	Fremdfinanzierungsgrad (Verschuldungsgrad)	320 · 100 : 510 =	62,8 %
	5	Selbstfinanzierungsgrad	90 · 100 : 190 =	47,4 %
	6	Liquiditätsgrad 1 (Cash Ratio)	60 · 100 : 110 =	54,6 %
		Liquiditätsgrad 2 (Quick Ratio)	180 · 100 : 110 =	163,6 %
		Liquiditätsgrad 3 (Current Ratio)	320 · 100 : 110 =	290,9 %
	7	Anlagedeckungsgrad A	190 · 100 : 190 =	100,0 %
		Anlagedeckungsgrad B	(190 + 210) · 100 : 190 =	210,5 %

5.25 Kennzahlensystem (Du Pont-Schema)

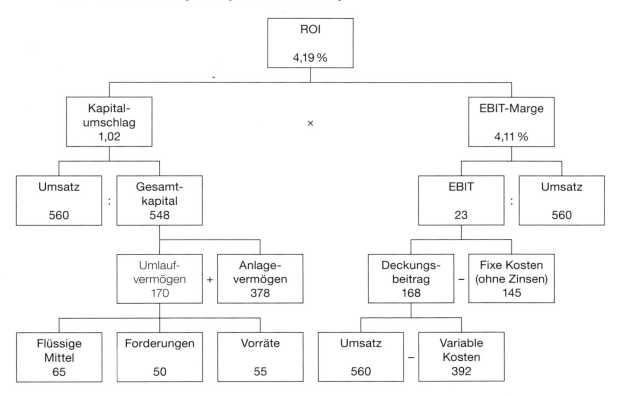

5.26 Aktienbewertung der Marcomis Holding

A

1	Payout Ratio	= 86 · 100 : (243 − 25)		= 39,5 %
2	Eigenkapitalrendite	= 243 · 100 : [(1 430 + 1 141) : 2]		= 18,9 %
3	Eigenkapital	= 1 234 Mio. − 536 Mio.		= 698 Mio.

4

	1.1. 20_1	30. 6. 20_1	31.12. 20_1	⌀
Inhaberaktien	900 000	1 000 000	1 000 000	950 000
Namenaktien	900 000	900 000	900 000	900 000

5 950 000 Inhaberaktien entsprechen   4 750 000 Namenaktien
                                        900 000 Namenaktien
Total   5 650 000 Namenaktien

Gewinn je Inhaberaktie   = (243 Mio. − 25 Mio.) : 5 650 000 · 5   = 192.92

6 Agio je Aktie   = (102 Mio. − 50 Mio.) : 100 000   = 520.−

B Korrigierter Konzerngewinn   = 243 Mio. − (536 Mio. : 5)   = 135,8 Mio.

C Kein Einfluss, da die Abschreibung nicht liquiditätswirksam ist.

D

Eigenkapital	1 141 Mio.	= 100 %

Börsenkapitalisierung
1 000 000 · 1 420.− = 1 420   Mio.
  900 000 ·   275.− =   247,5 Mio.   1 667,5 Mio.   = 146,1 %

5.27 Aktienbewertung und Aktienanalyse der Duo-Gruppe

A

1) $\dfrac{\text{Anzahl ausstehende Aktien} \cdot \text{Kurs}}{} = (168\,000 - 8\,000) \cdot 1\,400.- = 224\text{ Mio.}$

2) $\dfrac{\text{Jahresgewinn}}{\varnothing \text{ Anzahl ausstehende Aktien}} = \dfrac{22\text{ Mio.}}{(158\,000 + 160\,000) : 2} = 138{,}36$

3) $\dfrac{\text{Kurs}}{\text{Gewinn je Aktie (EPS)}} = \dfrac{1\,400.-}{138{,}36} = 10{,}12\times$

4) $\dfrac{\text{Dividende} \cdot 100}{\text{Gewinn je Aktie}} = \dfrac{35.- \cdot 100}{138{,}36} = 25{,}3\,\%$

B

1) $\dfrac{\text{EV}}{\text{EBITDA}} = \dfrac{224\text{ Mio.} + 51\text{ Mio.} - 16\text{ Mio.}}{12\text{ Mio.}} = 21{,}58\times$

2) Die Vergleichbarkeit verschiedener Unternehmen wird verbessert, da im Gegensatz zur PER folgende Punkte nicht berücksichtigt werden:
   - Finanzierungsverhältnis und damit das Finanzergebnis
   - Steueraufwendungen
   - Bewertung der Aktiven und damit die Höhe der Abschreibungen
   - Behandlung des Goodwills

C

80 % von 160 000 Aktien = 128 000 Aktien

Kaufpreis 128 000 · 1 500.–	=	192 000 000.–
80 % von der Substanz von 139 600 000.–	=	–111 680 000.–
Goodwill	=	80 320 000.–

5.28 Analyse des Konzernabschlusses Schindler 2000

A
1. Die meisten an der Schweizer Börse kotierten und weltweit tätigen Gesellschaften (Konzerne) wenden IFRS an.
2. Das Aktienrecht lässt die Bildung von stillen Reserven (Willkürreserven) zu. Die nach IFRS (auch Swiss GAAP FER und US-GAAP) erstellten Abschlüsse sollen ein den tatsächlichen Verhältnissen entsprechendes Bild der Vermögens-, Finanz- und Ertragslage (True and fair view-Prinzip) des Konzerns vermitteln.
3. Der Konzernabschluss umfasst die Jahresrechnung der Schindler Holding und der Gesellschaften, welche von der Schindler Holding mittels direkter oder indirekter Stimmenmehrheit oder auf andere Weise beherrscht werden.
4. Mittelflussrechnung

B
1.
   - Liquiditätsgrad 2   (3 381 − 526)   · 100 : 2 359   = 121 %
   - Fremdfinanzierungsgrad   4 206   · 100 : 5 660   = 74,3 %
   - Anlagedeckungsgrad 1   (1 317 + 137)   · 100 : 2 279   = 63,8 %
   - Anlagedeckungsgrad 2   (1 317 + 137 + 1 847) · 100 : 2 279   = 144,8 %

   Begründung
   - Liquiditätsgrad 2: Der Richtwert von 100 % wird klar überschritten.
   - Fremdfinanzierungsgrad: Einen allgemein gültigen Richtwert für den Fremdfinanzierungsgrad gibt es nicht. Ein Vergleich mit Unternehmen bzw. Konzernen, die in gleichen oder ähnlichen Marktsegmenten tätig sind, zeigt, dass der Fremdfinanzierungsgrad zwischen 70 % und 80 % liegt.
   - Anlagedeckungsgrad 1: Das Anlagevermögen ist nur zu etwa ⅔ mit Eigenkapital finanziert. Dies entspricht dem Branchendurchschnitt.
   - Anlagedeckungsgrad 2: Das Anlagevermögen ist weit über 100 % mit langfristigem Kapital finanziert. Die Finanzierung ist sehr solide. Die goldene Bilanzregel wird eingehalten.

2.
   - Immaterielle Werte
     Goodwill, Patente, Lizenzen, Software
     (Aus dem Anhang, der Ihnen nicht vorliegt, geht hervor, dass der Goodwill 864 und die übrigen immateriellen Werte 54 betragen.)
   - Beteiligungen an assoziierten Gesellschaften
     Aktienpakete von Gesellschaften, an denen die Schindler Holding zwischen 20 % und 50 % der Stimmen besitzt (massgeblicher, aber nicht beherrschender Einfluss). Beteiligungen an assoziierten Gesellschaften werden nicht konsolidiert. Die Bewertung und der Ausweis der Beteiligung erfolgt zu ihrem anteiligen Eigenkapital.
   - Minderheitsanteile
     Bei den Tochtergesellschaften, bei denen die Holding weniger als 100 % des Aktienkapitals hält, gibt es noch andere Aktionäre (Minderheitsaktionäre). Die Eigenkapitalansprüche dieser «Drittaktionäre» werden in der Bilanzposition Minderheitsanteile ausgewiesen.
   - Kapitalreserven
     Die Kapitalreserven setzen sich aus von Aktionären und Partizipanten einbezahlten Beträgen zusammen, die über dem Nennwert liegen. Es handelt sich somit um das Agio der Holding und andere Zahlungen (Zuschüsse) von Aktionären und Partizipanten sowie um Erfolge aus dem Verkauf von eigenen Aktien und Partizipationsscheinen.

	3	Vernichtung bzw. Rückkauf eigener Aktien und PS über pari (= Agiorückzahlung)	
	4	Gewinnreserven	
	5	Gewinnreserven (inkl. Umrechnungsdifferenzen) · 100 : Eigenkapital	
		1 062 + (– 80) · 100 : 1 317	= 74,56 %
	6	Abnahme um 23	
	7	3 335 – 2 219 = 1 116	
		3 381 – 2 359 = 1 022	
		Abnahme = 94	
C	1	(8 530 – 7 657) · 100 : 7 657 = 11,4 %	
	2	422 · 100 : 8 530 = 5 %	
	3	Finanzergebnis, Beteiligungsergebnis, Gewinnsteuern	
	4	Betriebsergebnis (EBIT)	422
		Abschreibungen (Sachanlagen und immaterielle Werte)	+202
		EBITDA	624
	5	422 · 100 : [(5 554 + 5 660) : 2] = 7,5 %	
	6	299 · 100 : [(1 185 + 1 317) : 2] = 23,9 %	
	7	Gewinnsteuern (= Ertragssteuern)	71
		Zunahme latente Steuerforderungen	15
		Zunahme latente Steuerverbindlichkeiten	– 3
		Bezahlte Gewinnsteuern	83
		Buchungen (nicht verlangt):	
		Latente Steuerforderungen / Gewinnsteuern	15
		Gewinnsteuern / Latente Steuerverbindlichkeiten	3
		Gewinnsteuern / Flüssige Mittel	83
		Übrigens: Am Ende der Konzerngeldflussrechnung werden die bezahlten Gewinnsteuern auch mit 83 ausgewiesen.	
	8	Dividende + (evtl. Nennwertrückzahlung) · 100 : Konzerngewinn	
		60 + (evtl. 20) · 100 : 238 = 25,2 % oder 33,6 %	

D 1
– Flüssige Mittel: Zunahme von 1
– Liquiditätsfonds: Zunahme von 39
– Der in der Geldflussrechnung definierte Liquiditätsfonds ist nicht identisch mit den Flüssigen Mitteln. Die definierte Nettoliquidität enthält auch Bankkontokorrente und diese wiederum sind Teil der Finanzschulden.
Der Anhang im Geschäftsbericht enthält folgende Informationen:

Nettoliquidität	1999	2000	Veränderung
Flüssige Mittel	736	737	+ 1
Abzüglich Bankkontokorrente	–155	–117	– (–38)
Total	581	620	+ 39

Bankkontokorrentschulden gehören grundsätzlich zu den Finanzierungstätigkeiten. Bei Schindler werden offenbar die Kontokorrentkredite als integraler Bestandteil der Zahlungsmitteldisposition betrachtet. Darum werden diese Finanzschulden den Zahlungsmitteln und den geldnahen Mitteln zugerechnet.

2	Geldfluss aus Geschäftstätigkeit (Cashflow)	539
	– Geldfluss aus Investitionstätigkeit	–344
	Free Cashflow	195

3 – Effektivverschuldung = Fremdkapital – Flüssige Mittel – Forderungen
Effektivverschuldung = Fremdkapital – Umlaufvermögen + Vorräte
1 351 = 4 206 – 3 381 + 526

Da der Anhang nicht zur Verfügung steht, wird davon ausgegangen, dass es sich ausser den Vorräten beim restlichen Umlaufvermögen um Flüssige Mittel und (liquiditätswirksame) Forderungen handelt.

– Verschuldungsfaktor = Effektivverschuldung : Cashflow
2,51 = 1 351 : 539

Es würde rund 2,5 Jahre dauern, bis die Nettoverschuldung mit dem Cashflow getilgt werden könnte.

4	1999:	313	
	2000:	539	
	Zunahme	226	+72,2 %

5 Grosse positive Wirkung auf die Liquidität und somit auf den Cashflow 2000 durch
 – Abnahme der Forderungen 48
 – Zunahme der Verbindlichkeiten 113

5.29 Analyse des Geschäftsberichtes Straumann 2001

A Beteiligung 13 231 (000)

B

Gewinnreserven	· 100 : Eigenkapital		
(110 944 + 2 723)	· 100 : 147 439	=	77 %

Die Umrechnungsdifferenzen sind Teil der Gewinnreserven.

C

(Umlaufvermögen – Vorräte)	· 100 : Kurzfristiges Fremdkapital		
(113 598 – 39 262)	· 100 : 39 422	=	189 %

Annahme: Alle Positionen des Umlaufvermögens und des kurzfristigen Fremdkapitals sind geldwirksam.

D

Zinsaufwand	· 100 : Ø Finanzkapital		
1 300	· 100 : [(7 000 + 303 + 14 200) + (12 000 + 622 + 14 200) : 2]	=	5,4 %

E

Dividende	· 100 : Konzerngewinn		
7 721	· 100 : 37 599	=	20,5 %

F

EBIT	· 100 : Nettoumsatz		
61 889	· 100 : 231 599	=	26,7 %

G

Krediteinkäufe	: Ø Bestand Verbindlichkeiten aus L + L		
(22 491 + 9 206)	: [(7 247 + 5 750) : 2]	=	4,89-mal

(Dies entspricht einer durchschnittlichen Lagerdauer von 74 Tagen.)

H

1.
Enterprise	: EBITDA		
[2 000 000 + (303 + 14 200 + 7 000) – 38 240]	: (61 889 + 15 150)	=	24,7-mal

2. b, c und e sind richtig.

I

Börsenkapitalisierung	2 000 000
– Eigenkapital (Substanzwert)	– 147 439
Goodwill	1 852 561

J

1.
Konzerngewinn	· 100 : Ø Konzerneigenkapital		
40 728	· 100 : [(147 439 + 114 366) : 2]	=	31,1 %

2.
EBIT	· 100 : (Gesamtkapital : 2)		
61 889	· 100 : [(211 266 + 178 677) : 2]	=	31,7 %

3. Anleihe; da der Fremdkapitalzinssatz von 5,4 % kleiner als die Gesamtkapitalrentabilität von 31,7 % ist. Dies hat einen positiven Effekt auf die Eigenkapitalrentabilität.

K

Anlagerendite	= (40 + –.50) · 100 : 90	=	45 %

5.30 Analyse des Geschäftsberichtes Tritech 2002

A 1 143 013 : 79 289 · 100 = 180,4 %
Alle kurzfristigen Forderungen sind geldwirksam, somit ist das Ergebnis 177,4 % falsch.
(Siehe ergänzende Angaben in der Aufgabenstellung.)

2 283 156 : 181 952 · 100 = 155,6 %
Auch die Minderheitsanteile sind zu berücksichtigen. Sie stellen langfristiges Kapital dar.

3
Anfangsbestand	134 239
– Abschreibungen	– 15 682
+ **Nettoinvestitionen**	59 612 (Nettokäufe)
Endbestand	178 169

In den Abschreibungen von 18 469 ist auch die Amortisation des Goodwills von 2 787 enthalten. Um die Nettoinvestitionen zu ermitteln, sind somit nur 15 682 zu berücksichtigen.

4
Zinsaufwand					2 298
Finanzkapital	AB	EB	Summe	∅	
– kurzfristig	1 333	8 018	9 351		
– langfristig	0	23 298	23 298		
	1 333	31 316	32 649	16 324,5	
Zinssatz				14,08 %	

5
Warenvorrat		Material-, Warenaufwand	
AB	20 005	73 279	
+ ∅ HF, FF	2 273		
+ ∅ Material, Waren	15 202	– 15 202	
EB	37 480	58 077	

6
Krediteinkäufe (90 % von 73 279)	65 951,10
∅ Verbindlichkeiten L + L (36 036 + 24 127) : 2	= 30 081,50
50 % von 30 081,5	15 040,75
Umschlagshäufigkeit	**4,38-mal**
(Nicht verlangt: Kreditdauer	82 Tage)

B – Kauf Beteiligung (Tochter) Biotech. Ein Teil der Aktionäre der Biotech hat die Aktien der Tritech nicht ausgehändigt.
– Tritech hat Aktien von Tochtergesellschaften an «Drittaktionäre» verkauft.

C
1	EBITDA (wie bisher)	15 046	
2	EBIT (bisher)	– 3 423	
	Amortisation Goodwill	– 23 502,1	(235 021 : 5 Jahre : 2)
	EBIT	– 26 925,1	
3	Eigenkapital (bisher)	206 942	
	Aktivierung Goodwill	+ 235 021	
	Amortisation Goodwill für 2002	– 23 502,1	
	Eigenkapital (neu)	418 460,9	

Handbook on Particle Separation Processes

Handbook on Particle Separation Processes

Edited by

Arjen Van Nieuwenhuijzen and
Jaap Van der Graaf

Publishing
London • New York

Published by   IWA Publishing
              Alliance House
              12 Caxton Street
              London SW1H 0QS, UK
              Telephone: +44 (0)20 7654 5500
              Fax: +44 (0)20 7654 5555
              Email: publications@iwap.co.uk
              Web: www.iwapublishing.com

First published 2011
© 2011 IWA Publishing

Apart from any fair dealing for the purposes of research or private study, or criticism or review, as permitted under the UK Copyright, Designs and Patents Act (1998), no part of this publication may be reproduced, stored or transmitted in any form or by any means, without the prior permission in writing of the publisher, or, in the case of photographic reproduction, in accordance with the terms of licenses issued by the Copyright Licensing Agency in the UK, or in accordance with the terms of licenses issued by the appropriate reproduction rights organization outside the UK. Enquiries concerning reproduction outside the terms stated here should be sent to IWA Publishing at the address printed above.

The publisher makes no representation, express or implied, with regard to the accuracy of the information contained in this book and cannot accept any legal responsibility or liability for errors or omissions that may be made.

Disclaimer
The information provided and the opinions given in this publication are not necessarily those of IWA and should not be acted upon without independent consideration and professional advice. IWA and the Author will not accept responsibility for any loss or damage suffered by any person acting or refraining from acting upon any material contained in this publication.

British Library Cataloguing in Publication Data
A CIP catalogue record for this book is available from the British Library

Library of Congress Cataloging-in-Publication Data
A catalog record for this book is available from the Library of Congress

ISBN13: 9781843392774
ISBN: 1843392771

Printed and bound in Great Britain by Bell & Bain Ltd., Glasgow

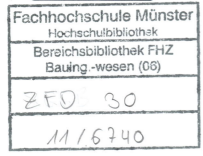

Contents

Preface xi

Chapter 1
Introduction 1
A. van Nieuwenhuijzen and J. van der Graaf

1.1 Introduction 1
1.2 This Handbook 2
1.3 Focus on Particles 3
1.4 Occurrence of Particles in Water 3
1.4 Particle Separation Processes 6
    1.4.1 Removal of particles >30 µm 6
    1.4.2 Removal of particles between 0.5 µm and 30 µm 6
    1.4.3 Removal of particles <0.5 µm 8
    1.4.4 Flocculation 8
    1.4.5 NOM-removal 8
    1.4.6 Flotation 10
1.5 Characterising the Membrane Filtration of Wastewater 10
    1.5.1 Particle characterisation for effluent filtration 10
    1.5.2 Sludge particle characterisation for MBR-applications 11
1.6 Special Applications of Particle Separation 12
    1.6.1 Jet-Mixed separator 12
    1.6.2 Rainwater treatment 12
    1.6.3 Direct membrane filtration 13

Chapter 2
Characterization of Aquatic Particles 15
M. Boller and R. Kaegi

2.1 Introduction 15
2.2 Occurrence of Particles in Water 16
2.3 Scale of Particle Observation 17
2.4 Single Particle Characterization 18
    2.4.1 Size and shape 18
        2.4.1.1 Definition of particle size 19
        2.4.1.2 Shape factor 21
        2.4.1.3 Particle agglomerates 23
    2.4.2 Microscopic analysis 26
        2.4.2.1 Optical microscopy 27
        2.4.2.2 Electron microscopy 27
        2.4.2.3 Sample preparation 30
        2.4.2.4 Atomic Force Microscopy (AFM) 31
        2.4.2.5 Overview on microscopic techniques 31
    2.4.3 Particle Density 33
    2.4.4 Particle mobility 33
    2.4.5 Sedimentation characteristics 33
    2.4.6 Shear strength 35
    2.4.7 Electrical surface charge 35
    2.4.8 Chemical composition 35
2.5 Suspension Characterization 36
    2.5.1 Bulk parameters 37
        2.5.1.1 Dry Solids Mass (TSS) 37
        2.5.1.2 Turbidity 37
    2.5.2 Particle size distribution 38
    2.5.3 Particle shear strength distribution 44
    2.5.4 Particle characterization including nanoparticles 44
        2.5.4.1 Sampling for nanoparticle analysis *by sedimentation
                and centrifugation* 45
        2.5.4.2 Field flow fractionation 45
        2.5.4.3 Laser-Induced Breakdown Detection (LIBD) 47
    2.5.5 Nanoparticles in drinking water treatment 48
        2.5.5.1 Nanoparticles in conventional drinking water and in
                membrane treatment 48
        2.5.5.2 AFM measurements 48
        2.5.5.3 TEM investigation 49
        2.5.5.4 LIBD measurements 51
        2.5.5.5 Comparing TEM and LIBD measurements 51
        2.5.5.6 Comparison between two different treatment schemes 51
    2.5.6 Synthetic nanoparticles in surface runoff 54
2.6 Overview: Particle Separation Processes 54
    2.6.1 Removal of particles >30 µm 55

	2.6.2	Removal of particles between 0.5 μm and 30 μm	56
	2.6.3	Removal of particles <0.5 μm	56
2.7	Acknowledgement		57

Chapter 3
Characterization Profiling of NOM – as a Basis for Treatment Process Selection and Performance Monitoring 61
S.K. Sharma, S.G. Salinas Rodriguez, S.A. Baghoth, S.K. Maeng and G. Amy

3.1	Introduction		61
	3.1.1	Background	61
	3.1.2	Types of NOM and their sources	62
	3.1.3	Methods for removal of different types of NOM/EfOM during water treatment	62
3.2	NOM in Water and Wastewater Treatment/Reuse		64
	3.2.1	Relevance of NOM in drinking water treatment	64
	3.2.2	Relevance of EfOM in wastewater effluent treatment/reuse	65
3.3	Quantification and Measurement of NOM		65
	3.3.1	Sampling and processing	65
	3.3.2	TOC and DOC	66
	3.3.3	UVA_{254} and SUVA	66
	3.3.4	Differential UVA (ΔUVA)	68
	3.3.5	XAD resin fractionation	69
	3.3.6	Dissolved Organic Nitrogen (DON)	69
	3.3.7	Fluorescence Excitation Emission Matrices (F-EEM)	70
	3.3.8	Size Exclusion Chromatography (SEC-DOC)	70
	3.3.9	Biodegradable Dissolved Organic Carbon (BDOC)	75
	3.3.10	Polarity Rapid Assessment Method (PRAM)	77
3.4	Case Studies of Nom Analysis for Assessment, Improvement and Design and Operation of Water Treatment Systems		77
	3.4.1	Surface water treatment	77
	3.4.2	Groundwater treatment	78
	3.4.3	Seawater desalination	79
	3.4.4	Bank filtration and artificial recharge and recovery	81
3.5	Perspectives and Recommendations		84

Chapter 4
Technologies for the Removal of Natural Organic Matter 89
H. Ødegaard, S. Østerhus, E. Melin and B. Eikebrokk

4.1	Introduction		89
4.2	Membrane (NANO) Filtration		90
4.3	Coagulation/Filtration		91
	4.3.1	General	91
	4.3.2	Alternative filter configurations	93
	4.3.3	Coagulation/membrane filtration	95

4.4	Oxidation/Biofiltration	96
	4.4.1 Oxidation	96
	4.4.2 Ozonation/biofiltration	97
	4.4.3 The OBM-process	98
4.5	Sorption Processes	99
	4.5.1 GAC adsorption	99
	4.5.2 Chemisorption (Ion exchange)	99
4.6	Conclusions	99

Chapter 5
Flocculation and its Inclusion in Membrane Filtration 103
Y. Watanabe

5.1	Introduction	103
5.2	Fundamentals of flocculation	104
	5.2.1 Floc density function	104
	5.2.2 Flocculation kinetics and GC_0T value	105
5.3	Flocculation in monolith ceramic membrane	107
	5.3.1 Theoretical consideration	107
	5.3.2 Experimental consideration	110
	5.3.2.1 Experimental set-up	110
	5.3.2.2 Experimental results	111
5.4	Conclusions	114
5.5	Acknowledgement	115

Chapter 6
Dissolved Air Flotation Development, Application, and Research Needs 117
M.Y. Han

6.1	Introduction	117
6.2	History of Developments in the DAF Process	118
6.3	Modelling of Collision Efficiency Between Microbubbles and Particles	120
6.4	Characterization of Bubble Size	122
6.5	Characterization of Bubble Charge	123
6.6	Mechanism for Producing Positively Charged Bubbles	124
6.7	Verification of Removal using Positively Charged Bubbles	125
6.8	Research Needs	126

Chapter 7
Characterising the Membrane Filtration Process of Wastewater 129
J. van der Graaf, S. Geilvoet and J. Roorda

7.1	Introduction	129
7.2	The Specific Ultra Filtration Resistance Method (SUR)	129

	7.2.1	Introduction	129
	7.2.2	Theoretical basis of the SUR	130
	7.2.3	Experimental set-up and configuration	132
		7.2.3.1 Membrane module for SUR measurement	133
		7.2.3.2 Constant pressure difference device	133
		7.2.3.3 Total filtration time	135
	7.2.4	Influence of process parameters on the SUR	137
		7.2.4.1 Experimental procedure for measuring SUR	137
		7.2.4.2 Trans Membrane Pressure (TMP)	137
		7.2.4.3 Temperature of the feedwater	140
	7.2.5	SUR for evaluation of filtration characteristics	142
		7.2.5.1 Foulants concentration	143
		7.2.5.2 Evaluation of feedwater pre-treatment	144
		7.2.5.3 SUR determination at various WWTP's in the Netherlands	146
	7.2.6	Discussion	146
		7.2.6.1 Parameter for dead-end ultra filtration	146
		7.2.6.2 Process conditions	148
	7.2.7	Conclusion	151
7.3	The Delft Filtration Characterisation Method (DFCM)		151
	7.3.1	Introduction	151
	7.3.2	Methods and materials	152
		7.3.2.1 Filtration unit	152
		7.3.2.2 Measuring protocol	153
		7.3.2.3 Output	153
		7.3.2.4 Sludge quality analyses	153
		7.3.2.5 Possibilities and limitations of DFCm	154
	7.2.3	DFCm results versus full-scale permeability development	155
	7.3.4	Filterability results	157
		7.3.4.1 Pilot comparison	158
		7.3.4.2 Long term sludge quality monitoring	159
		7.3.4.3 Batch experiments	160

Chapter 8
Enhanced Flocculation/Sedimentation Process by a Jet-Mixed Separator ... 165
Y. Watanabe, S. Kasahara and Y. Iwasaki

8.1	Introduction		165
8.2	Fundamental Study of JMS		166
	8.2.1	Phenomenon of simultaneous flocculation and sedimentation	166
	8.2.2	Hydrodynamic characteristics of JMS	169
8.3	Application of JMS to Water and Wastewater Treatment		172
	8.3.1	Pre-treatment for rapid sand filter	172
	8.3.2	Pre-treatment for biofilm reactor	174
8.4	Conclusions		181

Chapter 9
Particle Behaviour and Removal in a Rainwater Storage Tank and Suggestions for Operation 183
J.S. Mun and M.Y. Han

9.1 Introduction 183
9.2 Materials and Methods 184
    9.2.1 Rainwater utilization facility 184
    9.2.2 Experimental conditions 185
9.3 Results and Discussion 186
    9.3.1 Water quality of "first-flush" runoff and stored rainwater in the tank ... 186
    9.3.2 Particle behaviour and removal in a rainwater tank 187
    9.3.3 Design considerations for a rainwater tank 191
9.4 Conclusions 191

Chapter 10
Direct Membrane Filtration of Wastewater 193
A. Ravazinni, A.F. van Nieuwenhuijzen and J.H.J.M. van der Graaf

10.1 Introduction 193
10.2 Review on Direct Membrane Separation (DMS) of Wastewater 193
10.3 Direct Ultrafiltration of Municipal Wasteater 195
10.4 Applications and Reuse Possibilities of Direct UF 196
10.5 Research Studies at TU-DELFT 197
    10.5.1 Background 197
        10.5.1.1 Crossflow filtration 197
        10.5.1.2 Fouling mechanisms 198
        10.5.1.3 Filter cake compressibility 198
        10.5.1.4 Filterability and reversibility 198
        10.5.1.5 Critical flux concept 198
    10.5.2 Experimental set-up 199
    10.5.3 Fundamental role of operating conditions 199
        10.5.3.1 Experiments 199
        10.5.3.2 Results 200
        10.5.3.3 Conclusions 203
    10.5.4 Compressibility of filter cake 203
    10.5.5 Feasibility of constant TMP and constant flux operations 204
        10.5.5.1 Experimental 204
        10.5.5.2 Results 205
    10.5.6 Little effect of primary sedimentation 206
        10.5.6.1 Experimental 206
        10.5.6.2 Results 206
    10.5.7 Little effect of coagulant dosage 208
        10.5.7.1 Experimental 208
        10.5.7.2 Results 209
10.6 Costs 210
10.7 Conclusions 210

Preface

M. Jekel

Advances in particle science and particle removal in water and wastewater treatment are important features in understanding and optimising treatment processes and concepts. In 2008, a major summer course on this topic was organized by Delft University and UNESCO-IHE Delft, more than 30 years after the International Summer School on The Scientific Basis of Coagulation and Flocculation, held in 1977 at Cambridge University and organized by the late Ken Ives. The Academic Summer School on Advances in Particle Separation in Water and Wastewater Treatment was a selective symposium and workshop for invited lecturers and participants only, organised under supervision of the IWA Specialist Group on Particle Separation. The purpose of the Summer School is to exchange knowledge and expertise from a selected group of honourable experts with a long track record in the field of particles and particle separation in water and wastewater treatment to emerging new and young specialist in this area. Since the older generation of experts is more and more retiring, information exchange is essential to provide future experts with available expertise.

The Summer School provided five full days of lectures by established professors and short presentations from emerging scientists. Invited professors lectured in their field of expertise during a morning or afternoon session. The participating lecturer selected three promising experts from their institute or working environment to present their topics during special midday and afternoon presentations. The Summer School was meant to be interactive, with possibilities for questions and discussions at any stage of the day. This book provides an overview of the latest developments on particle separation in water and wastewater treatment as discussed during the summer course.

The IWA Specialist Group on Particle Separation acted as mother organisation of the summer school and has been founded in 1988 by the late experts Ken Ives from United Kingdom and Heinz Bernhardt from Germany. It was unique, as it was formed as a Joint Specialist Group on Coagulation, Flocculation, Sedimentation, Flotation and Filtration between the former organisations IAWQ (International Associations on Water Quality) and IWSA (International Water Supply Association). Both associations merged in 2000 as IWA, the International Water Association. The Joint Group became the regular IWA Specialist Group on Particle Separation.

This Specialist Group, with around 500 members within IWA, has a management committee of about 12 members from all continents reflecting also all the topics of particle separation. It is organising typically its own specialist conferences in between the main IWA world water conferences. The next event is planned for the late spring in 2012 in Berlin. Please inform about more details via the IWA home page.

As chairman of the Specialist Group on Particle Separation I want to thank especially our member Jaap van der Graaf and his supporter Arjen van Nieuwenhuijzen from the Netherlands, who prepared and organised the Summer School in 2008 and invested a lot of time in preparing this book, which will be a reference book on particle separation for the coming decades. Also, I thank the authors of the chapters for their effort and time in preparation of the reviews.

Figure A Participants of the first Summer School on Particle Separation, 1977 Cambridge *(photo courtesy Hallvard Ødegaard)*

Figure B Participants of the 2008 Summer School on Particle Separation, Delft *(photo courtesy Witteveen + Bos, A.F. van Nieuwenhuijzen)*

Chapter 1
Introduction

A. van Nieuwenhuijzen and J. van der Graaf

1.1 INTRODUCTION

Particles in water play an important role in all kinds of water quality and treatment issues. Since the early beginnings of centralised water production and treatment, the main goal of water purification was primarily the removal of water turbidity in order to produce clear water free from visible particles. Although the connection between hazardous organisms in water and diseases caused by water consumption was only proven in the second half of the 19th century (John Snow c.s, see Figure 1.1), experience learned human civilisation to treat water especially from surface water sources by removing the turbidity. Sedimentation in ponds and large pots, filtration through porous materials and textiles and other means of water treatment were applied in smaller communities and single households. With population growth and settlements of larger cities, water treatment and disease control were often neglected. Especially in medieval civilizations the idea that diseases would originate from (drinking) water was lost to a great extent. Only the discovery and recognition of pathogenic micro-organisms in water and their distinct effects on humans and animals during several water-born epidemics in (the first mega) cities in the World, created by an explosive growth due to industrialisation around 1850, brought the idea of hygiene in daily life back to the population. Pushed by medical and pharmaceutical specialists, water filtration in central treatment plants, water boiling in households and after 1900 also centralised water disinfection were introduced to produce safe drinking water. The necessity of controlled discharge of particle-rich human wastewater and treatment of it was recognised as well. Of course, particle removal and the transfer of soluble material into biological particles play an important role also in wastewater treatment. Around 1940, so called primary treatment was commonly applied consisting of simple sedimentation facilities to remove about 50% of the particles contained in raw sewage. Later, biological treatment was introduced where biological flocculation and the removal of the activated sludge is an important solids separation step for small colloidal particle fractions.

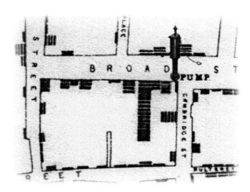

"Further inquiry, however, showed me that there was no other circumstance or agent common to the circumscribed locality in which this sudden increase of cholera occurred, and not extending beyond it, except the water of the [Broad Street] pump.
....
I had an interview with the Board of Guardians of St. James's parish, on the evening of Thursday, 7th September [1854], and represented the above circumstances to them. In consequence of what I said, the handle of the pump was removed on the following day."

John Snow M.D., On the Mode of Communication of Cholera,
second (extended) edition
London: John Churchill, New Burlington Street, England, 1855

Figure 1.1 John Snow's submission to human health (Van Nieuwenhuijzen, 2002)

1.2 THIS HANDBOOK

Advances in particle removal in water and wastewater treatment are still important developments in understanding and optimising treatment processes and concepts. In 2008 a major summer course on this topic was organized by Delft University and UNESCO-IHE Delft, more than 30 years after the first International Summer Course on Particle Separation, in 1977 in Cambridge. The Academic Summer School on Advances in Particle Separation in Water and Wastewater Treatment was a selective symposium and workshop for invited lecturers and participants only, organised under supervision of the IWA Specialist Group Particle Separation. The purpose of the Summer School was to exchange knowledge and expertise from a selected group of honourable experts with a long track record in the field of particles and particle separation in water and wastewater treatment to emerging new and young specialist in this area. Since the older generation of experts is more and more retiring, information exchange is essential to provide future experts with available expertise.

The IWA Handbook on Particle Separation Processes (Van Nieuwenhuijzen and Van der Graaf, 2010) provides an overview of the latest developments on particle separation in water and wastewater treatment. This book has been edited from the presentations and workshops held at the Academic Summer School Particle Separation in Water and Wastewater Treatment. The purpose of the Handbook is to provide knowledge and expertise from a selected group of international experts with a wealth of experience in the field of particles and particle separation in water and wastewater treatment. The book contains material ranging from Methods and Instrumentation for Particle Analysis and Characterisation (by Prof. Markus Boller), over Natural Organic Matter: Particles, Colloids and Macromolecules (by Prof. Gary Amy), NOM Removal Technologies (by Prof. Hallvard Ødegaard), Several Physical Chemical Treatment Technologies (Prof. Yoshima Watanabe), Filtration Characteristics for Effluent Treatment by Prof. Jaap van der Graaf and Flotation for Particles Removal by Prof. Mooyoung Han. Three chapters are dedicated to some new promising particle removal developments. Other topics like Modelling Particle Removal (Prof. Desmond Lawler), Particle Separation in Drinking Water Treatment (Prof. Rolf Gimbel) and Nanoparticles in Water and Wastewater (Prof. Mark Wiesner) are presented in other gremials and publications.

1.3 FOCUS ON PARTICLES

It becomes obvious that the removal of particles from water and wastewater is crucial for safe potable water production and efficient wastewater treatment. If particles are present in a water source, it is the primary purpose of all purification techniques to eliminate or inactivate the particles and with them also eventual hygienic hazards.

For several reasons particles represent undesired pollutants in most product waters. Apart from the mass of suspended matter as often used bulk parameter, many other quality indicators are strongly associated with particles such as hygienic contaminants and adsorbed chemicals. On one hand, particles may negatively interfere in various treatment processes and supply systems, on the other hand particulate matter in the form of biomass is a necessary prerequisite in many water treatment schemes. The removal of particulate matter was and will be one of the most crucial steps in water and wastewater treatment. In order to understand the behaviour of particles in water and to develop and design efficient treatment facilities, the characteristics of particles has to be known on the basis of individual solids and of whole particle populations. In water treatment, particles are of extremely heterogeneous nature with respect to size, density, shape, chemical composition, shear strength, surface charge, etc. which represent information that is in most cases not available. This book aims at gathering knowledge on particle characterisation by presenting research studies including results with innovative new instruments and methods.

In order to understand the role of particles in water quality evaluation and water purification and wastewater treatment processes, the particles and their behaviour in aqueous systems have to be known and characterized.

1.4 OCCURRENCE OF PARTICLES IN WATER

Solids in water are of very different origin and appear in a large variety of sizes, shapes, chemical composition, etc. An incomplete list of particles in water is shown below and illustrates the complex nature of aqueous solids:

(1) **Domestic Wastewater**
   – *Coarse solids*: gravel, sand, faeces, paper, hair, cotton, wood pieces, plastic pieces (e.g. ear sticks), cigarette-ends;

- *Fine solids*: faeces, road dust, atmospheric solids deposits, aggregates of micro-organisms, single micro-organisms, worm eggs, viruses, biological debris, clay minerals, chemical precipitates, nano-size particles;
(2) **Industrial wastewater**
- Great variety according to production and treatment processes cellulose fibres, asbestos fibres, incineration ashes, precipitation products, pigments, emulsified oil droplets, polymers, coal dust, silicates, metals, blood, milk;
(3) **River water**
- Gravel, sand, silt, clay, algae, decay products of plants, protozoa, bacteria, viruses;
(4) **Lake water**
- Phytoplankton, zooplankton, detritus, precipitation products, bacteria, viruses, protozoa;
(5) **Groundwater/Spring water**
- Precipitation products (Fe, Mn, Ca), soil colloids, bacteria, viruses, protozoa;
(6) **Potable water**
- Nano-size particles, bacteria, viruses, corrosion products, calcite particles, particles of natural organic matter (NOM).

While most of the above description do not give much information on particle characteristics, detailed analysis of particle numbers include the evaluation of the particle size. A coarse indication of the size range of some well known particle classes is given in Figure 1.2 and Figure 1.3.

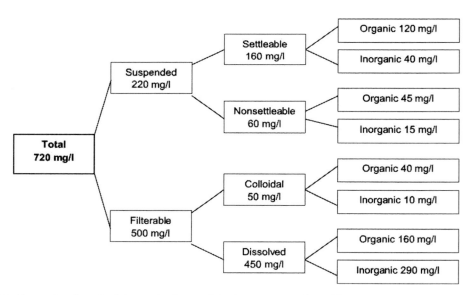

Figure 1.2 Example of particulate matter in municipal wastewater (Van Nieuwenhuijzen, 2002)

It also becomes clear that the standard procedure for solids analysis by filtering water samples with 0.45 μm membrane filters is not an accurate procedure to define solid and dissolved matter. There is still suspended matter in the size range below 0.45 μm which would have to be clearly classified as particulate.

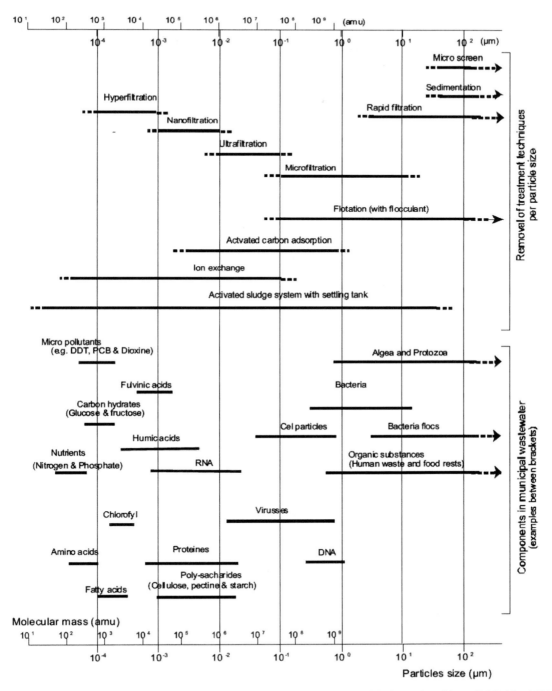

Figure 1.3 Size categories of aqueous particles (Van Nieuwenhuijzen, 2002 based on Metcalf & Eddy, 1998)

In Figure 1.2 the breakdown of constituents in typical municipal wastewater (in the Netherlands) is presented; it finally shows the divisions into four fractions: settleable, unsettleable, colloidal and dissolved.

Markus Boller presents in chapter 2 an overview on possible techniques for the measurement and characterisation of particles in water. Especially the submicron particles need very precise attention.

In chapter 3 the natural organic matter (NOM) is introduced by Gary Amy; the various analytical techniques finally give information on the selection of suitable removal processes.

1.4 PARTICLE SEPARATION PROCESSES

In most treatment trains for water treatment, particle separation is the first treatment step. There are different alternatives for solids separation and their beneficial application depends strongly on the quality of the water or more precisely on the characteristics of the particle suspension to be treated. The processes most widely applied in water treatment are:

- sedimentation
- flocculation
- flotation
- granular media filtration
- contact filtration
- screening, straining
- membrane filtration
- NOM-removal technologies.

Among these processes flocculation is not really a solids separation process but it helps to improve solids separation considerably by particle agglomeration. A primary factor for the decision which processes are suitable under which conditions, is the solids concentration in terms of mass quantity, volume or number concentrations. On the other hand, the particle size is an important parameter which determines the removal mechanisms which are best to be promoted in order to achieve optimal solids separation performance. Particle size fractionation of waters can be of interest for selection of an appropriate separation technology. Figure 1.4 presents a standardised method for particle size characterisation developed by the author.

1.4.1 Removal of particles >30 μm

Particles >30 μm can be removed by screening processes such as microstrainers. The smaller range of mesh sizes is in the order of 8 μm. Also a granular media filter may remove particles >20 μm completely. The combination rapid filter/slow sand filter can reach a particle removal efficiency of 100% for particles >10 μm. Screens and granular filters are subject to clogging and need to be cleaned regularly. At higher concentrations, sedimentation for particles with a higher density and flotation for particles with a low density are more suited. Filters and screens may be used below concentrations in the order of 50 mgTSS/l. At higher concentrations sedimentation or flotation are necessary.

1.4.2 Removal of particles between 0.5 μm and 30 μm

Many important particles in surface waters are in the size range between 0.5 and 30 μm such as bacteria, blue and green algae, diatoms, and partly also inorganic particles. In this size range orthokinetic flocculation (particle transport by shear) has to be applied in order to agglomerate the particles to larger flocs and thus enable removal by sedimentation, flotation or filtration. A combination with sedimentation or flotation is suitable at concentrations above 50 mgTSS/l or filtration or contact filtration at concentrations below this value. Also membrane filters such as micro- and ultra filters may cope with this particle class. In full scale, membrane filters are usually protected against too large particles by screening filters with openings in the order of 20 µm (Amy, 2004).

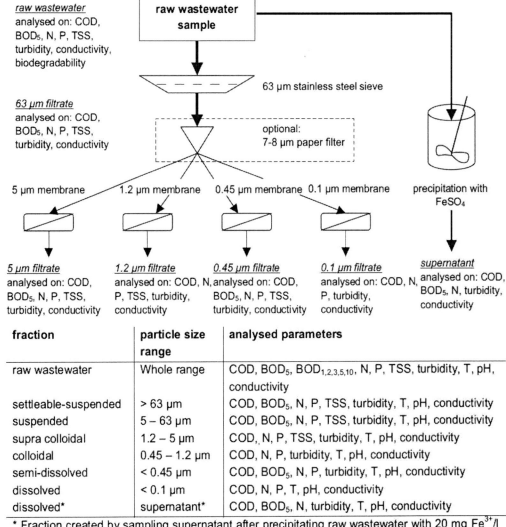

Figure 1.4 Particle size fractionation (Van Nieuwenhuijzen, 2002)

1.4.3 Removal of particles <0.5 μm

The smaller the particles in the nano-size range, the more difficult it is to describe their behavior in water. Viruses and some types of inorganic precipitates such as calcite and iron (hydr)-oxides typically belong to this size range. From particle analysis in this size range, it becomes clear that the number of particles is increasing with decreasing size. Particle numbers of nano-sized colloids in natural waters may easily reach 10^8 to 10^9/ml. In addition to the mentioned colloids, decay products of suspended organic material are present in large quantities. In future also an increasing number of synthetic nano-particles in wastewater, natural water and drinking water have to be expected.

The aggregation of submicron particles is relatively fast if their surface chemistry is suited and if their concentration is high enough (>108/ml). The transport of submicron particles for aggregation is brought about by Brownian motion, also know as perikinetic flocculation. Often the agglomerates are still small and cannot be removed by sedimentation or filtration, further agglomeration with the help of orthokinetic flocculation, contact filtration or sludge blanket clarifiers is necessary.

The particle class <0.5 μm can efficiently be removed by ultra filtration. Again pre-filters with openings of 10 to 20 μm are applied in order to protect the membranes. In view of the small pore size of ultra filters in the order of 0.01 μm, viruses and other colloids may be removed completely by ultra filter membranes. Ultra filters may cope with particle concentrations up to more than 1000 mgTSS/l. However, membrane fouling caused by accompanying organic material such as polysaccharides, proteins and humic substances can limit the application of ultra filters to much lower concentrations in the order of 100 mgTSS/l and lower.

1.4.4 Flocculation

This paragraph summarizes the researches on the flocculation conducted by Tambo and Watanabe, and on the inclusion of flocculation in the monolith ceramic membrane filtration conducted by the authors as described in more detail in chapter 5 of this book. The floc density function describes the quantitative relationship between the size and effective (buoyant) density of flocs. The exponent $K\rho$ in the function is related to the fractal dimension (D) for the aggregates formed in Cluster-Cluster Aggregation (CCA) as $D = 3 - K\rho$. The $K\rho$ is a function of the ALT ratio and has the numerical value of 1.00 and 1.25 for the ALT ratio of around 1/100 and 1/20, respectively. These values coincide with the D value determined for the reaction and diffusion limited case (2.05 and 1.75), respectively, determined in the field of the Fractal Physics.

The authors have also clarified the characteristics unique to monolith ceramic membrane with pre-coagulation by referring to the behaviour of micro-particles. The region exists in the monolith channel with the optimum G and GC0T value for good flocculation. The flocculation of micro-particles reduces the membrane fouling. If pre-coagulation and chemically enhanced backwashing are included in the monolith ceramic membrane filtration system, extremely high filtration flux is possible for a long operation period.

1.4.5 NOM-removal

Natural organic matter (NOM – with its main constituent humic substances), has several negative influences in water that is to be used for water supply and needs therefore to be removed (Boller, Odegaard). A better understanding of NOM character and its removal by various treatment methods is essential to improve treated water quality meeting increasingly stringent standards. In order to have a better insight into the types of organic compounds present before and after different water treatment processes several characterization techniques have been developed worldwide. These have provided considerable knowledge in understanding the impact of NOM on treatment processes. The characterization techniques differ considerably in terms of analytical approach, NOM fractionations or components analyzed, time and skills required, costs, and the form of the output or results (whether it can be interpreted easily and used by the treatment plant operators).

Comparative analysis of different methods of characterization of NOM has clearly shown that there is no single method which can fully reveal its characteristics that are important for water treatment practice. It is obvious that use of combinations of different methods would be required for proper analysis of the fate of different fractions of NOM during different treatment processes. However, the methods of characterization to be applied under given conditions depend on the source of NOM and treatment methods applied.

In the absence of high skills and costly instruments, tracking DOC and SUVA changes along the treatment process train could be a basic approach in understanding the removal of NOM. High pressure liquid chromatography using gels have proved useful in combination with UV/vis, fluorescence, light scattering and sensitive dissolved organic carbon detection techniques, yielding information on molecular absorbance, size distribution, molar mass and reactivity. Information on biodegradability of NOM can be deduced from experimental measurement of bacterial growth under defined conditions. The nature and amount of biologically assimilable organic carbon (AOC) in combination with the bacterial cell number and growth rate constants can provide a meaningful characterization of microbial stability in aquatic systems (see chapter 3 by Gary Amy).

The characteristics of humic substances (MW, charge, hydrophobic and, aromatic nature etc) give the opportunity of several removal methods (as described by Hallvard Ødegaard in chapter 4):

(1) Because of the large molecular size NOM may be removed by molecular sieving, i.e. filtration through NF membranes. According to the Norwegian experiences, predominantly with cellulose acetate membranes (typically 3 nm effective pore size), the plants should be designed for a moderate flux (<20 LMH) and recovery (<70%) and operated with daily light cleaning for fouling control. NF is suitable when the NOM concentration and color is high.

(2) Because of the charge and colloidal nature, NOM can be removed by coagulation and floc separation. Coagulant dose and pH of coagulation are the two most important factors for achieving optimal treatment result. In most cases, the maximum residual metal concentration level (0.15 mg Me/L) determines the required coagulant dose level. Contact filtration are often used for raw water color levels up to about 50 mg Pt/L and turbidity levels less than 1–2 NTU. Above this a pre-separation step (settling/flotation) is recommended.

(3) The color of NOM may effectively be removed by ozonation (or another strong oxidative method). Oxidation has to be proceeded by biofiltration in order to take the growth potential out of the water. Typical O3-dosages are 0.15–0.20 mg O3/mg Pt or 1–1.5 mg O3/mg TOC. Necessary biofilter EBCT is around 20–30 min. Ozonation/ biofiltration is only advised for relatively low color levels, typically below 35 mg Pt/l. Otherwise the biogrowth potential created by the ozonation may be too high for the biofilter to handle.

(4) Sorption processes are less used. GAC adsorption as the only process is unsuitable because of pore blocking resulting in low capacity and short filter runs. GAC may, however, be suitable in combination with pre-ozonation. Ion exchange (based on macroporous anion exchangers) is used in small plants, but is only recommended at relatively low raw water color levels, typically below 30 mg Pt/L.

1.4.6 Flotation

DAF plants have several advantages compared to conventional sedimentation plants. DAF is more efficient than sedimentation in removing particles (turbidity). Lower particle loading to the filters yields longer filter runs and high filtered water production. Integrating this into the design of new plants allows for filters to be designed at higher rates (see chapter 6 by Mooyoung Han).

DAF plants have a smaller footprint compared to conventional sedimentation and high rate plate and tube sedimentation plants. Shorter flocculation times reduce the size of the flocculation tanks. Another advantage is that DAF has been shown to be more effective than sedimentation in removing Giardia and Cryptosporidium (Edzwald et al., 2000, 2003). Finally, the sludge solids from DAF have a higher percentage of solids than sedimentation, thereby reducing sludge treatment and disposal costs.

Below, we provide a list of some research needs. This is not meant to be comprehensive, but rather point out some important areas for additional research. The first has to do with making positively-charged bubbles. Coagulants are used in drinking water treatment to produce flocs of little or no electrical charge to enhance bubble attachment. For water supplies low in natural organic matter, the primary objective of coagulation is altering the negative particle charge. Eliminating coagulant addition to the raw water flow may be possible by adding chemicals to the recycle flow to produce positively-charged bubbles (Han et al., 2006).

A second need has to do with optimising and controlling bubble size. DAF produces bubbles over a wide range of sizes from 10 to 100pm, depending on the saturator pressure and nozzle type and design. Optimising the bubble size could improve treatment efficiency and also reduce energy consumption.

DAF is known to strip out some taste and odour compounds. A third need is to quantify what compounds are removed and identify how the process can be optimised. A fourth need has to do with integrating DAF as a pre-treatment for membrane processes, especially reverse osmosis and nanofiltration. To prevent fouling of membranes and to make the membrane plants more cost effective, pre-treatment is often necessary. DAF could be used to reduce particle fouling and fouling from algal polysaccharides. Finally, research is needed to reduce the energy consumption from producing air bubbles or to utilize the physical characteristics that might occur when bubbles break for the removal of microorganisms or micro pollutants.

1.5 CHARACTERISING THE MEMBRANE FILTRATION OF WASTEWATER

In the field of wastewater treatment, membrane filtration is a fully accepted and still very fast growing technology. Two typical applications are the ultrafiltration of effluent and the membrane bioreactor (MBR) where the filtration characteristics are of major importance (see chapter 7 by Jaap van der Graaf).

1.5.1 Particle characterisation for effluent filtration

The Specific Ultra filtration Resistance (SUR) is proposed as a new parameter for measuring the filtration characteristics of effluent in dead-end ultra filtration. The SUR is calculated from the filtration data measured with a lab-scale device. The SUR is calculated from the ratio of filtration time and filtrate volume (t/V) as a function of the total filtrate volume and is the product of the specific cake resistance and the solids concentration. The process conditions during measurement affect the SUR of the effluent, therefore the SUR is defined at a constant TMP of 0.5 bar and an effluent temperature of 20°C. The SUR has an accuracy of more than 95% and is measured within 30 minutes of filtration.

The experiments on the SUR revealed also additional information about the filtration characteristics of WWTP-effluent. The MWCO of a PES/PVP membrane did not influence the SUR. This indicates that effluent constituents larger than the pore sizes determine filtration characteristics. Experiments with varying Trans Membrane Pressure showed that the occurring fouling layer is highly compressible (s = 0.6–0.75).

This implies that the fluxes should not increase too much, as the accompanying TMP increases more than linear. Pre-treatment induced an increase in filterability of 20% to 30%. Both pre-filtration and coagulation influenced mainly particles larger that 5–10 μm. This relatively small increase in filterability by pre-treatment indicates therefore that the filterability is only partly determined by particles larger than 5–10 μm.

The SUR was measured for effluent of various WWTP's in the Netherlands and showed great variations for the different WWTP's. The SUR was found to range from $5 \cdot 10^{12}$ to $30 \cdot 10^{12}$ m^{-2}. Although the effect of pre-treatment on the filterability (measured as SUR) was relatively small, the change in filterability can be measured accurately with the SUR. In these tests coagulation as well as multi-media filtration showed a decrease of the SUR (of approximately 20% to 30%), greatly depending on the local conditions.

1.5.2 Sludge particle characterisation for MBR-applications

A modification of the SUR for membrane bioreactors (MBR's) is the Delft Filtration Characterisation method (DFCm). For research into fouling in MBR Delft University of Technology has developed the Delft Filtration Characterisation method (DFCm), described in detail by Evenblij et al. (2005). With the DFCm different activated sludge samples can be filtrated with the same membrane and under identical hydraulic circumstances. In this way differences in filterability can be related exclusively to differences in sludge characteristics. The DFCm consists of a small scale filtration unit and an accompanying measuring protocol.

The heart of the filtration unit is a single tubular side stream X-Flow UF membrane with a length of 95 cm, a diameter of 8 mm and a nominal pore size 0.03 μm. A peristaltic pump circulates an activated sludge sample through the system; the cross-flow velocity in the membrane tube is fixed at 1 m/s. Another peristaltic pump is used for permeate extraction; permeate flow rate can be adjusted by tuning the pump speed. The permeate production is measured in time with a mass balance, so the flux J (l/m$^2 \cdot$ h) can be calculated. Using three pressure gauges (feed, concentrate and permeate) the transmembrane pressure TMP (bar) during an experiment is monitored. The viscosity η (Pa · s) of permeate can be assumed equal to pure water. From these three parameters the filtration resistance R (m^{-1}) can be calculated according to Darcy's law: $R = TMP/(\eta \cdot J)$.

Fouling is a complex process that can be analysed from different points of view. The DFCm can not cover all aspects of fouling that will occur in a full-scale installation. Therefore it is important to identify the possibilities and the limitations of DFCm.

The shortest-term fouling mechanism is cake formation (Table 1.1), which is only combated by mechanical measures. Apart from creating turbulent flow conditions near the membrane surface through coarse bubble aeration also relaxation and back flushing can be used to prevent or remove cake layer fouling. Periodical chemical cleaning of the membranes is indispensible to maintain sufficient permeability on a longer term. Depending on the system configuration low-intensive maintenance cleanings and high-intensive recovery cleanings can be carried out. Fouling that can not be removed by any physical or chemical cleaning measure is referred to as irrecoverable or long-term irreversible fouling. Ultimately the irrecoverable fouling determines the lifetime of a membrane (apart from other forms of damage).

The DFCm is not capable of covering long-term fouling phenomena; it only provides insight about cake fouling. Though on first sight DFCm thus only seems to cover a small part of the total fouling spectrum, it is however very important to have insight in the cake fouling potential of MBR activated sludge. In the first place low cake fouling offers room for optimisation of the membrane operation; when the filterability is good, energy and thus costs can be saved concerning relaxation time, back flushing and/or coarse bubble aeration rate. Besides this it is not improbable that there is a relation between short-term and long-term fouling rates. This can be investigated by comparing short-term DFCm results with long-term permeability data from investigated plants.

Table 1.1 Typical ranges of different fouling rates (based on Kraume 2007)

Fouling "form"	Fouling rate [mbar/min]	Time interval	Cleaning
Cake fouling	0.1 – 1	10 minutes	Mechanical
Residual fouling	0.01 – 0.1	1–2 weeks	Maintenance
Irreversible fouling	0.001 – 0.01	6–12 months	Recovery
Long-term irreversible fouling	0.0001 – 0.001	Several years	Not applicable

1.6 SPECIAL APPLICATIONS OF PARTICLE SEPARATION

However the applications of particle separation in the field of water and wastewater treatment are numerous, special attention is given to three typical and promising examples, namely Jet-Mixed Separation, rain water treatment by flotation and direct membrane filtration.

1.6.1 Jet-Mixed Separator

The Jet-Mixed Separator (JMS, see chapter 8) is an economical and effective solid-liquid separator with the phenomenon of simultaneous flocculation and sedimentation. It has porous plates inserted vertically in the channel perpendicular to the flow direction. The water passes through holes in the plates, thus creating jets which gently mix the water on itself resulting in the promotion of the flocculation of suspended particles. According to the local velocity measurement, it was demonstrated that large-scale eddies in the vertical plane are almost absent in the JMS. Therefore, larger flocs can settle in the JMS. The JMS incorporated with inclined tube settlers was applied to the rapid sand filtration system instead of the combination of mechanical flocculator and sedimentation basin. In a hydraulic detention time of less than 1 hour, the effluent turbidity from the JMS was below 1 TU. The JMS without inclined tube settlers was applied to the municipal wastewater treatment where it was used as pre-treatment process to the RBC. The JMS produced an effluent with low concentration of suspended solids and TOC at a hydraulic detention time of less than 1 hour.

1.6.2 Rainwater treatment

In an additional study, the water quality of first-flush runoff and stored rainwater, as well as the efficiency of removal and behaviour of particles in a rainwater storage tank, was investigated using three rainfall events that had different histories of previous dry days and rainfall volume. Several considerations to be born in mind while designing a rainwater storage tank were suggested [see chapter 9, (Han and Lee, 2005)].

Turbidity of first-flush runoff was over 100 NTU in the case of long antecedent dry days (13 days) and slight rainfall (6 mm), but, within 1 hour, runoff turbidity decreased to under 30 NTU. Right after runoff stopped, the initial turbidity of stored rainwater in the tank was 2.1~11.2 NTU for the three rainfall events. As antecedent dry days increased and the amount of rainfall decreased, so turbidity increased. The pH was high due to contact with the marble terrace. The average particle size in all cases was 8~10 μm.

The main tank, which consists of 2 rooms of 125 m^3, was operated at a fixed water level, without inflow and outflow, after stopping the access of runoff to examine the removal efficiency and behaviour of particles during sedimentation. The removal rate increased regularly according to retention time for stored rainwater of around 2 NTU. However, the removal rate increased rapidly early on, but then increased gently, for stored rainwater of 6~11 NTU. The particle number and peak of PSD in stored rainwater decreased according to the retention time.

The removal efficiency was increased by having a considerable distance between inlet and outlet, even when there were long antecedent dry days and little rainfall. If possible, it is recommended to design the effective water depth to be over 3 m, and to supply rainwater near the water surface by using a floating suction.

1.6.3 Direct membrane filtration

In chapter 10, a novel concept of direct ultrafiltration of municipal wastewater is presented. Previous studies indicated that direct membrane filtration has great potential, essentially because it produces clear bacteria-free filtrate in one single purely physical step. However, the knowledge about feasibility and cost is still limited and further development is need. The research presented here focused on the treatment of untreated municipal wastewater with ultrafiltration membranes. The main objectives were the influence of operating conditions (TMP and crossflow velocity) and pre-treatment (primary sedimentation and coagulation) on fouling characteristics.

In the frame of the worldwide interest for the development of novel applications for membrane processes, the concept of direct ultrafiltration of wastewater with crossflow tubular membrane has been explored.

The application has great potential with regard to water recycling and sanitation, especially because being a purely physical process, it can produce water on demand starting from common wastewater. The main applications could be irrigation and advanced pre-treatments, especially for the production of high quality water with dense membranes and nutrients recovery.

The research has shown that the process is technically feasible, with sustainable fluxes in the order 70–80 l/m^{2}h. This makes the application virtually economically reasonable. The cost of water extraction is indeed estimated below 0.30 eurocents/m^3.

The application should now be evaluated at pilot scale for continuous operation. Meanwhile, a deeper analyses of the permeate characteristics should be carried on, to evaluate in details treatment and reuse path.

It must be remarked that the application of simple pre-treatments, such as sedimentation and flocculation, does not affect significantly neither fouling formation nor permeate quality, and therefore appear useless.

1.7 REFERENCES

Amy, G. and Her, N. (2004). Size exclusion chromatography (SEC) with multiple detectors: a powerful tool in treatment process selection and performance monitoring. *Wat. sci. Tec.: Wat. Sup.*, **4**, 19–24.
Boller, M. and Blaser, S. (1998). Particles under stress, *Wat. Sci. Tech.*, **37**(10), 9–29.
Boller, M. and Pronk, W. (2004). Nano and Microparticles in Water and Wastewater Treatment. *Wat. Sci. Tech.*, **50**(12).
Buffle, J., Perret, D. & Newman, M. E. (1992). *Environmental Particles*, Boca Raton, Lewis Publishers.
Evenblij, H., Geilvoet, S.P., Van der Graaf, J.H.J.M., Van der Roest, H.F. (2005). Filtration characterisation for assessing MBR performance: three cases compared. *Desalination*, **178**, 115–124.
Filella, M., Buffle, J. & Leppard, G. G. (1993). Characterization of Submicrometer Colloids in Fresh-Waters – Evidence for Their Bridging by Organic Structures, *Wat. Sci. Tech.*, **27**, 91–102.

Geilvoet, S. (2010). *The Delft Filtration Characterisation method – assessing membrane bioreactor activated sludge filterability*, PhD Thesis, Delft University of Technology, ISBN: 978-90-8957-010-9.

Han M. Y. and Lee S. J. (2005). Evaluation of Stored Rainwater Quality at Galmoe Middle School Rainwater Harvesting System. *Korean Society of water and Wastewater*, **19**(1), 31–37.

Han M. Y., Han M. S. and Kim S. R. (2004). A Consideration in Determining the Tank Volume of Rainwater Harvesting System in Building. *J. of Korean Society of water and Wastewater*, **18**(2), 99–109.

Han, M.Y., Kim, M.K. and Ahn, H.J. (2006). Effects of surface charge, microbubble size and particle size on removal efficiency of electroflotation. *Wat. Sci. Tech.*, **53**(7), 127–132.

Kraume. (2007). Fouling in MBR – What use are lab investigations for full-scale operation. *Proc. 6th IMSTEC*, Sydney 5–9 Nov 2007.

Lawler, D.F. (1996). Particle size distribution in treatment processes: Theory and practice, *Wat. Sci. Tech.*, **36**(4), 15–23.

Melin, E. and Ødegaard H. (2000) The effect of biofilter loading rate on the removal of organic ozonation by-products. *Wat. Res.*, **34**(18), 4464–4476.

Nieuwenhuijzen (2002). *Scenario Studies into Advanced Particle Removal in the Physical-Chemical Pre-Treatment of Wastewater*, 2002 PhD-thesis Delft University of Technology, DUTPress, ISBN 9040722498.

Ødegaard, H, Eikebrokk, B. and Storhaug, R. (1999). Processes for the removal of humic substances from water - An overview based on Norwegian experiences. *Wat. Sci. Tech.*, **40**(9), 37–46

Ødegaard, H., Melin, E. and Leiknes, T. (2006). Ozonation/biofiltration for treatment of humic surface water. In. *Recent Progress in Slow Sand and Alternative Biofiltration Processes*, (editors Gimbel, R., Graham, N.J.D. and Collins, M.R), IWA Publishing, 397-405. ISBN 9781843391203

Poele, S. te and Graaf, J.H.J.M. van der (2002). Physical and chemical conditioning of effluent for decreasing membrane fouling during ultra filtration. In *Proceedings Membranes in Drinking and Industrial Water Production*, September 22-26, 2002, 37, 765–773.

Ravazzini, A.M., A.F. van Nieuwenhuijzen and J.H.M.J. van der Graaf (2004). Direct Ultrafiltration of Municipal Wastewater: comparison between filtration of Raw Sewage and Primary Clarifier Effluent from *Proceedings of Membranes in Drinking and Industrial Water Production (MDIW) 2005*, 14-17 November 2004, L'Aquila, Italy.

Ravazzini, A.M., A.F. van Nieuwenhuijzen and J.H.M.J. van der Graaf (2005). Towards sustainable operations via low fouling conditions, In *Proceedings of Particle Separation 2005*, 2-5 June 2005, Seoul, Korea.

Roorda, J.H. and Graaf, J.H.J.M. van der (2001). New parameter for monitoring fouing during ultra filtration of WWTP-effluent. *Wat. Sci. Tech.*, **43**(10), 241–248.

Saltnes, T., Eikebrokk, B., Ødegaard, H. (2002). Contact Filtration of Humic Waters, performance of an expanded clay aggregate filter (Filtralite) compared to a dual anthracite/sand Filter. *Wat. Sci. Tech.: Water Supply*, **2**(5–6).

Tambo, N. and Watanabe, Y. (1979a). Physical characteristics of flocs – I— The floc density function and aluminum floc, *Wat. Res*, **13**(5), 409–419.

Tambo, N. and Y. Watanabe, Y. (1979b). Physical aspect of flocculation process – I— Fundamental treatise, *Wat. Res.*, **13**(5), 429–439.

Wiesner, M.R. and Aptel, P. (1996). Mass transport and permeate flux and fouling in pressure driven processes (Ch. 4). In: *Water Treatment Membrane Processes*. Mallevialle, J., Odendaal, P.E. and Wiesner, M.R. (eds.), McGraw-Hill, New York, 4.1–4.30.

Wilkinson, K.J., Lead, J.R. (2007). *Environmental Colloids and Particles Behaviour, Separation and Characterisation*, John Wiley, Ltd., ISBN 13 9780470024324.

Chapter 2
Characterization of Aquatic Particles

M. Boller and R. Kaegi

2.1 INTRODUCTION

Since ancient times the aim of water purification was primarily the removal of water turbidity in order to produce clear water free from visible particles. Although the connection between hazardous organisms in water and diseases caused by water consumption was only proven in the second half of the 19th century, experience learned many civilizations to treat water especially from surface water sources by removing the turbidity. Sedimentation in large pots, filtration through porous materials and textiles and other means of water treatment were applied in single households. With population growth and settlements of larger cities, water treatment was often neglected, especially in medieval civilizations the idea that diseases would originate from drinking water was lost to a great extent.

Only the discovery of pathogenic micro-organisms in water and their distinct effects on humans and animals in the time from 1850 to about 1900 brought the idea of hygiene in daily life back to the population. Pushed by medical and pharmaceutical specialists, water filtration in central treatment plants, water boiling in households and after 1900 also water disinfection were introduced to produce safe drinking water. Parallel to this development, however, the rapid development of cities and industry, the supply of larger quantities of surface water by pressurized pipe systems led to numerous epidemic outbreaks of mainly typhus and cholera in many European cities at that time.

Increasingly, slow sand and rapid sand filters were applied for surface water treatment and brought marked improvement of the hygienic situation in larger cities. But it was only after 1910 when chlorination and ozonation were introduced in water treatment that epidemic outbreaks disappeared completely.

It becomes obvious that the removal of particles from water, especially from surface waters is crucial for safe potable water production. If particles are present in a water source, it is the primary issue of all purification techniques to eliminate or inactivate the particles and with them also eventual hygienic hazards.

Of course, particle removal and the transfer of soluble material into biological particles play an important role also in wastewater treatment. In the time before and still some time after the 2nd World War, so called primary treatment was applied consisting of simple sedimentation facilities to remove about 50% of the particles contained in raw sewage. Later, biological treatment was introduced where biological flocculation and the removal of the activated sludge is an important solids separation step for small colloidal particle fractions.

In order to understand the role of particles in water quality evaluation and water purification processes, the particles and their behaviour in aqueous systems have to be known and characterized.

2.2 OCCURRENCE OF PARTICLES IN WATER

Solids in water are of very different origin and appear in a large variety of sizes, shapes, chemical composition, etc. An incomplete list of particles in water is shown below and illustrates the complex nature of aqueous solids.

Domestic Wastewater	
Coarse solids	gravel, sand, faeces, paper, hair, cotton, wood pieces, plastic pieces (e.g. ear sticks), cigarette-ends, etc.
Fine solids	faeces, road dust, atmospheric solids deposits, aggregates of micro-organisms, single micro-organisms, worm eggs, viruses, biological debris, clay minerals, chemical precipitates, nanoparticles.
Industrial wastewater	great variety according to production and treatment processes cellulose fibres, asbestos fibres, incineration ashes, precipitation products, pigments, emulsified oil droplets, polymers, coal dust, silicates, metals, blood, milk, etc.
River water	gravel, sand, silt, clay, algae, decay products of plants, protozoa, bacteria, viruses, etc.
Lake water	phytoplankton, zooplankton, detritus, precipitation products, bacteria, viruses, protozoa, etc.
Groundwater/Spring water	precipitation products (Fe, Mn, Ca), soil colloids, bacteria, viruses, protozoa, etc.
Potable water	nano-size particles, bacteria, viruses, corrosion products, calcite particles, particles of natural organic matter (NOM).

There are many analytical bulk parameters to express the solids content of water. Among the most frequently used ones are:

TSS	Total suspended solids: expressing the dry weight of the filtered solids mass (0.45 µm membrane filtration) in $gTSS/m^3$.
POC	Particulate organic matter as difference between TOC – DOC (0.45 µm filtered) in gC/m^3.
PCOD	Particulate organic matter as difference between COD_{total} – $COD_{filtered}$ (0.45 µm filtered) in gO_2/m^3, (COD = chemical oxygen demand).
VSS	Volatile suspended solids: expressing the organic combustible part of TSS.

TS	Total solids: total solids mass after drying the water sample (including mass of dissolved matter) in gTS/m^3.
Turbidity	Light absorption or light scattering through a water sample; compared to standard turbidity of defined particles expressed in NTU (nephelometric turbidity), FTU (formazine turbidity) and others.
Particle number	Number of particles per volume (#/ml), usually with laser methods; size range of the analytical method has to be indicated, e.g. 0.5 to 200 µm or 1 to 1000 µm for conventional particle counters.

While most of the above parameters do not give much information on particle characteristics, detailed analysis of particle numbers include the evaluation of the particle size. A coarse indication of the size range of some well known particle classes is given in Figure 2.1. It becomes clear that the standard procedure for solids analysis by filtering water samples with 0.45 µm membrane filters is not an accurate procedure to define solid and dissolved matter. There is still suspended matter in the size range below 0.45 µm which would have to be clearly classified as particulate.

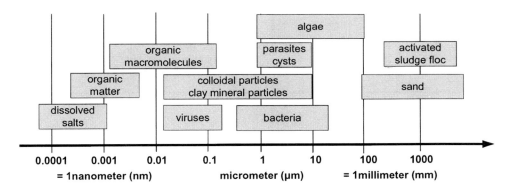

Figure 2.1 Size categories of aqueous particles

2.3 SCALE OF PARTICLE OBSERVATION

As will be shown below, particles may be characterized as single particles or as whole particle populations. The parameters used for characterization are very different between these two issues. However, the methods of particle characterization used in the nano- and micro-scale ranges are identical for natural and technical systems. While looking at mechanisms concerning origin, transport, aggregation, shear and deposition, Table 2.1 indicates that the methods of characterization are identical for natural and technical issues.

On a larger scale (meso-scale, macro-scale) particles and their behaviour are considered in their natural or technical environment. Transport and fate of solids in natural water, soil and air on one hand and particles in engineered processes such as solids separation on the other are of major concern. The methods of quantifying solids behaviour may be considerably different between natural and technical concerns in these scales of magnitude.

Table 2.1 Overview: particle characterization issues in natural and technical systems.

Nanoscale	Microscale	Mesoscale	Macroscale
Natural and technical systems		**Natural systems**	
Surface properties	Bulk-Parameters	Transport mechanisms in water, soil, air	Sediments in lakes, rivers, ocean
single particles agglomerates flocs surface chemistry charge potentials nucleation dissolution macromolecules surrounding matrix	distribution particle number floc aggregation sorption density sedimentation flotation surrounding matrix	particle flux deposition Remobilization	sediment formation sediment archives
		Technical systems	
		Process engineering Transport systems	Water treatment
		separation processes performance transport mechanisms solids formation attachment dissolution	achieve treatment goals
Mechanisms		Effects	

2.4 SINGLE PARTICLE CHARACTERIZATION

The following parameters are used for single particle characterization:

- size
- shape
- density
- mobility
- sedimentation velocity
- shear strength
- chemical surface properties
- chemical composition
- adsorption properties

2.4.1 Size and shape

The size of particles in water is strongly depending on particle origin and history as well as on the flow regime. Thus, river water and wastewater may contain large solids in the cm or mm range, but these may easily be removed by straining or under quiescent flow conditions such as lakes, river barrages, sand traps and sedimentation basins. Here, the interest is mainly focused on particles that are not rapidly removed such as particles in the size range below 1 mm, preferably below 200 μm. It is only recently, that the particles in the colloidal and nano-size range have become of special interest because (1) new analytical methods are developed for their characterization, and (2) synthetic nanoparticles are getting subject of water quality criteria.

2.4.1.1 Definition of particle size

A commonly used term for particle characterization is the size expressed as equivalent diameter. This refers to a diameter which is measurable by a certain technique. This measurement corresponds to a specific physical property of the particle. An equivalent diameter is reported as the diameter of a sphere having the same value of a specific property as the irregularly shaped particle being measured. A summary of the used techniques for particle assessment is given in Figure 2.2. When for instance the motion of a particle is of concern, the mobility equivalent diameter is the diameter of a sphere with the same mobility as the particle in question.

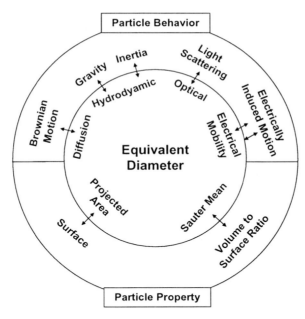

Figure 2.2 Particle size definition depending on observation of particle properties and behaviour (adapted from Baron and Willeke, 2001)

We talk about 'diameters' or particle radii assuming that particles are close to spherical shape. In reality this is seldom the case. We distinguish different particle size definitions. Figure 2.3 gives some often used definitions.

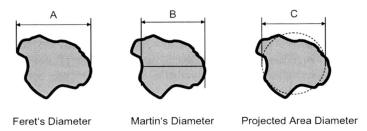

Figure 2.3 Particle size definition according to Feret, Martin and Projected Area

Feret's Diameter. This is depicted as dimension 'A', it is the overall length from 'tip-to-tail' of the particle.

Martin's Diameter. This is depicted as dimension 'B', it is the length of a theoretical horizontal line, which passes through the centre of gravity of the particle, to touch the outer boundary walls of the particle.

Projected Area Diameter. This is depicted as dimension 'C' and is the diameter of a theoretical circle, which would contain the same projected area as the irregular particle. Here of course it is the question from what side the particle is observed and if it is of highly irregular shape. Figure 2.4 shows an example of such a particle with the corresponding equivalent projected area diameter resulting from the perspective of observation.

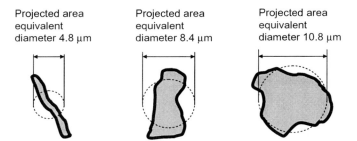

Figure 2.4 Projected area equivalent diameters of the same particle resulting from observation from different angles

Equivalent Volume Diameter. This is the diameter of a sphere, which would contain the same volume as the irregular particle.

Hydrodynamic Diameter. This is the diameter of a spherical particle that exhibits the same settling velocity as the irregular particle assuming equal density.

A simple example is the particle size determination by gravity (sedimentation). The settling velocity v_s of a real particle can be measured by observing its vertical transport by gravity. If it is a spherical particle, the settling velocity can be related to the particle diameter according to Stokes law as follows:

$$v_S = \frac{g \cdot (\rho_S - \rho_W) \cdot d_p^2}{18 \cdot \mu} \tag{2.1}$$

d_p = Hydrodynamic particle equivalent diameter [m]
μ = Dynamic viscosity [kg/ms]
g = Gravity constant [m/sec^2]
ρ_s = Density of particle [kg/m^3]
ρ_w = Density of water [kg/m^3]

In reality, the particles are usually not spherical and the density in water is often not well known, giving rise to considerable deviations between a spherical particle and measured particles with different shape and density.

If a density of 1,700 kg/m^3 is assumed, but the real density in water including void water volume is only 1,200 kg/m^3, a mistake in diameter estimation is made. If for example a diameter of 7 μm has been determined, the real equivalent diameter of a particle with the same settling velocity would then be

$$d_{real} = \sqrt{\frac{(\rho_s - \rho_w)}{(\rho_{real} - \rho_w)}} \cdot d_p = \sqrt{\frac{700}{200}} \cdot 7 = 13.1 \; \mu m \qquad (2.2)$$

2.4.1.2 Shape factor

One way of determining the shape of particles is to establish the relationship between particle surface and particle volume for a high number of differently sized particles. This can best be illustrated with the help of an example given by Garboczi and Bullard (2004). They investigated irregularly shaped cement particles like the one shown in Figure 2.5. For spheres, the particle surface as a function of the volume is given by $S = 4.84 \; V^{2/3}$. This function is plotted as reference particles in Figure 2.6 as solid line showing the minimum surface for a given sphere volume. Deviations from this curve indicate the non-spherical nature of irregularly shaped particles. The more the particles deviate from spheres, the more the surface/volume relationship lies above the curve for spheres. Figure 2.6 shows the data of the cement particles and may be described with a surface/volume function $S = a \times V^b$ where in this case "b" was

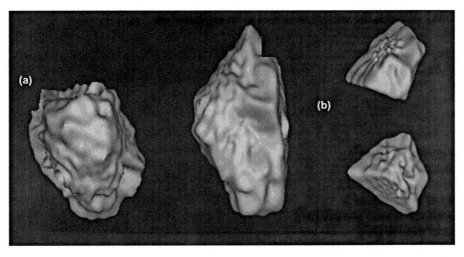

Figure 2.5 Two views each of the same cement particle with an equivalent spherical diameter of about 36 μm (Garboczi and Bullard, 2004)

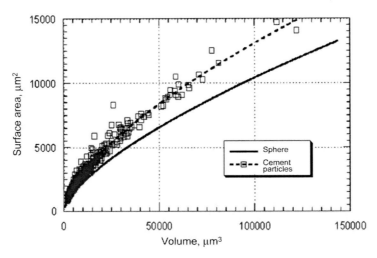

Figure 2.6 True surface area versus true volume for cement particles. The solid line is the theoretical relation for a sphere, $S = (36\pi)^{1/3} V^{2/3} \approx 4.84 V^{2/3}$. The dashed line is a power law fit of the cement particles of the form $S = 8.0 V^{0.64}$ (Garboczi and Bullard, 2004)

found to be 0.64 and "a" was equal to 0.8. The factor b is close to 2/3 which shows that the broken cement particles deviate from spheres but are still considered as Euclidian bodies without showing fractured surfaces. The irregular shape is mainly expressed by the factor "a".

More complex shapes can be described by a single spherical diameter which can be corrected by a shape factor ψ. The shape factor is always equal to or larger than 1. Shape factors for compact particles are typically between 1 and 2, while more extreme elongated shapes such as fibres and high-volume agglomerates may have larger values. Shape factors are useful for converting a readily measurable equivalent diameter (for instance from microscopy) to one that depends on particle behaviour such as the hydrodynamic diameter during settling. Shape factors may be defined as follows.

For spherical particles, the settling velocity can be expressed as:

$$v_s = \sqrt{\frac{4}{3} \cdot \frac{\rho_s - \rho_w}{\rho_w} \cdot \frac{g}{c_D} \cdot d_p} \qquad (2.3)$$

with

$g =$ Gravity constant [m/sec^2]
$d_p =$ Particle diameter [m]
$\rho_s =$ Density of particle [kg/m^3]
$\rho_w =$ Density of water [kg/m^3]
$A =$ Cross sectional area of particle [m^2]
$V =$ Volume of particle [m^3]
$v_s =$ Sedimentation velocity of particle [m/s]
$c_D =$ Drag coefficient of particle [−] is a function of viscosity and particle shape

For non-spherical particles v_s is:

$$v_s = \sqrt{\frac{2}{c_D} \cdot \frac{\rho_s - \rho_w}{\rho_w} \cdot g \cdot \frac{V}{A}} = \sqrt{\frac{2}{c_D} \cdot \frac{\rho_s - \rho_w}{\rho_w} \cdot g \cdot \psi \cdot d_p} \qquad (2.4)$$

with $\frac{V}{A} = \psi \cdot d_p$ and ψ = Shape factor.

Assuming laminar settling conditions which is especially true for the smaller particles in question, Stokes law can be applied for equivalent diameters determined microscopically where

$$v_s = \frac{g \cdot (\rho_s - \rho_w) \cdot d_{p,eqiv}^2}{18 \cdot \mu} \qquad (2.5)$$

In reality, the particles may have elongated shapes and settle faster:

$$v_s = \frac{g \cdot (\rho_s - \rho_w) \cdot d_p^2}{18 \cdot \mu} \qquad (2.6)$$

The ratio of the two settling velocities corresponds either to the shape factor defined before or to another definition of the shape factor χ :

$$\Psi^2 = \chi = \frac{d_{p,eqiv}^2}{d_p^2} \qquad (2.7)$$

Values for the dynamic shape factor are:

Shape	Shape factor χ
Sphere	1.0
Cluster spheres	
2 sphere chain	1.12
3 sphere chain	1.27
4 sphere chain	1.32
Spheroid (L/D = 5)	1.39
Sand	1.57
Quartz dust	1.36–1.82

2.4.1.3 Particle agglomerates

Particles in water may be present as single original particles, so called primary particles, or more often as agglomerates formed from numerous primary particles. They may contain from a few to hundreds of smaller particles attached to each other and hold together by interparticle forces. Particle counters do not distinguish between primary particles or aggregated forms. Only microscopic imaging can give more insight in this respect. Figure 2.7 shows schematically primary particles and aggregates of increasing complex nature.

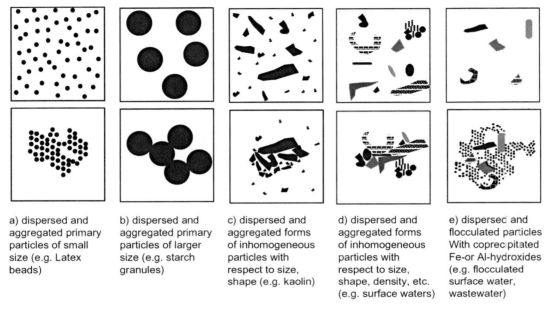

Figure 2.7 Schematic presentation of particles and particle aggregates in water with increasing complexity

Single particles in natural waters show a large variety in size, shape and chemical composition. The examples of microscopic pictures in Figure 2.8 indicate that particle size is not clearly defined. The more the particle deviates from spherical shape, the more difficult it is to assign a size to it. Nevertheless, particle size is usually expressed as equivalent diameter of a spherical particle where the diameter is corrected by the already discussed shape factor ψ.

Best access to the size and shape of particles can be gained by microscopy. Nowadays, different microscopes are available which give ample insight into the great variety of size and shape of solids in water (see following chapter).

Particles in water can have distinct size and shape such as algae or bacteria which can clearly be differentiated from the surrounding water by surface membranes. Other particles have a completely undefined shape (amorphous hydroxides) and their size may be strongly dependent on the hydraulic shear regime.

Another way of expressing the complex nature of particles, especially of agglomerated particles, is the fractal dimension. The fractal dimension is an expression which describes the deviation of the particle from perfect spherical shape. Particles may have the same mass, but the more irregular the shape, the larger their diameter. The relationship between the mass and the length of a fractal aggregate can be written as follows

$$d \propto m^{1/D_f} \tag{2.8}$$

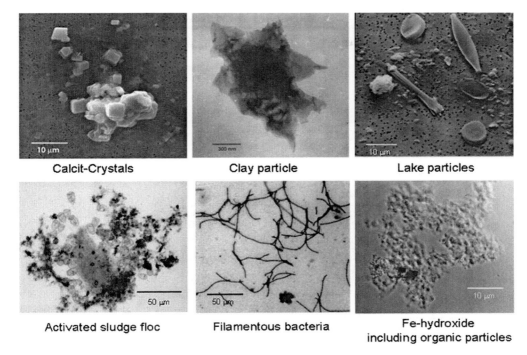

Figure 2.8 Examples of particles in water and wastewater *(photo courtesy: Particle Laboratory, Eawag)*

with:

d = characteristic length dimension of the aggregate
m = mass of the aggregate
D_f = fractal dimension = 3 for spheres = 1.7–2.5 for agglomerates and flocs in water

Figures 2.9 and 2.10 give some examples of particles of increasing complexity and decreasing fractal dimension.

Figure 2.9 Particles showing different fractal dimensions.

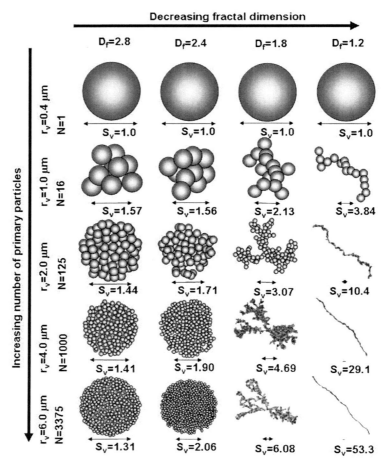

Figure 2.10 Particle agglomerates with different number of an identical primary particle with a diameter of 0.4 μm and different fractal dimensions D_f reaching from 2.8 to 1.2 (r_v = equivalent volume diameter, N = number of primary particles, S_v = ratio of the longest size/equivalent diameter) (adapted from Garboczi and Bullard, 2004)

2.4.2 Microscopic analysis

In microscopic analysis, there are different levels of magnification which may be of interest. Figure 2.11 shows a schematic picture of an agglomerate particle in two-dimensional space viewing the particle at ever higher levels of magnification. On a highest level is the size and shape of an agglomerate. At lowest magnifications, the complex structure can be represented by a fractal dimension (see previous chapter). On a next level of magnification, the geometry of the agglomerate may be of interest to see how the primary particles do arrange themselves to form flocs. Further down scanning gives insight into the size and shape of primary particles. The surface of these particles may be of interest with respect to roughness and another level of fractal dimension and finally, reaching the chemical structure of the particle and its surface chemistry.

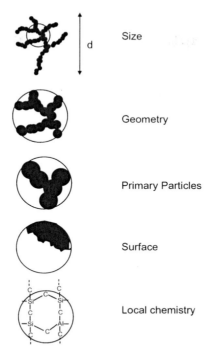

Figure 2.11 Structure of an agglomerate in two-dimensional space at increasing levels of magnification and resolution (adapted from Baron and Willeke, 2001)

Technique and purpose of the microscopes differ from each other and the visual information of different instruments may be combined to give a more comprehend over-all picture including also chemical composition of the particles. The following microscopy techniques are used most frequently.

2.4.2.1 Optical microscopy

The optical microscope, often referred to as the "light microscope", is a type of microscope which uses visible light and a system of lenses to magnify images of small samples. Optical microscopes are the oldest and simplest of the microscopes.

Compound optical microscopes can produce a magnified image of a specimen up to $1000\times$ and, at high magnifications, are used to study thin specimens as they have a very limited depth of field.

Optical microscopes can be combined with particle counting instruments and software to characterize heterogeneous particle suspension.

2.4.2.2 Electron microscopy

Particles <1 µm, also referred to as colloids (Definition IUAPC) are typically investigated with an electron microscope, which enable the characterization of the colloids down to the nanometer size range. In addition to the morphology of the colloids also the chemical composition can be determined using an energy dispersive X-ray analysis (EDX) system which can be directly attached to the microscope. Depending on the mode of operation, two different types of electron microscopes are most widespread, namely the scanning electron microscope (SEM) and the transmission electron microscope (TEM). Detailed information of the respective techniques can be found in several textbooks, such as Goldstein (SEM), Williams and Carter (TEM) and Egerton (SEM and TEM).

In the SEM, the electrons are focused to a fine beam which is scanned over the sample surface. The interaction of the electrons with the sample material produces a range of signal that can be used to image different properties of the sample. Most often secondary electrons (SE), backscattered electrons (BSE) and x-rays are detected. SE are used to image the topography of the sample, BSE reflect a density contrast and the x-rays carry an elemental information of the sample material. An example is given in Figure 2.12 where the surface of Calcite crystals has been imaged using the SE signal. Generally samples have to be conductive to prevent charging of the sample due to the electron bombardment. Conducting material such as C, Au or Pt are sprayed in a thin layer on the specimen. Coating of the sample can be avoided by either using an SEMs equipped with field emission guns (FEG) that is operated at low voltages or by using an imaging gas (low vacuum SEMs) which both prevent charging of the sample.

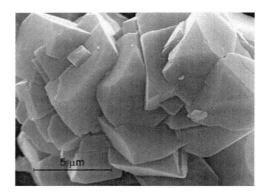

Figure 2.12 $CaCO_3$ crystal recorded with SEM (secondary electrons) *(photo courtesy by Mavrocordatos et al., 2004)*.

In the TEM technique, the sample is irradiated by a parallel beam of electrons. The electrons that are passing through the sample are collated on a Polaroid film or more recently on a CCD camera. The image thus presents a density and/or thickness contrast. In Figure 2.13 particles from wood combustion (pellet furnace) are imaged in the TEM. Thicker areas of the sample (superposition of particles) appear dark, thus representing a thickness contrast. The samples have to be very thin as they have to be able to penetrate the sample. Depending on the kind of analysis and sample material the maximal thinness ranges from a few tens to a few hundreds of nm. If only morphological analysis of individual particles is desired then the particles can be up to a few μm in diameter. If the beam is condensed to a small spot, also the chemical composition of individual particles can be determined using an EDX system. An example is given in Figure 2.14, where individual particles from road runoff are recorded and analysed in the TEM. The TEM can also be equipped with a scanning unit which is then referred to as STEM. The operation principle of a STEM is similar to a SEM.

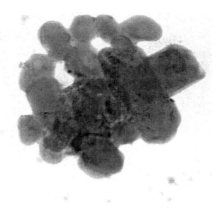

Figure 2.13 TEM micrograph of wood combustion particles. Electrons penetrate the specimen. It allows to image the particle silhouette by mass absorption *(photo courtesy by R. Kaegi, Eawag)*

Results of a typical TEM analysis are given in Figure 2.14 showing similar looking particles in the range of 100 to 300 nm. Although the particles look similar in the microscopic pictures, the corresponding elemental spectra reveal that only two of them are TiO_2 particles while the other one is a colloid consisting of the element Cerium.

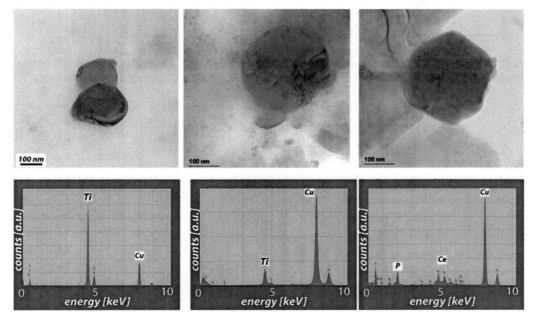

Figure 2.14 TEM images of single particles and corresponding elemental spectra showing two examples of TiO_2 particles on the left hand side and a Cerium particle to the right *(photo courtesy by R. Kaegi, Eawag)*

2.4.2.3 Sample preparation

Colloids and nanoparticles are often thin enough for the investigation in the TEM and thus do not require any treatment. Larger materials (particles) have to be thinned until they are electron transparent. There is a wide range of preparation techniques available to obtain an electron transparent sample, developed either from material scientists or from biologists. The sample preparation is of utmost importance and therefore, most textbooks on TEM technique also include a section on sample preparation. The classical approach for sample thinning such as ion milling yields electron transparent sections from rather unspecific areas. The focused ion beam (FIB), a relatively new technique to prepare thin samples for TEM, allows a very site specific preparation of the sample.

Figures 2.15 and 2.16 show an example of specimen preparation of a nanosize piece cut out from an akaganeite granule by FIB technique used for further investigation of copper adsorption with the help of TEM anaylsis. The procedure and results are described in detail in Mavrocordatos et al. (2003).

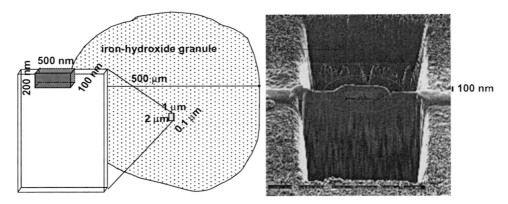

Figure 2.15 Focused ion beam cut of an iron-hydroxide particle with a dimension of some 100 nanometers with the help of FIB manipulation (Mavrocordatos et al., 2003, *photo courtesy by Mavrocordatos*)

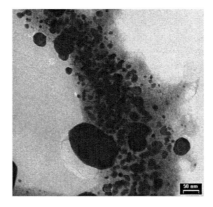

Figure 2.16 TEM micrograph of the granulated iron-hydroxide specimen allowing for mapping several elements like Fe, Cu, C (Mavrocordatos et al., 2003, *photo courtesy by Mavrocordatos*)

2.4.2.4 Atomic Force Microscopy (AFM)

The atomic force microscope (AFM) or scanning force microscope (SFM) is a very high-resolution type of scanning probe microscope, with demonstrated resolution of fractions of a nanometer. The AFM is one of the foremost tools for imaging, measuring and manipulating matter at the nanoscale.

The AFM consists of a microscale cantilever with a sharp tip (probe) at its end that is used to scan the specimen surface. The cantilever is typically silicon or silicon nitride with a tip radius of curvature on the order of nanometers. When the tip is brought into proximity of a sample surface, forces between the tip and the sample lead to a deflection of the cantilever according to Hooke's law. Figure 2.17 shows the cantilever with the tip.

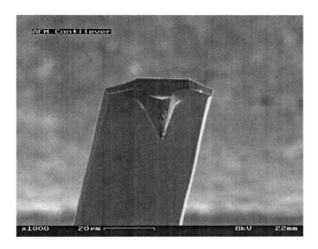

Figure 2.17 AFM cantilever and tip *(photo courtesy by M. Boller)*

Depending on the situation, forces that are measured in AFM include mechanical contact forces, Van der Waals forces, capillary forces, chemical bonding, electrostatic forces, magnetic forces. Typically, the deflection is measured using a laser spot reflected from the top of the cantilever into an array of photodiodes. Other methods that are used include optical interferometry, capacitive sensing or piezoresistive AFM cantilevers. These cantilevers are fabricated with piezoresistive elements that act as a strain gauge. Using a Wheatstone bridge, strain in the AFM cantilever due to deflection can be measured. This can also be used to measure the necessary forces to rupture particle agglomerates and, thus, give some indication of floc strength. An example of an AFM image is given in Figure 2.18 showing in the center a bacterial cell surrounded by extracellular polymer strains.

2.4.2.5 Overview on microscopic techniques

Depending on the mechanisms to be focused on, analytical microscopy offers a variety of suited methods to give insight into particle characteristics and behavior. Figure 2.19 gives an overview of which microscopic techniques may best be applied for certain mechanisms in question.

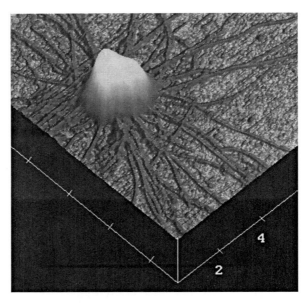

Figure 2.18 Biofilm growth showing bacterium and its extracellular polymers depicted by AFM. Particles can be observed in their native form (hydrated or dry); size range down to molecular level (Mavrocordatos et al., 2004, *photo courtesy by Mavrocordatos*).

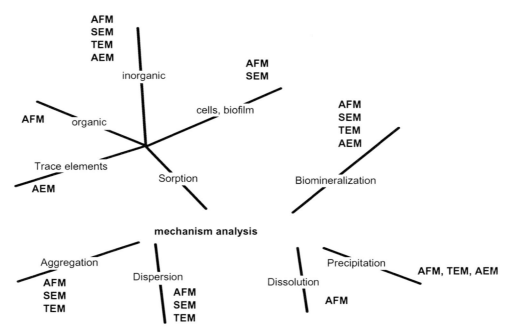

Figure 2.19 Microscopic techniques to be used for the investigation of different environmental mechanisms. AEM refers to SEM, AFM and TEM in combination with elemental analysis (D. Mavrocordatos et al., 2004).

2.4.3 Particle density

Depending on chemical composition, particles may differ considerably in density. Examples of particle densities are:

Garnet sand	4.2 g/cm^3
Quartz sand	2.6 g/cm^3
Clay particles	2.65 g/cm^3
Antharacite	1.6 g/cm^3
Organic material	1.1–1.4 g/cm^3

These densities refer to the dry solids density. Particles in water, however, have a density considerably different to the dry solids density. Many particles contain water in the internal matrix of the solids which may be filled with air or water or they are composed of numerous primary particles in the form of aggregates including a certain proportion of water in the pore space. If the volume of such a particle or floc V_{fl} is known, the real density in water may be calculated from the dry density by

$$\rho_{fl} = \frac{V_{ds}}{V_{fl}} \cdot (\rho_{ds} - \rho_w) \tag{2.9}$$

with

ρ_{fl} = density of floc or agglomerate
ρ_{ds} = density of dry solids
V_{ds} = dry volume of the particle
V_{fl} = floc volume in water
ρ_w = density of water

Most aggregated particles contain with increasing size an increasing amount of interstitial water, thus, leading to decreasing floc density with size. The example of a size-density relationship for Fe- and Al-hydroxide flocs measured by different authors is shown in Figure 2.20.

2.4.4 Particle mobility

Many biological particles such as bacteria, algae, protozoa and zooplankton are motile. The way of movement and the traveling speed varies among the species. Some bacteria are able to move at low velocities of ca. 4 µm/s, called gliding, while others can move with the help of flagella in a speed range of 20–200 µm/s. Most algae and protozoa are equipped with flagella and their movement speed has been observed to be in the order of 50–250 µm/s.

2.4.5 Sedimentation characteristics

The sedimentation velocity of a single particle depends on its density, size, shape and on the water viscosity (Stokes law). The observation of the downward movement of a particle allows determination of the settling velocity as an important parameter in solids separation without knowing density, size and shape. The parameter settling velocity is experimentally much easier accessible and is the crucial design parameter for settling processes. There are easy experimental methods to determine the settling velocity distribution

34 Handbook on Particle Separation Processes

of a whole inhomogeneous particle suspension. Figure 2.21 shows the example of the settling velocity of Fe-Hydroxide particles as a function of size including a density-size relationship similar to the one discussed before.

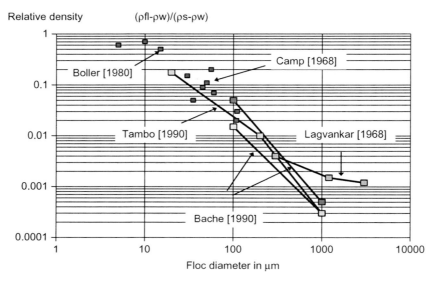

Figure 2.20 Floc size – density relationships for Fe- and Al-hydroxide flocs determined by different authors

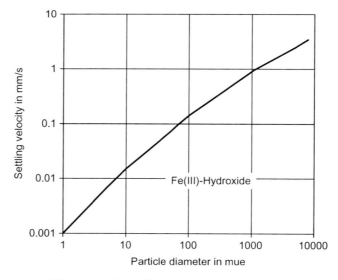

Figure 2.21 Settling velocity of Fe-hydroxide particles as a function of size

2.4.6 Shear strength

Particles in water may show different behavior when they are exposed to shear flow fields. Usually, particles with a defined shape are less subject to rupture while Fe- and Al-hydroxide flocs may break apart or are surface eroded under relatively low shear forces. If the hydrodynamic stress is larger than the internal bonding strength of a floc, it will be disrupted. This may lead to small flocs of poor settling and filtering characteristics. Information on floc strength is therefore crucial for the design of floc formation installations with respect to dosing point, placement of pumps, types of pumps, mixing devices and filtration rates. Very little is known on the floc strength and the available data do not give a coherent picture of floc binding forces in water treatment. In flocculation experiments using different mixing conditions or dissipated energy, respectively, a maximum floc size can be observed which is proportional to the dissipated energy. Experimental information is available in the range of 0.01 to about 1000 W/m^3 dissipated energy. The dissipated energy produces turbulence which is roughly expressed by the average shear or velocity gradient G. The maximum floc size as a function of the velocity gradient G can be expressed as a power law:

$$d_{fl} = K_{sh} \cdot G^{-\rho} \tag{2.10}$$

with

d_{fl} = max. floc diameter
K_{sh} = shear constant
G = average velocity gradient

Considering different studies, the exponent χ varies between 0.3 and 1.5.

2.4.7 Electrical surface charge

Dominant surface property is the electric surface charge which is responsible for the chemical stability of a particle. The higher the surface charge, the more stable is its behavior, meaning that the particle does not readily undergo agglomeration processes with particles of the same surface charge.

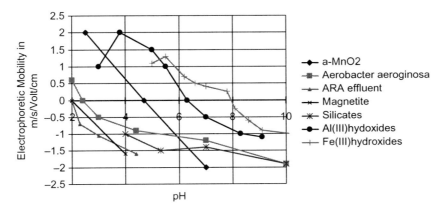

Figure 2.22 Examples of electrophoretic mobility of particles found in the aquatic environment.

The particle charge may be determined with the help of special analytical methods such as the electrophoretic mobility or the streaming current potential. The principle of the electrophoretic mobility measurement is that a particle is exposed to an electrical field. The more charges are on the particle, the faster is its traveling speed to the electrode of opposite charge. The velocity is proportional to the surface charge potential at the shear plane of surrounding liquid which is called the zeta(ζ)-potential. Another method of charge determination is the streaming current potential. With this method the surface charges are sheared off and measured as charge potential proportional to the surface charge. There is a strong dependency of the surface charge on pH. The majority of particles in natural water and wastewater are negatively charged in the pH range encountered in practice. Figure 2.22 shows examples of the electrophoretic mobility of various particles in water. Only Al- and Fe-hydroxides may show neutral or positive charges under neutral pH conditions whereas most other particles are strongly negative.

2.4.8 Chemical composition

Depending on their origin, particles may be composed of very different material. A crucial distinction can be made between inorganic and organic particles. While inorganic particles from rock weathering may contain many different elements, organic particles such as bacteria and algae often show a distinct stoichiometry of nutrients. Examples are particles in lakes which may show a composition which can be described with the following formula:

$$(CaCO_3)_{108}(MgCO_3)_4(CH_3O)_{114}(NH_3)_{16}(H_3PO_4)_1 \qquad (2.11)$$

with a nutrient ratio of C : N : P = 106 : 16 : 1 or wastewater particles, shown in Table 2.2, of which the nutrient composition depends on process conditions.

Table 2.2 Chemical composition of particles in wastewater

	Particles in raw water %	Particles in treated water without P-precipitation %	Particles in treated water with P-precipitation %
Fe	0.8	1.2	8.6
Organic fraction	70	70	57
Organic carbon	35	31	25
N	2.7	5.4	4.1
P	0.8	1.6	4.0

2.5 SUSPENSION CHARACTERIZATION

In general, the characterization of a suspension, that is the total population of suspended particles in a given water, is of major interest for process engineering. Natural waters contain numerous particles of inhomogeneous nature and it is of major concern to have measures and methods to describe and compare inhomogeneous particle populations in order to gain insight into particle transport and separation mechanisms and to describe the performance of solids separation processes.

2.5.1 Bulk parameters

2.5.1.1 Dry solids mass (TSS)

Particle concentrations above 2 mgTSS/l may be measured by filtering the water through commonly 0.45 μm membrane filters. In cases where large proportions of smaller particles are present, it is recommended to use 0.2 μm filters. According to the concentration of particles, between 0.5 to 2 l of water have to be filtered. The particles remaining on the filter are dried at 90°C. The dry solids mass is measured by weighing the filter before and after filtration and after a drying procedure. The result is expressed as dry solids mass in $gTSS/m^3$.

2.5.1.2 Turbidity

The determination of TSS is quite laborious. If an on-line signal on particle concentration is needed, TSS cannot be used. For these cases and especially at low particle concentrations turbidity or light scattering measurements may be more helpful to characterize the particle content. Direct light penetration or light scattering instruments measure either the absorbed light by the particles or the light deflection induced by diffraction, refraction or reflection. With larger particles (>1 μm) light reflection which correlates with the particle surface is dominant while in the size range of 0.1 to 1 μm the so called MIE scattering is important where refraction dominates. At even smaller sizes light diffraction becomes dominant (Raleigh diffraction). Therefore, particles of different size show different light scattering and it is not easy to interpret the over all turbidity signal in terms of particle content. In order to be able to compare turbidity measurements relatively homogeneous suspensions are used as reference turbidity. Depending on the standard suspension applied, different units are used for turbidity such as:

- Jackson turbidity unit (JTU) = amount of diatomaceous earth/l
- Formazine turbidity unit (FE or FTU) = amount of synthetic colloidal formazine particles
- mg SiO_2/l = amount of siliceous earth/l
- Nephelometric turbidity unit (NTU)

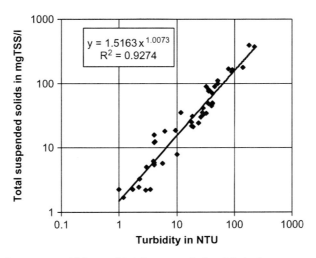

Figure 2.23 Correlation between turbidity and total suspended solids in the same water

Practical experience shows that generally direct light penetration (absorption) correlates well with the visibility depth while light scattering measurements may correlate with the dry solids content. An example of a correlation between TSS and turbidity is shown in Figure 2.23 for one type of suspension. Usually, correlations are much less significant if suspensions of different origin are compared.

2.5.2 Particle size distribution

Particle size distribution and particle concentration are most valuable information to characterize raw waters. Particles found in water resources and wastewaters are usually produced by erosion processes, aerosols, chemical precipitation, biological growth and decay. In natural and technical systems a broad range of particle sizes reaching from nm to mm exist and their shapes typically deviate from spherical throughout all size classes.

According to the method of particle analysis, number and size of particles in a suspension are measured in different ways. Particle counters, particle surface and particle volume measurements are used methods which may lead to substantially different results. Results determined with different instruments can usually not be compared without any comparative experiments with standardized suspensions. Most particle analyzers which do not only measure size distribution but also the particle concentration, generally laser methods, have an analytical size range starting at the lower end with about 0.5 µm. Frequently used methods are:

- Microscopic counting; laborious, exact
- Coulter counter: volume measurements; not suited for particles with low shear strength; change of chemical matrix necessary
- Light scattering with laser beams; rapid method, on-line measurement possible.

The particle size frequency distribution is defined as

$$n(dp) = \frac{\Delta N}{\Delta dp} \qquad (2.12)$$

where:

ΔN = number of particles per volume in the size interval $\{dp, dp + \Delta dp\}$
Δdp = size interval of the particle measurement

The total number of particles N_∞ of a suspension becomes

$$N_\infty = \int_0^\infty n(dp) \cdot \Delta dp \qquad (2.13)$$

Figure 2.24 shows the result of a particle count distribution in a treated wastewater effluent in the size range between 1 and 150 µm. Figure 2.25 shows the same results but presented in a log-log plot which is commonly applied for this kind of data.

Characterization of Aquatic Particles

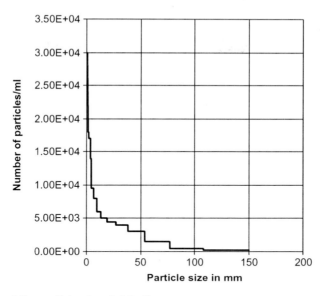

Figure 2.24 Histogram of the particle size distribution

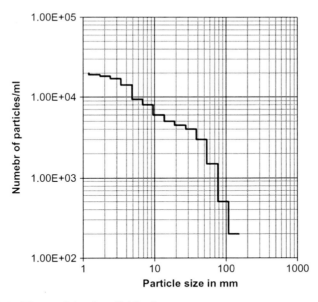

Figure 2.25 Log-log plot of the particle size distribution

Particle populations (especially number distributions) can best be visualized by particle size distribution functions following e.g. the power law

$$\frac{\Delta N}{\Delta dp} = A \cdot dp^{\beta} \qquad (2.14)$$

or transformed into log-form

$$\log\left(\frac{\Delta N}{\Delta dp}\right) = \log(A) + \beta \cdot \log(dp) \qquad (2.15)$$

where:

N = particle number per volume
dp = particle size (usually diameter)
A, β = constants of the distribution function

β is the slope of the distribution function and can in most cases be determined from log-log plots. Most particle analyzers do not count particle numbers but measure the cross sectional area, the circumference or the volume of particles in certain size classes and particle numbers are calculated by assuming spherical shape. If particle size distributions are discussed, the method of particle analysis should always be quoted.

The cumulative power law distribution becomes

$$F(d_p) = \sum N = -\left(\frac{A}{\beta + 1}\right) \cdot dp^{(\beta+1)} \qquad (2.16)$$

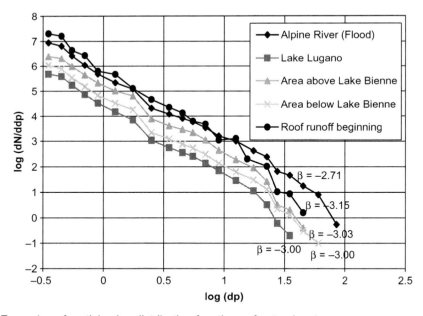

Figure 2.26 Examples of particle size distribution functions of natural waters

Examples of various particle size distribution functions in natural waters are given in Figure 2.26. Particle numbers were evaluated using a single particle counter in the size range of 0.2–150 μm. The analyzer works as a combination of laser scattering light detector for small particles (0.2–15 μm) and a laser light blockage detector for larger particles (2–150 µm). Particles can be detected and counted up to concentrations of about 10'000 #/ml. Higher concentrated suspensions are diluted by a built-in dilution unit. The signal used for particle size characterization is proportional to the projected area of the particles. As can be seen from Figure 2.26 most of the waters have characteristic slopes in a relative narrow range reaching from −2.7 for the alpine river to −3.15 for a roof runoff. Lake waters and low land rivers show intermediate β-values.

We can distinguish four different distribution functions representing the frequency of particle number, particle surface, particle volume or particle mass concentrations. Which one of the functions should be considered depends strongly on the scope of research associated with the particles. As an example particle size distributions in water and wastewater treatment plants can be of interest with respect:

(i) to particle number when hygienic criteria are applied (bacteria counts).

$$n(dp) = \frac{\Delta N}{\Delta dp} \tag{2.17}$$

(ii) to particle surface when adsorption capacities of suspended matter are evaluated (heavy metals, synthetic organics)

$$s(dp) = \frac{\Delta S}{\Delta dp} = \frac{\Delta N \cdot \pi dp^2}{\Delta dp} \tag{2.18}$$

(iii) to particle volume when particle loads of filters are considered with respect to headloss buildup

$$v(dp) = \frac{\Delta V}{\Delta dp} = \frac{\Delta N \cdot \pi dp^3}{6 \cdot \Delta dp} \tag{2.19}$$

(iv) to particle mass when mass related effluent standards have to be reached (effluent suspended solids). With ρ = dry solids density, the mass distribution becomes

$$m(dp) = \frac{\Delta M}{\Delta dp} = \frac{\Delta V}{\Delta dp} \cdot \rho \tag{2.20}$$

The importance of particles of a certain size range in different kinds of size distributions can best be visualized by frequency histograms. In Figure 2.27, the number, surface, volume and mass distributions are given for the same water sample of a secondary effluent with simultaneous precipitation. In this example, particle analysis is based on microscopic image counting giving the particle count of certain size classes as primary information. All other frequency distributions are calculated assuming spherical shape and an assumed density distribution to calculate the particle mass. Figure 2.28 depicts the same results but as cumulative number, surface, volume and mass distribution.

It becomes obvious that small particles are of primary importance when bacteria counts are evaluated. The correlation between particle counts and total number of microorganisms present in the in- and effluent of some full-scale tertiary wastewater filters in Switzerland is given in Figure 2.29 and indicates that particle number information may well be used as a hygienic indicator (Kobler and Boller, 1996). In the same plants particulate Cu concentrations were measured and revealed a pronounced relationship between particulate Cu removal and the removal rate of particles in the measured size range. Looking at the particle mass distribution it deviates from the volume distribution as a cause of inhomogeneous particle density. As was explained earlier, the density distribution follows again a power law which states that the particle density decreases with increasing particle size. Including the density distribution of secondary effluent particles reported by Boller and Kavanaugh (1995), the mass distribution was calculated and shows that only particles above 8 µm contribute to the total mass.

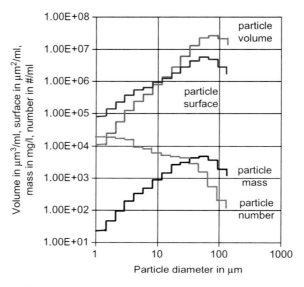

Figure 2.27 Particle size distribution in a tertiary wastewater effluent

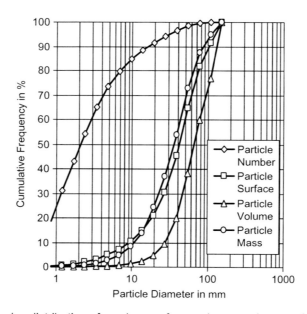

Figure 2.28 Cumulative size distribution of number, surface, volume, and mass of particles contained in a tertiary effluent

Characterization of Aquatic Particles

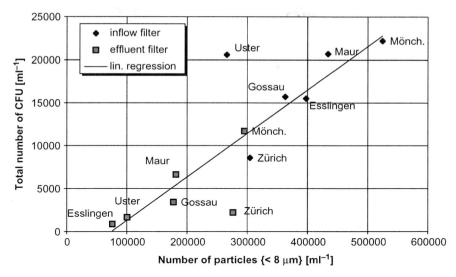

Figure 2.29 Correlation between particle number counts and total bacteria counts in secondary effluents and filtrate water of some Swiss tertiary filter plants (from Kobler and Boller, 1997)

Therefore, the assessment of tertiary filter efficiency on the base of particle mass considers only size classes >8 μm and does not give a full picture of particle separation. Hence, a sound evaluation of different filter types should best be based on particle counting as exemplified by Kobler and Boller (1996).

From literature data and also from the size distributions in the various waters, it seems as if the exponent β would be constant and allows extrapolation in particle size ranges beyond the detection limits of the instrument. In reality, β cannot be constant at both ends of the distribution function. Extrapolations shown by Lawler (1996) indicate that continuation of the distribution towards $\log dp = -\infty$ would yield an infinite number of particles. The same holds on the other side of the distribution if the volume function is considered. In order to come to a finite number of particles in a size distribution, the function has to be closed on the upper and lower end. Lawler concluded that the slope of the distribution function β has to be <1 at the lower end and >4 at the upper end of the size range. Most modern particle analyzers are not able to measure particles <0.2 μm meaning that the size distribution function would continue with a slope of ~−3, whereas the upper size range can well be analyzed. Therefore, the deviation from a straight line can often be observed at the upper but not at the lower end. The examples of particles in natural waters in Figure 2.26 show indeed this pattern and indicate that mechanisms such as sedimentation may limit the number of particles of larger size (~30–100 μm) and close the distribution with zero number counts in the upper size classes. This phenomenon can typically be observed if the distribution function of an alpine river containing substantial amounts of larger particles (deviation from constant slope starts only at last size interval of ~120 μm) is compared with the one of a roof runoff where no large particles are present (deviation starts at ~60 μm).

Since volume distribution functions are especially sensitive in the upper size range, they usually show a clear dependency of β from the particle size. Lawler proposed for the whole range of a finite particle number that $\beta(dp) = 3.33 \log(dp)$. The conclusion is that particle size analyzers which give a straight line (constant β) do not measure over the whole particle size range present in suspension and that extrapolation along the constant slope may lead to considerable errors.

2.5.3 Particle shear strength distribution

The relationship between floc size, strain rate and the resulting strain force is graphically presented in Fig 2.30. The calculations reveal that strain forces may well vary over six orders of magnitude for particles in the interesting size range of 1–1000 μm. Furthermore, it becomes clear that flocs of a diameter <10 μm would require extremely high strain rates in order to affect their integrity. According to the results, flocs of appreciable size for sedimentation in the order of 100 to 2000 μm are broken up in the force range above about 1 nN, preferably between 1–100 nN for the Fe-flocculated kaolin systems. These flocs, usually above a size of 100 μm, are subject to break-up under strain or shear rates normally encountered in technical flocculation installations designed for subsequent floc settling. Therefore, the floc size distribution may well be controlled by the dissipated energy from the rotor characterized by the shear or strain rates. The Fe-hydroxide particles investigated with the help of micromechanical methods by Yeung and Pelton (1996) were considerably smaller than the flocs of the other studies. The small Fe-hydroxide flocs are broken up preferably at strain forces between 10 and 100 nN which in fact would only act on particles of the investigated size in an aquatic environment with strain rates well above about 30'000 sec^{-1}. These are conditions which certainly do not occur in technical mixing and flocculation tanks, but possibly in centrifugal pumps.

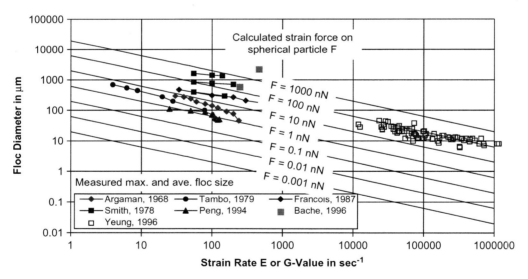

Figure 2.30 Calculated strain force as a function of strain rate and spherical floc diameter and measured maximum or average floc size as a function of shear or strain rate (Boller and Blaser, 1998)

2.5.4 Particle characterization including nanoparticles

Analytical methods which are capable of determining number densities and sizes of submicron particles in natural systems are very limited. Filtration based methods are prone to artifacts (Buffle et al., 1992) and for light scattering analyses, the concentrations of particles are too low (dynamic light scattering; Filella et al., 1997) and/or too polydisperse (static light scattering, Schurtenberger and Newman, 1992). Fujimori et al.

(1992) have demonstrated the potential of the LIBD (Laser Induced Breakdown Detection) to detect colloids down to approximately 10 nm. Recent advances in the LIBD technique described by Bundschuh et al. (2005) and Wagner et al. (2005) enable quantification of the particle number density and average diameter between 10 nm and 1μm within a few minutes.

An alternative method to investigate colloids in the submicron range is the transmission electron microscopy (TEM). Several studies have investigated aquatic colloids using this technique. A good overview is given in Mavrocordatos et al. 2007 Qualitative particle size distributions based on microscopic observations have been presented by Couture et al. (1996) and Mavrocordatos et al. (2000) and the potential of a combination of microscopic images and image analysis tools (IA) has been pointed out by Leppard et al. (1986, 2004). The combination with image analysis tools allows the semi-automated detection of a large number of particles that are automatically sized and the results can then further be processed.

2.5.4.1 *Sampling for nanoparticle analysis* by sedimentation and centrifugation

Two methods are widely used to fractionate the colloids in different size classes, namely filtration and sedimentation/centrifugation. The filtration technique consisting of a series of filtration steps with filters with a decreasing pore diameter is prone to artefacts (Buffle et al. 1992) and the sedimentation/centrifugation technique is very time consuming and its size resolution is rather poor.

At Eawag, a sampling procedure adapted from Perret et al. (1994) has been developed to fractionate water samples containing different fractions of nanoparticles in the same water. The sampling setup is as follows: A sedimentation tank (length = width = 45 cm, height = 15 cm, 30 l) is first rinsed and then filled with water and left for 2 h (see Fig 2.31). After this sedimentation time is elapsed, a layer of 0.5 cm thickness, corresponding to 1 l of water, from 2 cm underneath the surface of the water level is pumped with a peristaltic pump (flow rate 100 ml/min) into a clean glass bottle. A volume of 400 ml (four cups, 100 ml each) is centrifuged for 30 min ($330 \times g$) and the uppermost 2 cm layer is again removed with a peristaltic pump (flow rate 50 ml/min). In the third step the water is centrifuged for 1 h ($2,700 \times g$, 2 bottles 75 ml each) and the uppermost 2 cm layer is removed again. These fractionation steps are all performed in the field and the last step (ultracentrifugation for 12 h) is performed in the laboratory. The water is transported in an ice chest back to the lab and immediately processed.

Such samples may further be analyzed with different types of microscopes such as TEM and AFM and image analysis tools.

2.5.4.2 *Field Flow Fractionation*

An alternative technique to separate colloids into different size fractions is the Field Flow Fractionating (FFF) technique, which allows the separation of macromolecules, colloids and particles. The technique is well established in the analysis of biopolymers or macro-molecules in biochemistry or pharmaceutical research (Fraunhofer and Winter 2004; Liu et al. 2006) but is also a most promising technique for the investigations of colloids and nanoparticles. The FFF theory in general is based on simple physical principles and has been described by Giddings (Giddings 1993; Giddings et al. 1976).

The FFF technique in general includes four different principles and sub-techniques: Sedimentation FFF, thermal FFF, symmetric flow or asymmetric flow FFF. The covered size ranges vary for flow FFF approximately between 10 μm down to 1 nm, for sedimentation FFF between 10 μm and 80 nm, and for thermal FFF between ca. 1 nm and 50 nm. The most promising technique for the separation of environmental colloids and particles are the sedimentation FFF and the flow FFF. Both techniques are described in detail in Beckett and Hart (1992). The basic separation principle of all FFF techniques is a different response of particles in a force field. In the case of the sedimentation FFF the force field is induced by centrifugation and in the case of the flow FFF it is a cross flow field. The field FFF is suited for the fractionation of nanoparticles in water and is briefly described here and sketched in Figure 2.32.

Figure 2.31 Sampling station "Octopus" for fractionated sampling of nanoparticles *(Photo courtesy by R. Kaegi, Eawag)*

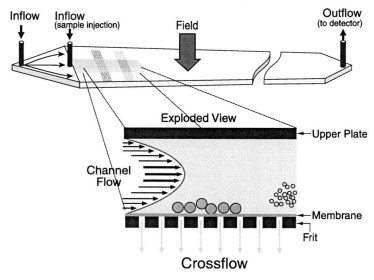

Figure 2.32 Principle of field flow fractionation

The core element of the flow FFF is a narrow channel of 50–300 μm in height, about 30 cm long and about 5 cm wide, where the bottom part of the channel consists of a permeable membrane. After injection of the sample, a flow field from the top to the bottom of the channel is applied. This flow drives particles of different sizes (strictly speaking of different diffusion coefficients) into different heights above the bottom wall (= accumulation wall) of the channel. Then, a carrier flow perpendicular and along the length axis of the channel is applied. Due to the parabolic flow profile, particles residing higher above the bottom wall are picked up at a higher velocity and thus, can be collected at the end of the channel at an earlier time compared to larger particles, which reside closer to the bottom wall of the channel. Thus, the separation of the particles is unfolded by the carrier flow along the flow axis. Particles of different sizes elute at different times and can be analyzed with suitable detectors.

The particles will be separated according to the hydrodynamic diameter (sedimentation FFF) or according to the diffusion coefficient, which is correlated to the hydrodynamic diameter by the Stokes-Einstein equation. Theoretically, both FFF techniques could be used to separate particles ranging from approximately 1nm to several tens of μm. However, technical limitations regarding the centrifugation velocity sets a lower limit of roughly 100 nm (varies with the density of the particles) for the sedimentation FFF. If smaller particles have to be separated, the flow FFF is the technique of choice.

The high resolving power and the gentle treatment of the particles during the size separation process makes the FFF technique a very powerful method to size fractionate polydisperse systems, and to extract particles of a given size. However, the FFF technique is not a stand-alone technique and needs to be operated in combination with detection techniques. In a basic version, the FFF is often equipped with an UV-vis detector, both in-line operated. The UV-vis detector is sensitive to the absorption of light caused by small organics (such as humic substances) and can thus be used to establish a mass distribution of small organic material (the hydrodynamic diameter of the particles can be calculated from the basic FFF theory).

A mass weighted size distribution might be enough to characterize well known synthetic systems; however, it is not enough to characterize highly complex natural particles and colloidal systems. Also a differentiation of engineered nanoparticles in presence of various other nanoparticles of natural or anthropogenic origin requires different detection capabilities. Therefore, combination of the FFF techniques with other, more elaborate techniques has been attempted. One suited method for a combination with FFF may be the laser induced breakdown detection (LIBD) described in the following section.

2.5.4.3 Laser-Induced Breakdown Detection (LIBD)

A pulsed laser beam generates plasma events (dielectric breakdowns) selectively on particles in liquid media. The number of plasmas per number of total laser pulses and their spatial distribution in the laser focus reveals colloid concentration and size. The detection limit depends on the optical setup and is typically <1 ng/l (ppt) for 10 nm colloids (app. 10^5 particles/ml) and several mg/l for 1 μm particles (10^4 particles/ml). Typical measurement duration is several minutes, no sample preparation is required, and the analysis is largely non-invasive. The LIBD does not distinguish between organic, inorganic and biological particles; also it returns a mean diameter for particle mixtures of different size. The first paper on the LIBD (Laser-induced Breakdown Detection) technique has been published by Fujimori et al. (1992) who have demonstrated the potential of the LIBD to detect colloids down to a size of approximately 10 nm. A fully automated system has been built and named Nano-Particle Analyzer based on LIBD (NPA/LIBD) (Wagner, 2005).

2.5.5 Nanoparticles in drinking water treatment

2.5.5.1 Nanoparticles in conventional drinking water and in membrane treatment

As an example, the number densities of colloids in drinking water after multi-stage conventional treatment (deep bed filtration, ozonation, activated carbon filtration, slow sand filtration) and after membrane ultra filtration are compared. Results are derived from LIBD measurements and from TEM-IA as well as AFM techniques described in Kaegi et al. (2008:1). The LIBD is a very fast, 'non-invasive' method while the TEM on the other hand is a very time consuming, invasive method. Despite this, both methods yield comparable results. The combination of the two methods is very promising as e.g. the water can be 'screened' with the LIBD and then a detailed analysis of selected samples can be performed with the TEM. The TEM/LIBD analysis was supported further with AFM analysis in order to visually confirm the findings of the TEM results.

2.5.5.2 AFM measurements

A representative AFM image of a sample after conventional treatment is given in Figure 2.33. Two types of particles can readily be recognized: Spheroid particles and fibrous particles. In the AFM technique, a sharp tip is scanned over the surface of the sample. Due to geometric constraints, the lateral dimensions of the particles are overestimated and the most correct parameter is the height of the particles. The spheroid particles are up to 50 nm. They are aggregates of several smaller particles. The fibrous particles have a height of only a few nm, but are several 100 nm long. Similar structures have been described in the marine (Santschi et al., 1998) and in freshwater environments (Filella et al., 1993). These two particle types are most likely aquagenic (or pedogenic) refractory organic matter (NOM) and polysaccharides (fibrils) (Leppard et al., 1986). The strength of the AFM is that the analysis can be performed under environmental conditions. AFM measurements (especially the height) are therefore probably closest to the 'real' size.

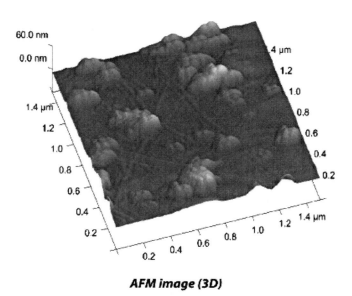

AFM image (3D)

Figure 2.33 Spheroid and fibrous particles representing humic substance and polysaccharide nanoparticles, respectively *(photo courtesy R. Kaegi, Eawag)*

2.5.5.3 TEM investigation

The particle number density of the particles >1μm in the finished water following conventional treatment and ultra filtration membrane filtration is very low as confirmed by on-line particle counters which are routinely operated. This corresponds to the microscopic investigation where only a few isolated particles (mainly of geological origin) were found in the finished water following conventional treatment. In terms of number concentration however, these particles are insignificant. Besides organic particles (e.g. bacteria), these larger particles consist of weathered mineral products (clays), iron oxides, silica and calcium carbonate.

A representative image of a sample after ultracentrifugation following the conventional treatment is given in Figure 2.34. The image is dominated by dark particles which are a few tens of nm in diameter. Besides these round particles, also fibrils can be seen on the image. These fibrils can reach a length of up to a few μm. These results are in good agreement with the results from the AFM analysis, where similar particles have been observed. Elemental analysis performed in the TEM revealed C as the dominant element. Although C-coated TEM grids have been used and therefore C is also related to the C film of the TEM grid, the lack of other elements shows that geological particles (carbonates and silicates) or iron-hydroxides can be excluded. It can therefore be concluded that the vast majority of the particles are of organic material.

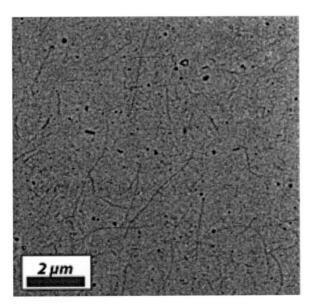

TEM (bright field) of purified water following conventional treatement.

Figure 2.34 TEM picture of natural nanoparticles (NOM) in the finished lake water after conventional treatment *(photo courtesy by Kaegi et al., 2008:1)*

A particle size distribution can be derived based on several images in combination with IA tools. The ultracentrifugation leads to a total deposition of colloids >10 nm (density 1.1 g/cm^3) directly on the

TEM grid and thus, the derived particle number distribution can be quantified. The size distribution is given in Figure 2.35. In Figure 2.36 the size distribution is given in a log- log-scale. The data points fall on a straight line with a slope of −3.3 indicating that the size distribution follows an exponential law down to 40nm, corresponding to the lower size limit of particles detected using the IA tools. This is in agreement with slopes of about −3 which are typically found in natural waters for size classes above 0.3 μm (Boller, 1998).

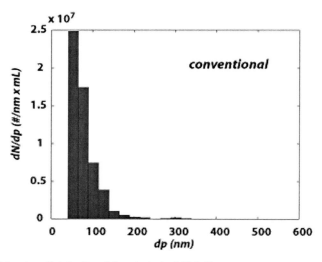

Figure 2.35 Nanoparticle size distribution (Kaegi et al., 2008:1)

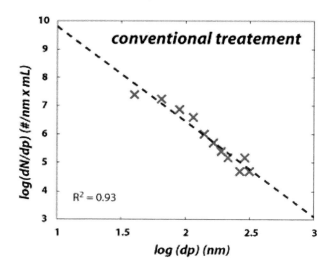

Figure 2.36 Log size distribution function (Kaegi et al., 2008:1)

2.5.5.4 LIBD measurements

The results from the LIBD measurements are given in Table 2.3. LIBD measurements were carried out on centrifuged and raw (untreated) water samples. This gives a first indication of the size spectra of the particles. The measurements clearly show that the mean particle diameters in all samples are in the lower nanometer range, and that the number densities are in the order of 10^8 #/ml. This is in accordance with earlier LIBD measurements of comparable water samples (Bundschuh et al., 2001, Wagner et al., 2002). The finished water, following conventional treatment, yields an average particle diameter of 31 (± 5) nm, both centrifugation steps further decrease the number of larger particles, resulting in 26 (± 6) nm after the first step, and 15 (± 4) nm after the second step. The number density decreases after the first centrifugation step and then significantly increases again. This apparent contradiction can be explained as follows: The LIBD method becomes more sensitive for smaller particles when larger colloids are removed. However, compared to standard methods such as dynamic light scattering, this masking effect is smaller by orders of magnitude, but still has to be considered when interpreting results from LIBD measurements. It can therefore occur that the apparent number density of the colloids remains constant or even increases during filtration/centrifugation processes. The effect becomes more severe with increasing size and fraction of larger particles.

Table 2.3 Results from the LIBD measurements (Kaegi et al., 2008:1).

Sample	Average size (nm)	Number density (#/l)	Volume (nl/l)
Conventional	31 (± 5)	2.7 (± 0.3)$\times 10^{11}$	4.2 (± 2.4)
Conventional 1st step	26 (± 6)	1.5 (± 0.3)$\times 10^{11}$	1.4 (± 0.9)
Conventional 2nd step	15 (± 4)	7.0 (± 0.9)$\times 10^{11}$	1.3 (± 0.9)

2.5.5.5 Comparing TEM and LIBD measurements

The number densities derived form TEM-IA are about an order of magnitude lower than the LIBD measurements. This apparent discrepancy is caused by the different cut-offs of the two methods. While the LIBD includes particles down to 10 nm, results from the TEM-IA are restricted to particles >40 nm. Although this size limit is far higher than the resolution limit of the TEM (0.12 nm), the automatic particle detection and measuring algorithm used becomes less accurate with particles smaller than 40 nm. This is mainly due to the low contrast of the organic particles in the TEM. However, if the size distribution derived from the TEM-IA is extrapolated down to 10 nm, assuming an exponential increase of the particle number density with decreasing size, a total number of roughly 10^8 particles/ml is obtained, which is in good agreement with the LIBD measurements. Also the average size of the particles resulting from the extrapolated size distribution is in good agreement with the LIBD measurements (Figure 2.37).

2.5.5.6 Comparison between two different treatment schemes

In order to compare the finished water following either conventional treatment or UF membranes, AFM and LIBD measurements were conducted. TEM analysis was not performed on the membrane filtered water because the membrane had a cut-off of 10 kDa corresponding to roughly 10 nm and the lower size limit of the TEM-IA setup was about 40 nm.

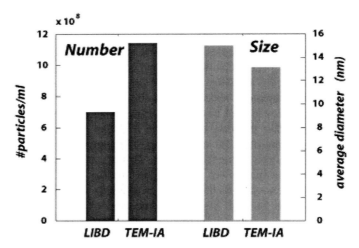

Figure 2.37 Comparison of nanoparticle number concentration and average size measurement with LIBD and TEM-IA in Lake Zurich water (Kaegi et al., 2008:1)

A typical AFM image of the finished water following UF is given in Figure 2.38 and may be compared with the image in Figure 2.33 showing a sample after conventional treatment. A height profile of the sample after conventional treatment was taken in the indicated directions given in Figures 2.39 and 2.40 showing the effluent particles of conventional treatment. Comparing images after UF treatment with the ones from conventional filtration, two features can readily be observed:

1. the water following UF lacks the fibrils which were always observed in the water following conventional treatment,
2. the particles in the permeate are much smaller, the maximum height is about 15 nm.

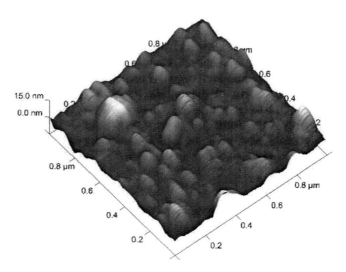

Figure 2.38 AFM picture of the membrane finished water (permeate) (Picture: R. Kaegi, Eawag).

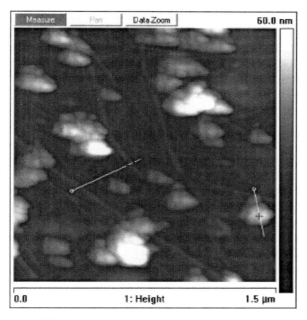

Figure 2.39 Profile locations in TEM *(photo courtesy by M. Boller)*

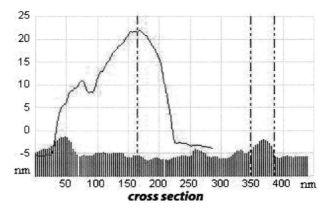

Figure 2.40 Height of the particles cut by the analysis profile (Kaegi et al., 2008:1)

Both findings are in excellent agreement with the 10 kDa cutoff of the UF-membrane, which should retain particles larger than 10 nm with a high efficiency. LIBD measurements were only performed directly in the UF permeate. There was no need for any fractionation steps as there were almost no larger particles present in the permeate. Based on the LIBD measurements, the particle number density was still 1.3×10^8/ml and the average diameter was 13 nm compared to number counts of $>10^{11}$/ml and average diameter of 31 nm after conventional treatment (see Table 2.3). Also these measurements agree well with the qualitative findings of the AFM measurements in the ultra filter permeate where most of the particles were <10–15 nm in size.

As a conclusion, we have to get acquainted with the fact that excellent drinking water contains nanomaterial in number densities of about 10^8 #/ml, using either conventional treatment or membrane technology. The particles following membrane filtration, however, are considerably smaller compared to the particles resulting from conventional treatment. In addition, the size distribution of the particles in the UF permeate is more narrow than the size distribution from conventional treatment. This is in agreement with the rather sharp cutoff of the membrane.

2.5.6 Synthetic nanoparticles in surface runoff

Since a few years, synthetic nanoparticles are used on facades and walls of buildings. Among a number of organic biocides, the nanoparticles titanium dioxide (Nano-TiO_2 in the form of anatas) and nanosilver (n-Ag) are most widely applied. The idea is to protect the building surfaces from algae and fungi growth. The nanoparticles usually supplement organic biocides contained in plaster and paint materials. In addition, with photoactive TiO_2, organic pollutants should be degraded. The application of engineered nanoparticles on facades is a strongly competitive business for the protection of building surfaces which is so far not controlled ("Easy-to-Clean", "Self-Cleaning Coatings").

Until now, the mobilization of synthetic nanoparticles from facade coatings has not been investigated in the urban water cycle. Therefore, a quantification of nanoparticle inputs into the urban drainage systems and a consequent evaluation of possible effects on aquatic organisms is unclear. Therefore, no basis is available to classify the application of synthetic nanoparticles regarding environmental sustainability and the development of possible measures at the source. The environmental risk assessment of synthetic nanoparticles will be a challenge for the future urban water management. The importance of this topic is supported by the recently published intention to restrict the application of n-Ag by the USEPA.

Engineered nanoparticles within a size range of a few tens to a few hundreds of nm in diameter were successfully detected and identified in the environment using combinations of analytical microscopy (TEM-EDX) and bulk chemical methods (ICP-MS) (see Figure 2.41). The results are described in more detail in Kaegi et al. (2008:2). It could be shown that TiO_2 particles are released in significant amounts to the aquatic environment. The nano-TiO_2 concentration was estimated in the façade runoff to reach 3.5×10^5 particles/ml < 300 nm and 3.5×10^4 particles/ml < 100 nm.

2.6 OVERVIEW: PARTICLE SEPARATION PROCESSES

In most treatment trains for water treatment, particle separation is the first treatment step. There are different alternatives for solids separation and their beneficial application depends strongly on the quality of the water or more precise on the characteristics of the particle suspension to be treated.

The processes most widely applied in water treatment are:

- sedimentation
- flocculation
- flotation
- granular media filtration
- contact filtration
- screening, straining
- membrane filtration.

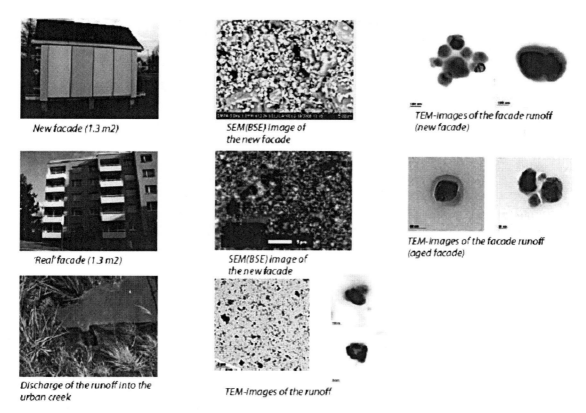

Figure 2.41 TiO$_2$ nanoparticle analysis from the facade to the receiving water *(photo: Burkhardt, Eawag, SEM and TEM pictures: Kaegi et al., 2008:2)*

Among these processes flocculation is not really a solids separation process but it helps to improve solids separation considerably by particle agglomeration. A primary factor for the decision which processes are suited under which conditions, is the solids concentration in terms of mass quantity, volume or number concentrations. On the other hand, the particle size is an important parameter which determines the removal mechanisms which are best be promoted in order to achieve optimal solids separation performance. Based on the relationships depicted in Figure 2.42, different areas can be identified in which certain solids separation processes are best be applied.

2.6.1 Removal of particles >30 μm

Particles >30 μm can be removed by screening processes such as microstrainers. The smaller range of mesh sizes is in the order of 8 μm. Also a granular media filter may remove particles >20 μm completely. The combination rapid filter/slow sand filter can reach a particle removal efficiency of 100% for particles >10 μm. Screens and granular filters are subject to clogging and need to be cleaned regularly. At higher concentrations, sedimentation for particles with a higher density and flotation for particles with a low density are more suited. Filters and screens may be used below concentrations in the order of 50 mgTSS/l. At higher concentrations sedimentation or flotation are necessary.

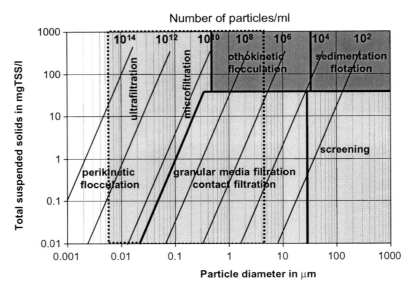

Figure 2.42 Appropriate action fields of solids separation processes

2.6.2 Removal of particles between 0.5 μm and 30 μm

Many important particles in surface waters are in the size range between 0.5 and 30 μm such as bacteria, blue and green algae, diatoms, and partly also inorganic particles. In this size range orthokinetic flocculation (particle transport by shear) has to be applied in order to agglomerate the particles to larger flocs and thus enable removal by sedimentation, flotation or filtration. A combination with sedimentation or flotation is suited at concentrations above 50 mgTSS/l or filtration or contact filtration at concentrations below this value.

Also membrane filters such as micro- and ultra filters may cope with this particle class. In full scale, membrane filters are usually protected against too large particles by screening filters with openings in the order of 20 μm.

2.6.3 Removal of particles <0.5 μm

The smaller particles in the nano-size range, the more difficult it is to describe their behavior in water. Viruses and some types of inorganic precipitates such as calcite and iron (hydr)-oxides typically belong to this size range. From particle analysis in this size range, it becomes clear that the number of particles is increasing with decreasing size. Particle numbers of nano-sized colloids in natural waters may easily reach 10^8 to 10^9/ml. In addition to the mentioned colloids, decay products of suspended organic material are present in large amounts. In future also an increasing number of synthetic nano-particles in wastewater, natural water and drinking water have to be expected.

The aggregation of submicron particles is relatively fast if their surface chemistry is suited and if their concentration is high enough ($>10^8$/ml). The transport of submicron particles for aggregation is brought about by Brownian motion, also know as perikinetic flocculation. Often the agglomerates are still small and cannot be removed by sedimentation or filtration, further agglomeration with the help of orthokinetic flocculation, contact filtration or sludge blanket clarifiers is necessary.

The particle class <0.5 μm can efficiently be removed by ultra filtration. Again pre-filters with openings of 10 to 20 μm are applied. In view of the small pore size of ultra filters in the order of 0.01 μm, viruses and other colloids may be removed completely by ultra filter membranes.

Ultra filters may cope with particle concentrations up to more than 1000 mgTSS/l (Pianta et al.). However, membrane fouling caused by accompanying organic material such as polysaccharides, proteins and humic substances can limit the application of ultra filters to much lower concentrations in the order of 100 mgTSS/l and lower.

2.7 ACKNOWLEDGEMENT

The authors would like to thank Dr. Michael Burkhardt, scientist at the Department for urban Water Management at Eawag for his information on the application of synthetic nanoparticles in the construction sector.

2.8 REFERENCES

Baron, P. and Willeke, K. (2001). *Aerosol Measurement*, Wiley Interscience, ISBN 0-471-35636-0.
Beckett, R. & Hart, B. T. (1992) *Environmental Particles*, Boca Raton, Lewis Publishers.
Boller, M., Kavanaugh, M., Particle characteristics and headloss increase in granular media filtration, *Wat Res.*, **29**, 1139–1149.
Boller, M. and Blaser, S. (1998), Particles under stress, *Wat. Sci. Tech.*, **37**(10), 9–29.
Boller, M. and Pronk, W. (2004). Nano and Microparticles in Water and Wastewater Treatment. *Wat. Sci. Tech.*, **50**(12).
Bouby, M., Geckeis, H., Manh, T.N., Yun, J.I., Dardenne, K., Schafer, T., Walther, C. and Kim, J.I. (2004), Laser-induced breakdown detection combined with asymmetrical flow field-flow fractionation: application to iron oxi/hydroxide colloid characterization, *Journal of Chromatography* A **1040**, 97–104.
Brydson, R. (2001) *Electron Energy Loss Spectroscopy*, Guildford, BIOS Scientific Publishers Ltd.
Bundschuh, T., Wagner, T.U., Koester, R. (2005) "Laser-induced Breakdown Detection (LIBD) for the highly sensitive quantification of aquatic colloids. Part I: Principle of LIBD and mathematical model," *Particle & Particle Systems Characterization* 22, 172–180.
Bundschuh, T., Knopp, R. & Kim, J. I. (2001a) Laser-induced breakdown detection (LIBD) of aquatic colloids with different laser systems, *Colloids and Surfaces a – Physicochemical and Engineering Aspects*, **177**, 47–55.
Bundschuh, T., Knopp, R., Winzenbacher, R., Kim, J. I. & Koester, R. (2001b) Quantification of aquatic nano particles after, different steps of Bodensee water purification with laser-induced breakdown detection (LIBD), *Acta Hydrochimica Et Hydrobiologica*, **29**, 7–15.
Buffle, J., Perret, D. & Newman, M. E. (1992) *Environmental Particles*, Boca Raton, Lewis Publishers.
Couture, C., Lienemann, C. P., Mavrocordatos, D. & Perret, D. (1996) New directions towards the understanding of physico-chemical processes in aquatic systems, *Chimia*, **50**, 625–629.
Egerton, R. F. (1996) *Electron Energy Loss Spectroscopy in the Electron Microscope*, New York, Plenum Press.
Egerton, R. F. (2007) *Physical Principles of Electron Microscopy*, New York, Springer+Business Media.
Filella, M., Buffle, J. & Leppard, G. G. (1993) Characterization of Submicrometer Colloids in Fresh-Waters – Evidence for Their Bridging by Organic Structures, *Wat. Sci. Tech.*, **27**, 91–102.
Filella, M., Zhang, J. W., Newman, M. E. & Buffle, J. (1997) Analytical applications of photon correlation spectroscopy for size distribution measurements of natural colloidal suspensions: Capabilities and limitations, *Colloids and Surfaces a – Physicochemical and Engineering Aspects*, **120**, 27–46.
Fraunhofer, W. & Winter, G. (2004) The use of asymmetrical flow field-flow fractionation in pharmaceutics and biopharmaceutics, *European Journal of Pharmaceutics and Biopharmaceutics*, **58**, 369–383.
Fujimori, H., Matsui, T., Ajiro, T., Yokose, K., Hsueh, Y.M. and Izumi, S. (1992) Detection of Fine Particles in Liquids by Laser Breakdown Method, Japanese *Journal of Applied Physics* Part 1-Regular Papers Short Notes & Review Papers 31, 1514–1518.

Garboczi, E.J. and Bullard, J.W. (2004), Shape analysis of a reference cement, *Cement and Concrete Research*, **34**(10), 1933–1937.

Giddings, J. C., Yang, F. J. & Myers, M. N. (1976) Theoretical and Experimental Characterization of Flow Field-Flow Fractionation, *Analytical Chemistry*, **48**, 1126–1132.

Giddings, J. C. (1993) Field-Flow Fractionation – Analysis of Macromolecular, *Colloidal, and Particulate Materials, Science*, **260**, 1456–1465.

Goldstein, J., Newbury, D., Joy, D., Lyman, C., Echlin, P., Lifshin, E., Sawyer, L. & Michael, J. (2003) *Scanning Electron Microscopy and X-Ray Microanalysis*, New York, Kluwer Academic.

Hassellov, M., v. d. Kammer, F., and Beckett, R. (2007), *Characterization of Aquatic Colloids and Macromolecules by Field-flow Fractionation*, West Sussex, England, John Wiley & Sons Ltd.

Kaegi, R., Wagner, T., Hetzer, B., Sinnet, B., Tzvetkov, G., Boller, M. (2008:1) Size, number and chemical composition of nanosized particles in drinking water determined by analytical microscopy and LIBD, *Water Res.*, **42**(10-11), 2778–2786.

Kaegi, R., Ulrich, A.; Sinnet,B.; Vonbank,R.; Wichser,A.; Zuleeg,S.; Simmler,H.; Brunner,S.; Vonmont,H.; Burkhardt, M.; Boller,M. (2008:2) Synthetic TiO2 nanoparticle emission from exterior facades into the aquatic environment, E*nviron. Pollut.*, **156**(2), 233–239.

Kobler, D. and Boller,M. (1997), Particle removal in different filtration systems for tertiary wastewater treatment – A comparison, *Wat. Sci. Tech.* **36**(4) 259–267

Lawler, D.F., (1996) Particle size distribution in treatment processes: Theory and practice, *Wat. Sci. Tech.*, **36**(4), 15–23.

Leppard, G. G., Buffle, J. & Baudat, R. (1986) A Description of the Aggregation Properties of Aquatic Pedogenic Fulvic-Acids – Combining Physicochemical Data and Microscopic Observations, *Wat. Res.*, **20**, 185–196.

Leppard, G. G., Mavrocordatos, D. & Perret, D. (2004) Electron-optical characterization of nano- and micro-particles in raw and treated waters: an overview, *Wat. Sci. Tech.*, **50**(12), 1–8.

Liu, J., Andya, J. D. & Shire, S. J. (2006) A critical review of analytical ultracentrifugation and field flow fractionation methods for measuring protein aggregation, *Aaps Journal*, **8**, E580-E589.

Mavrocordatos, D., Mondi-Couture, C., Atteia, O., Leppard, G. G. & Perret, D. (2000) Formation of a distinct class of Fe-Ca(-C-org)-rich particles in a complex peat-karst system. *Journal of Hydrology*, **237**, 234–247.

Mavrocordatos, D., Steiner, M.; Boller, M. (2003) Analytical electron microscopy and focused ion beam: complementary tool for the imaging of copper sorption onto iron oxide aggregates, *J. Microsc. Oxford.*, **210**, 45–52.

Mavrocordatos, D; Pronk,W.; Boller,M. (2004) Analysis of environmental particles by atomic force microscopy, scanning and transmission electron microscopy, *Wat. Sci. Tech.*, **50**(12), 9–18.

Mavrocordatos, D., Perret, D. & Leppard, G. (2007) Strategies and advances in the Characterisation of Environmental Colloids by Electron Microscopy. In Wilkinson, K. J. & Lead, J. R. (Eds.) *Environmental Colloids and Particles. Behavior, Separation and Characterization*. John Wiley & Sons Ltd.

Perret, D., Newman, M. E., Nègre, J. C., Chen, Y. W. and Buffle, J. (1994) Submicron Particles in the Rhine River. 1. Physicochemical Characterization. *Wat. Res.*, **28**, 91–106.

Pianta,R., Boller,M.; Janex,M.L.; Chappaz,A.; Birou,B.; Ponce,R.; Walther,J.L. (1998) Micro- and ultra filtration of karstic spring water, *Desalination*, **117**(1-3), 61–71.

Santschi, P. H., Balnois, E., Wilkinson, K. J., Zhang, J. W., Buffle, J. & Guo, L. D. (1998) Fibrillar polysaccharides in marine macromolecular organic matter as imaged by atomic force microscopy and transmission electron microscopy, *Limnology and Oceanography*, **43**, 896–908.

Schurtenberger, P. & Newman, M. E. (1992) *Environmental Particles*, Boca Raton, Lewis Publishers.

Wagner, T., Bundschuh, T., Schick, R., Schwartz, T. & Koster, R. (2002) Investigation of colloidal water content with laser-induced breakdown detection during drinking water purification, *Acta Hydrochimica Et Hydrobiologica*, **30**, 266–274.

Wagner, T.U., Bundschuh, T., and Koster, R., (2005), Laser-induced Breakdown Detection (LIBD) for the highly sensitive quantification of aquatic colloids. Part II: Experimental setup of LIBD and applications, *Particle & Particle Systems Characterization* **22**, 181–191.

Williams, D.B., Barry Carter, C. (1996). Transmission Electron Microscopy, Plenum Press, ISBN 0-306-45324-X.

Wilkinson, K.J., Lead, J.R. (2007). *Environmental Colloids and Particles Behaviour, Separation and Characterisation*, John Wiley, Ltd., ISBN-13 978-0470-02432-4.

Chapter 3

Characterization Profiling of NOM – as a Basis for Treatment Process Selection and Performance Monitoring

S.K. Sharma, S.G. Salinas Rodriguez, S.A. Baghoth, S.K. Maeng and G. Amy

3.1 INTRODUCTION

3.1.1 Background

Natural organic matter (NOM) is a complex heterogeneous matrix of organic compounds found in all natural waters. The type and amount of NOM in water depend on climatic conditions and hydrological regime as well as other environmental factors. Rainwater has a relatively low amount of NOM to which other components are added during surface runoff and subsurface infiltration. During river and aquifer transport, various processes (e.g., adsorption and biotransformation) further alter the NOM characteristics. Upon river discharge into an algal-impacted lake/reservoir, NOM of a microbial origin is introduced. The ocean represents the ultimate sink whereby coastal and estuarine regions are impacted by NOM in runoff and discharges whereas open-ocean NOM reflects highly stabilized NOM. The presence of NOM in water and soil has a profound influence on water chemistry due to its acid/base and complexing characteristics. NOM plays a crucial role in the transport and fate of metals in aquatic environments (Aiken *et al.*, 1985). Because of its strong acidifying and complexing abilities, NOM has significant impacts on several environmental and commercial issues including drinking water quality, forestry, freshwater fish stocks, and carbon budget and global warming (NOMINIC, 2009).

NOM in general significantly influences water treatment processes and some of its constituents in particular are problematic. In addition to aesthetic problems such as color, taste and odor, it contributes to the fouling of membranes, serves as precursor for the formation of disinfection by-products, increases the exhaustion and usage rate of activation carbon and also certain fractions of NOM promotes microbial growth and corrosion in the distribution system (Amy, 1994; Owen *et al.*, 1993). The presence of NOM increases the cost of water treatment by increasing the adsorbent and chemical use and consequently increased sludge treatment disposal requirements. An understanding of the behaviour of different fractions or constituents of NOM present in water sources is important to understand their fate and impact during water treatment and distribution.

Global warming, changes in soil acidification, increased drought severity and more intensive rain events have led to increasing natural organic matter (NOM) concentration levels in water sources in many countries around the world during the past 10–20 years. In addition to the trend towards increasing NOM concentration, the character of NOM can vary with source and time (season). The great seasonal variability and the trend towards elevated NOM concentration levels impose challenges to the water industry and water treatment facilities in terms of operational optimization and proper process control (Fabris et al., 2008). By systematic characterization, the problematic NOM fractions can be targeted for removal and transformation. Therefore, proper characterization of the NOM in raw water or after different treatment steps would be an important basis for selection of the water treatment processes, monitoring of the performance of different treatment steps, and assessing distribution system water quality.

3.1.2 Types of NOM and their Sources

NOM mainly consists of carbon, oxygen and hydrogen. Depending on the source of NOM, nitrogen and sulphur can also be present. Furthermore, different cations and anions may be incorporated into NOM structure due to adsorption, complexation and ion exchange. NOM, in general, can be divided into three main types:

(1) Allochthonous NOM – This type of NOM originates from the decay of terrestrial biomass or through soil leaching in the watershed, mainly from runoff or vegetative debris. The production and characteristics of this type of NOM is therefore related to vegetative patterns and to hydrologic and geological characteristics of the watershed.

(2) Autochthonous NOM – This type of NOM originates from in-situ sources, mainly algal organic matter (AOM), other phytoplankton, and macrophytes; components could be excellular or intracellular organic matter consisting of macromolecules and cell fragments. The production of this type of NOM is therefore related to photosynthetic activity and decay products of algal matter.

(3) Effluent organic matter (EfOM) – EfOM consists of "background" drinking water NOM which is not removed during wastewater treatment plus soluble microbial products (SMPs) formed during biological treatment of wastewater. The characteristics of EfOM therefore depend on the type of drinking water source and treatment as well as the type of wastewater treatment applied.

NOM consists of both humic and non-humic components. Humic substances (HS) in soils and sediments can be divided into three main fractions: humic acids (HA), fulvic acids (FA) and humin. The HA and FA can be extracted from soil and other solid phase sources using a strong base (NaOH or KOH). Humic acids are operationally defined as insoluble at low pH, and are precipitated by adding strong acid (adjust to pH 1 with HCl). Humin cannot be extracted with either a strong base or a strong acid. Aquatic HS contain only HA and FA (IHSS, 2009). Aquatic humic substances account for approximately 50% of the DOC present in most natural waters, although this percentage varies. The non-humic fraction of NOM consists of hydrophilic acids, proteins, amino acids, amino sugars and carbohydrates. All these groups of compounds are likely to be present in natural waters, although their absolute and relative concentrations are expected to vary from site to site (Drewes and Summers, 2002).

3.1.3 Methods for Removal of Different Types of NOM/EfOM during Water Treatment

Removal of NOM from water sources is highly dependent on the characteristics of the NOM present (e.g., molecular weight distribution (MWD), carboxylic acidity, and humic substances content), its concentration and the removal methods applied. High molecular weight (HMW) NOM is more amenable to removal than low molecular weight (LMW) NOM, particularly the fraction with an MW of <500 Dalton (Da). NOM components with the highest carboxylic acidity and hence the highest charge density are generally more difficult to remove by conventional treatment (Collins *et al.*, 1985; Collins *et al.*, 1986). Different water treatment methods have been used for the removal of NOM from water sources with varying degree of success. These include:

(1) Enhanced coagulation
(2) Activated carbon filtration
(3) Ion exchange
(4) Ozonation followed by bio-filtration
(5) Membrane filtration
(6) Bank filtration
(7) Different combinations of methods listed above

Some of these removal methods are elaborated below:

Enhanced coagulation has been used in many countries as the conventional method for removal of NOM. Enhanced coagulation processes designed for the removal of NOM requires elevated coagulant doses and strict control of coagulation pH, leading to excess sludge production and increased costs of treatment. The condition for maximum NOM removal (pH and mixing) may or may not coincide with the conditions for maximum turbidity removal. Both alum- and iron-based coagulants have been used, but iron-based coagulants, such as ferric chloride, has been reported to be consistently more effective than alum in removing NOM (Crozes *et al.* 1995). However, this method is effective mainly for the removal of hydrophobic humic substances and NOM of relatively nonpolar or lower acidity character. More advanced processes are required to remove the hydrophilic, non-humic NOM (Owen *et al.* 1993; Amy, 1994).

Activated carbon (AC) is widely used to remove organic matter from water. AC adsorbs NOM to some degree, which is controlled predominantly by the relationship between the molecular size distribution of NOM and the pore size distribution of the AC (Matilainen *et al.*, 2006). McCreary and Snoeyink (1980) observed that the extent of adsorption of the HS fraction decreased with increasing total carboxyl groups. In many studies the low molecular weight (LMW) organic matter was observed to be more amenable to adsorption onto AC than the high molecular weight (HMW) organic matter mainly due to a size exclusion effect.

Ion exchange is an effective method for removing humic substances from drinking water supplies. Anion exchange resins (AER) or MIEX (Magnetic Ion Exchange resin) have been effective in treatment of potable waters containing large amounts of the LMW forms of humic substances which can be difficult to treat by coagulation processes, especially if the waters are low in turbidity. The performance of AER for NOM removal is influenced by the characteristics of the resins (strong or weak base AER), water quality (pH, ionic strength, hardness, etc.) and the nature of organic compounds (molecular weight (MW), charge density, polarity). Ion exchange has been claimed to be more effective than activated carbon, carbonaceous resins or metal oxides for NOM adsorption (Fettig, 1999). The technology is most competitive for low colour waters, and has low installation costs and operational simplicity (Hongve *et al.*, 1999).

Ozonation is often used in combination with other treatment processes for NOM removal. The amount of NOM reduction by ozonation and subsequent biofiltration depends on ozone dose, characteristics of the

NOM present in water and other water quality parameters like pH and alkalinity (Ødegaard et al., 2006). Ozonation leads to the degradation or breakdown of NOM and formation of low molecular weight compounds that have lower UV absorbance and are easily biodegradable. The subsequent biofiltration or activated carbon filtration provides the opportunity for removal of the biodegradable fractions or small fragments of the NOM formed. However, when these fractions are not well removed in biofilters or adsorbed on GAC, they tend to be more difficult to remove due to their mobility and generally increased polarity. Typically, the adsorbability of NOM decreases with ozonation because of the creation of more polar, hydrophilic compounds.

Membrane filtration systems like ultra filtration and nanofiltration can be used to remove larger residual organic matter left after coagulation and certain dissolved NOM. Ultra filtration may be used to remove larger apparent molecular weight (AMW) organics, but may fail to remove a significant portion of lower AMW organic matter. Nanofiltration membranes of low molecular weight cutoff (MWCO) could be used for removal of those fractions of NOM which are not removed by ultra filtration (AWWARF, 2000; Frimmel et al., 2006).

Bank filtration (BF) systems have been used as a pre-treatment or as the complete treatment of river or lake water for drinking water supply in many countries worldwide. BF is known to effectively remove majority of the bulk organic matter (NOM) and some organic micropollutants. The concentration of NOM and soluble microbial products (SMPs) that comprise the bulk of the dissolved and particulate organic carbon are reduced during soil passage as high molecular weight compounds are hydrolyzed to lower molecular weight compounds, and lower molecular weight compounds serve as substrates for microorganisms (NRC, 2008). It has been reported that during BF there can be 50% to 90% reduction of biodegradable dissolved organic carbon (BDOC) and assimilable organic carbon (AOC), biodegradable portions of NOM, and 26% reduction in specific UV absorbance values in UV absorbing NOM (Weiss et al., 2004). Furthermore, BF can greatly reduce chlorine demand as well as trihalomethane formation potential (THMFP) and haloacetic acid formation potential (HAAFP) in river water.

Combined treatment processes and hybrids with different combination of above mentioned methods have been employed for removal of NOM. The main objective of these hybrid/combined systems is to maximise the removal of different fractions of the NOM more effectively. Some of these methods include, (a) coagulation followed by ultra filtration, (b) ozonation followed by activated carbon filtration, (c) activated carbon filtration followed by reverse osmosis, (d) biofiltration followed by nanofiltration, (e) ion exchange followed by activated carbon filtration and (f) ozonation followed by biofiltration and membrane filtration (Owen et al., 1993; Matilainen et al., 2002; Osterhus et al., 2007; Gur-Reznik et al., 2008; Humbert et al., 2008).

3.2 NOM IN WATER AND WASTEWATER TREATMENT/REUSE

3.2.1 Relevance of NOM in Drinking Water Treatment

NOM present in water has significant impacts on all aspects of drinking water treatment as well as water quality in the distribution system, leading to operational problems and increased cost of water treatment. Some of these are summarised below:

(i) The presence of NOM in water causes aesthetic water quality problems including color, taste or odour.
(ii) The demand or dose of coagulants, oxidants and disinfectants used for water treatment is increased in the presence of NOM.

(iii) NOM present in water may react with chlorine or other disinfectants/oxidants to produce disinfection by-products (DBPs), many of which are either carcinogenic or mutagenic.
(iv) NOM is responsible for fouling of membranes, reducing the flux, resulting in high frequency of backwashing and cleaning of membranes.
(v) Presence of NOM decreases the lifetime of activated carbon filters used for the removal of organic micropollutants, as it competes for adsorption sites. NOM present in water can adversely impact both adsorption capacity and adsorption kinetics of micropollutants.
(vi) Presence of biodegradable NOM in water entering the distribution system may lead to regrowth, when a sufficient disinfectant residual is not maintained.
(vii) Some NOM fractions may promote corrosion in the distribution system.

3.2.2 Relevance of EfOM in Wastewater Effluent Treatment/Reuse

The organic matter present in wastewater treatment plant effluents (commonly known as EfOM) is a mixture of (i) natural organic matter (NOM), (ii) soluble microbial products (SMPs), (iii) easily biodegradable organic matter and (iv) synthetic organic compounds (SOCs). The concentrations and proportions of each of these components in the effluent depends on the source of drinking water, type of drinking water treatment, water use in the service area and type of wastewater treatment. Removal of EfOM is one of the main concerns in treatment of wastewater treatment plant effluents for water reuse applications as it impacts the treatability of the water for intended application. The refractory organic compounds remaining after advanced water treatment are of special concern.

EfOM is a DBP precursor, exerts higher coagulant and oxidant demands, influences nitrification and denitrification processes as well as the removal of micropollutants by biodegradation. Some components of EfOM, e.g., protein-like organic matter are also responsible for the fouling of membranes and adsorbents. Furthermore, some aesthetic (color, taste, and odor) and operational problems (corrosion, regrowth) associated with NOM in drinking water also affect wastewater reuse applications. In general, EfOM affects essentially all chemicals and biological processes in aquatic environments (Shon *et al.*, 2006).

3.3 QUANTIFICATION AND MEASUREMENT OF NOM

3.3.1 Sampling and Processing

All water samples for NOM or EfOM analysis should be handled properly and should be analysed within a short period of time. Except for few newly developed spectrophotometry-based (e.g., UV-Vis) technology for on-line monitoring, generally it is not possible to conduct detailed in-situ analyses of organic matter. Therefore, the representative samples must be taken carefully and transported to a qualified laboratory for analysis. Besides external contamination during handling, some components of NOM or EfOM are subject to slow biodegradation and hydrolysis. Rapid analysis should be envisaged specifically for samples rich in biodegradable organic matter. Prior to shipment, the samples should be kept at temperature of 4°C or below after sampling.

Specially cleaned glassware (preferably "soak cleaned") should be used with hard plastic screw cups and Teflon, polypropylene (PP) or polyethylene (PE) inlays. When dealing with samples with low TOC content, higher precautionary measures are required. For low-TOC waters, use of glass or Teflon sampling bottles are recommended, as some perfluoroalkoxy (PFA) products may leach monomers. Other precautionary measures include (i) proper labeling of the sampling bottles, (ii) rinsing the sampling bottle with the sample, where feasible, and (iii) not freezing the samples or treating with any additives or preservatives. Samples dedicated to dissolved organic analysis are generally filtered through 0.45 µm filter immediately after sampling.

It is necessary to use cooling boxes for the shipment of samples. The shipment method should consider the arrival time for the sample and the time between sampling and analysis. Non-cooled samples should be analysed within 24 hours after sampling (cooled: up to 72 hours). Another alternative is pasteurisation of closed sampling bottles at 70°C for 30 minutes.

3.3.2 TOC and DOC

The first characterization of NOM can be based on the fractionation of total organic carbon (TOC) into the operationally defined fractions of dissolved organic carbon (DOC) and particulate organic carbon (POC). POC is the fraction of the TOC that is retained on a 0.45 µm filter. DOC is the organic carbon smaller than 0.45 µm. POC generally represents a minor fraction (below 10%) of the TOC (Thurman, 1985). The determination of DOC is done by combustion or oxidation to carbon dioxide and by measurement of carbon dioxide by infrared spectrometry.

TOC is often synonymous with natural organic matter (NOM) because trace organic contaminants in natural systems generally represent an insignificant fraction of the TOC (Leenheer and Croué, 2003). Nevertheless, separate measurements should be made for DOC and POC; DOC is chemically more reactive because it is a measure of individual organic compounds in the dissolved state, while POC is both discrete plant and animal organic matter and organic coatings on silt and clay.

Dissolved organic matter (DOM) is analogous to DOC, but organic matter refers to the entire organic molecule and includes other elements, such as oxygen and hydrogen. For this reason, organic matter is difficult to quantify, and measurements of organic carbon are preferred (Thurman, 1985). DOM is a complex mixture of aromatic and aliphatic hydrocarbon structures that have attached amide, carboxyl, hydroxyl, ketone, and various minor functional groups. Heterogeneous molecular aggregates in natural waters increase DOM complexity (Leenheer and Croué, 2003).

Different methods of DOC/TOC analysis are available, of which the most commonly used are persulfate oxidation, ultraviolet irradiation, and a combination of the two (Sharp, 1993), specifically for the determination of low concentrations (Dafner and Wangersky, 2002). However, the high amount of chloride and other ions in seawater are known to inhibit the oxidation of organic matter organic matter by persulfate in the wet oxidation method. The combustion method, are therefore, generally more accurate in DOC measurements for seawater samples (McKenna and Doering, 1995; Kim et al., 2009). Kainulaien et al. (1994) determined correlation coefficients for different analytical methods (TOC, $KMnO_4$), colour, and fractions of humic matter.

Figure 3.1 shows the division between dissolved and particulate organic carbon, based on filtration through a 0.45 µm filter. But overlapping the dissolved and particulate fractions is the colloidal fraction. According to IUPAC (1971), the term colloidal refers to a state of subdivision, implying that the molecules or polymolecular particles dispersed in a medium have at least in one direction a dimension roughly between 0.001 µm and 1 µm. (Figure 3.1 indicates an equivalence of 10 kDa for 0.001 µm.)

3.3.3 UVA_{254} and SUVA

Ultraviolet (UV) absorbance at particular wavelengths can be related to the presence of specific organic matter chromophores. Absorbance at 254 nm can be mainly correlated to the amount of double bonds in aromatic rings (Petterson et al., 1994) and, thus, to the aromaticity. Humic acid (HA) is more aromatic than fulvic acid (FA), and FA is more aromatic than hydrophilic acids (Krasner *et al.*, 1996). Absorbance has been observed to be highly pH dependent (Abbt-Braun *et al.*, 1990). For monitoring and representing NOM concentration and the humic content or aromaticity of NOM, ultraviolet absorbance at 254 nm (UVA_{254}) is used. However, UV measures the aromaticity of compounds and does not give correct results if the aromaticity is altered, as is the case in some treatments. Values will be overestimated, as most treatment processes preferentially remove aromatic compounds. UV absorbance can therefore not be easily used to measure treatment efficiency (Schäfer, 2001).

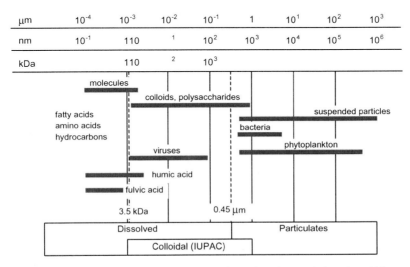

Figure 3.1 Continuum of particulate and dissolved organic carbon in natural waters (Aiken and Leenheer, 1993)

The UV_{254}/DOC ratio, defined as specific ultraviolet absorbance (SUVA), is often used to determine the humic fraction in the organic matter or to determine the aromaticity of a sample. The SUVA of fulvic acid is higher than that of natural bulk waters. In the case of comparing ozonated water and raw waters, ozonated water exhibits lower SUVA than the corresponding raw water because of the breakdown of aromatic structure by ozone. Thus, the aromatic structure of NOM can absorb more UV light than an aliphatic structure.

Kabsch-Korbutowicz (2005a & 2005b) observed a preferential decrease of colour over UV absorption at 254 nm (UV_{254}) and TOC. This was evident because the color of a natural water is related to the presence of large fractions of NOM. UV_{254} monitors the amount of NOM fraction containing aromatic structures in their molecules. The smaller the molecular size of NOM, the less reliable the quantitative estimation of NOM concentration due to scarcity of aromatic structures. The smallest fraction may contain compounds that have no UV absorbance. The concept of SUVA has been developed as an operational indicator of the nature of NOM and the effectiveness of coagulation in removing NOM, TOC, and disinfection-by-products (DBP) precursors (Edzwald and van Benschoten, 1990). SUVA values offer a simple characterization of the nature of the NOM based on measurements of UV absorbance and DOC. SUVA is defined as the normalized UV absorbance of a water sample with respect to the DOC.

$$SUVA = \frac{UV_{254}(cm^{-1}) \times 100}{DOC(mg/l)} \text{ in L/mg.m} \tag{3.1}$$

Guidelines for the interpretation of SUVA values for freshwaters are presented in Table 3.1. For water sources with low SUVA (2 or less), TOC will not control coagulant dose. For water sources with SUVA greater than 2, the amount of NOM typically exerts a greater coagulant demand than the amount of particles. For these waters, the required coagulant dose increases with increasing TOC.

Table 3.1 Guidelines on the nature of NOM and expected TOC removals Source: (Edzwald and Tobiason, 1999)

SUVA	Composition	Coagulation	DOC Removals
<2	Mostly Non-Humics, Low Hydrophobicity, Lower molecular weight	NOM has little influence, Poor DOC removals	<25% for Alum, Little greater for Ferric
2–4	Mixture of Aquatic Humics and other NOM, Mixture of Hydrophobic and Hydrophilic NOM, Mixture of Molecular Weights	NOM influences, DOC removals should be Fair to Good	25–50% for Alum, Little greater for Ferric
>4	Mostly Aquatics Humics, High Hydrophobicity, High Molecular Weight	NOM controls, Good DOC removals	>50% for Alum, Little greater for Ferric

Cho and Amy (1999) ultra filtered different source waters (covering a range of SUVA values and humic content) and studied the resulting flux declines. At lower J/k ratio (J = flux, k = mass transfer coefficient), there was little difference among the source waters, whereas there was an increase in flux decline (or fouling) with increasing SUVA at the higher J/k ratio. They also observed a clear trend of increasing NOM rejection with increasing SUVA, and proposed a general rule that NOM rejection increased with humic content and SUVA. It was noted that there was preferential rejection of NOM measured as UV_{254} over NOM measured as DOC. Fan et al. (2001) arrived at a similar conclusion, and also found that NOM that had a higher degree of aromaticity (higher SUVA) also contained a greater amount of colloidal NOM molecules (< 30 kDa). However, Jarusutthirak et al. (2002) in their study of UF of wastewaters identified high molecular weight (HMW) non-UV absorbing compounds as having the largest impact on membrane fouling. In addition, the literature suggests that a correlation exists between the SUVA value and membrane fouling (Anselme et al., 1994). However, Laine et al. (2003) did not find this parameter sufficient to fully characterize or predict fouling during membrane operation.

3.3.4 Differential UVA (ΔUVA)

Differential absorbance (ΔA) is defined as the change in the absorbance of a sample in response to any forcing function such as halogenation or ozonation (Korshin et al., 1999). However, when only ultraviolet light is considered, it is referred to as differential UV absorbance (ΔUVA). Differential spectroscopy focuses on the behavior of only those chromophores that are affected by the forcing parameter. It can be used to monitor the transformation of NOM species by water treatment processes such as oxidation with chlorine or ozone. ΔUVA is measured as the difference between UV absorbance of a sample after and before a process (e.g. ozonation). Differential absorbance at wavelengths near 272 nm (ΔUVA_{272}) for chlorinated surface waters has been found to strongly correlate with the concentrations of total organic halogens and those of individual DBPs (Korshin et al., 1997a, 2002).

3.3.5 XAD Resin Fractionation

Various XAD resins, non-ionic solid sorbent (Amberlite), have been used to isolate organic matter from water. Chemical fractionations involving XAD or ionic resins are frequently used to separate and to isolate specific compartments (e.g. humic substances) from dissolved organic matter (DOM) (Leenheer and Croue, 2003). The interest is that fractions obtained by this methodology are linked to environmental processes. Humic substances (humic and fulvic acids) are thus linked to humification process whereas simple compounds are rather attributed to the decomposition of plants and animals (Thurman, 1985).

The isolation procedure generally uses two types of XAD resin in series: XAD-8 resin first, followed by XAD-4 resin. The XAD-8 resin procedure has been extensively used in water chemistry research. It has been established that the so-called hydrophobic acid fraction (i.e. fulvic and humic acids) and the hydrophobic neutral fraction can be quantitatively concentrated from water by XAD-8 resin and then quantitatively recovered from the resin. These hydrophobic components commonly represent 50 to 65% of DOC in water. Another large fraction of the organic solutes in water, the so-called hydrophilic acids which will not sorb on XAD-8 resin, commonly represents 20–30% of DOC.

DOM was divided into four fractions according to the protocol of Malcom and McCarthy (1992): humic acids (HA), hydrophobic substances (HPO), transphilic substances (TPI) and hydrophilic substances (HPI). The humic acid fraction is separated from samples by acidification at pH 2 with HCl and precipitation. The acidified, filtered water is first passed through a column of XAD-8 resin. The effluent from the XAD-8 column is then passed through a column of XAD-4 resin. Fulvic acids, humic acids, and the hydrophobic neutral fraction are quantitatively sorbed onto XAD-8 resin. The fulvic acids and humic acids (the so-called hydrophobic acid fraction) are back-eluted from the XAD-8 with dilute 0.1 M NaOH (Labanowski and Feuillade 2009).

3.3.6 Dissolved Organic Nitrogen (DON)

Nitrogen is one of the essential nutrients for the growth of microorganisms in the aquatic environment. However, excessive amounts of dissolved inorganic nitrogen (DIN) (i.e., bio-available forms), such as NH_4^+ and NO_3^-, often leads to eutrophication in lakes or ponds. The increasing use of nitrification–denitrification processes for municipal wastewater treatment leads to the presence of dissolved organic nitrogen as the main form of nitrogen in the wastewater effluent. Wastewater-derived DON may simulate algal growth or act as a precursor for the carcinogenic disinfection by-product N-nitrosodimethylamine (NDMA).

The measurement of DON has not received much attention compared to DIN and it is present in relatively low concentrations in natural waters compared to wastewater treatment plant effluents. Thus, DON measurement requires good analytical precision and accuracy of total dissolved nitrogen (TDN) and DIN analyses in natural waters (Badr et al. 2003). In all of the available methods for quantifying DON as a bulk parameter, DON is estimated by subtracting DIN (e.g., NH_3/NH_4^+, NO_2^- and NO_3^-) from TDN. Because the concentration of the inorganic nitrogen species (DIN) often is considerably higher than that of the organic nitrogen species, DON measurements are subject to substantial error. Pretreatment such as dialysis can improve the accuracy of NDMA measurement, separating DIN from DON (Lee, 2005); however this method may not be very useful for DON measurement in wastewater due to matrix effects.

Natural organic matter also contains 1–5% of nitrogen by weight (Lee and Westerhoff, 2006). Egeberg et al (1999) found that HMW size fractions in NOM consist of more nitrogen compared to the LMW size fractions. The major route of DON into drinking water sources includes autochthonous biological processes (i.e., AOM) as well as wastewater effluents and run-off from non-point sources (Badr et al., 2003). DON may act as nutrient and is a precursor of carcinogenic DBP NDMA which is formed during disinfection using chlorine. Concerns about NDMA mainly focused on the persistent behavior of NDMA in the environment. NDMA has a high mobility in soil (Yang et al., 2005) and the activated carbon process is not effective for removal of NDMA during drinking water treatment process because of its LMW, high molecular polarity and high solubility in water (Dai et al., 2009).

3.3.7 Fluorescence Excitation Emission Matrices (F-EEM)

Some NOM species fluoresce when excited by UV and blue light and the fluorescence intensity and spectral response depend on, besides other factors, the concentration and composition of the species. This property has enabled the use of fluorescence measurements, which allow rapid data acquisition of aqueous samples at low natural concentrations, to study the character of NOM. To perform the measurement, a sample is excited by a light source (such as a xenon arc lamp) and the emitted light is recorded. An excitation emission matrix (EEM) is obtained by collecting the emission spectra at a series of excitation wavelengths. The magnitude and location of the EEM peaks vary with the concentration and composition of NOM.

Fluorescence intensity is known to increase with DOC, but due to the absorbance characteristic of different DOC molecules, this increase may not be linear, particularly at higher concentrations. Other light absorbing molecules or ions such as nitrate may also cause a reduction of the measured intensity. To account for these inner-filter effects, absorbance corrections have to be applied; however, these corrections are not necessary if the sample absorbance is less than $0.05\,\text{cm}^{-1}$ or if the DOC concentration of the sample is diluted to about 1 mg/L prior to measurement. Fluorescence is sensitive to factors such as pH, solvent polarity, temperature, redox potential of the medium, and interactions with metal ions and organic substances. To minimize metal-binding of DOC, water samples may be acidified to pH ~3 prior to measurement. However, this may lead to significant reduction in fluorescence intensities and loss of resolution for the more pH sensitive EEM peaks such as the protein-like peaks located at emission/excitation wavelengths of 320 nm/250 nm respectively (Westerhoff et al., 2001).

The traditional method for analyzing EEMs involves the use of excitation-emission wavelength pairs to identify fluorophores based on the location of fluorescence intensity peaks (Coble, 1996).

Figure 3.2 is a typical contour plot of EEMs of a natural water sample showing the locations of fluorescence intensity peaks B (tyrosine-like, protein-like), T (tryptophan-like, protein-like), C (humic-like) and C2 (humic-like, marine humic-like) that have been previously identified (Coble, 1996). Other methods include: fluorescence regional integration (FRI) (Chen et al., 2003); multivariate modelling (Boehme et al., 2004; Stedmon et al., 2003; Persson and Wedborg, 2001); and F-EEMs and parallel factor analysis (PARAFAC) (Bro, 1997),which have been used to identify individual fluorophores that have been attributed to humic-like, fulvic-like and protein-like NOM.

3.3.8 Size Exclusion Chromatography (SEC-DOC)

Size exclusion chromatography (SEC) is used for high resolution size separation. The principle of SEC is molecular size determination with gel permeation chromatography. A solution of NOM (water sample) is passed through a column of gel, and the extent to which fractions are retarded is a measure of their molecular size. Larger molecules that do not enter the gel pores pass through the columns while smaller ones diffuse into the gel and take longer to pass through. SEC provides an indication of the apparent molecular weight (MW) or molecular size (MS) of different classes of NOM fractions including biopolymers (which include polysaccharides, organic colloids and proteins), humic substances, building blocks, acids and low molecular weight (LMW) humics and LMW neutrals and amphiphilic species (Figure 3.3).

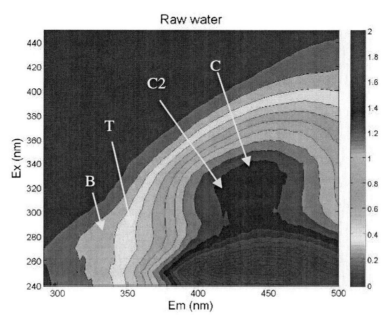

Figure 3.2 Fluorescence EEM spectra showing the location of fluorescence intensity peaks B, T, C and C2 for a sample of surface water

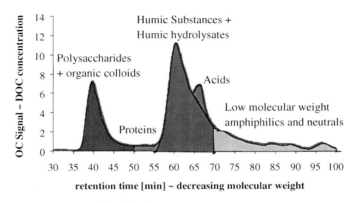

Figure 3.3 SEC-DOC chromatogram identification

The technique has been widely used in MW/MS determinations of NOM but some results reported in the literature may be misleading because of the almost exclusive reliance on a single wavelength UV detector. While UV detection is effective for humic substances, it is less effective (or ineffective) for non-humic components of NOM such as proteins and saccharides (simple sugars and polysaccharides). Non-humic components of NOM can also be problematic in water treatment – e.g., polysaccharides are reported to be a major membrane foulant (Amy and Her, 2004; Lee *et al.*, 2004). Other factors such as charge, molecular structure, steric effects and hydrophobicity may also influence the result (Wershaw and Aiken, 1985).

Her *et al.* (2003) have coupled fluorescence and variable wavelength UV detectors (which have long been used in traditional HPLC analysis of specific organic compounds) with SEC. This permits differentiation between NOM components that exhibit high UV absorptivity at 254 nm and other NOM components that are more sensitively detected at other UV wavelengths – e.g., 210 nm for amino acids and proteins (Figure 3.3). Her *et al.* (2004b) defined a UV absorbance ratio index (URI) corresponding to the ratio of UV absorbance at 210 nm to that at 254 nm – see Figure 3.4. While humic substances are characterized by a URI of 1.5 to 2.0, proteins and their amino acid building blocks show higher URI values of 5 to 10.

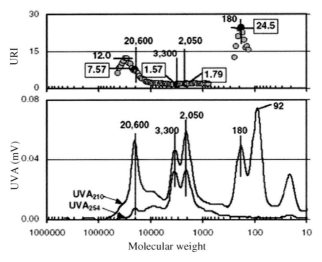

Figure 3.4 URI and HPSEC-UVA (at 210 nm and 254 nm) chromatograms of extracted foulant from a nanofiltration (NF) membrane (Adapted from Amy and Her, 2004)

Humic substances fluoresce; however, their fluorescence intensity depends on the excitation and emission wavelengths. Based on 3-D fluorescence excitation-emission matrices (F-EEM), humic substances exhibit a characteristic peak intensity around the excitation and emission ranges of 300–350 nm and 400–450 nm, while proteins exhibit a characteristic peak intensity around excitation of 250–300 nm and emission of 300–350 nm. Thus, depending on which NOM component is of interest, a fluorescence detector can be set to optimize recognition of either humic-like or protein-like NOM components, based on their respective EEM spectra (see Figure 3.5 and Figure 3.6). Fluorescence detection is, however, inappropriate for saccharides (Amy and Her, 2004).

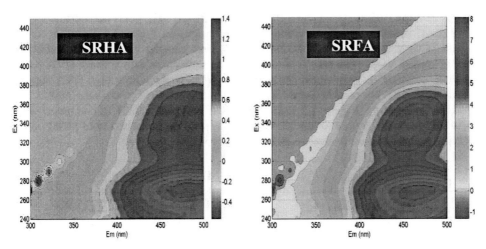

Figure 3.5 Fluorescence EEM of Suwannee River Humic Acid (SRHA) and Suwannee River Fulvic Acid (SRFA)

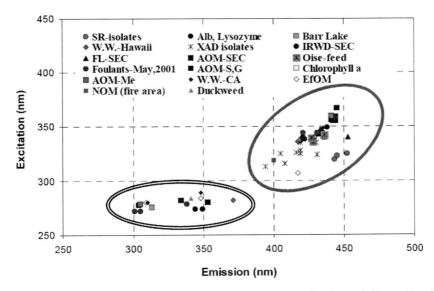

Figure 3.6 F-EEM Map of NOM. Isolates and Known Compounds: Protein- (lower left) and Humic-Like (upper right) NOM

One main application of F-EEM is as a NOM fouling indicator in membrane technology. The only problem is that erroneous analysis may result if the water has a high concentration of polysaccharides for which this method is inappropriate. This can be overcome by coupling SEC with fluorescence and variable wavelength UV detection (Amy and Her, 2004).

SEC consists of High Performance Liquid Chromatography (HPLC), UVA and on-line DOC detectors. With an on-line DOC detector, all organic compounds are recognized. Figure 3.7 illustrates chromatograms with UVA- and DOC- responses of bulk EfOM samples. Both samples exhibit UVA and DOC response peaks at similar elution times. The results show that large molecules with a small UVA peak appeared first. These compounds reflect non-humic materials. The DOC peaks with a high UVA signal at elution times between 2000–3500 s represent humic and fulvic acids, whereas peaks near 4000 s indicate low MW hydrophilic compounds. Figure 3.7 also shows that colloidal EfOM is comprised of high MW materials with low aromaticity (due to low SUVA). In this way the contribution of NOM components to the total NOM concentration can be determined.

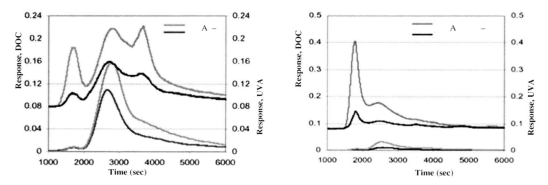

Figure 3.7 SEC chromatograms of bulk EfOM waters (left) and Colloids (right) for two different samples (A and B Secondary Effluent) (Adapted from Jarusutthirak et al., (2002))

SEC values calculated as the height of the peaks in the SEC chromatogram indicate the amount of NOM in a specific molecular size fraction. The sum of the peak areas in the chromatogram represents the total amount of NOM in the sample, with the peak having the lowest retention time referring to the highest MW and vice versa (Figure 3.8).

A recent major achievement has been the interfacing of an on-line organic carbon detector (based on the *Gräntzel* thin film reactor) with SEC to permit recognition of all NOM components. In order to purify the inorganic carbon, phosphoric acid (at pH 1.5) is added and nitrogen is used as a carrier gas to bring the carbon dioxide to the organic carbon detectors.

Liquid chromatography with organic carbon detection (LC-OCD, also called SEC-DOC) can be used to effectively monitor polar NOM components with a lower SUVA. LC-OCD has been successfully applied to monitoring changes in NOM associated with bank infiltration, soil aquifer treatment, ozone oxidation, coagulation, adsorption, bio-filtration and membrane separation (Her et al., 2002). It has also been used to identify problematic NOM components in membrane fouling (Her *et al.*, 2004a; Salinas Rodríguez *et al.*, 2008). LC-OCD chromatography separates components according to their size ranging from higher to lower, providing a MW/MS distribution. The resultant peaks can be classified as the biopolymers peak (consisting of macromolecules such as polysaccharides, proteins, amino-sugars – more precisely N-acetyl heteropolysaccharides, and possibly organic colloids), the humic substances peak, building blocks and the low MW compounds (acids) peak. Different columns have been used to optimize separation over higher versus lower MW ranges. An LC-OCD or SEC chromatogram can be represented in terms of either retention time or, if calibration chemicals are used, in terms of MW distribution – Daltons (Amy and Her, 2004).

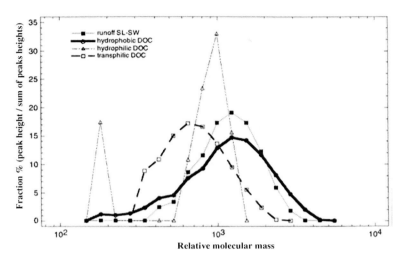

Figure 3.8 Relative molecular mass distribution (by SEC) of the NOM fractions contained in the (■) runoff Silver Lake surface water (SL-SW): (heavy solid line) hydrophobic DOC, (thin solid line) hydrophilic DOC, and (dashed line) transphilic DOC (Adapted from Cho et al., 2000)

A typical chromatogram of NOM contained in surface water is shown in Figure 3.9. The first fraction identified after approximately 25–45 minutes (first peak – largest molecular size) is the biopolymers peak with significant of organic carbon detection (OCD) only. The organic colloids and proteins present in this fraction provide response in OCD and UV detection. The second and third fraction response in OCD and UVD is attributed to humic substances and building blocks. The fourth response to OCD and UV detection is attributed to low MW organics. Low MW neutrals and amphiphilic species compose the last main fraction.

3.3.9 Biodegradable Dissolved Organic Carbon (BDOC)

Biodegradable dissolved organic carbon (BDOC) determines the amount of dissolved organic carbon (DOC) utilized for growth and activity of microorganisms (Servais et al., 1987). There are a number of different methods to measure the BDOC in water. Firstly, BDOC can be measured by a plug-flow biofilm reactor which consists of a glass column filled with bioactive glass beads. BDOC is a difference in DOC concentrations for influent and effluent of the reactor (Kaplan and Newbold, 1995; Trulleyová and Rulík, 2004). The second method of BDOC determination is to use a natural assemblage of bacteria from the environment where samples are taken for BDOC, and determine different DOC concentrations during an incubation period. Also, there is a BDOC method developed by Joret and Levi (1986) for drinking water using bioactive sand from a water treatment plant. Again, BDOC is determined as the difference of DOC concentration in an Erlenmeyer flask contained bioactive sand during an incubation period. Currently, there is no one absolute or well accepted method for BDOC measurement. The estimation of biodegradable dissolved organic matter is also affected by the amount of active biomass and microbial diversity in a system. Khan *et al.* (1999) suggested that mixed liquor suspended solids from a biological wastewater treatment plant is an effective BDOC inoculum because the microbial biomass and diversity in activated sludge systems is sufficient to biodegrade dissolved organic matter. Moreover, some methods for BDOC measurement have been standardized (APHA, 1998).

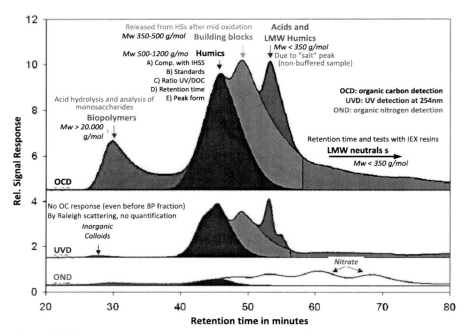

Figure 3.9 Typical NOM chromatogram of a surface water sample (Huber, 2007)

BDOC plays an important role in supplying safe water through drinking water distribution systems. The potential of bacteria (i.e., biofilm) growth is a function of the BDOC which is one of main factors controlling bacterial regrowth in a drinking water distribution system (Block *et al.*, 1993). Growth of bacteria can also lead to a variety of problems including the possibility of pathogen contamination and the formation of taste and odor (Miltner *et al.*, 1992). Several previous studies were carried out to determine threshold values of BDOC using different methods, and they suggested that BDOC should be less than 0.15 mg/L for the water to be considered biologically stable (Volk *et al.*, 1994; Servais *et al.*, 1995; Laurent *et al.*, 1999; Volk and LeChevallier, 2000; Niquette *et al.*, 2001). Also, Marcoonet *et al.* (2009) observed a positive correlation between the BDOC concentration of feed water and the biofouling on the surface of nanofiltration (NF) membranes. This study demonstrated that higher BDOC concentrations lead to more biofilm development which decreases permeability of NF membranes. Higher BDOC concentration can also increase microbial density associated with sediment at the first few centimeters of bank filtration transects, and an increase of active biomass attached to sediment causes a reduction in hydraulic conductivity during infiltration. In contrast to a slow sand filter or an artificial recharge and recovery system, it is not possible for riverbank filtration or lake bank filtration sites to remove a clogging layer; thus, BDOC is an important factor to monitor during riverbank filtration to maintain a constant pumping rate as well as understanding hydrogeochemical conditions during infiltration. Also, higher BDOC concentrations in surface water turn redox conditions in an aquifer to more anoxic condition because it requires more oxygen demand by microorganisms during infiltration.

3.3.10 Polarity Rapid Assessment Method (PRAM)

Polarity rapid assessment method (PRAM) characterizes the polarity of bulk organic matter by measuring the fraction of substances adsorbed onto different solid-phase extraction (SPE) sorbents (Rosario-Ortiz et al., 2004; Rosario-Ortiz et al., 2007a). Non-polar sorbents (C18, C8, C2), polar sorbents (CN, silica and diol) and anionic sorbents (NH2 and SAX) are commonly used to characterize the polarity of bulk organic matter under ambient conditions. Non-polar sorbents and polar sorbents extract hydrophobic organic matter and hydrophilic organic matter, respectively. Anionic sorbents characterize the negative charge of bulk organic matter. PRAM uses the normalized UVA breakthrough curve to determine the amount of total materials adsorbed defined by a retention coefficient (RC). RC is expressed as $1 - C_{max}/C_0$ (C_{max}: maximum absorbance after break through curve and C_0: absorbance of original sample) (Rosario-Ortiz et al., 2007a; Philibert et al., 2008). Using different properties of sorbents, PRAM analysis depicts different degrees of polarity in bulk organic matter originating from different sources or water treatment steps.

PRAM was used to characterize dissolved organic matter originating from different source waters, and samples were taken from the four major tributaries of Lake Mead, USA (Rosario-Ortiz et al., 2007b). There were clear distinctions in the hydrophobic/hydrophilic characters between different water sources. Rosario-Ortiz et al. (2009) demonstrated PRAM applications for different water treatment processes (e.g., membrane, ozonation, coagulation and biofiltration). Hydrophobic and hydrophilic characteristics of NOM were decreased during coagulation, flocculation and biofiltration. SPE cartridges of C18, silica and amino were used for column studies simulating bank filtration. Philibert et al. (2008) compared PRAM with the XAD resin method, and they suggested the C18 appeared to be a direct surrogate for XAD-8 resin, but the diol is not feasible to represent XAD-4. PRAM can be used as an analytical tool for bulk organic matter characteristics and provides insightful information about variability of bulk organic matter.

3.4 CASE STUDIES OF NOM ANALYSIS FOR ASSESSMENT, IMPROVEMENT AND DESIGN AND OPERATION OF WATER TREATMENT SYSTEMS

3.4.1 Surface Water Treatment

Water samples were collected from the two-stage drinking water treatment train of Amsterdam Water Supply operated by Waternet which consists of Loenderveen pre-treatment and Weespekarspel post-treatment plants. The former treats seepage water from the Bethune Polder, near Maarssen, by coagulation, retention in a surface water reservoir for about 100 days and rapid sand filtration. The pretreated water is then transported to Weesperkarspel where it is treated further by ozonation, pellet softening, activated carbon filtration and slow sand filtration. Table 3.2 shows the characteristics of raw and treated water samples taken during the period January–December 2007. The relatively high mean DOC (8.7 mg/L) and moderate mean SUVA (3.5 L/mg/m) indicate that the raw water contains NOM of moderate aromaticity. The DOC of the final water is reduced by about 65% to an average of 2.9 mg/L, and the mean SUVA is reduced to 1.5 L/mg/m. This low SUVA is indicative of NOM with low aromaticity and which is, hence, more biodegradable.

Table 3.2 Bulk NOM characteristics of raw surface water and treated water samples

Sample	DOC (mg/L)		UV_{254} (m^{-1})		SUVA (L/mg/m)	
	Mean	S.D.	Mean	S.D.	Mean	S.D.
Raw surface water	8.7	1.3	27.1	3.3	3.5	0.3
Treated water	2.9	0.5	3.8	0.6	1.5	0.1

LC-OCD results show that humic substances comprise around 70% of the DOC of the raw water as well as of the treated water. Low molecular weight neutrals and 'building blocks', which are hydrolysates of humic substances, each contribute 13% of the raw water DOC. The contribution of the 'building blocks' increased to 17% after treatment, partly as a result of oxidation of some humic substances by ozonation. The more readily biodegradable biopolymers, which contribute about 2% of the DOC in the raw water, are completely removed during treatment. Fluorescence EEMs also show that the raw water is dominated by humic-like DOC. Figure 3.10 shows typical F-EEM spectra for raw and treated water samples as well as a differential spectrum, which shows the reduction in fluorescence after treatment.

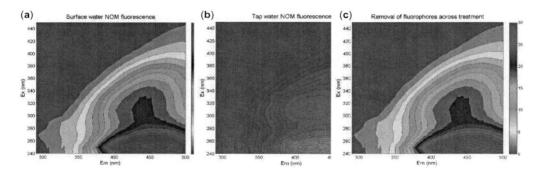

Figure 3.10 Typical fluorescence EEM spectra: a) Surface water, b) Tap water and c) Differential F-EEM indicating reduction of humic-like and protein-like NOM fractions across the treatment train

3.4.2 Groundwater Treatment

Water samples from two groundwater drinking water treatment plants operated by Vitens, a Dutch water supply company, were characterized using DOC, UV_{245} and fluorescence EEM measurements. Source waters for both plants, located in Oldeholtpade and Spannenburg, respectively, have relatively high DOC (8–10 mg/L) and both produced water with yellowish colour (15–22 mg/L Pt-Co) prior to the upgrading of the former with an ion exchange reactor. Originally, both were conventional groundwater treatment plants consisting of plate aeration, rapid sand filtration, pellet softening, and rapid sand filtration, but in order to reduce the colour, an ion exchange reactor was added at the end of the Oldeholtpade process train.

The DOC was reduced by about 50% at Oldeholtpade and by only about 10% at Spannenburg. For the latter case, SUVA was increased by less than 10% (2.3 to 2.5 L/mg/m), indicating that there was no significant change in the aromaticity and the molecular weight of NOM after treatment. In the former, SUVA was reduced by about 55%, from 3.7 to 1.6 L/mg/m, clearly showing the effectiveness of ion exchange in the removal of the more hydrophobic and aromatic NOM fractions (acids). The low SUVA (<2 L/mg/m) of the treated water from Oldeholtpade is typical of hydrophilic and relatively low molecular weight NOM which is less aromatic and generally more biodegradable. The treated water from the two plants had comparable values of assimilable organic carbon (AOC), 14 µg/L for Oldehaltpad and 10 µg/L for Spannenburg, while the latter had twice as much DOC.

3.4.3 Seawater Desalination

Organic matter characterization for representative estuarine/bay waters and seawaters from different locations are presented in this section.

The results of the characterization by LC-OCD for "raw water" are shown in Figure 3.11. For the three "seawater-representative" locations, the DOC content is, on average, 1 mg/L where the humic substances represent about 50 % of the DOC content. In the case of the specific estuarine water, the DOC content is around 5 mg/L (see Table 3.3). Additionally, the LC-OCD results for fresh water are included to illustrate the main differences among these three waters.

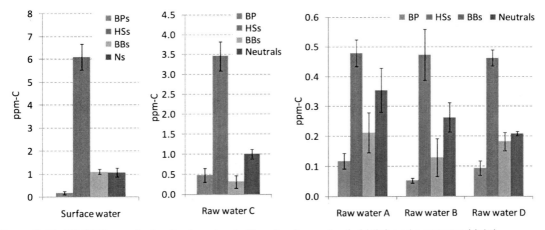

Figure 3.11 LC-OCD results for: fresh water (left), estuarine water (middle) and seawater (right)

Table 3.3 DOC and SUVA values for different raw waters (L/mg · m)

Parameter	Surface Water	Site A (seawater)	Site B (seawater)	Site C (estuarine water)	Site D (seawater)
DOC (mg/L)	8.7 ± 1.3	1.16 ± 0.16	0.92 ± 0.09	5.26 ± 0.56	0.95 ± 0.03
SUVA (L/mg.m)	3.5 ± 0.3	1.14 ± 0.59	0.70 ± 0.05	3.03 ± 0.54	0.89 ± 0.22

The samples from site A and site B are from the Western Mediterranean Sea while sample D comes from the Eastern Mediterranean Sea. Site C samples are derived from an estuary of the North Sea (Electric conductivity between 1 and 9 mS/cm). The DOC and SUVA values for the plants are shown in Table 4.2.

Figure 3.12 shows the average values for all analyzed samples. Variations represent the maximum and minimum values of the samples. Higher variation is present in humic substances and building blocks in comparison to neutrals and biopolymers.

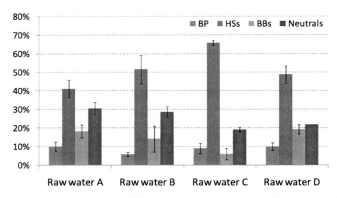

Figure 3.12 Typical organic matter fractions (%) (Mediterranean Sea and the North Sea)

LC-OCD results show that humic substances are the higher-concentration fraction in seawater and estuarine water compared with biopolymers, building blocks and neutrals. Typically, humic substances (0.5 – 5 kDa in size) represent ~50 % of the DOC content while the biopolymer fraction (>20 kDa) is less than 8 % of the total DOC. In the case of estuarine water, the humic substances represent ~65 % of the total DOC and biopolymers ~10 %.

F-EEM is an effective tool to characterize protein-like versus humic-like components. Figure 3.13 shows the F-EEM for Site A water, highlighting the different peak locations of typical organic components.

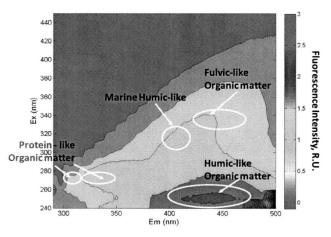

Figure 3.13 Typical F-EEM for Mediterranean water (DOC ~1 mg/L)

3.4.4 Bank Filtration and Artificial Recharge and Recovery

Two 5-meter long sand columns (SC1 and SC2) were used to investigate the fate of natural organic matter and the impacts of wastewater effluent (i.e., effluent organic matter, EfOM) on the removal of dissolved organic matter during riverbank filtration. The bottom of each column was packed with filter media support of 15 cm thick-graded gravel and then filled with silica sand sized between 0.8 and 1.25 mm. Sand columns were operated under a down-flow mode with an empty bed contact time (EBCT) of 8.9 days. SC1 was fed with the river Maas water (The Netherlands), while SC2 was fed with a mixture of the river Maas water and secondary effluent from a wastewater treatment plant (1:1 ratio) from a municipal wastewater treatment plant (Hoek van Holland, The Netherlands). More detail of this system has been described in Maeng et al. (2008). Table 3.4 shows pH, DOC, BDOC, and SUVA values for SC1 and SC2. For SC2, SUVA increased as a result of biodegradation of aliphatic organic matter originating from EfOM.

Table 3.4 Characteristics of influent and effluent–sand column (SC) experiment

		pH	DOC (mg/L)	BDOC (mg/L)	SUVA (L/mg m)
SC1 (The river Maas)	Influent	7.85	3.66	0.67	2.46
	Effluent	7.81	2.99		2.34
SC2 (The river Maas and secondary effluent, 1:1)	Influent	7.50	9.67	3.24	2.90
	Effluent	7.99	6.43		3.27

F-EEM spectra were measured for SC1 and SC2. Figure 3.14 shows F-EEM spectra of SC1 and SC2 at different depths (e.g., 0, and 5 meter). SC2 consists of EfOM which originated from a biological wastewater treatment process. In contrast to NOM, more biopolymer fraction was present in the EfOM, and the biopolymer was comprised of proteins (up to 60%) and polysaccharides (40–95%) (Felmming and Wingender, 2001). This explains the high FI of the protein-like peak (P3) that appeared in a sample from SC2. As shown in Figure 3.14, fluorescence intensities of humic-like peaks (P1 and P2) and P3 were gradually reduced along soil passage of the SC1 and SC2 columns. Figure 3.15 shows the differential spectra between influent and effluent of SC1 and SC2. The spectrum of each effluent from SC1 and SC2 was subtracted from the influent spectrum from SC1 and SC2. Reductions in fluorescence index (FI) of P1, P2 and P3 for SC2 were significantly greater than that of SC1. Humic-like substances in secondary effluent (P1 and P2) also appear to be more biodegradable, and a significant reduction of the FI was also observed in P3 for the SC2.

Figure 3.16 shows the LC-OCD results of SC1 and SC2. Biopolymers defined by LC-OCD (MW > 20,000 Da) in SC1 and SC2 were removed 55% and 91%, respectively. The biopolymer fraction in the SC2 appeared to be removed rapidly during the column study. These results are consistent with those of a previous study done by Jekel and Grünheid (2003) at the Lake Tegel bank filtration site (Berlin, Germany). Jekel and Grünheid (2003) showed that the removal of polysaccharides (i.e., biopolymers) was higher compared to the rest of the fractions as determined by LC-OCD. The removal of high MW DOC (i.e., biopolymers) of DOC during riverbank filtration is beneficial for the post treatment processes. Removal efficiencies of humic fractions from SC1 and SC2 were 11% and 22%, respectively. Part of the humic fraction in SC2, originating from the wastewater treatment plant, may have more biodegradable characteristics; however, significant removal of the humic fraction was not achieved. This result corresponds with the F-EEM result where the removals of humic-like peaks (P1 and P2) in SC2 were relatively high.

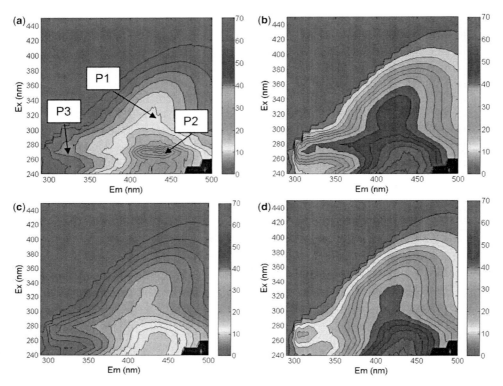

Figure 3.14 F-EEM spectra of SC1 (left) and SC2 (right) at: 0-meter, (a) and (b), and 5.0-meters, (c) and (d), under oxic conditions [Y-axis: excitation wavelengths (nm), X-axis: emission wavelengths (nm)]

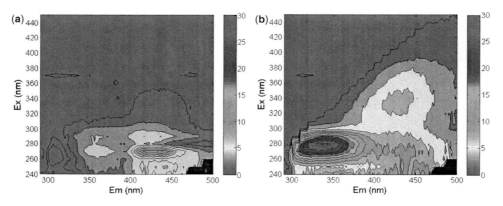

Figure 3.15 Differential F-EEM spectra of (a) SC1 and (b) SC2 under oxic conditions

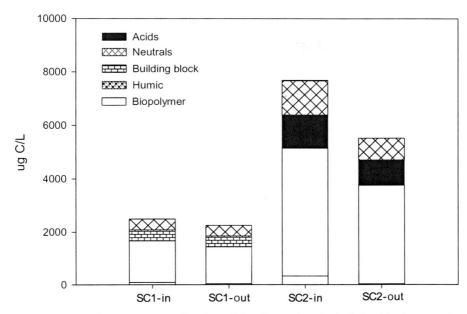

Figure 3.16 The change of organic matter fractions (biopolymer, humic, building block, neutrals and acids) determined by LC-OCD for SC1 and SC2

Three different sorbents, C18, silica and amino, were applied to influent and effluent samples of SC1 for PRAM. The non-polar character of organic matter (C18) (i.e., hydrophobic component) slightly decreased during infiltration, and these fractions in influent and effluent samples were 20 and 15%, respectively. The uncharged polar character of dissolved organic matter significantly decreased during infiltration, and this corresponded to the reduction in biopolymer fraction (i.e., hydrophilic-neutral) from LC-OCD analysis, as explained above. The anionic fraction of NOM slightly increased after infiltration due to the reduction of neutral organic matter. PRAM can be used as an analytical tool and provides insightful information about variability in bulk organic matter characteristics during subsurface infiltration.

3.5 PERSPECTIVES AND RECOMMENDATIONS

A better understanding of NOM character and its removal by various treatment methods is essential to improve treated water quality meeting increasingly stringent standards. In order to have a better insight into the types of organic compounds present before and after different water treatment processes several characterization techniques have been developed worldwide. These have provided considerable knowledge in understanding the impact of NOM on treatment processes. The characterization techniques differ considerably in terms of analytical approach, NOM fractionations or components analyzed, time and skills required, costs, and the form of the output or results (whether it can be interpreted easily and used by the treatment plant operators) (Chow et al., 2003).

Comparative analysis of different methods of characterization of NOM has clearly shown that there is no single method which can fully reveal its characteristics that are important for water treatment practice. It is obvious that use of combinations of different methods would be required for proper analysis of the fate of different fractions of NOM during different treatment processes. However, the methods of characterization to be applied under given conditions depend on the source of NOM and treatment methods applied.

In the absence of high skills and costly instruments, tracking DOC and SUVA changes along the treatment process train could be a basic approach in understanding the removal of NOM. High pressure liquid chromatography using gels have proved useful in combination with UV/vis, fluorescence, light scattering and sensitive dissolved organic carbon detection techniques, yielding information on molecular absorbance, size distribution, molar mass and reactivity. Information on biodegradability of NOM can be deduced from experimental measurement of bacterial growth under defined conditions. The nature and amount of biologically assimilable organic carbon (AOC) in combination with the bacterial cell number and growth rate constants can provide a meaningful characterization of microbial stability in aquatic systems (Frimmel, 1998).

3.6 REFERENCES

Abbt-Braun, G., Frimmel, F. H. and Schulten, H. R. (1990), Strukturelle Charakterisierung isolierter aquatischer huminstoffe – Anwendbarkeit, Grenzen und Vergleich ausgewahlter Methoden. *Vom Wasser*, **74**, 325–338.

Aiken, G. and Leenheer, J. (1993) Isolation and chemical characterization of dissolved and colloidal organic matter. *Chemistry and Ecology*, **8**, 135–151.

Aiken, G.R., Mcknight, D.M., Wershaw, R.L. and Maccarthy, P. (1985) Humic Substances in Soil, Sediment, and Water: In: *Geochemistry, Isolation and Characterization*, John Wiley & Sons, New York, p. 691.

Amy, G. (1994) Using NOM Characterisation for Evaluation of Treatment. In *Proceedings of Workshop on "Natural Organic Matter in Drinking Water, Origin, Characterization and Removal"*, September 19–22, 1993, Chamonix, France. American Water Works Association Research Foundation, Denver, USA, 243 pages.

Amy, G. and Her, N. (2004) Size exclusion chromatography (SEC) with multiple detectors: a powerful tool in treatment process selection and performance monitoring. *Wat. Sci. Tech.*: Water Supply, **4**, 19–24.

Anselme, C., Mandra, V., Baudin, I. and Mallevialle, J. (1994) Optimum use of membrane processes in drinking-water treatment. *Water Supply*, **12**, 1–2.

APHA, AWWA and WEF (1998) *Standard Methods for the Examination of Water and Wastewater*. 20th edn. Washington, DC: American Public Health Association.

AWWARF (2000) Natural Organic Matter in Drinking Water: Recommendations to Water Utilities. *American Water Works Association Research Foundation*, Denver, USA.

Badr, E.-S. A., Achterberg, E. P., Tappin, A. D., Hill, S. J., and Braungardt, C. B. (2003) Determination of dissolved organic nitrogen in natural waters using high-temperature catalytic oxidation. *TrAC Trends in Analytical Chemistry*, **22** (11), 819–827.

Block, J.C., Haudidier, K., Paquin, J.L., Miazga, J. and Levi, Y. (1993) Biofilm accumulation in drinking water distribution systems. *Biofouling*. **6**, 333–343.

Boehme, J., Coble, P., Conmy, R. and Stovall-Leonard, A. (2004) Examining CDOM fluorescence variability using principal component analysis: seasonal and regional modeling of three-dimensional fluorescence in the Gulf of Mexico. *Marine Chemistry*, **89** (1-4), 3–14.

Bro, R. (1997) PARAFAC. Tutorial and applications. Chemometrics and Intelligent Laboratory Systems, **38** (2), 149–171.

Chen, J., LeBoeuf, E. J., Dai, S. and Gu, B. (2003) Fluorescence spectroscopic studies of natural organic matter fractions. *Chemosphere*, **50**, 639–647.

Cho, J. and Amy, G. (1999) Interactions between natural organic matter (NOM) and membranes: rejection and fouling. *Wat. Sci. Tech.*, **40**, 131–139.

Cho, J., Amy, G. and Pellegrino, J. (2000) Membrane filtration of natural organic matter: factors and mechanisms affecting rejection and flux decline with charged ultra filtration (UF) membrane. *Jour. Memb. Sci.*, **164**, 89–110.

Chow, C., Fabris, R. and Drikas, M. (2003) A Rapid Organic Characterisation Tool To Optimise Water Treatment Processes. In: Natural Organic Matter In *Drinking Water: Problems and Solutions. Cooperative Research Centre for Water Quality and Treatment*, Australia, Occasional Paper Number 6, 11–16.

Coble, P. G. (1996) Characterization of marine and terrestrial DOM in seawater using excitation-emission matrix spectroscopy. *Marine Chemistry*, **51**, 325–346.

Coble, P. G., Schultz, C. A. and Mopper, K. (1993) Fluorescence contouring analysis of DOC intercalibration experiment samples: a comparison of techniques. *Marine Chemistry*, **41**, 173–178.

Collins, M.R., Amy, G.L. and King, P.H. (1985) Removal of organic matter in water treatment. *Jour. Envir. Engi.*, **11**, 850–64.

Collins, M.R., Amy, G.L. and Steelink, C. (1986) Molecular weight distribution, carboxylic acidity and humic substances content of aquatic organic matter: implications for removal during water treatment. *Envir Sci. Tech.*, **20**, 1028–32.

Crozes G., White P. and Marshall M. (1995) Enhanced coagulation: its effects on NOM removal and chemical costs: *Journal AWWA*, **87** (1), 78–89.

Dafner, E. V. and Wangersky, P. J. (2002) A brief overview of modern directions in marine DOC studies Part I.— Methodological aspects. *J. Environ. Monit.*, **4**, 48–54.

Dai, X., Zou, L., Yan, Z., and Millikan, M. (2009) Adsorption characteristics of N-nitrosodimethylamine from aqueous solution on surface-modified activated carbons. *Journal of Hazardous Materials*. **168** (1), 51–56.

Drewes, J. E. and Summers, R.S. (2002) Natural organic matter removal during riverbank filtration: current knowledge and research needs. In: *Riverbank Filtration: Improving Source-Water Quality*. C. Ray, G. Melin, and R. B. Linsky (eds.), Kluwer Academic Publishers, Dordrecht, The Netherlands, 303–310.

Edzwald, J. K. and Tobiason, J. E. (1999) Enhanced Coagulation: USA requirements and a broader view. In: *Removal of Humic Substances from Water*. Trondheim, Norway, IAWQ/IWSA Joint specialist group on particle separation.

Edzwald, J. K. and van Benschoten, J. E. (1990) Aluminum Coagulation of Natural Organic Matter. *Chemical Water and Wastewater Treatment*, 341–359.

Egeberg, P. K., Eikenes, M., and Gjessing, E. T. (1999) Organic nitrogen distribution in NOM size classes. *Environment International*. **25** (2-3), 225–236.

Fabris, R., Chow, C.W.K., Drikas, M. and Eikebrokk, B. (2008) Comparison of NOM character in selected Australian and Norwegian drinking waters. *Wat. Res.*, **42** (15), 4188–4196.

Fan, L., Harris, J. L., Roddick, F. A. and Booker, N. A. (2001) Influence of the characteristics of natural organic matter on the fouling of microfiltration membranes. *Wat. Res.*, **35**, 4455–4463.

Fettig, J. (1999) Removal of humic substances by adsorption/ion exchange. *Wat. Sci,Tech.*, **40** (9), 173–182.

Felmming, H.-C. and Wingender, J. (2001) Relevance of microbial extracellular polymeric substances (EPSs) - Part I: Structural and ecological aspects. *Wat. Sci. Tech.*, **43** (6), 1–8.

Frimmel, F.H. (1998) Characterization of natural organic matter as major constituents in aquatic systems. *Journal of Contaminant Hydrology*, **35** (1-3), 201–216.

Frimmel, F.H., Saravia, F. and Gorenflo, A. (2006) NOM removal from different raw waters by membrane filtration. *Wat. Sci. Tech. Water Supply*, **4** (4), 165–174.

Gur-Reznik, S., Katz, I. and Dosoretz, C.G. (2008) Removal of dissolved organic matter by granular-activated carbon adsorption as a pretreatment to reverse osmosis of membrane bioreactor effluents. *Wat. Res.*, **42**, 1595–1605.

Her, N., Amy, G., Foss, D. & Cho, J. (2002) Variations of molecular weight estimation by HP - size exclusion chromatography with UVA versus on-line DOC detection. *Envir. Sci. Tech.*, **36**, 3393–3399.

Her, N., Amy, G., McKnight, D., Sohn, J. and Yoon, Y. (2003) Characterisation of DOM as a function of MW by fluorescence EEM and HPLC-SEC using UVA, DOC and fluorescence detection. *Wat. Res.*, **37**, 4295–4303.

Her, N., Amy, G., Park, H. and Song, M. (2004a) Characterising algogenic organic matter (AOM) and evaluating associated NF membrane fouling. *Wat.Res.*, **38**, 1427–1438.

Her, N., Amy, G., Park, H. and Von-Gunten, U. (2004b) UV absorbance ratio index with size exclusion chromatography (URI-SEC) as a NOM property indicator. *Journal of Water Supply: Research and Technology – AQUA*, **57** (1), 35–44.

Hongve, D., Baann, J., Becher, G. and Beckmann, O-.A. (1999) Experiences from operation and regeneration of an anionic exchanger for NOM removal. *Wat. Sci.Tech.*, **40** (9), 215–221.

Huber, S. (2007) LC-OCD applications. DOC-Labor Dr. Huber, Germany (online). http:www.doc-labor.de/english_pages/What_is_LC-OCD_About/What_is_LC-OCD_about_2007-2.pdf

Humbert, H., Gallard, H., Suty, H. and Croué, J.-P. (2008) Natural organic matter (NOM) and pesticides removal using a combination of ion exchange resin and powdered activated carbon (PAC). *Wat. Res.*, **42**, 1635–1643.

IHSS (2009) What are Humic Substances? International Humic Substances Society. http:ihss.gatech.edu/ihss2/whatarehs.html

IUPAC (1971) Manual of symbols and terminology for physicochemical quantities and units, Appendix II definitions, *Terminology and symbols in colloid and surface chemistry*, D. H. Everet.

Jarusutthirak, C., Amy, G. and Croue, J. P. (2002) Fouling characteristics of wastewater effluent organic matter (EfOM) isolates on NF and UF membranes. *Desalination*, **145**, 247–255.

Jekel, M. and Grünheid, S. (2003) NASRI-Removal of Organic Substances, In: *Proceedings of Conference Wasser Berlin 2003*, pp. 31–40.

Kabsch-Korbutowicz, M. (2005a) Application of ultra filtration integrated with coagulation for improved NOM removal. *Desalination*, **174**, 13–22.

Kabsch-Korbutowicz, M. (2005b) Effect of Al coagulant type on natural organic matter removal efficiency in coagulation/ultra filtration process. *Desalination*, 185, 327–333.

Kainulainen, T., Tuhkanen, T., Vartiainen, T., Heinonen-Tanski, H. and Kalliokoski, P. (1994) The effect of different oxidation and filtration processes on the molecular size distribution of humic material. *Wat. Sci. Tech.*, **30**, 169–174.

Kaplan, L.A. and Newbold, J.D. (1995) Measurement of streamwater biodegradable dissolved organic carbon with a plug-flow bioreactor. *Wat. Res.*, **29**, 2696–2706.

Kim, S., Chon, K., Kim, S.J., Lee, S., Lee, E. and Cho, J. (2009) Uncertainty in organic matter analysis for seawater reverse osmosis (SWRO) desalination. *Desalination*, **238** (1-3), 30–36.

Krasner, S. W., Croue, J. P., Buffle, J. and Perdue, E. (1996) Three approaches for characterizing NOM. *Journal AWWA*, **88** (6), 66–79.

Korshin, G. V., Li, C. W. and Benjamin, M. M. (1997) The decrease of UV absorbance as an indicator of TOX formation. *Wat. Res.*, **31** (4), 946–949.

Korshin, G. V.; Kumke, M. U.; Li, C. W.; Frimmel, F. H. (1999) Influence of chlorination on chromophores and fluorophores in humic substances. *Environ. Sci. Tech.*, **33**, (8), 1207–1212.

Korshin, G. V., Wu, W. W., Benjamin, M. M. and Hemingway, O. (2002) Correlations between differential absorbance and the formation of individual DBPs. *Wat. Res.*, **36** (13), 3273–3282.

Labanowski, J. and Feuillade, G. (2009) Combination of biodegradable organic matter quantification and XAD-fractionation as effective working parameter for the study of biodegradability in environmental and anthropic samples. *Chemosphere*, **74** (4), 605–611.

Lainé, J.-M., Campos, C., Baudin, I. and Janex, M.-L. (2003) Understanding membrane fouling: a review of over a decade of research. *Wat. Sci. Tech.: Water Supply*, **3**, 155–164.

Laurent, P., Pévost, M., Cigana, J., Niquette, P., Servais, P. (1999) Biodegradable organic matter removal in biological filters: Evaluation of the CHABROL model. *Wat. Res.*, **33** (6) 1387–1398.

Leenheer, J. A. and Croué, J.-P. (2003) Characterizing Dissolved Aquatic Organic Matter. *Environ. Sci. Tech.*, **37** (1), 18A-26A.

Lee, N., Amy, G., Croue, J.-P. and Buisson, H. (2004) Identification and understanding of fouling in low-pressure membrane (MF/UF) filtration by natural organic matter (NOM). *Wat. Res.*, **38**, 4511–4523.

Lee, W. (2005). *Occurrence, molecular weight and treatability of dissolved organic nitrogen*. Doctoral Dissertation, Arizona State University, USA.

Lee, W., and Westerhoff, P. (2006). Dissolved organic nitrogen removal during water treatment by aluminum sulfate and cationic polymer coagulation. *Wat. Res.*, **40** (20), 3767–3774.

Maeng, S.K., Sharma, S.K., Amy, G. and Magic-Knezev, A. (2008) Fate of effluent organic matter (EfOM) and natural organic matter (NOM) through riverbank filtration. *Wat. Sci. Tech.*, **57** (12), 1999–2007.

Malcolm, R.L. and MacCarthy, P. (1992) Quantitative evaluation of XAD 8 and XAD 4 resins used in tandem for removing organic solutes from water, *Environment International*, **18** (6), 597–607.

Matilainen, A., Lindqvist, N., Korhonen, S. and Tuhkanen, T. (2002) Removal of NOM in the different stages of the water treatment process. *Environment International*, **28** (6), 457– 465.

Matilainen, A., Vieno, N. and Tuhkanen, T. (2006) Efficiency of the activated carbon filtration in the natural organic matter removal. *Environment International*, **32** (3), 324–331.

Marconnet, C., Houari, A., Galas, L., Vaudry, H., Heim, V., Di Martino, P. (2009) Biodegradable dissolved organic carbon concentration of feed water and NF membrane biofouling: a pilot train study. *Desalination*, **242**, 228–235.

Matthews, B. J. H., Jones, A. C., Theodorou, N. K. & Tudhope, A. W. (1996) Excitation-emission-matrix fluorescence spectroscopy applied to humic acid bands in coral reefs. *Marine Chemistry*, **55**, 317–332.

McKenna, J.H. and Doering, P.H. (1995) Measurement of dissolved organic carbon by wet checmial oxidation with persulfate: influence of chloride concentration and reagent volume. *Marine Chemistry*, **48**, 109–114.

McCreary, J.J. and Snoeyink, V. L. (1980) Characterization and activated carbon adsorption of several humic substances. *Wat. Res.*, **14**, 151– 160.

Miltner, R.J., Shukairy, H.M., Summers, R.S. (1992) Disinfection by-product formation and control by ozonation and biofiltration. *Journal AWWA*, **84**, 53–62.

Niquette, P., Servais, P. and Savoir., R. (2001). Bacterial dynamics in a drinking water distribution system in Brussels. *Wat. Res.*, **35** (3), 675–682.

NOMINIC (2009) Natural Organic Matter in the Nordic Countries. NOMINIC homepage http://www.kjemi.uio.no/envir/nominic/documents/background.html

NRC (2008) *Prospects for Managed Underground Storage of Recoverable Water*. Committee on Sustainable Underground Storage of Recoverable Water, National Research Council, USA. Published by National Academy Press, USA.

Owen, D.M., Amy, G.L. and Chowdhury, Z.K. (1993) Characterization of natural organic matter and its relationship to treatability. American Water Works Association Research Foundation, Denver, USA, 250 pages.

Ødegaard, H., Melin, E., and Leiknes, T. (2006) Ozonation/biofiltration for treatment of humic surface water", in: *Recent Progress in Slow Sand and Alternative Biofiltration Processes*, Gimbel, R., Graham, N. J. D., and Collins, M. R. (eds.), IWA Publishing, London, 397–405.

Osterhus, S. Azrague, K., Leiknes, T. and Odegaard, H. (2007) Membrane filtration for particles removal after ozonation-biofiltration. *Wat.Sci.Tech.*, **56** (10), 101–108.

Petterson, C., Ephraim, J. and Allard, B. (1994) On the composition and properties of humic substances isolated from deep groundwater and surface waters. *Organic Geochemistry*, **21**, 443–451.

Persson, T. and Wedborg, M. (2001) Multivariate evaluation of the fluorescence of aquatic organic matter. *Analytica Chimica Acta*, **434** (2), 179–192.

Philibert, M., Bush, S., and, F.L.R.-O. and Suffet, I.H. (2008) Advances in the characterization of the polarity of DOM under ambient water quality conditions using the polarity rapid assessment method. *Wat. Sci. Tech.*, **8**, 725–733.

Potschka, M. (1993) Mechanism of size exclusion chromatography. *J. Chromatography*, **648**, 41–69.

Rinnan, A. (2004) *Application of PARAFAC on spectral data*. Faculty of Sciences, Univerisity of Copenhagen, Copenhagen, Denmark.

Rosario-Ortiz, F.L., Gerringer, F.W. and Suffet, I.H., (2009) Application of a novel polarity method for the characterization of natural organic matter during water treatment. *J. Water Supply Research and Technology – AQUA*, **58**, 159–169.

Rosario-Ortiz, F.L., Kozawa, K., Al-Samarrai, H.N., Gerringer, F.W., Gabelich, C.J. and Suffet, I.H. (2004) Characterization of the changes in polarity of natural organic matter using solid-phase extraction: introducing the NOM polarity rapid assessment method (NOM-PRAM). *Wat.Sci.Tech.*, **40**, 11–18.

Rosario-Ortiz, F.L., Snyder, S. and Suffet, I.H. (2007a) Characterization of the Polarity of Natural Organic Matter under Ambient Conditions by the Polarity Rapid Assessment Method (PRAM). *Environ. Sci. Tech.*, **41**, 4895–4900.

Rosario-Ortiz, F.L., Snyder, S.A. and Suffet, I.H. (2007b) Characterization of dissolved organic matter in drinking water sources impacted by multiple tributaries. *Wat. Res.*, **41**, 4115–4128.

Salinas Rodríguez, S. G., Kennedy, M. D., Schippers, J. C. & Amy, G. (2008) Identification of organic foulants in estuarine and seawater reverse osmosis systems – Comparison for different pre-treatments. In EDS-INSA (Ed.) In: *Proceedings of Membranes in Drinking Water Production and Wastewater Treatment Conference (20–22 October 2008)*. Toulouse, France, European Desalination Society.

Schäfer, A. I. (2001) *Natural Organics Removal using Membranes*, Technomic Publishing Co, Australia.

Servais, P., Billen, G. and Hascoët, M.-C. (1987) Determination of the biodegradable fraction of dissolved organic matter in waters. *Wat. Res.*, **21**, 445–450.

Servais P., Laurent, P. and Gatel D. (1995b) Characterization of dissolved organic matter biodegradability in waters: impact of water treatment and bacterial regrowth in distribution systems. In: *AWWA-WQTC Proceedings*, New Orleans, USA, pp. 2175–2190.

Sharp, J.H. (1993) The Dissolved Organic Carbon Controversy: An Update. *Oceanography*, **6**(2), 45–50.

Shon, H. K., Vigneswaran, S. and Snyder, S. A.(2006) Effluent Organic Matter (EfOM) in Wastewater: Constituents, Effects, and Treatment. Critical Reviews in *Environ. Sci. Tech.*, **36** (4), 327- 374.

Stedmon, C. A., Markager, S. and Bro, R. (2003) Tracing dissolved organic matter in aquatic environments using a new approach to fluorescence spectroscopy. *Marine Chemistry*, **82**, 239–254.

Thurman, E. M. (1985) *Organic Geochemistry of Natural Waters*, Dordrecht, Martinus Nijhoff/Dr Junk W Publishers.

Trulleyová, S. and Rulík, M. (2004) Determination of biodegradable dissolved organic carbon in waters: comparison of batch methods. *Sci. Total Environ.*, **332** (1-3), 253–260.

Volk, C., Renner, C. and Joret, J.C. (1994) Comparison of two techniques for measuring the biodegradable organic carbon in water. *Environ. Tech.*, **15**, 545–556.

Volk, C.J. and LeChevallier, M.W. (2000) Assessing biodegradable organic matter. *Journal AWWA*, **92**, 64–76.

Weiss, W. J., Bouwer, E. J., Ball, W. P., O'Melia, C. R., Aboytes, R., and Speth, T. F. (2004) Riverbank filtration: Effect of ground passage on NOM character. *Journal of Water Supply: Research and Technology - AQUA*, **53** (2), 61–83.

Wershaw, R. L. & Aiken, G. R. (1985) Molecular size and weight measurements of humic substances. In *Humic Substances in Soil, Sediment and Water*. MacCarthy, P., (eds.), pp 477–492, John Wiley & Sons, New York.

Westerhoff, P., Chen, W. and Esparza, M. (2001) Organic Compounds in the Environment Fluorescence Analysis of a Standard Fulvic Acid and Tertiary Treated Wastewater. *J. Environ. Qual.*, **30**, 2037–2046.

Yang, W. C., Gan, J., Liu, W. P., and Green, R. (2005) Degradation of N-Nitrosodimethylamine (NDMA) in Landscape Soils. *J. Environ Qual*, **34** (1), 336–341.

Chapter 4
Technologies for the Removal of Natural Organic Matter

H. Ødegaard, S. Østerhus, E. Melin and B. Eikebrokk

4.1 INTRODUCTION

NOM in water is a major concern and should be removed from drinking water for a number of reasons, including that NOM: a) affects organoleptic properties of water (colour, taste and odour); b) reacts with disinfectants used in water treatment, thus reducing their disinfection power; c) influences disinfectant demand and process design, operation and maintenance; d) produces disinfection by-products (DBPs) of various kinds; e) affects stability and removal of inorganic particles; f) influences heavily on coagulant demand; g) may control coagulation conditions and coagulation performance; h) affects corrosion processes; i) affects biostability and biological regrowth in distribution systems; j) forms complexes with and increase mobility of chemical substances found in nature; k) fouls membranes; l) reduces adsorption capacity of GAC/PAC by pore blocking, m) competes with taste and odour for adsorption sites in GAC/PAC (Eikebrokk et al., 2006).

The main NOM component in Norwegian water is attributed to humic substances (HS) that have several characteristics that are influencing on how NOM may be removed from water:

(1) Because of the large size of the humic substance molecules (MW 10,000 – 100,000), it is possible to separate HS directly from water by molecular sieving through a sufficiently tight membrane (nano-filtration)
(2) Because the HS molecules are negatively charged at drinking water pH, they can be coagulated, adsorbed to metal hydroxide and subsequently removed by floc separation
(3) Because of the negative charge, HS may be removed by chemical sorption (ion exchange). HS may also be adsorbed on activated carbon (physical adsorption)
(4) Since the color of HS is associated with its aromatic content and C=C bonds, the color can be removed by breaking these bonds through the addition of a strong oxidant
(5) Since HS is the end-point of nature's biodegradation, HS is close to being non-biodegradable. By use of a strong oxidising agent, however, the large HS molecules may be broken into smaller, biodegradable components, removable by biofiltration

4.2 MEMBRANE (NANO) FILTRATION

Research on membrane filtration (nano/ultra-filtration) for the removal of humic substances was started at the university in Trondheim already around 1975 (Ødegaard and Kootatep, 1982) and the first full-scale plant was put into operation in 1990. Since then membrane filtration has become very popular in Norway and more than 100 nanofiltration (NF) plants are in operation at this time. Most of the plants are small, the largest plant having a design flow of 16,000 m^3/d.

All the Norwegian NF plants are based on spiral wound modules and the majority on cellulose acetate (CA) membranes, with a few exceptions based on polyamide (PA) membranes. The typical pore size of the membranes is 1–5 nm (1000–2000 Da) operated at a pressure of 4–8 bar (Ødegaard et al., 2000). The typical flow diagram of a membrane filtration plant is shown in Figure 4.1. The raw water passes first through a pre-treatment unit, normally a micro-sieve with a sieve opening of typically 50 μm. After the sieve, the pressure is raised up to the operating pressure of the membrane unit by a circulation pump. Cross-flow filtration takes place in the membrane unit resulting in a cleaned water stream (the permeate) that has passed through the membrane and a dirty water stream (the concentrate) that passes a reduction valve bringing the pressure in the concentrate back to that of the atmosphere. Some of the concentrate is recycled to the inlet in order to increase the recovery.

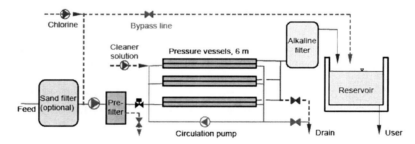

Figure 4.1 Typical flow diagram and picture of a nanofiltration plant for NOM removal

Since the reduction of calcium and bicarbonate concentration through the membrane filter is about 15–30%, an alkaline filter (calcium carbonate) is often included in order to increase the level of calcium and bicarbonate in the typically soft and corrosive Norwegian water.

In order to prevent capacity reduction over time as a result of membrane fouling, the membranes are cleaned by two different cleaning procedures; a frequent (daily) cleaning (chemical rinse) and a main cleaning that is carried out once or twice a year. In the daily cleaning, that normally lasts for about an hour and takes place during night, a chemical solution, also containing an oxidant (normally chlorine) for disinfection purposes, is pumped into the membrane module and circulated here for 20–30 minutes after which it is pumped out. Raw water is then lead through the membrane module for rinsing for 20–40 minutes before the plant is again put into operation. The plants are fully automated and the operator has only to see to that there are sufficient amounts of washing solutions and that the pressures in the plant are as intended. The main cleaning is normally carried out a couple of times per year coupled to a general service of the plant by the contractor. The washing chemicals may contain wetting agents (tensides, phosphates etc), sequesters (phosphates, EDTA etc), oxidation chemicals (peroxides, chlorine etc) and enzymes (Ødegaard et al., 2000).

The NF process is selected when the NOM-content/color is high (<30 mg mg Pt/L) and turbidity low (<1 NTU). The most typical problems encountered are those connected to capacity loss caused by fouling. In most cases this is either caused by too high design flux relative to the characteristics of the water in question, especially too high flux for waters with high particle concentration and high NOM-content. Model calculations made by Thorsen (1999) indicated that particles in the size range of about 0.1–3 μm are particularly critical for fouling. Thorsen and Fløgstad (2006) demonstrated when using a lab scale plant (flux 24 L/m^{2}h) on a colored surface water that the permeability decline was 31% over a 700 h period when using a 100 μm pre-filter before the spiral wound NF membrane and almost the same when using a 5 μm prefilter, while it was close to 0% when using a 0.1 μm prefilter. This demonstrates the importance of correct design relative to the water characteristics. Practical full-scale experiences show that the best spiral wound membranes can be operated for weeks with an almost constant flux up to 20 L/m^{2}h (Thorsen and Fløgstad, 2006) and the design flux recommended is therefore in the range of 15–18 L/m^{2}h. The criteria for success in operating a NF-plant for NOM-removal in Norway seem to be a) low flux (≤20 L/m^{2}h) combined with b) low recovery (≤70%), selection of CA-membranes (to avoid adsorptive fouling) with proper cleaning procedures, i.e. daily with a diluted solution to prevent a bound fouling layer – combined with a more comprehensive chemical cleaning once or twice a year.

4.3 COAGULATION/FILTRATION

4.3.1 General

The conventional coagulation/floc separation method (see Figure 4.2) is globally probably the most commonly used method for NOM substance removal. Principally it is constructed in a similar way as plants for turbidity removal. Since Norwegian lake water commonly is low in turbidity, the more compact flow diagrams (direct- or contact filtration), are dominating in Norway. The conventional process is used only when turbidity is higher than normal. Compact separation units (flotation and microsand ballasted lamella sedimentation) before the filter are favored when the conventional process is used.

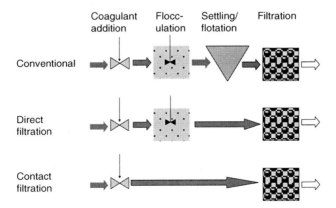

Figure 4.2 Coagulation/floc separation flow schemes

Coagulation is normally carried out by the addition of aluminium sulfate, prepolymerised aluminium chloride of iron chloride as coagulants. The primary NOM-coagulation mechanisms are: a) complexation of NOM with dissolved metal coagulant species (Al or Fe), leading to direct precipitation of a Me-NOM solid phase, b) complexation of NOM with dissolved coagulant species, leading to adsorption of this complexed material onto precipitated Me(OH)$_3$ solids, and c) direct adsorption of NOM onto the surface of precipitated Me(OH)$_3$ solids. The coagulation of waters containing both particles and NOM becomes more complicated, involving several important factors: a) the dissolved coagulant species present upon coagulant addition, b) the presence of precipitated metal hydroxide solids, c) the concentration of particles and NOM, d) the chemical properties of these contaminants and their reactivity with dissolved coagulant species, and e) the pH of coagulation, which is affected by the chemistry of the coagulant and the water alkalinity (Eikebrokk et al., 2006).

The two most important factors in order to achieve optimal coagulation, flocculation and subsequent floc attachment and retainment on the filter grains, are the coagulant dosage and the coagulation pH (see Table 4.1).

Table 4.1 Recommended pH and dose using alum (ALG), iron (JKL) or chitosan (Chi) in contact filtration of raw waters at color levels of 15, 30 and 50 mg Pt/L (Eikebrokk, 2001)

Raw water colour	Raw water SUVA L/mg C·m	Recommended specific coagulant dosage and pH mmol Me or mmol Chi/gTOC; (µg Me or µg Chi/mgPt)			
		ALG pH 5.8-6.6	JKL pH 4.0-5.5	PAX pH 5.7-6.7	CHI pH 5.0-6.0
RW15	3.8	16 (78)	16 (162)	14 (67)	0.6 (110)
RW30	4.3	20 (63)	20 (128)	17 (54)	0.7 (80)
RW50	4.8	26 (61)	26 (100)	20 (49)	0.8 (70)

–ALG-aluminium sulphate, JKL-ferric chloride; PAX-poly aluminium chloride; Chi-Chitosan
–For Me-coagulants: Dose levels needed to obtain <0.1 mg residual Me/L, >90% and 50–60% colour and TOC reduction Absolute minimum doses are 25% lower than the given practical minimum doses.
–For Chitosan: Dose levels needed to obtain >60% colour and 20–35% TOC reduction respectively

Pre-polymerised aluminium chloride (PAX) in Table 4.1 has the advantage of consuming less alkalinity than alum and is often preferred in the soft, low-alkalinity Norwegian waters. In most cases the most difficult water quality criteria to comply with, is the residual metal concentration after filtration (Eikebrokk, 2001). This has led to an increased use of iron based coagulants, especially in plants that use calcium carbonate as a filter media for corrosion control. The low optimum coagulation pH of ferric coagulants combines very well with the alkaline post-filtration because of the rapid dissolution of calcium carbonate (i.e. low contact time) and the supplementary removal of Fe-residuals in the alkaline filter bed.

The high molecular weight NOM fractions that are dominant in Norway are easier to coagulate than low molecular weight NOM. Since it is the high molecular weight fraction that contribute most to the color of the water, the color/DOC-ratio (or UV-absorption/DOC or SUVA-index) gives an indication of the dominating MW-fractions in the water and consequently of the efficacy of coagulation. A color to DOC ratio higher than 5–10 mg Pt/mg C is considered favorable, and in such cases specific dosages in the range of 0.3–0.6 mg Al/mg C or 0.03–0.06 mg Al/mg Pt, are typical (Eikebrokk, 2001).

Cationic, synthetic polymers can also be used for NOM-coagulation (Bolto et al., 1998, Kvinnsland and Ødegaard, 2004) but there is no tradition for this in Norway. However, the cationic biopolymer chitosan is used for coagulation to some extent. Chitosan can remove color reasonably well, but it is not comparable to metal coagulants with respect to DOC removal. The main advantages are related to the ease of sludge handling (biodegradable and non-toxic) and the non-existing residual metal problem. Chitosan can be used alone or in combination with a metal coagulant. In contact flocculation plants a non-ionic or anionic synthetic polymer is often used to enhance flocculation and increase filter run lengths.

Sub-optimal coagulation conditions (pH and dosage) represent various operational challenges for the whole plant as such. First of all it may lead to too high residual metal content as well as reduced filtrate quality levels (NOM, turbidity, pathogens etc), but sub-optimal conditions impact on the filter performance as well. Too high coagulant dosage, for instance, may lead to: a) short filter runs (early breakthroughs, head loss), b) reduced alkalinity/increased base consumption, c) increased sludge production (metal hydroxide), d) increased backwash water consumption and e) increased operation costs. Eikebrokk et al. (2006, 2007) developed several empirical models for the purpose of optimization of operation performance in Norwegian contact filtration plants:

(1) *Minimum required coagulant dose*:

Dose (mg Me/L) = A · Raw water Colour (mg Pt/L) + B

where A and B are constants depending on the coagulant and operational conditions. For alum A was found to be 0.043 and for iron 0.107, while B was found to be 0.30 for alum and 0.58 for iron. The practical minimum dose was recommended to be 25% higher than this.

(2) *Sludge production at optimum coagulation*:

SS (mg/L) = SS_{RW} + k · Dose

where SS_{RW} is the suspended solid concentration in the raw water including the contribution from additional processes like pH- and corrosion control, k is a constant depending on the type of coagulant and Dose is the coagulant dose (mg Me/L). For alum and ferric chloride as coagulant, k is found to be 4.2 and 2.5 respectively.

(3) *Filter run time to break through at optimum coagulation*:

t_{BT} = a $(v_f \cdot SS)^b$

where t_{BT} is time of filtration until breakthrough (hrs), v_f is rate of filtration (m/h), SS is the suspended solids concentration in coagulated water, i.e. sludge production (mg SS/L), and a and b are constants specific to the filter and coagulant. For alum without any polymer as filter aid and $SS_{RW} = 0$, the time of filtration has been found to be: $t_{BT} = 298 \, (v_f \cdot Dose_{Al})^{-1.29}$

4.3.2 Alternative filter configurations

As mentioned above, the two-media anthracite/sand filter is the most commonly used filter configuration, as shown in Figure 4.3. An alternative two-media configuration is the one based on, Filtralite (Figure 4.4), a lightweight expanded clay media produced in Norway. By using Filtralite of two different grain sizes and densities, a coarse-to-fine media filter is established.

Saltnes et al. (2001, 2002) demonstrated in a Filtralite filter with coarse grains (see Figure 4.4) and consequently high sludge storage capacity/long filter runs, that bigger grain sizes could be compensated for by increasing filter depth, especially when using a polymer as filter aid.

Because of the need for corrosion control, an alternative filter configuration have become popular in Norway, where calcium carbonate is used as the bottom media in a down-flow three media filter with conventional anthracite/sand as the upper media (Figure 4.5) (Ødegaard et al., 1999). Floc separation

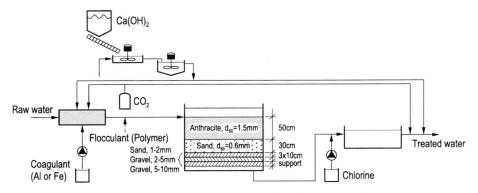

Figure 4.3 Typical flow scheme for a contact filtration plant for NOM removal in Norway

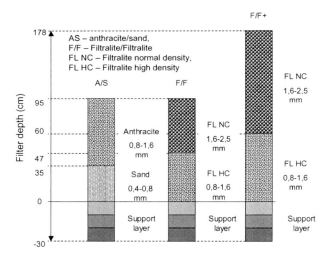

Figure 4.4 Mono-multi Filtralite filter

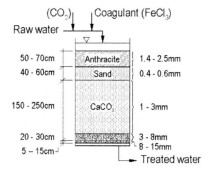

Figure 4.5 Three media filter for coagulation/carbonatisation

takes place in the anthracite/sand part of the filter while the calcium carbonate part has the function of carbonation. Most of these plants use iron chloride as coagulant (typical dosage 3.3–5 mg Fe/l) in order to reach the operating pH of 3.5–4,0 that is required to ensure sufficient dissolution of the $CaCO_3$. In some of these plants CO_2 is added as well (typically 6–15 mg/l) in order to minimize the iron dosage. pH, grain size as well as contact time influence on the dissolution of the marble in order to arrive at the combination of pH, alkalinity and Ca-concentration aimed for (see above).

In a typical Norwegian situation, it is experienced that the empty bed contact time in the marble part of the filter must be at least 15–25 minutes. A filter depth of the marble layer of 150–250 mm at a filter rate of 5 m/h is required (see Figure 4.5). After reaching a critical lower grain size, the smallest grains are washed out during back-washing and new marble grains have to be supplied. New grains are supplied during back-washing in order to ensure the proper grain grading at the start of a new filter cycle. In the three media filters a typical back-washing routine is composed of 3 min water backwash at 60–80 m/h, 3 min backwash with air (together with water) and finally 6.5 min water backwash. Overall this results in quite high backwash water consumption, in the range of 6–11 % (Ødegaard et al., 1999).

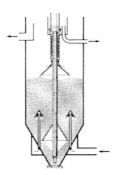

Figure 4.6 Continuous, uplow (Dynasand) filter

Another filter that is much used in Norway in contact filtration plants for NOM-removal is the continuously operated filter – the so-called Dynasand filter (see Fig 4.6).

4.3.3 Coagulation/membrane filtration

There is now an increasing interest in replacing the granular media filtration after coagulation with membrane (ultra- or micro-) filtration. At this time only one full scale plant based on coagulation (PACl)/hollow fibre UF (10 nm) membrane filtration (Xiga, Norit) is in operation in Norway. It has a stable operation at a flux of ca 80 L/m²h at 90 % recovery on a raw water with color 40 mg Pt/L. The plant is backwashed with treated (and chlorinated) water and chemical cleaning (75% phosphoric acid, soaking for 20 min and 15% sodium hypochlorite, soaking for 15 min) is performed every 8th backwash.

Research is being carried out at Norwegian University of Science and Technology (NTNU) both on ultra- and microfiltration. Two systems have been investigated for NOM removal:

(1) A system based on coagulation, flocculation and submerged, hollow fibre, outside-in UF filtration (Zenon Zeeweed) (Machenbach and Ødegaard, 2004)

(2) A system based on coagulation, flocculation and inside-out ceramic microfiltration membranes (Metawater) (Meyn et al., 2007)

In both cases a water with a high color (50 mg Pt/L corresponding to a TOC of 5.5 mg/l) has been investigated. It has been shown that the optimized coagulation (pH and coagulant dose) conditions for membrane filtration are pretty much the same as for sand filtration. In the UF study (Machenbach and Ødegaard, 2004), that was carried out with operating fluxes in the range of 45–75 L/m²h, it was demonstrated that optimization of floc aggregation (flocculation) was important in order to minimize trans-membrane pressure (TMP) build-up. A packed bed flocculator at low velocity gradients (G-value ≤ 30 s^{-1}) and ≥ 5 min empty bed residence time gave lower TMP-build-up than a high velocity gradient (G-value $\simeq 400$ s^{-1}) and 30 seconds residence time in pipe flocculator. In the MF study, however, that was operated at fluxes in the range of 140–220 L/m²h, a pipe flocculator operated at varying conditions (G = 60 and 300 s^{-1} and HRT 7.5 and 30 s) gave only moderately higher TMP build-up than the standard, traditional two-stage flocculation tank with 20 min HRT (Meyn et al., 2007). The difference in experience is probably caused by the fact that conditions suitable for good flocculation exist inside the ceramic membrane module itself.

The higher flux of the MF-unit was not sustainable and it seems that the recommended fluxes for UF-membranes after coagulation of NOM is typically 50–70 L/m²h while it is the range of 130–160 L/m²h in MF membranes.

4.4 OXIDATION/BIOFILTRATION

4.4.1 Oxidation

In humic surface water where color removal and disinfection is the main target, ozonation is normally be the preferred oxidation method. The oxidation of NOM by ozone can follow two main pathways; 1) direct oxidation by ozon which is selectively targeting mainly activated aromatics and double bonds, and 2) indirect reaction where ozone is decomposed to form hydroxyl radicals which are very powerful but less selective oxidants than ozone. Consequently, the direct reaction pathway results in high color removal, but little TOC removal, whereas the indirect pathway removes less color and more TOC. The water matrix may determine the importance of the two pathways, and also the degree of scavenging. pH is of particular importance, and at high pH the indirect reaction pathway dominates and the ozonation may be considered as an AOP (Advanced Oxidation Process, defined as using hydroxyl radicals for oxidation). The use of an AOP may be advantageous if oxidation of ozone resistant compounds is desired (i.e. several micro-pollutants, atrazine, alachlor, etc). A disadvantage of the AOP's is that the hydroxyl radicals are very unstable, easily scavenged and very short lived. Ozonation may become an AOP when combined with H_2O_2 or UV, or by using a catalytic packing media in the ozone column. Other AOP's may also be applied, such as UV/H_2O_2, UV/TiO_2, Vacuum-UV, Fenton, etc.

When using ozonation in humic surface water without any pollutants, the direct oxidation reaction pathway is advantageous. This would imply that using an inert ozone column packing media is beneficial and that the pH should be neutral to low. At high alkalinity and NOM concentration the efficiency of the system would be somewhat reduced,

In practice the ozone dose required for 80% color removal that has typically been achieved in pilot- and full-scale plants, is around 0.15–0.20 mg O_3/mgPt which translates to 1.0–1.5 mg O_3/mgTOC, see Figure 4.7 (Ødegaard et al., 2006).

4.4.2 Ozonation/biofiltration

Ozonation is effective in colour removal from humic surface water – see Figure 4.7 in which the colour removal versus specific dose is shown for different waters (Ødegaard et al., 2006).

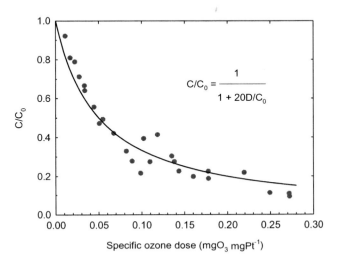

Figure 4.7 Color reduction versus specific ozon dose

Ozonation of colored water results however, also in reaction products that are far more biodegradable than the original humic substances themselves. Biofiltration is therefore required in order to remove the easily biodegradable organic ozonation by-products. The flow-scheme of various alternatives of an ozonation/biofiltration plant is shown in Figure 4.8.

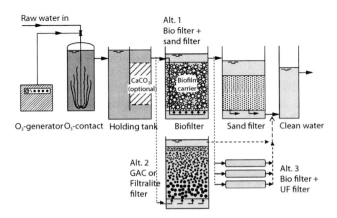

Figure 4.8 Alternative flow diagrams for ozonation/biofiltration plants

It is well known that activated carbon filters after ozonation of NOM-containing waters results in biological activity in the filter. The run-time of GAC filters is increased because of "biological regeneration". In Norway we have also experiences from plants with biofilters consisting of packed bed plastic carrier (Kaldnes K1) followed by sand filters for biomass separation, combined biofilters/ separation filters with Filtralite or with as three-media (anthracite/sand/calcium carbonate) as filter medium (Melin et al, 2006). Besides the fact that GAC-filters gives a quicker start-up caused by the adsorption effect, the rate of biodegradation does not seem to be strongly influenced by the media selected, while the kinetic studies show that residence time is of importance. The results show that for typical Norwegian water, the EBCT should not be less than around 20 min (Ødegaard and Melin, 2006). The total TOC removal is relatively low, typically in the range of 20–30% even through the color removal is high (70–80%) at dosages mentioned above (Melin and Ødegaard, 2000). The method is, therefore, not suitable for raw waters with high NOM-content, but for waters with an average color of around 30 mg Pt/l, which is quite common in Norway, the experiences with the method is quite satisfactory. It is a very simple process to operate without any external chemicals needed and it gives a good hygienic barrier because of the high ozone concentration.

4.4.3 The OBM-process

In the European project TECHNEAU our group has investigated an oxidation/biofiltration/membrane filtration process (OBM-process) that is based on the "multi-barrier" concept (Azrague et al., 2009). The process is comprised of three separate independent processes.

(1) The first step is oxidation, based on ozonation or an AOP (O_3/H_2O_2, UV/TiO_2 etc). It will in addition to being the 1. hygienic barrier, also result in a) NOM-oxidation (color removal), b) oxidation of trace organics, c) oxidation and removal of taste and odor and d) oxidation of inorganics (Fe, Mn etc)
(2) The second step (biofiltration) will biologically stabilize the water by removing the easiest biodegradable organic matter produced by the oxidation step
(3) The third step, membrane filtration (MF, UF or NF) is there to remove a) biomass produced in the second step, b) oxidized/precipitated inorganics, c) inorganic trace pollutants and d) pathogen microorganisms (constituting the 2. hygienic barrier)

In a pilot plant operated at the university (NTNU) it has been demonstrated (Østerhus and Azrague, 2009), that the OBM process achieved good colour removal (>80%) during ozonation even in high NOM water. After the biofiltration stage the produced water was bio-stable, with a very low sludge production in the biodegradation stage.

Final separation by ultra filtration using polymeric membranes in an immersed configuration (Zenon, ZeeWeed) worked very well as it could be operated at high fluxes (80 l/m^{2}h), with a high recovery (98%), still permitting operational time of approx 400 hrs before chemical cleaning was needed (approx. 600 hrs of operation at flux of 60 l/m^{2}h). By modifying the operation mode (air scouring) and reactor design, the process can probably be further optimized. The use of ceramic microfiltration membranes (Metawater) for the final separation on the other hand caused severe fouling. This may be because the MF membrane is more prone to pore blockage due to submicron particles coming from the biofilter

The OBM process is suitable for medium to low NOM containing water (20–40 mg Pt/L), and acts as an efficient hygienic barrier process producing high quality water. It has shown to be very robust and flexible, and it may be designed for removal of several micro pollutants. The cost estimation has shown that the OBM process is competitive with conventional treatment processes (Azrague et al., 2009).

4.5 SORPTION PROCESSES

GAC adsorption as well as ion exchange may be used for removing humic substances.

4.5.1 GAC adsorption

Direct activated carbon adsorption is not recommendable since the sorption capacity is quickly reduced by pore blocking caused by the large NOM molecules. GAC adsorption of NOM may be suitable as post-treatment after other processes (coagulation, ozonation etc) have removed or changed the NOM-molecules to the extent that the residuals may be sufficiently small to arrive at sites in the finer pores. GAC is not used as the only NOM-removing process in Norway, but is used as filter medium in ozonation/biofiltration plants.

4.5.2 Chemisorption (Ion exchange)

Humic substances may be removed by macroporous anion exchangers because of the negative charge of the humic molecules at normal pH. The raw water is pre-treated in a micro-sieve (pore opening 50 μm) or a rapid sand filter when the turbidity is higher than 0.5–1.0 NTU. Thereafter, the water is passed through ion exchange filters placed in parallel or in series. The process is only used in small plants in Norway in which only two ion exchange filters are used that normally are operated in series even though parallel operation is also possible.

An empirical model for the break-through curve as a function of raw water concentration C_0 (UV-ext., m^{-1}), empty bed contact time, t_k (min) and filter run time, t (hrs) and temperature, T (°C) has been developed (Ødegaard et al., 1989):

$$C/C_0 = 0,04 \cdot C_0^{0,46} \cdot t_k^{-0,67} \cdot t^{0,37} \cdot T^{0,13}$$

The contact time is a more relevant parameter than the filter velocity. Typically a contact time of at least 10 min at maximum flow is used when the goal is to bring the colour down to less than 10 mg Pt/l. If a lower treated-water colour is aimed for, a longer contact time will have to be used. Typically a bed depth (h) of 0.5–2 m is used resulting in filter rates of $v_f = h \cdot n \cdot 60/t_k$ where n is the number of columns in series and t_k is contact time. It is recommended that the filter rate at design load does not exceed 20 m/h.

After breakthrough the ion exchanger has to be back-washed and regenerated. Normally an alkaline salt solution (2% NaOH + 10% NaCl) is used. While the flow during normal operation is downwards, the flow during backwash is upwards while the flow during regeneration may either be downwards or upwards. The regeneration solution is typically reused 7–8 times and in such a manner that around 1/8 of the regeneration solution volume is substituted at each regeneration.

Until now, the magnetic ion exchange process (MIEX) is not applied in Norwegian water treatment plants.

4.6 CONCLUSIONS

Natural organic matter (NOM – with its main constituent humic substances), has several negative influences in water that is to be used for water supply and needs therefore to be removed. The characteristics of humic substances (MW, charge, hydrophobic and, aromatic nature etc) give the opportunity of several removal methods:

(1) Because of the large molecular size NOM may be removed by molecular sieving, i.e. filtration through NF membranes. According to the Norwegian experiences, predominantly with cellulose acetate membranes (typically 3 nm effective pore size), the plants should be designed for a moderate flux (<20 LMH) and recovery (<70%) and operated with daily light cleaning for fouling control. NF is suitable when the NOM concentration and color is high.

(2) Because of the charge and colloidal nature, NOM can be removed by coagulation and floc separation. Coagulant dose and pH of coagulation are the two most important factors for achieving optimal treatment result. In most cases, the maximum residual metal concentration level (0.15 mg Me/L) determines the required coagulant dose level. Contact filtration are often used for raw water color levels up to about 50 mg Pt/L and turbidity levels less than 1–2 NTU. Above this a pre-separation step (settling/flotation) is recommended.

(3) The color of NOM may effectively be removed by ozonation (or another strong oxidative method). Oxidation has to be proceeded by biofiltration in order to take the growth potential out of the water. Typical O_3-dosages are 0.15–0.20 mg O_3/mg Pt or 1–1.5 mg O_3/mg TOC. Necessary biofilter EBCT is around 20–30 min. Ozonation/ biofiltration is only adviced for relatively low color levels, typically below 35 mg Pt/l. Otherwise the biogrowth potential created by the ozonation may be too high for the biofilter to handle.

(4) Sorption processes are less used. GAC adsorption as the only process is unsuitable because of pore blocking resulting in low capacity and short filter runs. GAC may, however, be suitable in combination with pre-ozonation. Ion exchange (based on macroporous anion exchangers) is used in small plants, but is only recommended at relatively low raw water color levels, typically below 30 mg Pt/L.

4.7 REFERENCES

Azrague, K., Østerhus, S.W. and Leiknes, T. (2009) Assessment of the OBM-process for drinking water treatment. In: *Proceedins Intenational. Wisa Membrane Technology Conference 2009*, Stellenbosch, South-Africa, May 13–15.

Bolto, B.A., Dixon, D.R., Eldridge, R.J. and King, S.J. (1998) The use of cationic polymers as primary coagulants in water treatment. In: *Chemical water and wastewater treatment V*, Hahn, H.H., Hoffmann, E. and Ødegaard, H. (Eds) Springer Verlag, Berlin Heidelberg, pp 173–185.

Eikebrokk, B. (1996) Removal of humic substances by coagulation. *Chemical water and wastewater treatment V*, Hahn, H.H., Hoffmann, E. and Ødegaard, H. (Eds) Springer Verlag, Berlin Heidelberg, pp 173–187.

Eikebrokk, B. (2001) Aspects of enhanced coagulation-contact filtration process optimisation. In: *Proceedings Workshop on utilization of NOM characteristics to improve process selection and performance*. AWWARF, Vivendi Water, CRC for Water Quality and Treatment, Berlin Germany, Oct. 9–12.

Eikebrokk, B., Juhna, T. and Østerhus, S.W. (2006) Water treatment by enhanced coagulation – Operational status and optimization issues. *Techneau*, D 5.3.1, December. http://www.techneau.eu.

Eikebrokk, B., Juhna, T., Melin, E. and Østerhus, S.W. (2007) Water treatment by enhanced coagulation and oxonation-biofiltration: Intermediate report on operation optimization procedusre and trielas. *Techneau*, D 5.3.2A. http://www.techneau.eu.

Fløgstad, H. and Ødegaard, H. (1985) Treatment of humic waters by ozone. *Ozone Sci. Eng.* **7**, pp 121–136.

Kvinnesland, T. and Ødegaard, H. (2004) The effects of polymer charachteristics on nano particle separation in humic substance removal by cationic polymer coagulation. *Wat.Sci.Tech.*, **50**(12), pp 185–191.

Machenbach, I., Ødegaard, H. (2004) Relevance of flocculation in integrated membrane processes for NOM removal. In: *Chemical water and wastewater treatment VII*. Hahn, H.H., Hoffmann, E., Ødegaard, H. (eds), IWA Publishing, London, pp 245–254.

Melin. E., Skog, R., Ødegaard. H. (2006) Ozonation/biofiltration with calcium carbonate as biofilter media. In: *Recent Progress in Slow Sand and Alternative Biofiltration Processes*, Gimbel, R., Graham, N.J.D. and Colllins, M.R. (eds), IWA Publishing, pp 40 – 413. ISBN 9781843391203.

Melin, E. and Ødegaard H. (2000) The effect of biofilter loading rate on the removal of organic ozonation by-products. *Wat. Res.* **34**(18), pp 4464–4476.

Meyn, T., Leiknes, T, Ødegaard, H. (2007) 67812Coagulation/flocculation - ceramic membrane filtration for removal of natural organic matter (NOM) under Norwegian conditions. In: *Proceedings IWA Conference on Membranes for Water and Wastewater treatment*. Harrogate, UK, 15–17 May.

Ødegaard, H. and Koottatep, S. (1982) Removal of humic substances from natural waters by reverse osmosis. *Wat. Res.*, **16**, pp. 613–620.

Ødegaard, H., Brattebø, H. and Halle, O. (1989) Removal of humic substances by ion exchange. Chapter 45. In: *Suffet and MacCarthy: Aquatic Humic Substances. Influence on fate and Treatment of Pollutants. Advances in Chemistry Series 219*, American Chemical Society.

Ødegaard, H. and Thorsen, T. (1989) Removal of humic substances by membrane processes. Chapter 42. In: *Suffet and MacCarthy: Aquatic Humic Substances. Influence on Fate and Treatment of Pollutants. Advances in Chemistry Series 219*, American Chemical Society.

Ødegaard, H, Eikebrokk, B. and Storhaug, R.(1999) Processes for the removal of humic substances from water - An overview based on Norwegian experiences. *Wat. Sci. Tech.*, **40**(9), pp 37–46.

Ødegaard, H, Thorsen, T, Melin, E. (2000) Practical experiences from membrane filtration plants for humic substance removal. *Wat. Sci.Tech.*, **41**(10–11), pp. 33–41.

Ødegaard, H., Melin, E., Leiknes, T. (2006) Ozonation/biofiltration for treatment of humic surface water". In: *Recent Progress in Slow Sand and Alternative Biofiltration Processes*, Gimbel, R., Graham, N.J.D. and Collins, M.R. (eds), IWA Publishing, pp 397–405. ISBN 9781843391203.

Østerhus, S. W. and Azrague, K. (2009) Removal of NOM by an Oxidation-Biofiltration-Membrane filtration (OBM) process. Submitted for publication in *Organic Geochemistry*.

Saltnes, T., Eikebrokk, B., Ødegaard, H. (2002) Contact Filtration of Humic Waters, performance of an expanded clay aggregate filter (Filtralite) compared to a dual anthracite/sand Filter. *Wat. Sci. Tech.: Water Supply*, **2**(5–6), 2002.

Saltnes, T, Eikebrokk, B. and Ødegaard, H. (2001) Coagulation optimization for NOM removal by direct filtration in clay aggregate filters. *Water Supply: Research and technology – AQUA*, 51, 2, pp 125–134.

Thorsen, T. and Fløgstad, H. (2006) Nanofiltration in drinking water treatment. Literature review. *Techneau*, D 5.3.4B, http:www.techneau.eu.

Thorsen, T. (1999) *Fundamental studies on membrane filtration of coloured surface water*. Dr-thesis, Norwegian University of Science and Technology (NTNU), November.

Chapter 5
Flocculation and its Inclusion in Membrane Filtration

Y. Watanabe

5.1 INTRODUCTION

Coagulation-Flocculation process has been widely used to form aggregates (flocs), which include many fine particles contained in the raw water, for the efficient solid-liquid separation in the sedimentation basin and sand filter. Tambo and Watanabe (1979a, 1979b and 1984) published several papers describing the floc density and flocculation kinetics for the better understanding of flocculation process. They presented the floc density function and GC_0T value. The floc density function describes the quantitative relationship between the size and effective (buoyant) density of flocs. The exponent K_ρ in the function is related to the fractal dimension (D) for the aggregates formed in Cluster-Cluster Aggregation (CCA) as $D = 3 - K_\rho$ (Weitz and Oliveria, 1984). The K_ρ is a function of the ALT ratio and has the numerical value of 1.00 and 1.25 for the ALT ratio of around 1/100 and 1/20, respectively. These values coincide with the D value determined for the reaction and diffusion limited case (2.05 and 1.75), respectively, in the field of the Fractal Physics. Tambo and Watanabe have proposed that the GC_0T value is much useful compared with the GT value proposed by Camp (1955) as the criterion of flocculation. These research results have been included in the membrane filtration process to improve the filterability of the membrane.

In Japan, membrane filtration plant has increased its treatment capacity since the middle of 1990s. Tokyo Metropolitan Water Works Authority constructed a plant with the total capacity of 80,000 m³/day in April 2007 using hollow fiber MF membranes made of PVDF. It is currently the largest plant in Japan. There also has been innovation in the membrane material and membrane module. The monolith ceramic membrane was developed in 1988 and its advances have been remarkable as seen in Table 5.1.

At present, 60 plants with monolith ceramic membrane have been under operation in Japan and the maximum capacity of the plants is about 40,000 m³/day. The pre-coagulation has been provided to all of these plants to strengthen filterability for stable filtration performance for a wide range of raw water turbidity and enhancement of the removal of viruses and dissolved organic substances.

Table 5.1 Advance in monolith ceramic membrane

Configuration	unit	Tube	Monolith				
Stage		1985	1988	1990	1994	2001	(2006)
Length	mm		1,000				1,500
Diameter	mm	10	30			180	
Channel Number	–	1	19	37	61	2000	
Channel Diameter	mm	7	4	3		2.5	
Membrane Area	m²	0.02	0.24	0.35	0.48	15	24
Packing Density	m²/L	0.25	0.34	0.50	0.63	0.6	0.63
Application	–	Industrial Use			WaterPurification		

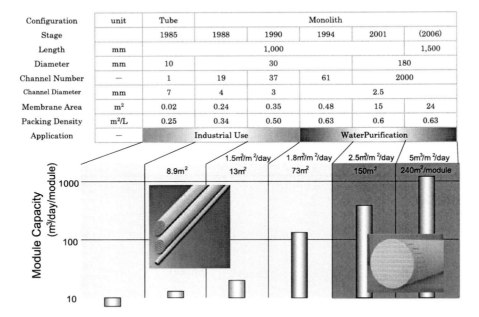

The authors (2004, 2005) have clarified the characteristics unique to monolith ceramic membrane with pre-coagulation by referring to the behaviour of micro-particles. The region exists in the monolith channel with the optimum G and GC_0T value for good flocculation. The flocculation of micro-particles offers the reduction in the membrane fouling.

This paper deals with the fundamentals of flocculation and its inclusion in the monolith ceramic membrane filtration based on the authors previous researches.

5.2 FUNDAMENTALS OF FLOCCULATION

5.2.1 Floc density function

Tambo and Watanabe (1979a) developed experimental method to measure the diameter and settling velocity of a discrete floc under a large number of coagulation and flocculation conditions and formulated the floc density function (equation 5.1) as described in Figure 5.1.

$$\rho_e = \rho_f - \rho = a(d_f/1)^{-K\rho} \tag{5.1}$$

where:

ρ_e, ρ_f and ρ = floc effective density, floc density and water density (g/m³), respectively;
d_f = floc diameter (cm);

a = imaginary effective density of a floc of $d_f = 1$ cm (g/m³); and
K_p = the exponent (−).

Equation 5.1 demonstrates that the Stokes settling velocity of a discrete floc is proportional to the power of $(2 - K_p)$ of its diameter. Making the mass balance of an i-fold floc consisting of i number of primary particles, the following relationship has been derived:

$$i = (d_i/d_1)^{(3-K_p)} = (d_i/d_1)^D \qquad (5.2)$$

where:

i = number of primary particles contained in i-fold floc (−);
d_i and d_1 = diameter of i-fold and primary particle (cm), respectively; and
D = fractal dimension of floc (−).

Equation 5.2 demonstrates that the fractal dimension of floc (D) is equal to $(3-K_p)$. Value of the exponent K_p is a function of ALT ratio, i.e. a ratio between raw water turbidity and dosed aluminum concentration, as shown in Figure 5.1. The K_p value is about 1.00 and 1.25 for the ALT ratio of around 1/100 and 1/20, respectively. These values coincide with the D value determined for the reaction and diffusion limited case (2.05 and 1.75) in the field of the Fractal Physics.

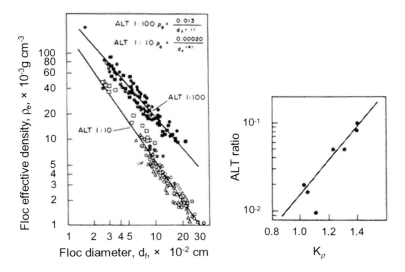

Figure 5.1 Floc density function and K_p as a function of ALT ratio

5.2.2 Flocculation kinetics and GC₀T value

The floc density function has been introduced into the flocculation kinetics to determine the diameter of i-fold floc which consists of i number of primary particles. Equation 5.3 is the dimensionless flocculation kinetics derived by Tambo and Watanabe (1979b).

$$\frac{dN_R}{dm} = \frac{1}{2}\sum_{i=1}^{R-1} \alpha_R \left\{ \frac{1}{i^{3-K_p}} + \frac{1}{(R-i)^{3-K_p}} \right\}^3 N_i N_{R-i}$$

$$- N_R \sum_{i=1}^{S-R} \alpha_R + i\left[\frac{1}{i^{3-K_p}} + \frac{1}{R^{3-K_p}} \right]^3 N_i N_R \quad (5.3)$$

$$N_i = \frac{n_i}{n_0}, \quad \sum_{i=1}^{S} iN_i = 1$$

where:

R = number of primary particles contained in R-fold floc (–);
n_i = number concentration of i-fold floc ($1/cm^3$);
α_R = collision-agglomeration factor of R-fold floc formation (–)
n_0 = number concentration of primary particles ($1/cm^3$)

Based on equation 5.3, Tambo and Watanabe have proposed three dimensionless parameters (m, S and K_ρ) for describing the flocculation process.

$$m = 1.22\sqrt{\varepsilon_0/\mu} d_1^3 n_0 T \approx 1.22\sqrt{0.1\varepsilon/\mu} \cdot (6/\pi)C_0 T \approx 0.723 G C_0 T \quad (5.4)$$

$$S = (d_{max}/d_1)^{(3-K_\rho)} \quad (5.5)$$

where:

ε_0 and ε = effective and total energy dissipation rate in turbulent flow ($erg/cm^3/sec$) respectively;
$\varepsilon_0 \approx 0.1\varepsilon$;
μ = water viscosity ($g/cm/s$);
$G = \sqrt{\varepsilon/\mu}$ (sec^{-1});
$C_0 = (\pi/6) d_1^3 n_0$;
T = flocculation time (sec); and
d_{max} = maximum floc diameter in a given ε_0 (cm).

The maximum floc diameter (d_{max}) under a given effective energy dissipation rate (ε_0) is evaluated by equation 5.6 (Tambo and Hozumi, 1979c)

$$d_{max} = k\varepsilon_0^{-3/2(3+K_\rho)}, \quad d_f \ll \lambda_0 \quad (5.6)$$

λ_0 = micro scale of turbulent flow (cm)

The optimum m value is a function of S and is around unity in the S of 10^3–10^4. Taking into account of the above equations, the G and GC_0T value should be used for the design criteria. Tambo (1991) presented the estimation method of C_0 under a given condition of raw water turbidity and ALT ratio, and concluded that the optimum GC_0T value is around unity in the conventional rapid sand filtration process. Tambo calculated the required optimum flocculation time under a fixed G value of 20 sec^{-1} in the case of clay suspension concentration of 5 and 25 mg/L, which correspond to the Japanese turbidity unit of 5 and 25 degree, respectively. Tambo calculated the optimum hydraulic detention time in flocculator is 168 min. and 33 min. to set the GC_0T value at unity for each case, which correspond to the GT value of 200,000 and 40,000, respectively. This example clearly demonstrates the usefulness of the GC_0T value.

5.3 FLOCCULATION IN MONOLITH CERAMIC MEMBRANE

5.3.1 Theoretical consideration

The laminar flow model within dead-end hollow fibre membranes has been presented in many studies. For example, Fujita and Takizawa (1994) developed equation 5.7 from the energy equation and the material balance in the course of filtration.

$$\frac{dp}{dv} = -\frac{v}{g} \cdot \left\{ 1 - \frac{8 \cdot \mu}{\rho \cdot d \cdot k \cdot (p - p_0)} \right\} \tag{5.7}$$

where:

p = static pressure (m);
v = axial velocity within hollow fibre (m/sec);
g = gravitational acceleration (m/sec^2);
μ = viscosity (kg/m/sec);
ρ = water density (kg/m^3);
d = internal diameter of hollow fibre (m);
k = membrane filterability (sec^{-1}); and
p_0 = external pressure of membrane (m).

Considering the characteristic values ($d = 4 \times 10^{-4}$ m, $k = 6 \times 10^{-6}$ sec^{-1}) of the typical hollow fibre, the first term in equation 5.7 is much smaller than the second term. Neglecting the first term, an appropriate equation to calculate an expanded approximate axial velocity in a fibre can be derived. In the case of monolith ceramic membrane ($d = 2.5 \times 10^{-3}$ m, $k = 5 \times 10^{-5}$ sec^{-1}), however, the first term in Eq. 5.7 can not be neglected to derive an appropriate equation for calculating axial velocity in a monolith channel. Without neglecting the first term in equation 5.7, the authors (2004) have developed equation 5.8 to calculate an expanded approximate axial velocity in a monolith channel.

$$v = v_f \cdot \cosh(\alpha \cdot x) - \beta \cdot (p_f - p_e + \frac{v_f^2}{2g}) \cdot \sinh(\alpha \cdot x) \tag{5.8}$$

$$\beta^2 = \frac{\rho \cdot g \cdot d \cdot k}{8\mu}, \quad \alpha = \frac{4 \cdot d \cdot k}{d^2 \cdot \beta}$$

where:

p_f and v_f = pressure (m) and velocity at inlet of monolith channel (m/sec), respectively.

On the other hand, the membrane filterability k in the monolith membrane has a certain distribution. To facilitate analysis of the flow pattern on the basis of this distribution, a five-channel model with three levels of the filterability was created, as described in Figure 5.2.

108 Handbook on Particle Separation Processes

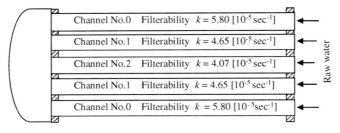

Figure 5.2 Five-channel model

Solving equation 5.8 under the material balance and appropriate boundary conditions, the equation for axial velocity in the five channel model has been derived as equation 5.9 (Yonekawa, 2005).

$$v_i = v_{fi} \cdot \cosh(\alpha_i \cdot x) - \beta_i \cdot (p_{fi}^* - p_e) \cdot \sinh(\alpha_i \cdot x) \qquad (i = 0, 1, 2) \tag{5.9}$$

where:

p_{fi}^* = total pressure at channel inlet (m); and
p_e = external static pressure of membrane (m).

The calculated flow pattern in the monolith ceramic membrane module is shown in Figure 5.3.

A concentrate flowing out through outlets of channels 1 and 2 with lower filterability is drawn into channel 0 with higher filterability. It was also confirmed that the dead end point is located at the position with an axial velocity $v_i = 0$ in channel 0.

In the channel of 1 m long, axial velocities calculated by equation 5.9 are shown in Figure 5.4 for the membrane flux of 2 m³/m²/day.

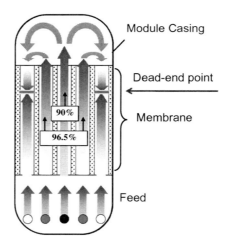

Figure 5.3 Flow pattern in monolith module

The G value in the channels 0 to 2 was calculated at about 40 sec⁻¹, which is in the range of optimum values proposed by Camp (1943). On the other hand, the mean hydraulic residence time in the channels 0 to

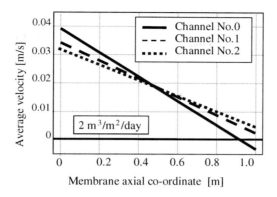

Figure 5.4 Analytical results of axial velocity

2 was about 50 seconds. Therefore, the GT value in the channel is only about 2,000, which is too small compared with the Camp's proposed values. However, good flocculation was observed in the channel, because the GC_0T value in the part of channel is high enough for good flocculation, explained as below. Using the data shown in Figure 5.4, the distribution of the local G values within the channel 2 under the membrane flux of 2 m³/ m²/day is described as seen in Figure 5.5.

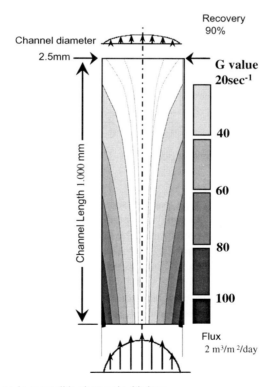

Figure 5.5 Profile of G values in monolith channel with low κ

Considering the velocity distribution in the channel and high concentration of coagulated micro-particles reflected by membrane filtration, the GC_0T value may be high enough for a good flocculation in the region with the local G value of 40 to 100 sec^{-1}. In this context, C_0 is defined as the coagulated micro-particle concentration near the entrance of such a region.

5.3.2 Experimental consideration

5.3.2.1 Experimental set-up

Figure 5.6 shows the experimental set-up (large and small monolith membrane module) and sampling points. The top and bottom portion of the both modules were made of transparent material to enable a visual observation of flocs using video camera. Raw water was taken from the Kiso River near Nagoya city. The dosage of coagulant (poly aluminium chloride, PACl) was fixed at 1 mg Al/L. The rapid mixing condition was the G value of 150 sec^{-1} and hydraulic detention time of 5 minutes. The filtration mode was dead-end and membrane flux was fixed at 2 m^3/m^2/day. The specifications and operation conditions of the two membrane modules are described in the authors' paper (2004). Detail of the cross section of large monolith ceramic membrane is shown in Figure 5.7.

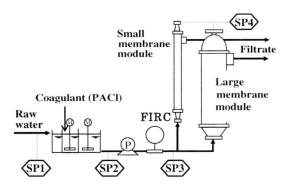

Figure 5.6 Experimental setup and sampling points

With the laser diffraction scattering type particle size distribution cell holder (Horiba LY-073), the particle size distribution was measured to verify the predicted flocculation phenomena and its effect on the filterability of the monolith ceramic membrane. The behaviour of the micro-particles with the size of 0.5–15 μm in the channel with lower filterability was also measured to identify the critical particle size. Polystyrene type latex particles (JSR Stadex/Dynospheres: 0.5, 3, 5, 10, 15 μm, specific density of 1.05) were used as model particles.

The authors also investigated the correlation between micro-particle concentration and trans-membrane pressure (TMP) using the effluent from a conventional rapid sand filtration process, as shown in Figure 5.8. There exists a clear relationship between them. It would suggest a significant effect of the flocculation on the filterability in the monolith channel, because the micro-particles, larger than 1 μm in the shear field, are subject to a lift force such as the lateral migration and shear-induced diffusion which are proportional to square and cubic power of the equivalent particle diameter, respectively (Cohen and Prostein, 1986; Wiesner *et al.*, 1989).

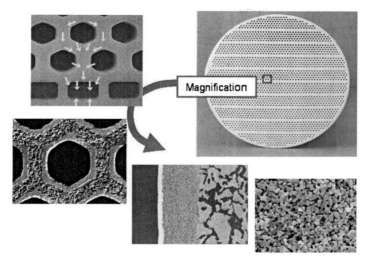

Figure 5.7 Detail of large monolith ceramic membrane

5.3.2.2 Experimental results
5.3.2.2.1 Visual experiment
There were no visual flocs in the bottom portion of the module where coagulated micro-particles entered. Visual flocs, however, blew out at the maximum velocity of 3–8 mm/s from the lower filterability channels in the upper portion of the module. From the analytical result with five channel model, the average outflow velocity at the membrane top was estimated to be 2–4 mm/s. The maximum flow velocity in laminar flow is twice the average velocity. Therefore, the analytical result has been confirmed by the visual experiment.

We measured the concentration of polystyrene type latex particles with the size range of 0.5 to 15 μm in the influent of membrane. There were almost no particles in the effluent. It demonstrated that the latex particles of smaller than 15 μm are deposited onto the membrane surface in the course of membrane filtration. This result can explain the correlation of the variation of micro-particle number in raw water and TMP as seen in Figure 5.8.

5.3.2.2.2 Flocculation of coagulated micro-particles in the monolith channel
This experiment was carried out to prove that good flocculation occurs in the channel and will improve the filterability of the membrane. From the theoretical analysis, the average flow velocity in the channel with lower filterability is about 0.5 mm/s in the region of 1 to 200 μm from the surface, so the detention time is between some ten minutes and some hours. The G value is in the zone is between 20 and 100 sec^{-1}. Figure 5.9 shows the floc size distribution in each sampling point. Figure 5.10 shows the relationship between the particle diameter and lift force, such as the lateral migration and shear-induced diffusion, in the case of our experimental conditions.

Flocs are lifted up by laminar flow and carried away from the outside of the channel. Therefore, the space near the membrane surface might be considered to be a high efficient field for flocculating the charged-neutralized micro-particles.

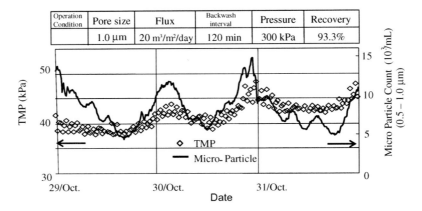

Figure 5.8 Correlation between TMP and micro-particle concentration

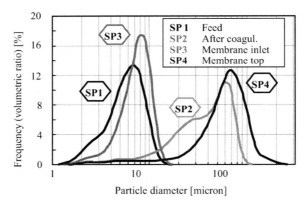

Figure 5.9 Result for distribution of floc particles diameter

Figure 5.11 shows a schematic image of phenomenon occurred in the channel when the pre-coagulation is prepared.

In order to confirm the flocculation effect on the improvement of ceramic membrane filterability, the authors carried out an additional experiment using the small module with the different river water. Figure 5.12 shows the experimental result and confirms the effect of flocculation on the fouling reduction. Further improvement is possible if the chemically enhanced backwashing (CEB) with acidic solution. Figure 5.13 shows the experimental verification of the effect of the CEB on the membrane filterability. The reason of the improvement may be the removal of micro-flocs attached to the membrane surface.

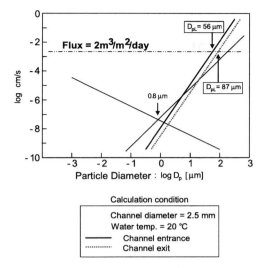

Figure 5.10 Relationship between particle diameter and lift force

Lateral migration
Shear-induced Diffusion

$$v_L = u_o^2 \cdot d_p^3 /(32 \cdot v \cdot r_o^2)$$

$$v_S = 0.05 \cdot u_o \cdot d_p^2 /(4 \cdot r_o^2)$$

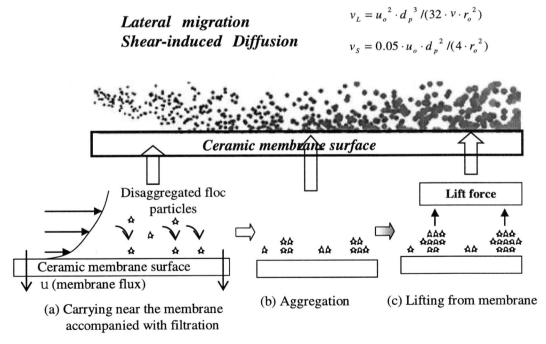

Figure 5.11 Floc behaviour in monolith channel

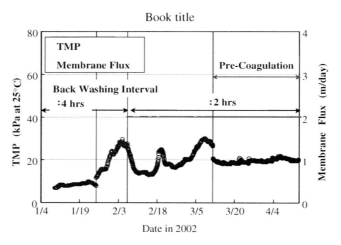

Figure 5.12 TMP change in monolith ceramic membrane

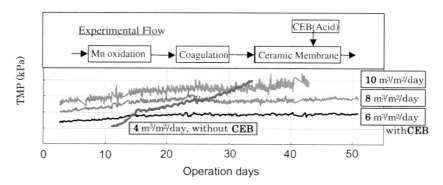

Figure 5.13 Result of high flux experiment using acid CEB

5.4 CONCLUSIONS

This chapter summarized the previous researches on the flocculation conducted by Tambo and Watanabe, and on the inclusion of flocculation in the monolith ceramic membrane filtration conducted by the authors. The floc density function describes the quantitative relationship between the size and effective (buoyant) density of flocs. The exponent K_ρ in the function is related to the fractal dimension (D) for the aggregates formed in Cluster-Cluster Aggregation (CCA) as $D = 3 - K_\rho$. The K_ρ is a function of the ALT ratio and has the numerical value of 1.00 and 1.25 for the ALT ratio of around 1/100 and 1/20, respectively. These values coincide with the D value determined for the reaction and diffusion limited case (2.05 and 1.75), respectively in the field of the Fractal Physics. Based on the dimensionless flocculation kinetics derived by Tambo and Watanabe, the GC_0T value has been proposed as the design criterion of flocculator and its usefulness was clearly demonstrated in this paper.

The authors have also clarified the characteristics unique to monolith ceramic membrane with pre-coagulation by referring to the behaviour of micro-particles. The region exists in the monolith channel with the optimum G and GC_0T value for good flocculation. The flocculation of micro-particles reduces the membrane fouling. If pre-coagulation and chemically enhanced backwashing are included in the monolith ceramic membrane filtration system, extremely high filtration flux is possible for a long operation period.

5.5 ACKNOWLEDGMENT

This research has been supported by CREST (Core Research for Evolutional Science and Technology) of Japan Science and Technology Corporation (JST).

5.6 REFERENCES

Camp T.R. and P. C. Stein (1943). Velocity gradients and internal work in fluid motion, *Journal of Boston Society of Civil Engineers*, **30**, pp. 219–237.

Camp T.R. (1955). Flocculation and flocculation basins, *Trans. Am. Civ. Engrs.*, **120**, pp. 1–16.

Cohen R.D. and R. F. Prostein (1986). Colloidal fouling of reverse osmosis membranes, *Journal of Colloid and Interface Science*, **114**(1), pp. 194–207.

Fujita K. and S. Takizawa (1994). Study on hydraulics of backwashing and air-scrubbing in hollow fiber filtration (in Japanese) *J. Japan Water Works Association*, **63**(3), pp. 94–101.

Tambo N. and Y. Watanabe (1979a). Physical characteristics of flocs–I— The floc density function and aluminum floc, *Wat. Res.*, **13**(5), pp. 409–419.

Tambo N. and Y. Watanabe (1979b). Physical aspect of flocculation process–I— Fundamental treatise, *Wat. Res.*, **13**(5), pp. 429–439.

Tambo N. and H. Hozu I (1979c). Physical characteristics of flocs–II— Strength of floc, *Wat, Res.*, **13**(5), pp. 421–427

Tambo N. and Y. Watanabe (1984). Physical aspect of flocculation process –III— Floccuylation process in a continuous flow flocculator with a back-mix flow, *Wat. Res.*, **18**(6), pp. 695–707.

Tambo N. (1991). G and GC_0T Value as design criterion of flocculator (in Japanese), *Journal of Japan Water Works Association*, **60**(10), pp. 11–18.

Watanabe Y. (2006). Water metabolic system and membrane technology (in Japanese), *Membrane*, **31**(4), pp. 180–187.

Weitz D.A. and M. Oliveria (1984). *Fractal Structures Formed by Kinetic Aggregation of Aqueous Gold Colloids*, *Physical Review Letters*, **52**, pp. 1433–1436.

Wiesner, M.R., M.M. Clark and J. Mallevialle (1989). Membrane filtration of coagulated suspension, *Journal of Environmental Engineering*, **115**(1), pp. 20–40.

Yonekawa, H. Y. Tomita and Y. Watanabe (2004). Behavior of micro-particles in monolith ceramic membrane filtration with pre-coagulation, *Wat. Sci. Tech.*, **51**(12), pp. 317–315.

Yonekawa H. (2005). *Study on the characteristics of monolith ceramic membrane for water purification*, doctoral dissertation, Hokkaido University.

Chapter 6
Dissolved Air Flotation
Development, Application, and Research Needs

M.Y. Han and T.I. Kim

6.1 INTRODUCTION

Solid/liquid separation lies at the heart of many treatment systems, because many pollutants are ultimately removed from water in the solid phase. Flotation of particles suspended in water is driven by density differences, with flotation occurring when the density of a particle is less than that of water. Many particles in water and wastewater treatment systems are low in density: for example, algae, bacteria, protozoa, light flocs from chemical precipitation processes, biological flocs, food wastes, oily wastes, and paper wastes and fibres. These particles are easily floated by introducing air bubbles to a treatment scheme in which the bubbles attach to the particles and reduce their density to less than water.

Dissolved air flotation (DAF) is one of various methods of flotation. In DAF, the air bubbles are created by dissolving air into water under pressure, and then releasing the pressurized water into a flotation tank in which the reduced pressure causes instantaneous precipitation of very small air bubbles with sizes in the range of 10 to 100 μm. These small air bubbles scatter light, producing a white water or milky appearance as shown in Figure 6.1.

DAF was recognized in 1924 as a feasible process for recovery of fibres in the paper industry. Since then, the process has become established for treatment of various industrial wastes and sludge thickening. Its history in drinking water is more recent. The first plants were built in Scandinavia and South Africa in the mid to late 1960s. Through the 1970s and 1980s, DAF saw wide use in Scandinavia and the UK. Since the mid 1980s, the application of DAF for clarification of water supplies has been increasingly used around the world.

The purposes of this paper are to summarize developments in the DAF process and to present some results of modeling, bubble characterization, alteration of bubble surface charge and its application to water treatment plant and natural water system and finally, to list some advantages and research needs.

Figure 6.1 DAF tank: illustrates white water appearance due to small air bubbles (*photo courtesy by Han*)

6.2 HISTORY OF DEVELOPMENTS IN THE DAF PROCESS

The evolution of the DAF process is depicted in Figure 6.2. The design and operation of the DAF process in the 1960s, 1970s, and early 1980s was based on experience. Low hydraulic loadings were used. Some laboratory and pilot-scale research was carried out by the Water Research Centre (UK) in the 1970s that led to better understanding of the operating conditions and in development of nozzles for injection of the pressurized water.

In the early 1980s the introduction of placing the DAF process on top of granular media filters was an interesting development. This is an important application as it greatly reduces a plant's footprint. Initially, this process was used by many small facilities, but it also has enormous advantages for large cities where land is scarce and costly. An example of this is a large plant (1.1 Mm^3/day) under construction in New York City for treatment of its Croton supply.

Beginning in the mid-1980s, and continuing to the present, extensive fundamental research on DAF has yielded a better understanding of the process. Some of the researchers (Edzwald et al 1990; Han, 2001; Haarhoff and Edzwald, 2004) studied the collisions and attachment of bubbles to particles and flocs in the contact zone (front baffled section).

This fundamental work, coupled with extensive pilot-scale studies of academics, utilities and industry has led to significant developments in decreasing pre-treatment flocculation times and high hydraulic loadings. Manufacturers have made major contributions to DAF tank design with deeper tanks, square configurations, improved hydraulic flows and withdrawal of the treated waters leading to high rate DAF processes. The trends to decreasing flocculation times and high hydraulic loadings are shown in Figure 6.3.

In the US, there are now some 100 DAF plants, most of which were built and went online since the early 1990s. As mentioned above, one plant under construction is the Croton plant for New York City. This plant is being built entirely underground with a footprint of only 3 ha to treat 1.1 Mm^3/d, which is made possible by stacking flotation over filtration and utilizing small flocculation tanks with just five minutes' detention time. When construction is completed and the plant covered, a golf driving range will be sited on top of it.

DAF is now used in South Korea, where there are two large DAF plants. One is the Songjeon plant in Wonju (see Figure 6.4). The water source for this plant is Hoeng-seong dam. Built between 1997 and 2005, the 150,000 m^3/day plant serves 407,300 people. This water treatment works is unique in that it treats a reservoir supply that undergoes large seasonal changes in turbidity. When the water quality is good, the plant can operate in a direct filtration mode, by-passing the DAF system. When the supply experiences high turbidity, the DAF unit is used. The plant can also make use of pre-sedimentation during very high turbidity events.

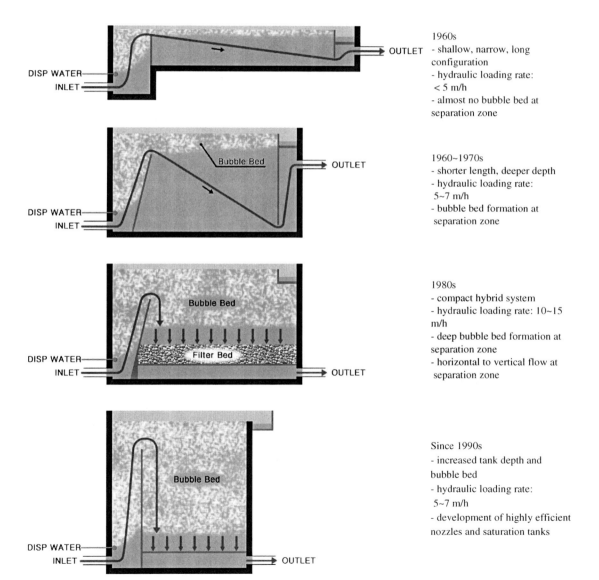

Figure 6.2 Developments in the DAF process

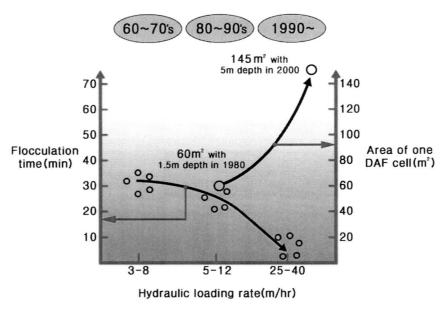

Figure 6.3 Trends of pre-treatment flocculation times, hydraulic loadings, and tank size

Figure 6.4 Songjeon plant, Wonju, South Korea. The water source for this plant is Hoeng-seong dam. Built between 1997 and 2005, the 150,000 m³/day plant serves 407,300 people (*photo courtesy by Wonju*)

6.3 MODELLING OF COLLISION EFFICIENCY BETWEEN MICROBUBBLES AND PARTICLES

For the modelling of collision of bubbles and particles, a single collector efficiency model (Edzwald et al., 1990) and the heterogeneous flocculation-based model (Tambo and Matsui, 1986) has been suggested. Han and Lawler (1992) modelled the collision efficiency of two particles under the three particle transport mechanism of Brownian motion, fluid shear and differential sedimentation including the hydrodynamic and inter particle force. They found that best collision occurs when the two particles are of similar size. However, electric force is not considered assuming that the particles are destabilized. Since then, the modelling (Han, 2002a) of dissolved air flotation (DAF) with the collision efficiency factor for bubbles and particles has been calculated from a trajectory analysis by a method similar to that used for the calculation of the collision efficiency factor in differential sedimentation (Han et al., 1991; Han et al., 1992). In this model, the effects of the contributing parameters, with bubbles and particles of various sizes and electric potentials, and particles of various densities, and ionic strength of the solution in the bubble–particle–solution system were investigated. The most important parameters in the DAF system are found to be the surface characteristics (zeta potential) of both bubbles and particles (Han et al., 2001).

Collision efficiency according to microbubble and particle sizes was determined based on changes in the zeta potentials of the bubbles and particles. Figure 6.5(a) shows that there were no collisions, regardless of the microbubble or particle sizes, when the zeta potentials of the microbubbles and particles had the same charge. Figure 6.5(b) shows that when the zeta potential of the particle was close to the isoelectric point, there were collisions. As the sizes of the microbubbles and particles became similar, collision efficiency increased, and when the sizes of the particles and bubbles decreased, the collision efficiency also increased. Figure 6.5(c) shows that when the zeta potentials of the microbubbles and particles are of opposite charge, the collision efficiency was the highest of all three cases.

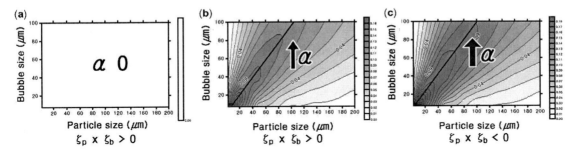

Figure 6.5 Collision efficiency according to the sizes and charge of the particles and bubbles. ζp and ζb represents the zeta potential of particle and bubble, respectively

Therefore, to increase the collision efficiency of the microbubbles and particles in the flotation process, their zeta potentials should be opposite, and the sizes of the particles and bubbles should be small and similar, to achieve the highest efficiency.

Pollutants in natural water are negative as is the case of most particles in water. Bubbles are negative too. In order to apply the harmony and balance (TaeGeuk) theory, we can change the characteristics of either pollutants or bubbles. We can change pollutants and algae into positive charge by adding chemicals, however it is prohibitively expensive and maybe harmful to the water body. Instead, we can think of making positively charged bubbles to make better collision with negatively charged pollutants.

6.4 CHARACTERIZATION OF BUBBLE SIZE

Microbubbles have been traditionally measured by image analysis, because of the rising and instable characteristic of bubble. A method of measuring microbubble size using one or two online particle counters in series (Chemtrac Model PC2400D, USA), has been developed (Han et al., 2002b) as shown in Figure 6.6. This arose from the idea that a microbubble behaves like a particle (Schulz, 1984), so a particle counting method (PCM) may sample bubbles to measure them, using the principles used for measuring particles using an online particle counter. To confirm its usefulness, the results were compared with those from image analysis. The PCM results were found to be very similar and were easier to handle, and the measuring time was much shorter.

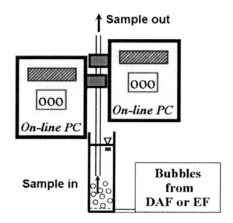

Figure 6.6 Schematic of particle counting method

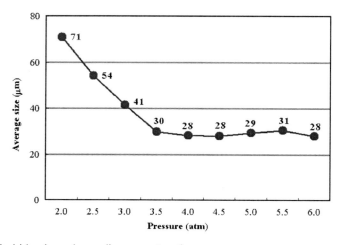

Figure 6.7 Average bubble sizes depending on saturation pressure

Then, using PCM, the sizes of bubbles in the DAF were measured under various pressure conditions, as pressure is known to affect bubble sizes the most (from 2 to 6 atmospheres) (Han et al., 2002c). Figure 6.7 shows the change of average bubble size under different pressure. The bubble size decreased as the pressure increased, up to 3.5 atmospheres. Above this critical pressure, the bubble size did not decrease with further increases in pressure. According to these experimental results, it is not only costly, but also unnecessary, to maintain a pressure above 3.5 atmospheres if the goal is only to generate smaller bubbles. By using this method, the sizes of bubbles generated under various operating conditions in DAF and Electro Flotation have been measured (Han et al., 2002b; Han et al., 2002c).

6.5 CHARACTERIZATION OF BUBBLE CHARGE

The zeta potential of bubbles are measured by electrophoresis measurement (EPM) method (Dockko et al., 1998; Han et al., 2004; Collins et al., 1978; Okada et al., 1987). Based on the principle of EPM, the zeta potential of the bubbles was measured with a set of equipment comprising an electrophoresis cell, microscope, CCD camera and a video image analyzer, as shown in Figure 6.8 (Dockko et al., 1998; Han et al., 2004).

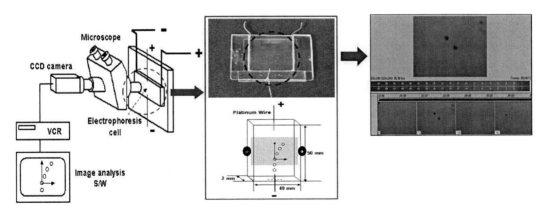

Figure 6.8 Equipment for electrophoresis measurement

When a horizontal electric field is applied to rising bubbles, the bubbles may move in a horizontal direction, according to their charge. The horizontal velocities of bubbles were obtained by analysis of the videotape with an image analyzer. The electrophoretic mobility of the bubbles was derived from this velocity. Then the zeta potential of the bubbles can be calculated from the measured horizontal velocity using the Smoluchowski equation.

Zeta potential of bubbles were measured under different concentrations of five metal species (Na^+, K^+, Mg^{2+}, Ca^{2+}, Al^{3+}). To exclude the effect of the anion in the solutions of divalent and trivalent salts, chloride salts dissolved in distilled water were used throughout. Four different concentrations of metal ions were prepared, ranging from 10^{-5} M to 10^{-2} M in increments of one order of magnitude. Solutions containing each metal ion, except potassium, were adjusted to the desired pH (from 3 to 12) by using hydrochloric acid or sodium hydroxide (Han et al., 2004; Han et al., 2006a; Han et al., 2006b). The zeta potential of bubbles in each solution is indicated in Figure 6.9.

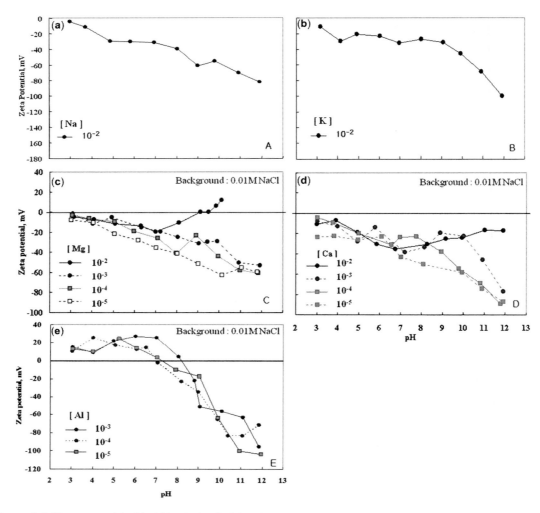

Figure 6.9 Zeta potential of bubbles in NaCl (a), KCl (b), MgCl$_2$ (c), CaCl$_2$ (d) and AlCl$_3$ (e) solutions

6.6 MECHANISM FOR PRODUCING POSITIVELY CHARGED BUBBLES

There have been experimental attempts to produce the positively charged bubbles (Li and Somasandaran, 1991; 1992). Positively charged bubbles were observed (Figure 6.9e) in AlCl$_3$ solutions of 10^{-5} M over a pH range of 3–7 (shaded on the graph). pC–pH diagram was used to analyze the reason for generating positive bubble.

Trivalent ions seem to be more useful than divalent ones if positively charged bubbles need to be generated in flotation. Moreover, addition of aluminium ions seems to be a reasonable way to make positively charged bubbles because a strongly alkaline solution is necessary to generate a positive zeta potential utilizing magnesium ions. Furthermore, because microbubbles with a positive zeta potential can be generated using the metal ions that occur naturally in water, any concerns about harmful by-products can be eliminated.

Han et al. (2006b) suggested a combined mechanism, with both specific adsorption of hydroxylated species and formation of hydroxide precipitates (Figure 6.10). Consequently, a prior knowledge of metal species distribution and solution conditions could lead to a tailoring of the zeta potential of bubbles in a flotation process.

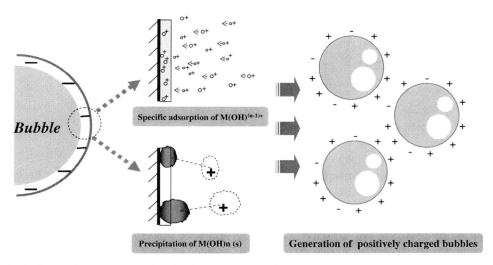

Figure 6.10 Probable principle explaining the procedure of charge reversal

6.7 VERIFICATION OF REMOVAL USING POSITIVELY CHARGED BUBBLES

A batch test was performed to investigate whether (Han et al., 2006a) algae could be removed using positively charged bubbles. Using charge-reversed bubbles produced by adjusting the pH of a solution of metal ions and water, we generated microbubbles after passing the solution into an electroflotation reactor, according to previously established solution conditions. Algae numbers were measured with a particle counter to analyze the numbers of blue-green algae before and after the removal process. The zeta potential of the bubbles was also measured by electrophoresis, and that of the algae was measured with a zeta meter (Sephy-II). The laboratory-scale experiment for the removal of algae using electroflotation was performed according to the schematic diagram in Figure 6.11.

We now examine whether positively charged bubbles can be used to remove algae with negative charges. Most algae are not easily removed with sedimentation processes, because of their low specific gravity, their tendency to float, their biological activity, and their mobility. Removal efficiency of algae is usually determined by the analysis of their chlorophyll-A. However, this study treats algae as particles. The removal ratio was analyzed using a high-sensitivity particle counter rather than by chlorophyll-A analysis, and the numbers of algae at different size range were counted before and after treatment. Because the blue-green alga used in this experiment is passively mobile, following the water flow, and occurs in a range of various sizes, the analysis of removal efficiency by size is more direct.

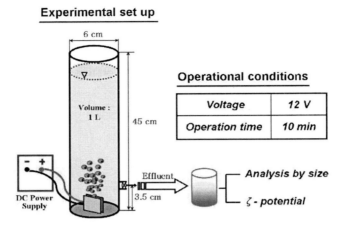

Figure 6.11 Schematic diagram of the laboratory-scale set up

A set of experiment was performed to analyze the removal efficiency of algae using positively charged bubbles. Figure 6.12 shows the zeta potentials of microbubbles and algae before and after the addition of 0.001 M $AlCl_3$. The algae take on different potentials, and this experiment investigated the removal efficiency of algae by section at pHs 3, 5, 7, and 9.

The relationship between zeta potential and removal efficiency indicates that the removal efficiency of algae increased in all pH regions, except pH 3, after the addition of $AlCl_3$. Because the removal efficiency at pH 3 without $AlCl_3$ is 100%, it could not be increased by adding $AlCl_3$. When the zeta potentials of the microbubbles and algae took on opposite charges, or in the range of pH 3–9, which is close to the isoelectric point, algae of more than 10 μm showed removal efficiencies of close to 100%. When the algae size is less than 10 μm, removal efficiency was 0% with or without $AlCl_3$. Conversely, when the zeta potentials of the microbubbles and algae took on the same charge or at pH 11, which is far from the iso-electric point, relatively low removal efficiencies were observed for all sizes of particles.

The size distribution of the algae investigated in this experiment indicated that the overall removal efficiency was less than 50%, because half of the algal particles were less than 10 μm. From this set of experiments to find the removal at different size and charge of both bubbles and algae, we found that the TaeGeuk theory can be applied to the removal of algae. This should advance our search for an effective way of removing algae.

6.8 RESEARCH NEEDS

DAF plants have several advantages compared to conventional sedimentation plants. DAF is more efficient than sedimentation in removing particles (turbidity). Lower particle loading to the filters yields longer filter runs and high filtered water production. Integrating this into the design of new plants allows for filters to be designed at higher rates.

DAF plants have a smaller footprint compared to conventional sedimentation and high rate plate and tube sedimentation plants. Shorter flocculation times reduce the size of the flocculation tanks. Another advantage is that DAF has been shown to be more effective than sedimentation in removing Giardia and

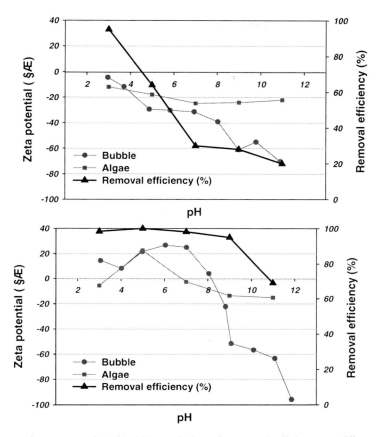

Figure 6.12 Change of zeta potential of bubble and algae & removal efficiency at different pH

Cryptosporidium (Edzwald et al., 2000, 2003). Finally, the sludge solids from DAF have a higher percentage of solids than sedimentation, thereby reducing sludge treatment and disposal costs.

Below, we provide a list of some research needs. This is not meant to be comprehensive, but rather point out some important areas for additional research. The first has to do with making positively-charged bubbles. Coagulants are used in drinking water treatment to produce flocs of little or no electrical charge to enhance bubble attachment. For water supplies low in natural organic matter, the primary objective of coagulation is altering the negative particle charge. Eliminating coagulant addition to the raw water flow may be possible by adding chemicals to the recycle flow to produce positively-charged bubbles (Han et al., 2006).

A second need has to do with optimising and controlling bubble size. DAF produces bubbles over a wide range of sizes from 10 to 100 pm, depending on the saturator pressure and nozzle type and design. Optimising the bubble size could improve treatment efficiency and also reduce energy consumption.

DAF is known to strip out some taste and odour compounds. A third need is to quantify what compounds are removed and identify how the process can be optimised. A fourth need has to do with integrating DAF as a pre-treatment for membrane processes, especially reverse osmosis and nanofiltration. To prevent fouling of membranes and to make the membrane plants more cost effective, pre-treatment is often necessary. DAF could be used to reduce particle fouling and fouling from algal polysaccharides. Finally, research is needed to reduce the energy consumption from producing air bubbles or to utilize the physical characteristics that might occur when bubbles break for the removal of microorganisms or micro pollutants.

6.9 REFERENCES

Collins, G.L., M. Motarjemi, G.J. Jameson (1978). A method for measuring the charge on small gas bubbles, *Jour. of Colloid Interface Science*, **63**(1) 69–75.

Dockko S., Han, M.Y., Park, C.H. (1998). Measuring Zeta potential of Micro-bubbles in DAF, *Jour. of Korean Society of Water and Wastewater*, **12**(4), 53–58.

Edzwald, J.K., Malley, J.P. Jr., and Yu, C. (1990). A conceptual model for dissolved air flotation in water treatment. *Water Supply*, **8**, 141–150.

Han, M. Y. (2002a). Modeling of DAF: the effect of particle and bubble characteristics, *Jour. of Water Supply: Research and Technology–AQUA*, **51**(1), 27–34.

Han, M.Y. and Lawler, D.F. (1992). The (relative) insignificance of G in flocculation, *Jour. AWWA*, **84**(10), 79–91.

Han, M.Y. and Lawler, D.F. (1991). Interactions of two settling spheres: settling rates and collision efficiencies, *Jour. Hydraulic Eng.* ASCE, **117**(10), 1269–1289.

Han, M.Y., Kim, W.T., and Dockko, S. (2001). Collision efficiency factor of bubble and particle (αbp) in DAF: Theory and experimental verification. *Wat. Sci. Tech.*, **43**(8), 139–144.

Han, M.Y., Park, Y.H. and Yu, T.J. (2002b). Development of new method of bubble size. *Wat. Sci. Tech.: Water Supply*, **2**(2), 77–83.

Han, M.Y., Park, Y.H., Lee, J. and Shim, J.S. (2002c). Effect of pressure on bubble size in dissolved air flotation. *Wat. Sci. Tech.: Water Supply*, **2**(5–6), 41–46.

Han, M.Y., Ahn, H.J., Shin, M.S., and Kim S.R. (2004). The effect of divalent metal ion on the zeta potential of bubbles. *Wat. Sci.Tech.*, **50**(8), 49–56.

Han, M.Y., Kim, M.K. and Ahn, H.J. (2006a). Effects of surface charge, microbubble size and particle size on removal efficiency of electroflotation. *Wat. Sci. Tech.*, **53**(7), 127–132.

Han M.Y., Kim, M.K. and Shin, M.S. (2006b). Generation of a positively charged bubble and its possible mechanism of formation. *Journal of Water Supply: Research and Technology–AQUA*, **55**(7–8), 166–176.

International Water Association (2007) *IWA Yearbook 2007*, Drinking water treatment, 38–40.

Li, C. and Somasundaran, P. (1991). Reversal of bubble charge in multivalent inorganic salt solution: Effect of magnesium, *Jour. of Colloid and Interface Science*, **146**(1), 215–218.

Li, C. and Somasundaran, P. (1992). Reversal of bubble charge in multivalent inorganic salt solution: Effect of Aluminum, *Jour. of Colloid and Interface Science*, **148**(2), 587–591.

Okada, K., and Y. Akagi (1987). Method and apparatus to measure the zeta potential of bubbles. *Jour. of Chemical Engineering of Japan*, **20**(1), 11–15.

Schulz, H.J. (1984). *Physico-chemical elementary process in flotation*. Elsevier, **12**(5), 275–276.

Tambo, N. and Matsui, Y. (1986). A kinetic study of dissolved air flotation. In *Proceedings World Congress of Chemical Engineering* (Tokyo), **3**, 200–203.

Chapter 7
Characterising the Membrane Filtration Process of Wastewater

J. van der Graaf, S. Geilvoet and J. Roorda

7.1 INTRODUCTION

Membrane ultra filtration for WWTP effluent and even feedwater as Membrane bioreactor (MBR) technology has become a widely used method for the treatment of municipal wastewater. Technologies developed are direct membrane filtration, effluent membrane filtration and MBR-technology. At the Delft University of Technology, intensive investigations have been carried out to search for optimisation of these processes by research and development of particle and filterability characterisation related to membrane filtration of effluent, raw wastewater and activated sludge. This chapter provide insight into the latest results of these research developments, namely the Specific Ultra Filtration Resistance (SUR) and the Delft Filtration Characterisation method (DFCm).

7.2 THE SPECIFIC ULTRA FILTRATION RESISTANCE METHOD (SUR)

7.2.1 Introduction

WWTP-effluent is a complex mixture with varying biological, chemical and physical properties. WWTP-effluent contains, as well as other raw water sources, dispersed particles, macromolecules, biological active substances and various ions (Brauns et al., 2002a). Even a single group of substances may represent thousands of chemical species, like for instance the group of humic substances (Drewes and Croue, 2002). The variations of constituents in the effluent in both quantity and quality make it difficult to relate one or a few components to the occurring fouling phenomena.

Wright et al. (2001) suggested the use of Flow Field Flow Fractionation (FlFFF) as a method to fingerprint feedwater for membrane filtration. FlFFF is based on solute characteristics and membrane solute interactions. FlFFF is a method to determine particle and macromolecule characteristics, most notably size and diffusion coefficient, in natural and synthetic systems. Brauns et al. (2002; 2002a) proposed a multi-value approach of fouling characterization using filtration data (Volume and

Permeability), presented in specific graphical formats and tables. That data presentation provides additional information to other fouling parameters like the Silt Density Index (SDI) and the Modified Fouling Index (MFI), both used for fouling prediction in reverse osmosis systems. The SDI and MFI are measured by filtering a feedwater sample over a flat sheet membrane with a pore size of 0.45 µm at a Trans Membrane Pressure (TMP) of 2.0 bar. The SDI is calculated from the time required to filter a fixed volume over the 0.45-µm membrane (Wiesner and Aptel, 1996). The MFI is calculated using the same filtration data as the SDI, but interpreting these with the cake filtration theory (Schippers and Verdouw, 1980). To incorporate colloidal particles into the MFI measurement Boerlage *et al.* (2002; 2003) proposed the application of ultra filtration (UF) membranes and named this parameter the MFI-UF.

Jarusutthirak *et al.* (2002) analysed Effluent Organic Matter (EfOM) in WWTP-effluent and distinguished different fractions of EfOM (colloids and hydrophobic and transphillic fractions) by different techniques. Jarusutthirak *et al.* concluded that the colloidal fraction of WWTP-effluent plays an important role in fouling of the membranes.

In all of these examples a mix of (filtration) properties of the feedwater was related to the occurring fouling phenomena in membrane filtration. This approach may be useful for the prediction of the fouling properties of a single feedwater. The ultra filtration process could be optimised when it would be possible to measure the filtration and fouling properties of the feedwater, i.e. WWTP-effluent in this research. Until now, there has not been any viable parameter for the determination of filtration characteristics in dead-end ultra filtration of WWTP-effluent. In practice and by performing pilot-plant experiments, it is also very difficult to measure accurately and differences in filterability.

Next to the complex composition of the effluent, also (dis)continuous changes in composition have a distinct effect on ultra filtration. The composition of the WWTP-effluent is subject to regular changes due to weather influences, discontinuous discharges in the raw wastewater and other aspects (Roorda and van der Graaf, 2001).

Other important aspects in determination of the fouling properties of WWTP-effluent are membrane-solute interactions, which are specific for each combination of membrane type and WWTP-effluent. Fouling parameters like the MFI-UF have to be measured with a specific membrane (Boerlage *et al.*, 2002) and therefore do not take into account the membrane-solute interactions. Finally, in dead-end ultra filtration the filtration time is usually 15 to 30 minutes, after which the membrane is backflushed. The filtration characteristics of the effluent have to be optimised for this time interval, as a high increase of resistance during this time interval frequently refers to increased fouling of the membrane on the long run (Doyen *et al.*, 1998; Galjaard *et al.*, 1998).

The objective of the research is to develop a parameter for evaluation of filtration characteristics during dead-end ultra filtration of WWTP-effluent. The Specific Ultra filtration Resistance (SUR) is proposed as a parameter. This parameter provides useful information about the filterability of the WWTP-effluent and can be measured within a short time (30 minutes). This enables online evaluation of the filtration properties and adjustment of the feedwater, which may therefore result in a more stable ultra filtration process.

7.2.2 Theoretical basis of the SUR

Darcy's law describes the relationship between flux, TMP, viscosity of the fluid and the total membrane resistance. In dead-end ultra filtration of $WWTP_{effluent}$ cake filtration is assumed to be the predominant filtration mechanism for the increase in resistance; therefore the total filtration resistance (R_{tot}) is the sum of membrane resistance (R_m) and cake resistance (R_c). Combining Darcy's law with the definition of flux, the following relationship for the total filtration resistance can be derived (equation 7.1).

$$R_{tot} = R_m + R_c = \frac{\Delta P}{\eta_T} \cdot A_m \cdot \frac{dt}{dV} \qquad (7.1)$$

where:

R_{tot} = total filtration resistance (m^{-1})
R_m = membrane resistance (m^{-1})
R_c = cake resistance (m^{-1})
ΔP = Trans Membrane Pressure, TMP (N/m^2 or Pa)
η_T = dynamic viscosity (N · s/m^2 or Pa · s)
A_m = membrane area (m^2)
t = time (s)
V = filtered volume (m^3)

The membrane resistance R_m is assumed to be constant. The cake resistance is not constant but increases with increasing cake layer thickness. The following equation shows the cake resistance as a function of the average specific cake resistance, the solids concentration and the filtered feedwater volume per m^2 of membrane area (Mulder, 1997). The resistance of the cake layer is the sum of the resistance caused by all particles retained within the cake layer (equation 7.2).

$$R_c = \alpha_{av} \cdot c_v \cdot \frac{V}{A_m} \qquad (7.2)$$

where:

α_{av} = average specific cake resistance (m/kg)
c_v = solids concentration in feedwater (kg/m^3)

When equation 4.1 and 4.2 are combined and integrated, assuming constant TMP and temperature ($t_0 = 0$; $t_t = t$; $V_0 = 0$; $V_t = V$), the relation for t/V and V can be derived. Equation 7.3 presents the linear relationship between t/V and V, depending on TMP and viscosity (temperature).

$$\frac{t}{V} = \frac{\eta_T \cdot R_m}{\Delta P \cdot A_m} + \frac{\eta_T \cdot \alpha_{av} \cdot c_v}{2 \cdot \Delta P \cdot A_m} \cdot V \qquad (7.3)$$

Except for the average specific cake resistance (α_{av}) and the solids concentration in the feedwater (c_v), all parameters in equation 7.3 are known or can be measured in experiments on dead-end ultra filtration of WWTP-effluent. The slope of the curve (t/V versus V) may therefore be used to calculate the product of the average specific cake resistance and the solids concentration ($\alpha_{av} \cdot c_v$). In Figure 7.1 the theoretically characteristic filtration curve is presented (according to Schippers and Verdouw, 1980). Three filtration mechanisms can be distinguished from this graph: initially pore blocking occurs, which is followed by cake filtration and finally cake filtration with compression of the cake layer.

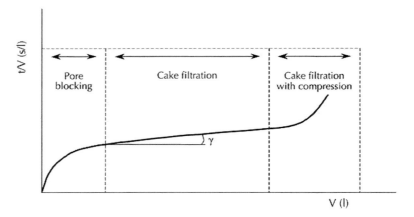

Figure 7.1 Ratio of filtration time and filtered volume (t/V) as a function of the total volume of filtered feed water (V) at constant TMP; this graph indicates three filtration mechanisms that occur theoretically: pore blocking, cake filtration and cake filtration with compression; tan γ is used to calculate the Specific Ultra filtration Resistance (SUR) (adapted from Schippers and Verdouw, 1980)

In this book the product of the average specific cake resistance α_{av} and the solids concentration of the feedwater c_v is defined as the Specific Ultra filtration Resistance (SUR) in m^{-2}. The SUR is used for characterisation of filtration behaviour.

$$\text{SUR} = \alpha_{av} \cdot c_v = \frac{d\left(\frac{t}{V}\right)}{d(V)} \cdot \frac{2 \cdot \Delta P \cdot A_m^{\ 2}}{\eta_T} \tag{7.4}$$

where:

SUR = Specific Ultra filtration Resistance, the cake layer resistance per unit of filtered feedwater per m^2 membrane area (m^{-2})

Schippers and Verdouw (1980) used the relation shown in equation 7.3 for the Modified Fouling Index (MFI) that was applied as a parameter for prediction of fouling in RO-systems. The MFI has been normalised to a TMP of 2.0 bar and a membrane area of a standard 0.45 μm microfilter ($13.8 \cdot 10^{-4}$ m^2). Boerlage et al. (2002) used the same equation to calculate the MFI-UF using ultra filtration membranes by using the same conditions as Schippers and Verdouw. Roorda and van der Graaf (2001) presented the normalised MFI-UF (MFI-UFn) as a standardised measurement for the prediction of filtration behaviour.

7.2.3 Experimental set-up and configuration

Experiments were performed to investigate the optimal procedure for measurement of the filtration curve and calculation of the SUR. In the experiments described in this section the lab-scale set-up and the process configuration were optimised, focusing on the following aspects: membrane module, constant pressure device, and total filtration time. In section 7.2.4 the influence of the process conditions (TMP and temperature) on the SUR is presented and the description of a procedure for measuring the SUR is suggested.

7.2.3.1 Membrane module for SUR measurement

Filtration and fouling phenomena in ultra filtration of WWTP-effluent depend both on membrane and feedwater characteristics (Galjaard *et al.*, 1998). The SUR will be especially useful when this interaction is taken into account. Many membrane types varying in physical and chemical properties are commercially available for full-scale application of ultra filtration. For measurement of the SUR a membrane module was made in which the same membrane type was used as in the pilot- or full-scale plant to which it refers. Two different membrane modules were tested. The first module is shown in Figure 7.2 in which the membrane is not supported. In this module the membrane was easily damaged during measurement of the filtration curve. Therefore a second module type has been tested, as shown in Figure 7.3.

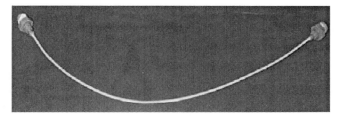

Figure 7.2 First membrane module with a membrane without module support for measurement of the filtration curve during dead-end ultra filtration; the membrane was easily damaged during an experiment *(photo by Roorda)*

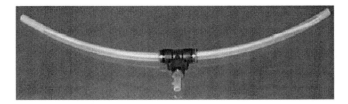

Figure 7.3 Second membrane module with PVC-tube supported membrane for measurement of the filtration curve during dead-end ultra filtration; this module showed good results and is proposed as the standard module for SUR measurement *(photo by Roorda)*

The membrane in the second module (Figure 7.3) was glued in a PVC tube (6 mm inner diameter), in which permeate is collected and continuously discharged through the outlet in the middle of the module. This module with the supported membrane showed good results and is proposed as the standard module for SUR measurements.

7.2.3.2 Constant pressure difference device

The relationship between t/V and V, used for calculation of the SUR was derived by using the cake filtration theory at a constant TMP. In this research three different devices for a constant TMP were tested. The first device was the lab-scale unit shown in Figure 7.4 in which constant pressure is provided by a pump that recirculates feedwater with a sub flow over the membrane. The feedwater temperature was measured with sensor T before and after an experiment, TMP was manually kept at a constant value and was analogically measured. Filtration data were sent to a personal computer (PC) that calculated the curve for t/V − V relationship. Experiments using this unit showed an increase of feedwater temperature with several degrees Celsius within 10–15 minutes. Next to this, the pump caused turbulence resulting in changes of the feedwater composition. Therefore, this lab-scale unit was transformed into the second device shown in Figure 7.5.

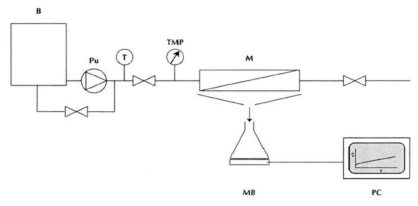

Figure 7.4 First lab-scale unit with a feedwater pump and recirculation of the feedwater through the pump; this unit is used for measuring filtration curves and calculating SUR; in which B: buffer tank, T: temperature sensor, Pu: pump, TMP: pressure sensor, M: membrane module, MB: analytical balance, PC: personal computer

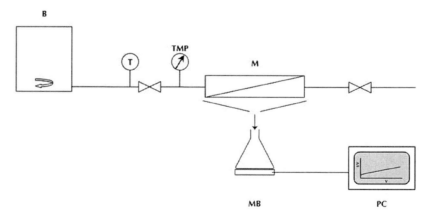

Figure 7.5 Second lab-scale unit with a pressurised buffer tank (B) collecting permeate in a separate permeate collector used for measuring filtration curves and calculating SUR; B: continuously stirred pressurised buffer tank, T: temperature sensor, TMP: pressure sensor, M: membrane, MB: mass balance and PC: personal computer

The air-pressured buffer tank (volume is 10 dm^3) provided a constant pressure difference over the membrane. Initially the TMP was measured analogically, and manually kept constant at 0.5 bar.

Permeate was collected in a beaker on an analytical balance (Mettler Toledo, 0–2000 g) that was connected to a computer with data analyses software. Some experiments were performed with a digital TMP measurement device, the data of which were sent to the PC together with the filtration data. The buffer tank was filled to a maximum of 50% with feedwater, the minimum sample volume was 1.5 dm^3. The feedwater is continuously stirred in the buffer tank.

Finally, the lab-scale unit was modified by putting two pressurised buffer tanks in parallel. As shown in Figure 7.6, buffer tank B1 was filled with demineralised water and the buffer tank B2 with feedwater. The use of two pressurised buffer tanks enabled initial filtration with demineralised water until TMP was constant. When TMP was constant valve 1 (V1) was changed from buffertank 1 to buffertank 2 providing constant TMP at the start of the feedwater filtration experiment. This led to more accurate filtration data. TMP was measured digitally and feedwater temperature was measured before and after an experiment. The device shown in Figure 7.5 (one pressurised buffer tank) has been used in most experiments presented in the subsequent part of this chapter.

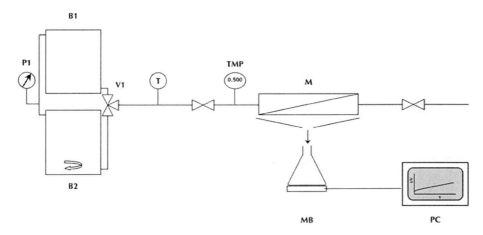

Figure 7.6 Lab-scale unit with two pressurised buffer tanks and used for measuring filtration curves and calculation of the SUR; B1: pressurised buffer tank 1 filled for 50% with demineralised water, B2: continuously stirred pressurised buffer tank 2 filled with feedwater, V1: valve choosing between Buffertank 1 or 2, T: temperature sensor, P1: constant pressure device before buffer tank (~0.5 bar), TMP: digital pressure sensor, M: membrane, MB: mass balance and PC: personal computer

7.2.3.3 Total filtration time

In dead-end ultra filtration of a feedwater the most frequently used cleaning method is the back flush. The time interval between two back flushes is normally 15 up to 30 minutes of filtration. It has been suggested that the filtration and fouling phenomena that occur during this short time interval influence the long-term fouling (Doyen *et al.*, 1998; Galjaard *et al.*, 1998). To characterise the short-term effect of interaction between feedwater and membrane with the SUR, the calculated value has to be stable within a time interval of 15 up to 30 minutes. For example, in Figure 7.7 a graphical presentation is shown of the filtration curve and related SUR curve, which was found in a lab-scale experiment using effluent from WWTP Berkel (sample date: 14-5-'02). In the first minutes of filtration the SUR increased due to the development of a cake layer. After ten minutes of filtration the SUR was more stable and showed a value of $(15.8 \pm 0.3) \cdot 10^{12}$ m^{-2} (a deviation of 1.8%) in the following twenty minutes of filtration, from 10 to 30 minutes of filtration.

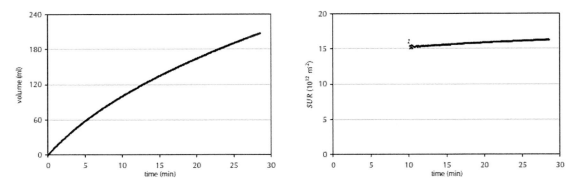

Figure 7.7 Result of lab-scale experiment on filtration of effluent from WWTP Berkel (14-5-'02) using the device with two buffer tanks in parallel (shown in figure 4.6); the filtration curve is shown in the graph at the left side, the calculated SUR curve is shown in the graph at the right side; between t = 10 and t = 30 minutes the SUR is determined $(15.8 \pm 0.3) \cdot 10^{12}$ m^{-2} (standard deviation of 1.8%)

Similar filtration experiments were performed on effluent from WWTP Berkel for a longer period, i.e. more than ten hours (Figure 7.8). These long-term experiments showed a continuously increasing SUR, with a large increase within the first two hours of filtration. During the last ten hours of filtration the SUR still increases, but at a lower rate. In Figure 7.8 the results are presented for the first thirty minutes of filtration (graph left) showing an average SUR of $(8.7 \pm 0.3) \cdot 10^{12}$ m^{-2}. After two hours of filtration the SUR increased to an average of $(10.4 \pm 0.1) \cdot 10^{12}$ m^{-2}, as shown in the graph on the right in Figure 7.8.

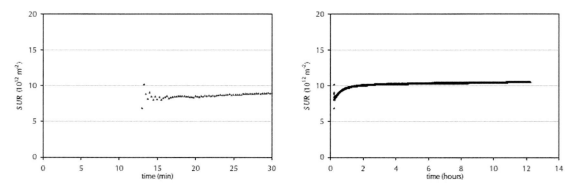

Figure 7.8 Results of long-term lab-scale experiment on filtration of effluent from WWTP Berkel (26-10-'00) using the device with one buffer tank (shown in Figure 7.5); the development of the SUR is presented for the first 30 minutes of filtration graph in the graph on the left side, with SUR is $(8.7 \pm 0.3) \cdot 10^{12}$ m^{-2}; the SUR is presented for twelve hours of filtration in the graph on the right side, after two hours the SUR increased to an average of $(10.4 \pm 0.1) \cdot 10^{12}$ m^{-2}

In this research, the SUR was calculated from data of a lab-scale experiment with dead-end ultra filtration performed for about 30 minutes. The standard deviation of the value of the SUR was similar in all experiments. The SUR had a standard deviation to a maximum of 3% within the first 30 minutes of filtration (for more details on the calculation of the SUR in practice see the description of the experimental procedure in the following section.

7.2.4 Influence of process parameters on the SUR

In this section the general experimental procedure that was followed is described. Next, the influence of the following process parameters on the SUR is investigated: Trans Membrane Pressure (TMP), feedwater temperature, and membrane type. All experiments described in §6.2.4 have been performed using the device with one pressurised buffer tank (Figure 7.5). In cases where the device with two buffertanks (shown in Figure 7.6) was used, this is mentioned explicitly.

7.2.4.1 Experimental procedure for measuring SUR

The applied experimental procedure for measuring the SUR was as follows. By gluing a commercially available capillary membrane (0.8 or 1.5 mm inner diameter) in a PVC tube (6 mm inner diameter) the membrane module was made. In order to remove conditioning liquid and other impurities, the membrane module was then soaked for 30 minutes in a NaOCl solution (200–400 ppm).

After soaking in a NaOCl solution the membrane module was placed in the lab-scale filtration unit (Figure 7.5) and the buffer tank was filled with demineralised water (5 dm^3, 50% of the volume of the buffer tank). Next, the membrane module was cross-flushed with demineralised water (for about 2 minutes). Back flushing of the membrane was not possible with the lab-scale unit. Finally, the permeability (in $l/m^2 \cdot h\,bar$ at 15°C) was determined by filtering demineralised water over the membrane at a TMP of 0.5 bar. Before and after filtration the temperature of the demi-water was measured.

The demineralised water was removed from the buffer tank after determination of the permeability. The feedwater for measurement was added to the buffer tank. The whole system was flushed with feedwater (for 2 minutes) and by closing the valve right after the module (see Figure 7.5) the filtration mode could be transformed from cross-flow to dead-end filtration. The TMP was manually set to 0.5 bar and the feedwater was filtered over the membrane. After 30 minutes of filtration the system was cross-flushed with feedwater and the membrane module was removed from the lab-scale unit and soaked in a sodium hypochlorite solution. After soaking for 30–60 minutes the permeability for demi-water was measured. If the change in permeability for demi-water was less than 10% as compared to the initial value, the module was (re)used in the next experiment.

The collected data were stored in a computer and were analysed in a spreadsheet model for calculation of the SUR. The slope of the t/V – V curve was evaluated and the interval for which the slope was constant was noted. Next, the SUR was calculated from the difference between the highest and the lowest value in this interval for which the slope was constant. This simplification of the calculation of the SUR led to an overestimation of the SUR of less than 3%. The overestimation was demonstrated by calculating the SUR for each point of the t/V – V curve (<500 points). The average value of the SUR calculated accordingly showed this minor overestimation (whereas the standard deviation was less than 3%). The measurement of the SUR was done in duplicate for each sample.

7.2.4.2 Trans Membrane Pressure (TMP)

Material and methods

The TMP is an important process parameter in membrane filtration processes. Increasing the TMP will increase the flow through the membrane and at the same time increase the deposition of particles. The fouling layer may be compressed at increasing TMP. Boerlage et al. (2003) found a non-linear relationship between TMP and MFI-UF, which was attributed to cake layer compression. Three series of experiments have been performed to investigate the influence of the TMP on the SUR during dead-end ultra filtration of WWTP-effluent. In all experiments a 1.5 mm capillary X-flow membrane (PES/PVP) was used. In Table 7.1 an overview of these experiments is shown.

Table 7.1 Three series of experiments for the study of the influence of TMP on SUR using effluent from WWTP Berkel

Experiment	TMP (bar)	Increasing/decreasing TMP	NaOCl cleaning	No. of experiments
TMP-1	0.5, 1.0, 2.0	Increasing (0.5 → 2.0)	No	4
TMP-2	0.25, 0.5, 1.0, 1.5, 2.0	Increasing (0.25 → 2.0)	Yes	2
TMP-3	0.25, 0.5, 1.0, 1.5, 2.0	Decreasing (2.5 → 0.25)	Yes	2

The first series of experiments (TMP-1) were performed with effluent from WWTP Berkel at a TMP of 0.5, 1.0 and 2.0 bar. The experiment started by measuring the SUR at a TMP of 0.5 bar. After 30 minutes of filtration, the membrane was crossflushed (without soaking in chemicals) and the TMP was set to 1.0 bar. The same procedure was applied for measurement of the SUR at a TMP of 2.0 bar. Finally, at the end of the experiment, the membrane was soaked for 5–20 hours (during the night) with NaOCl solution (200 ppm). This experiment was repeated on the following three days, using the same effluent sample that was stored in a refrigerator (at 4°C).

The second series of experiments (TMP-2) was also carried out with effluent from WWTP Berkel for five different TMP's (0.25, 0.5, 1.0, 1.5, and 2.0 bar) and started by measuring the SUR at the lowest TMP (0.25 bar). The experiment was finished by determination of the SUR at the highest TMP (2.0 bar). The membrane was soaked for 15 minutes with 200–400 ppm NaOCl and cross-flushed before increasing the TMP for the following experiment. This experiment was repeated on the following day, using the same effluent sample.

The last series of experiments (TMP-3) was performed under similar conditions as TMP-2, but now with decreasing TMP. The first SUR determination was done at a TMP of 2.0 bar and the last measurement of the SUR on a day was done at a TMP of 0.25 bar. This experiment was also repeated on the following day. Finally, the membrane permeability for demineralised water was determined at 0.5, 1.0 and 2.0 bar. The permeability of the membrane was used for calculation of the membrane resistance.

Results

The results of the experiments are summarised in Table 7.2, which shows the average SUR measured at the various applied TMPs. A graphical presentation is given in Figure 7.9, showing on the X-axis the applied TMP and on the Y-axis the average SUR found in the experiments. Before starting the experiment, the permeability of the membrane was measured by filtration of permeate. Contrary to Persson et al. (1995), Huisman et al. (1997) and Boerlage et al. (2003) no change in membrane resistance was found at increasing TMP.

Increasing the TMP with 100% from 0.5 to 1.0 bar, showed a 55% to 80% increase of the SUR. Similar results were found for a TMP increase from 1.0 to 2.0, which resulted in an additional SUR increase of 56% to 75%. The results of experiment TMP-1 and TMP-2 were the same, the results of experiment TMP-3 showed some difference for TMP of 1.5 and 2.0 bar. This might be due to the differences in the

Table 7.2 Results of three series of experiments for the study of the influence of TMP on SUR using effluent from WWTP Berkel

Experiment Applied TMP (bar)	TMP-1[a] SUR (10^{12} m^{-2})	TMP-2[b] SUR (10^{12} m^{-2})	TMP-3[c] SUR (10^{12} m^{-2})
0.25	nd[d]	6.2 ± 2.0	4.6 ± 0.0
0.5	7.7 ± 1.0	8.4 ± 0.3	6.4 ± 0.0
1.0	12.3 ± 1.7	12.9 ± 0.3	11.4 ± 0.7
1.5	nd	18.3 ± 1.7	13.7 ± 1.1
2.0	21.7 ± 1.9	21.3 ± 0.8	17.8 ± 1.0

[a]Measured at increasing TMP; measured four times
[b]Measured at increasing TMP; measured twice
[c]Measured at decreasing TMP; measured twice
[d]Not determined

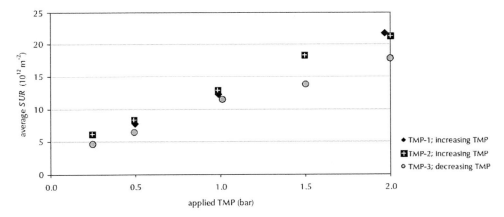

Figure 7.9 SUR of WWTP-effluent (Berkel) measured at variable TMP

experimental procedure. Experiment TMP-3 started SUR measurement at the highest TMP, whereas TMP-1 and TMP-2 started at the lowest TMP.

It is possible that the cross-flushing (TMP-1) and chemical cleaning (TMP-2) were not effective enough to remove all retained material within and on the membrane structure. The remaining material on the membrane could have promoted the development of a cake layer and thereby the increase of the SUR.

The SUR was defined as the product of the average specific cake resistance (α_{av}) and the solids concentration in the feedwater (c_v). As the latter (the composition) was kept constant, the increase in SUR at increasing TMP should have been caused by an increase of the average specific cake resistance (α_{av}). This might be due to cake layer compression (Hermia, 1982; Mulder, 1997; Boerlage et al., 2003). Compressibility of the cake layer can be expressed as a variation in the specific cake resistance as a function of the pressure (Boerlage et al., 2003; Lee et al., 2003; Matsumoto et al., 1999; Tiller and Yeh, 1987):

$$\alpha = \alpha_0 \cdot \Delta P^s \tag{7.5}$$

where:

α = specific cake resistance (m/kg)
α_0 = specific cake resistance at reference pressure, i.e. 0.5 bar (m/kg)
s = compressibility coefficient, expressing degree of compressibility

(when s = 0, no compression occurs; when s = 1, compression is complete)

This relationship is used for calculation of the compressibility of the cake layer in these experiments, assuming that the SUR (specific cake resistance * solids concentration) shows an identical relationship. The log-log curve of the SUR versus the TMP is presented in Figure 7.10. The compressibility coefficient is the slope of each curve. For the three series of experiments the compressibility coefficient for TMP-1, TMP-2 and TMP-3 are 0.75, 0.61 and 0.66 respectively, indicating a highly compressible cake layer.

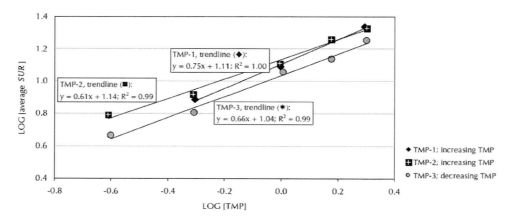

Figure 7.10 LOG-LOG curve of SUR of WWTP-effluent (Berkel) against measured TMP

As shown in these results the SUR strongly depends on the applied TMP. To use the SUR as a parameter for filtration characteristics of effluent, the TMP for SUR measurement should be defined as a constant value. In dead-end ultra filtration of WWTP-effluent in practice, the TMP is generally in the range of 0.2 to 0.8 bar with an average of 0.5 bar. Therefore in further research a TMP of 0.5 bar has been used for the determination of the SUR value of (pre-treated) WWTP-effluent.

7.2.4.3 Temperature of the feedwater
Material and methods

Since the (dynamic) viscosity of water is related to temperature, the feedwater temperature is an important factor in the calculation of the SUR. In the following experiments the relation between temperature and SUR has been investigated for temperatures of 10°C (exp. T-1), 20°C (exp. T-2) and 30°C (exp. T-3).

Experiments at a feedwater temperature of 10°C were done with effluent stored in a refrigerator. At 20°C the effluent was first adapted to the ambient temperature. Finally, for experiments with a feedwater temperature of 30°C the effluent was heated with a thermo regulator.

On the first day effluent is taken from WWTP Berkel, after which the first experiment was performed at 20°C. The next day two experiments were performed at 10 and 20°C. The following day the temperature was set to 10 and 30°C and on the final day to 30°C. In Table 7.3 a summary of the experiments is presented.

Table 7.3 Three experiments to study the influence of feedwater temperature on SUR using effluent from WWTP Berkel

Experiment	Feedwater temperature	Effluent age[a] (days)
T-1	10	1[b] and 2[c]
T-2	20	0[c] and 1[b]
T-3	30	2[d] and 3[e]

[a]The effluent had been stored in a refrigerator (at 4-6°C)
[b]Measured twice
[c]Measured four times
[d]Measured once
[e]Measured five times

The membranes used in these experiments were 0.8 mm X-flow membranes (PES/PVP). Before the start of each experiment the membrane was soaked in a 50–100 ppm NaOCl solution.

Results

The results of experiments T-1, T-2 and T-3 are presented in Table 7.4 and Figure 7.11 and show that the SUR increased with increasing effluent temperature. As found in these experiments, the SUR increased about $9 \cdot 10^{12}$ m^{-2} for every 10°C. Accordingly, for every degree Celsius the SUR of effluent from WWTP Berkel changes about $1 \cdot 10^{12}$ m^{-2}. Te Poele and Van der Graaf (2002) found similar results for increasing the temperature of WWTP-effluent (Berkel) from 13 to 30°C (SUR changed from $18.3 \cdot 10^{12}$ to $30.4 \cdot 10^{12}$ m^{-2}. At even higher temperatures (60 and 90°C) similar results were found.

Table 7.4 Results of experiments on the influence of feedwater temperature in the SUR for effluent from WWTP Berkel, together with results of te Poele and vd Graaf (2002) and Meezen (2002)

Experiment		Average temperature	
	Sampling date	Feedwater (°C)	SUR (10^{12} m^{-2})
T-1	9-2000	9.6 ± 1.3	15.4 ± 0.7
T-2		20.4 ± 0.4	24.4 ± 5.3
T-3		31.2 ± 1.6	33.3 ± 4.4
te Poele and vd Graaf (2002)	4-2001	13.0	18.3
		30.0	30.4
Meezen-1 (2002)	4-2002	13.0	12.4
		14.0	12.7
		15.0	13.1
Meezen-2 (2002)	4-2002	8.0	11.6
		11.0	13.1
		15.5	14.0

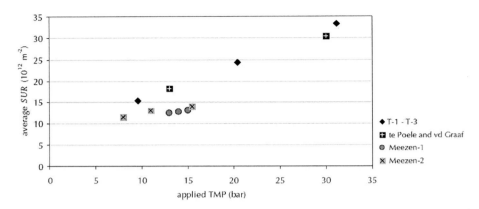

Figure 7.11 Graphical presentation of results of experiments studying the influence of feedwater temperature on SUR for effluent of WWTP Berkel

These results are in contradiction to the findings for the permeability of Chiemchaisri and Yamamoto (1994) for membrane bioreactor sludge, where at a constant flux an increase of the feedwater temperature resulted in a decrease of the TMP. Also the results of Boerlage et al. (2003) on the permeability of tap water showed the opposite, i.e. increasing temperature increased the permeability.

The effect of temperature on the SUR was only determined for effluent of WWTP Berkel. Also te Poele and van der Graaf (2002) used Berkel effluent, the results of which are added to figure 7.11. The effect on demineralised water is not determined, but no increase of SUR is expected at increasing temperature. Te Poele and van der Graaf (2002) found no change in filtration characteristics of demineralised water after increasing the temperature from 30 to 60°C and even from 60 to 90°C. Also no change in membrane resistance was found, an observation that corresponds to the findings of Huisman et al. (1997).

These experiments indicate that the temperature of the WWTP-effluent influences the filtration characteristics, which must be due to changes in the specific cake resistance.

As the SUR values for experiments T-1 to T-3 are relatively high, it is expected (see data of Meezen (2002)) that effluent with a lower SUR will show a smaller change for a temperature increase. The results of the experiments on WWTP-effluent (Berkel) showed that a pre-defined feedwater temperature is important for using the SUR as a parameter for the prediction of filtration behaviour.

7.2.5 SUR for evaluation of filtration characteristics

In this section the feasibility of the SUR as a parameter to evaluate filtration characteristics and predict the flux decline in dead-end ultra filtration systems is investigated. To determine the relation between the foulants/particle concentration and SUR in WWTP-effluent, the SUR was measured for diluted samples of WWTP-effluent.

Next, the possibility to measure differences in filterability of WWTP-effluent due to pre-treatment of the effluent by in-line coagulation and multi-media filtration was examined. Finally, this section summarises SUR values found for effluent from eight WWTP's in the Netherlands.

7.2.5.1 Foulants concentration

Material and methods

The relationship between foulants concentration and the SUR value was investigated in five experiments. The SUR was measured using the lab-scale device with one pressure vessel (figure 7.5) at a TMP of 0.5 bar. The SUR of WWTP-effluent (Berkel, T = 20°C) was measured, as well as the SUR after diluting the WWTP-effluent (ratio WWTP-effluent: dilution water is 100:0, 50:50, and 25:75).

In all experiments demineralised water was used for dilution. Experiments D-1 to D-3 were started by measurement of the SUR of demineralised water. Next, the undiluted effluent was measured, followed by 50%-effluent and 25%-effluent. In experiments D-4 and D-5 first the SUR of demineralised water was measured, followed by 25%- effluent, 50%-effluent and finally undiluted effluent. The membrane was soaked in NaOCl (200 ppm) in between the SUR measurements. In table 7.5 an overview of the five experiments is presented.

Table 7.5 Experiments to determine the effect of effluent dilution with demineralised water on the SUR

Experiment	Order[a]	No. of experiments
D-1	Demi, 100%, 50%, 25%	Two (over two days)
D-2	Demi, 100%, 50%, 25%	One
D-3	Demi, 100%, 50%, 25%	Two (over two days)
D-4	Demi, 100%, 50%, 25%	Two (over two days)
D-5	Demi, 25%, 50%, 100%	Four (over two days)

[a]Each experiment started with measurement of the SUR of demineralised water, followed by the (diluted) effluent samples; 100% indicates undiluted effluent, 50% indicates 50% effluent and 50% demi water, 25% indicates 25% effluent and 75% demi water

Results

In Table 7.6 the measured SUR values found in the dilution experiments are presented together with the relative value of the SUR compared to the SUR value for undiluted effluent (100% effluent). The SUR of demineralised water was between 0 and $0.4 \cdot 10^{12}$ m^{-2}. In Figure 7.11 the SUR of a 0%-effluent (100%-demi) is defined as 0% of the SUR of a 100%-effluent sample.

The SUR is defined as the product of the average specific cake resistance and solids concentration in the feedwater. A decrease in solids concentration should therefore result in a proportional decrease of the SUR. The results presented in Table 7.6 and Figure 7.12 showed a non-linear decrease in SUR. In all experiments a 50% dilution showed a more than 50% decrease of the SUR (55–61% decrease).

Another 50% effluent concentration decrease showed again a decrease of more than 50% (percentage not presented in Table 7.8; decrease of 57–68%). The SUR value of 100%-effluent was different in all experiments and reflects the variations in quality of WWTP-effluent (Berkel) in a period of a month. An almost linear relation between SUR decrease and effluent dilution has been found in all experiments. In the dilution experiments the flux of 25%-diluted effluent was 0–20% higher than for the undiluted effluent. This might have caused a change in average specific cake resistance, which could explain the small deviation of the measured data compared to a linear relationship. Another explanation might be that the dilution caused a different cake layer build-up.

Table 7.6 SUR measured as function of foulants concentration (effluent diluted with tap water (D-1, D-2) and demineralised water (D-3, D-4, D-5))

Foulants (%)	Experiment D-1		Experiment D-2		Experiment D-3		Experiment D-4		Experiment D-5	
	SUR (10^{12} m^{-2})	(%)	SUR (10^{12} m^{-2})	(%)	SUR (10^{12} m^{-2})	(%)	SUR (10^{12} m^{-2})	(%)	SUR (10^{12} m^{-2})	(%)
100	10.1 ± 0.9	100	8.3	100	9.4 ± 0.1	100	15.3 ± 0.7	100	13.9 ± 0.4	100
50	4.5 ± 0.2	45	3.7	45	3.8 ± 0.3	40	6.2 ± 0.2	41	5.4 ± 0.7	39
25	1.5 ± 0.1	14	1.2	15	1.6 ± 0.1	17	2.5 ± 0.2	16	2.3 ± 0.1	17

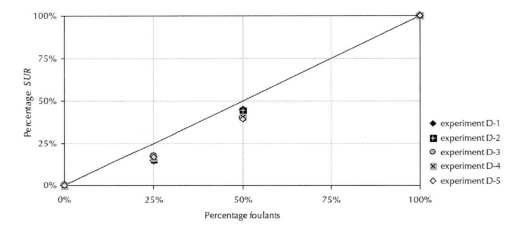

Figure 7.12 Percentage of SUR as a function of dilution for five experiments using WWTP-effluent (Berkel) as feedwater

7.2.5.2 Evaluation of feedwater pre-treatment
Material and methods

The possibilities for application of the SUR in evaluation of the effect of WWTP-effluent pre-treatment on the filtration characteristics are described in this section. The effect of pre-treatment by dual-media filtration and coagulation with ferric chloride on the value of the SUR was investigated in the following experiment. Firstly, the SUR of raw WWTP-effluent (Berkel, T = 20°C) was measured. Next, ferric chloride was added and the SUR was measured. The last measurement was performed using effluent that was pre-treated with dual-media filtration.

The first experiment (Pre-1) was performed for four consecutive days; all measurements were done in duplicate. The second experiment (Pre-2) was performed on two consecutive days. The (pre-treated) effluent was analysed for turbidity (Hach, model 2100N). The SUR was measured of:

(1) Untreated effluent;
(2) Effluent pre-treated with 1.0 mg Fe^{3+}/l. Ferric chloride (1.0 mg Fe^{3+}/l) was added to effluent (V = 4 dm^3) and stirred for 10 minutes. The SUR was determined after stirring the sample;

(3) Filtrate of dual-media filtration of WWTP-effluent. The dual-media filter was a double media layer (V = 13 dm³; A = 0.64 dm² and H = 20 dm) made of 0.5 m sand (d = 1.0 − 1.6 mm) and 1.5 m anthracite (d = 1.4 − 2.5 mm). The filtration rate was controlled with a valve in the filtrate line on the bottom of the filter bed and set at 5 m/h (32 l/h). After filtering 1.5 times the volume of the filter bed (∼20 dm³ of effluent) filtrate was sampled for the SUR measurement.

Results

In Table 7.9 and Figure 7.13 the results of the experiments for evaluation of pre-treatment on the SUR are presented, which show a decrease of the SUR for both dual media filtration and coagulation with 1 mg/l of ferric chloride. This showed that differences in filterability could be measured by the SUR.

Table 7.9 SUR measured of raw and pre-treated WWTP-effluent (Berkel, 20°C)

Experiment	Pre-1				Pre-2			
Feedwater	SUR (10^{12} m^{-2})	%SUR[a]	Turbidity (NTU)	%Turbidity	SUR (10^{12} m^{-2})	%SUR[a]	Turbidity (NTU)	%Turbidity
Effluent	12.4 ± 1.1	100%	3.4 ± 0.6	100%	17.0 ± 1.4	100%	3.4 ± 0.7	100%
Effluent + 1 mg Fe^{3+}/l	9.1 ± 0.5	73%	3.3	97%	12.9 ± 1.4	76%	2.9 ± 0.6	85%
Filtrate	10.6 ± 0.6	85%	1.1 ± 0.2	32%	13.9 ± 0.6	82%	1.4 ± 0.2	41%

[a]Relative to the value of effluent

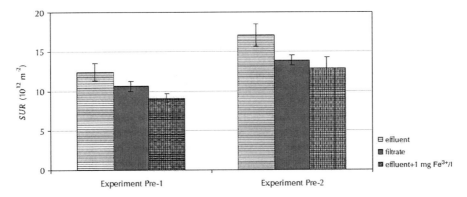

Figure 7.13 Diagram of SUR measured for raw and pre-treated WWTP-effluent (Berkel, 20°C)

Coagulation resulted in a turbidity decrease of 5% to 15%, whereas the dual-media filter removed 60% to 70% of the turbidity. But the largest decrease in the SUR was found for coagulation, about 25%, where the dual-media filter resulted in a SUR decrease of 14% to 18%. This showed that a decrease in turbidity of the effluent did not relate to a similar increase in filterability of the effluent (i.e. decrease of SUR). Coagulation of the effluent compared to dual-media filtration proved to be a better technique for reduction of components that determine the filterability of the WWTP-effluent.

7.2.5.3 SUR determination at various WWTP's in the Netherlands

Material and methods

During the research period described in this chapter (1998–2003) the SUR has been measured at eight different WWTP's in the Netherlands. In 1999 the SUR was measured using the lab-scale unit equiped with a pump (Figure 7.4) for WWTP Ede and Kaffeberg. In 2000 the second lab-scale unit, with one pressurised buffer tank (Figure 7.5), was used and SUR was measured at WWTP Tilburg-Noord and Vlaardingen. All measurements in 2002 were performed with the lab-scale unit equipped with two pressurised vessels (Figure 7.6) for the remaining WWTP's of Berkel, Emmtec, Hoek van Holland and Zaandam.

The SUR has to be measured at a feedwater temperature of 20°C. At some WWTP's the effluent or filtrate was coagulated (1.0 mg/l ferric chloride or aluminium chloride (poly aluminium chloride, PACl)). In some cases, the SUR was also measured for WWTP-effluent pre-treated with dual-media filtration.

Results

In Table 7.10 the results of the SUR measurements are given. These results show large variations in SUR for effluent at the different WWTP's. The filterability of the effluent was specific for each WWTP. This shows the possible advantages of the use of SUR for actual investigation of the filtration characteristics in a pilot-plant or full-scale installation.

7.2.6 Discussion

7.2.6.1 Parameter for dead-end ultra filtration

The SUR is the product of the specific cake resistance (α_{av} in m/kg) and the solids concentration (c_v in kg/m^3). WWTP-effluent is a complex mixture of constituents that may vary in both physical and chemical properties. It is therefore very difficult to find the proper values for solids concentration and specific cake resistance. But the product of specific cake resistance and solids concentration can be found by applying the cake filtration theory on filtration data that are measured in constant TMP experiments (Hermia, 1982). The SUR is then calculated from the slope of the t/V versus V curve.

To obtain reliable and reproducible data, a filtration device for constant pressure filtration was introduced. Firstly, a device with a pump that recirculates the effluent was tested, but changes in effluent composition made it necessary to transform this device into a lab-scale unit with a pressurised buffer tank. The turbulence in the recirculation pump changed the properties of the feedwater with rising temperatures (5°C for every 30 minutes of filtration). With the pressurised buffer tank (V = 10 dm^3) the composition of the feedwater sample could be kept constant throughout the experiment without increasing the temperature. At the start of the filtration cycle the TMP of the lab-scale unit with a single vessel was manually set to a constant TMP of 0.5 bar. This procedure took about 1 to 2 minutes and caused disturbances in the filtration data. By adding another buffer tank in parallel (filled with demineralised water), the TMP could be adjusted to a constant value within seconds.

In this case no disturbance of the filtration data was found. The lab-scale unit with two buffer tanks in parallel worked properly and provided reliable filtration data for measurement of the SUR.

Table 7.10 SUR values found for (pre-treated) effluent from eight different WWTP's in the Netherlands; for effluent the measured range is shown between brackets

WWTP	Berkel[c]	Ede[a]	Emmtec[c]	HvHolland[c]	Kaffeberg[a]	Tilburg-N[b]	Vlaardingen[b]	Zaandam[c]
Year	2002	1999	2002	2003	1999	2000	2000	2000
Feedwater	SUR (10^{12} m^{-2})	SUR (10^{12} m^{-2})	SUR (10^{12} m^{-2})	SUR (10^{12} m^{-2})	SUR (10^{12} m^{-2})	SUR (10^{12} m^{-2})	SUR (10^{12} m^{-2})	SUR (10^{12} m^{-2})
Effluent	11	18	9	21	29	5	15	20
(range)	(6-40)	(11-23)	(4-13)	(11-44)	(24-34)	(3-6)	(14-16)	(18-22)
Effluent + coag.	9	10	3			5		
Filtrate	10	4	7	16	28	4		
Filtrate + coag.			5	11				

[a]Measured using device with recirculation pump (Figure 4.4)
[b]Measured using device with one pressurised buffer tank (Figure 4.5)
[c]Measured using device with two parallel pressurised buffer tanks (Figure 4.6)

7.2.6.2 Process conditions

Total filtration time

The experiments that were performed for determination of the time needed for measurement of a reliable and reproducible SUR (§7.2.3.3) resulted in a total measurement time of 30 minutes. The SUR was calculated from the data that were found between 10 and 30 minutes of filtration. It was shown that the SUR increased slightly in time, about 1–3% within 30 minutes of filtration. This finding might be related to small particles that are retained by the fouling layer and penetrate the fouling layer. This will lead to a decrease in porosity of the fouling layer, which might increase the resistance of the fouling layer (i.e. an increase in SUR).

Trans Membrane Pressure

The SUR was measured as a function of the Trans Membrane Pressure (TMP). An increase in the TMP resulted in an increased SUR, due to compression of the fouling layer. The compression coefficient was in the range of 0.61 to 0.75. The values for the compression coefficient reflect the compression of a whole range of constituents that are found in WWTP-effluent. The specific cake resistance and its compressibility depend both on the character of the foulants. This is shown in for instance Nakanishi *et al.* (1985) where it is concluded that the specific cake resistance depends on the species of microorganisms, their shape and size (Matsumoto *et al.*, 1999). Foulants in WWTP-effluent are expected to have a biological background and behave similar to, or are similar to (fractions of) micro-organisms.

Compression of the fouling layer should be taken into account in the design of the process conditions of full-scale ultra filtration plants. The compressibility of a fouling layer determines the limits of the ultra filtration process. The impact of compression is explained in the following figures. In Figure 7.14(a) the filtration curve is drawn for a flux of 50 and 100 $l/m^2 \cdot h$. The resistance increase in this graph is a function of the amount of filtered feedwater (i.e. amount of foulants). The resistance over the membrane is doubled after 15 minutes of filtration at a flux of 50 $l/m^2 \cdot h$ without compression of the fouling layer. At a flux of 100 $l/m^2 \cdot h$, the similar amount of foulants is filtered over the membrane within 7.5 minutes, resulting in the same resistance of the fouling layer. But a similar resistance over the membrane relates at a double flux to doubling of the TMP, from 0.2 bar for 50 $l/m^2 \cdot h$ and 0.4 bar for 100 $l/m^2 \cdot h$ (without compression).

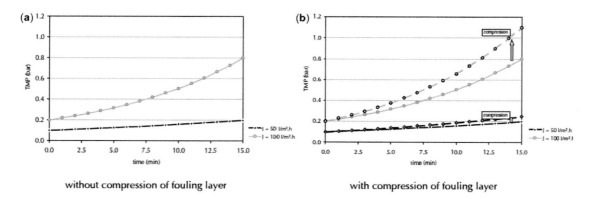

Figure 7.14 TMP as a function of the flux and its relationship with compression of the fouling layer

In Figure 7.14(b) the effect of compression on the TMP is drawn. Compression is a function of the applied TMP and increases at increasing TMP. The subsequent increase in resistance over the membrane and fouling layer amplifies the TMP increase. Compression of the fouling layer is especially something to deal with at a higher TMP than at a low TMP. From these findings it is concluded that fouling layer compression is a very important aspect in determination of the process conditions of dead-end ultra filtration systems.

Temperature

The temperature of the (pre-treated) effluent influenced the SUR. Unexpectedly, no major flux increase was found at increasing temperature in the experiments described in §7.2.4.3. This effect of the temperature has also been found in other effluent ultra filtration experiments in our laboratory (te Poele and van der Graaf, 2002; Meezen, 2002). In literature no similar results were found. The average specific cake resistance is the overall cake resistance of all foulants in the effluent. It is therefore expected that the temperature effect can be related to changes in the characteristics of most foulants. Maybe foulants stretch due to temperature increases (Campbell et al., 1993).

The SUR values that were found in experiments T-1 to T-3 were rather high for effluent of WWTP Berkel ($24.4 \cdot 10^{12} \pm 5.3 \cdot 10^{12}$ m^{-2}, measured at T = 20°C), compared to the average SUR of Berkel effluent ($11.1 \cdot 10^{12}$ m^{-2}). This might also affect the filtration characteristics found in experiments T-1 to T-3. This is indicated by the research of Meezen (2002), in which a smaller SUR values were measured. This resulted in a lower increase of the SUR as a function of temperature.

Measurement of the SUR

From the TMP as well as the temperature experiments it became clear that the interpretation of SUR data is only possible if TMP and temperature are well defined. The SUR is introduced as a parameter for evaluation of filtration characteristics in ultra filtration of effluent. In pilot-scale research as well as in full-scale applications the TMP is found within the range of 0.2 to 0.8 bar. Measurement of the SUR is therefore proposed at a TMP of 0.5 bar. The temperature of the sample feedwater is measured at ambient temperature of 20°C which is proposed as the reference temperature.

Membrane type

Results of experiments M-1 to M-4 using four different membranes with the same chemical composition but a different pore size and diameter of the fibres, showed that the pore size of the membranes (Molecular Weight Cut-Off, MWCO) did not influence the SUR. Components with dimensions within the MWCO-range of 80–150 kDa have only minor influence on the filtration characteristics. These results indicate that the components retained on the membrane surface predominantly determine the filtration characteristics. It has been shown in §7.2.4.4 that differences found in the SUR for 0.8 and 1.5 mm capillaries were mainly related to inaccurate data of the internal diameter of the capillaries. Still the corrected values of the membranes with a larger inner diameter (1.5 mm) showed a 12% lower SUR than those with the smaller inner diameter.

In general, differences in membrane composition are related to differences in filtration characteristics (Boerlage et al., 2003; Doyen et al., 1998; Galjaard et al., 1998). The SUR provides information of the interaction between the applied membrane and the feedwater. The information on filtration characteristics measured with the SUR might be related to experiments on a larger scale, using the same membrane type and WWTP-effluent. In that case also the measuring conditions have to be similar to the conditions in the pilot-plant or full-scale installation. The interaction between membrane and feedwater determines the filtration and fouling characteristics. Therefore the SUR is defined and measured at a TMP of 0.5 bar at a feedwater temperature of 20°C. The temperature of WWTP-effluent showed variations between 6–25°C, but evaluation of the influence of for instance pre-treatment should be performed under specified conditions. For on-line measurement of SUR it might be possible to incorporate the actual temperature of the feedwater.

SUR for characterisation of filtration

To investigate the relationship between the foulants concentration and the SUR, experiments were performed on the relation between SUR values and dilution of effluent samples (WWTP Berkel). The results showed an almost linear relationship between foulants concentration and SUR. By dilution of the effluent, only the solids concentration changes, which was found in these experiments. Boerlage *et al.* (2003) found similar results for the relationship between concentration and MFI-UF for dilution experiments on tap water and canal water.

Pre-treatment of WWTP-effluent by multi-media filtration and in-line coagulation is sometimes found to increase the filterability of the effluent (Abdessemed *et al.*, 2000; Bourgeous *et al.*, 2001; Ghosh *et al.*, 1994; van der Graaf *et al.*, 1999). Experiments Pre-1 and Pre-2, as well as the results of experiments found at various WWTP's (data from table 7.10), resulted in changes in the SUR after pre-treatment of the effluent. In Figure 7.15 the data of table 7.10 are graphically presented, showing a decrease of the SUR after in-line coagulation of 4% (WWTP Tilburg-Noord) to 63% (WWTP Emmtec). The decrease after multi-media filtration was for some effluents less than after in-line coagulation (WWTP's Berkel, Emmtec) and for some more than after coagulation (WWTP's Ede, Hoek van Holland, Tilburg). These results show that the choice of a proper pre-treatment technique for improved filterability can be evaluated with the SUR.

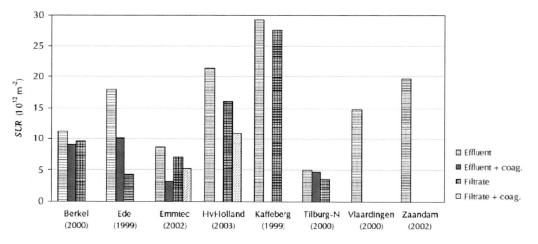

Figure 7.15 Average SUR values found for raw and pre-treated effluent from eight different WWTP's in the Netherlands

Finally, it has to be emphasized that the performance of ultra filtration in pilot or full-scale installations depends only partly on the filterability. Although a high initial filterability (low SUR) indicates higher fluxes, also the removal efficiency of the retained material at the membrane surface is important. When the retained material partly removed during a cleaning interval, the overall flux will decrease. However, comparing the SUR of effluent with the results from the pilot-scale tests, it is found that a low SUR (high filterability) is a requirement for good ultra filtration performance.

7.2.7 Conclusion

The Specific Ultra filtration Resistance (SUR) is proposed as a new parameter for measuring the filtration characteristics of effluent in dead-end ultra filtration. The SUR is calculated from the filtration data measured with a lab-scale device. The SUR is calculated from the ratio of filtration time and filtrate volume (t/V) as a function of the total filtrate volume and is the product of the specific cake resistance and the solids concentration. The process conditions during measurement affect the SUR of the effluent, therefore the SUR is defined at a constant TMP of 0.5 bar and an effluent temperature of 20°C. The SUR has an accuracy of more than 95% and is measured within 30 minutes of filtration.

The experiments on the SUR revealed also additional information about the filtration characteristics of WWTP-effluent. The MWCO of a PES/PVP membrane did not influence the SUR. This indicates that effluent constituents larger than the pore sizes determine filtration characteristics. Experiments with varying Trans Membrane Pressure showed that the occurring fouling layer is highly compressible (s = 0.6–0.75).

This implies that the fluxes should not increase too much, as the accompanying TMP increases more than linear. Pre-treatment induced an increase in filterability of 20% to 30%. Both pre-filtration and coagulation influenced mainly particles larger that 5–10 µm. This relatively small increase in filterability by pre-treatment indicates therefore that the filterability is only partly determined by particles larger than 5–10 µm.

The SUR was measured for effluent of various WWTP's in the Netherlands and showed great variations for the different WWTP's. The SUR was found to range from $5 \cdot 10^{12}$ to $30 \cdot 10^{12}$ m^{-2}. Although the effect of pre-treatment on the filterability (measured as SUR) was relatively small, the change in filterability can be measured accurately with the SUR. In these tests coagulation as well as multi-media filtration showed a decrease of the SUR (of approximately 20% to 30%), greatly depending on the local conditions.

7.3 THE DELFT FILTRATION CHARACTERISATION METHOD (DFCM)

7.3.1 Introduction

Despite several advantages, like superior effluent quality and compactness, combining the activated sludge process and membrane filtration in an membrane-bioreactor (MBR) inevitably introduces the problem of membrane fouling. Fouling in MBR is an extensively investigated research topic and significant progress has been made in understanding this problem, but nevertheless fouling is still a major point of attention in (full-scale) MBR operation. Fouling is the result of interaction between the membrane and the activated sludge to be filtered. Zhang et al. (2006) distinguish three basic factors that determine the degree of fouling occurring in MBR: (a) the nature of the feed to the membrane, (b) the membrane properties and (c) the hydrodynamic environment experienced by the membrane.

In practice researchers use a wide variety of these three interactive factors in their experimental set-ups to investigate fouling. As a result of this the outcome of various research projects can often not be generalized or can even lead to contradictory results. To overcome this problem Delft University of Technology has developed a filtration characterisation method; with this method activated sludge samples collected from different pilot- or full-scale MBR installations or under different circumstances are filtrated with the same membrane under identical hydrodynamic circumstances. In this way differences in filterability can be exclusively linked to differences in the quality of the filtered sludge. This method is called the Delft Filtration Characterisation method (DFCm).

This chapter deals with several aspects of the DFCm. First the employed filtration unit and the accompanying measuring protocol are described. Secondly for one research project the DFCm results are analysed in relation to the performance (permeability) of the considered full-scale installation to verify whether DFCm results indeed give an indication of the sludge filterability in practice. Finally an overview of several different research campaigns with the DFCm is given.

7.3.2 Methods and Materials

For research into fouling in MBR Delft University of Technology has developed the Delft Filtration Characterisation method (DFCm), described in detail by Evenblij et al. (2005). With the DFCm different activated sludge samples can be filtrated with the same membrane and under identical hydraulic circumstances. In this way differences in filterability can be related exclusively to differences in sludge characteristics. The DFCm consists of a small scale filtration unit (Figure 7.16) and an accompanying measuring protocol.

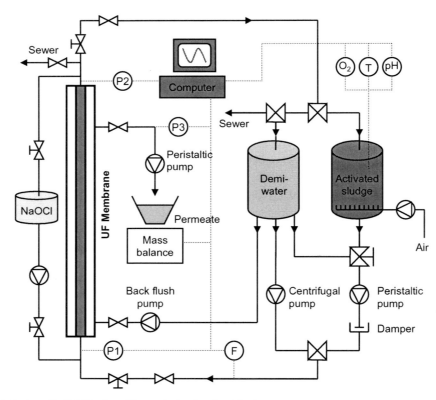

Figure 7.16 Set-up Delft Filtration Characterisation installation

7.3.2.1 Filtration unit

The heart of the filtration unit is a single tubular side stream X-Flow UF membrane with a length of 95 cm, a diameter of 8 mm and a nominal pore size 0.03 μm. A peristaltic pump circulates an activated sludge sample through the system; the cross-flow velocity in the membrane tube is fixed at 1 m/s. Another peristaltic pump is used for permeate extraction; permeate flow rate can be adjusted by tuning the pump speed. The permeate production is measured in time with a mass balance, so the flux J ($l/m^2 \cdot h$) can be calculated. Using three pressure gauges (feed, concentrate and permeate) the transmembrane pressure TMP (bar) during an experiment is monitored. The viscosity η (Pa $\cdot$ s) of permeate can be assumed equal to pure water. From these three parameters the filtration resistance R (m^{-1}) can be calculated according to Darcy's law: $R = TMP/(\eta \cdot J)$

7.3.2.2 Measuring protocol

In order to obtain unequivocal results all filtration experiments are conducted following a measuring protocol consisting of three steps:

(1) *Clean Water Resistance (CWR) measurement.*
The membrane has to be clean prior to a sludge filtration experiment. To check this demineralised water is filtrated with CFV = 1 m/s and J = 80 $L/m^2 \cdot h$. For a clean membrane the filtration resistance should be about $0.4 \cdot 10^{12}$ m^{-1} ($\pm 0.05 \cdot 10^{12}$ m^{-1}). If the CWR is too high supplementary cleaning measures are necessary (see #3).

(2) *Sludge filtration.*
An activated sludge sample (about 30 liter) is filtrated with CFV = 1 m/s at a flux of J = 80 $l/m^2 \cdot h$ for half an hour or until the maximum TMP of 0.75 bar is exceeded. Depending on filterability the flux can be increased or decreased in subsequent experiments.

(3) *Membrane cleaning.*
After sludge filtration the membrane is cleaned for the next experiment. This can be done by (a combination of) a forward flush (demi-water, 4 m/s), a back flush (demi-water, -0.75 bar) and chemical cleaning (NaOCl 500 ppm, soaking 15 minutes).

7.3.2.3 Output

The main step of the measuring protocol is the sludge filtration step. During the filtration step several parameters (TMP, resistance, flux, temperature, pH) are monitored and stored in a computer file using the software application Testpoint. The main output of an experiment is the course of the resistance during filtration. An example of the output of an experiment is presented in Figure 7.17. In this graph the filtration resistance is plotted against the permeate production per membrane surface. The starting- or membrane resistance is similar for all experiments and is left out of consideration when analysing the results. As a result of fouling of the membrane during filtration the filtration resistance will increase. The slope of the curve gives an indication of the sludge filterability; a steep curve corresponds with a poor filterability. To make a comparison between different curves each curve can be presented as the value ΔR_{20}: this value represents the increase of the resistance after a permeate production of 20 l/m^2.

7.3.2.4 Sludge quality analyses

All DFCm experiments are accompanied by sludge quality analyses to identify foulants. Basic sludge quality parameters like temperature, pH, mixed liquor suspended solids (MLSS) concentrations and sludge volume index (SVI) are always measured.

Many researchers attribute fouling in MBR systems to extracellular polymeric substances (EPS), and more specifically to EPS in the free water phase of the sludge: This form of EPS is now commonly

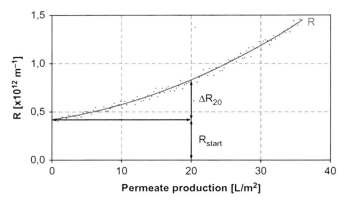

Figure 7.17 Example output DFCm experiment

referred to as soluble microbial products (SMP). The main constituents of SMP are considered to be proteins and polysaccharides. Proteins are measured according to the method of Lowry et al. (1951), modified by Frølund et al. (1996) and improved by Brahner (2000). Polysaccharides are measured according to the method described by Dubois et al. (1956) and improved by Brahner (2000).

7.3.2.5 Possibilities and limitations of DFCm

Fouling is a complex process that can be analysed from different points of view. The DFCm can not cover all aspects of fouling that will occur in a full-scale installation. Therefore it is important to identify the possibilities and the limitations of DFCm. This is done on the basis of Figure 7.18 (based on Kraume et al. 2007); this figure schematically presents the different fouling mechanisms that occur in practise in a full-scale installation on a long term.

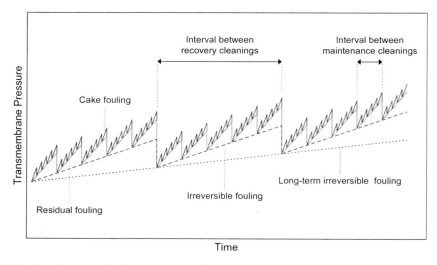

Figure 7.18 Filtration characterisation curves MBR Varsseveld

Each form of fouling illustrated in Figure 7.3 corresponds with a typical rate, time interval and cleaning measure. A rough range of typical numbers is given in Table 7.11.

Table 7.11 Typical ranges of different fouling rates (based on Kraume 2007)

Fouling "form"	Fouling rate [mbar/min]	Time interval	Cleaning
Cake fouling	0.1 – 1	10 minutes	Mechanical
Residual fouling	0.01 – 0.1	1–2 weeks	Maintenance
Irreversible fouling	0.001 – 0.01	6–12 months	Recovery
Long-term irreversible fouling	0.0001 – 0.001	Several years	Not applicable

The shortest-term fouling mechanism is cake formation, which is only combated by mechanical measures. Apart from creating turbulent flow conditions near the membrane surface through coarse bubble aeration also relaxation and back flushing can be used to prevent or remove cake layer fouling. Periodical chemical cleaning of the membranes is indispensible to maintain sufficient permeability on a longer term. Depending on the system configuration low-intensive maintenance cleanings and high-intensive recovery cleanings can be carried out. Fouling that can not be removed by any physical or chemical cleaning measure is referred to as irrecoverable or long-term irreversible fouling. Ultimately the irrecoverable fouling determines the lifetime of a membrane (apart from other forms of damage).

The DFCm is not capable of covering long-term fouling phenomena; it only provides insight about cake fouling. Though on first sight DFCm thus only seems to cover a small part of the total fouling spectrum, it is however very important to have insight in the cake fouling potential of MBR activated sludge. In the first place low cake fouling offers room for optimisation of the membrane operation; when the filterability is good, energy and thus costs can be saved concerning relaxation time, back flushing and/or coarse bubble aeration rate. Besides this it is not improbable that there is a relation between short-term and long-term fouling rates. This can be investigated by comparing short-term DFCm results with long-term permeability data from investigated plants.

7.2.3 DFCm results versus full-scale permeability development

As discussed previously an important aspect of the DFCm experiments is how the filterability measured with the FCI relates to the functioning of the membranes of the full-scale installation in practice. This matter is discussed with respect to a research campaign at the full-scale MBR installation of Varsseveld in 2005. A number of factors which could complicate the interpretation of the filtration characteristics produced by the DFCm can be pointed out:

- The membrane configurations of the DFCm and MBR Varsseveld are different; while the filtration unit is equipped with an external (inside-out) membrane the full-scale MBR has submerged (outside-in) membranes. This implies that the shear created tangential to the membrane surface to prevent fouling is different for both systems. In the full-scale installation shear is created by coarse bubble aeration, while in the DFCm shear is created by means of cross-flow velocity of the fluid in the membrane tube.
- To prevent fouling in the full-scale installation the membranes are usually operated under low subcritical fluxes, while in the DFCm fouling is forced by applying high supercritical fluxes.

- The difference between the type/brand of the membranes in the filtration unit and the full-scale MBR can be mentioned. However, both membranes are made of PVDF and the difference in pore size between the membranes in the filtration unit (X-flow, nominal pore size 0.03 μm) and the full-scale installation (Zenon, nominal pore size 0.04 μm) are negligible.

In the first months after the biological start-up of the MBR major problems were experienced concerning the filterability of the sludge/water mixture. Soon it was suspected that the wastewater stream from a local cheese factory was the malefactor. This wastewater contained the substance PVA (poly vinyl acetate), which is used to cover the cheese with a plastic-like coat. It appeared that this PVA was responsible for sticking of the membranes. To put a stop to the PVA problems it was decided to uncouple the cheese factory from the sewer (as from the 9th of May) and to transport this wastewater to another (conventional) treatment plant. The uncoupling of the cheese factory resulted in a considerable improvement of the filterability measured with the DFCm. Curves from before (Jan–Apr) and after (Jun–Oct) the uncoupling of the cheese factory are presented in Figure 7.19.

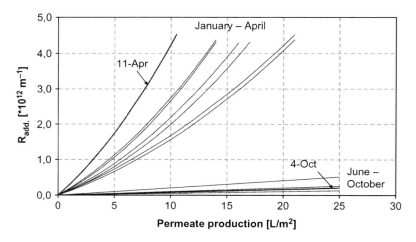

Figure 7.19 Filtration characterisation curves MBR Varsseveld

Two curves from Figure 7.19 (April 11th and October 4th) are analysed more in detail in relation to the permeability values at the time of sampling. The worst filterability measured with the DFCm was encountered on April 11th, see figure 7.20. The major problems with the filterability also come to light in the full-scale permeability data. Permeability values have dropped to low levels (<300 $l/m^2 \cdot h \cdot bar$). The applied flux is very low, approximately 17 $l/m^{-2} \cdot h$ and increasing the flux directly leads to a severe permeability drop. This observation supports the proposition that the sludge filterability quality is indeed bad, as was measured with the DFCm.

Filterability measured with the DFCm in October is excellent. By chance at the moment of sampling on October 4th the Water Board was executing a capacity test with one of the membrane tanks. Figure 7.21 presents the applied flux and the permeability in the concerned tank. Results show that the permeability is hardly influenced by the continuous high flux (approximately 35 $l/m^2 \cdot h$). The excellent filterability which was measured with the DFCm is again in accordance with the permeability data monitored for the full-scale installation.

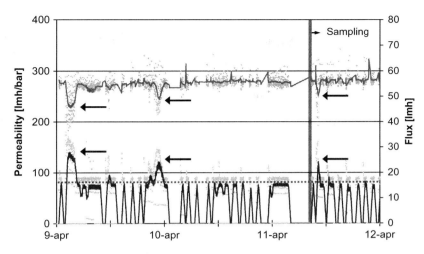

Figure 7.20 Permeability and applied flux MBR Varsseveld, 9–12 April

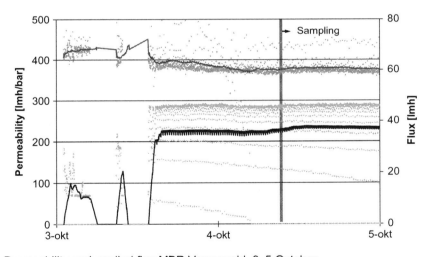

Figure 7.21 Permeability and applied flux MBR Varsseveld, 3–5 October

7.3.4 Filterability results

The DFCm can be employed in several ways. In this chapter three applications will be discussed:

(1) As a tool to compare the sludge quality between several different (pilot) installations;
(2) As a tool to characterise the sludge quality of a single MBR installation over a long period;
(3) As a tool to perform batch experiments.

7.3.4.1 Pilot comparison

In 2004 the filtration unit was installed at three different MBR pilot plants in the Netherlands, at each location for a period of about two weeks. Each pilot plant had a capacity of approximately 10 m^3/h. Every day about three filtration characterisation experiments were performed. Results showed that filterability per pilot was rather constant, but when the pilots are compared mutually, considerable differences between the curves reveal. Figure 7.22 presents the average curves obtained at experiments with a flux of 80 l/m$^2 \cdot$ h.

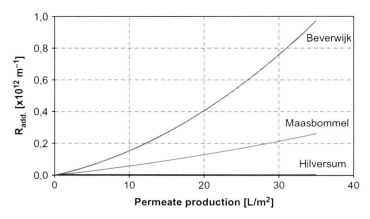

Figure 7.22 Filtration curves for three different MBR pilots

Besides a flux of 80 l/m$^2 \cdot$ h several other fluxes were tested to investigate the sensitivity for changes in flux. In Figure 7.23 the ΔR_{20} values are plotted against the applied fluxes.

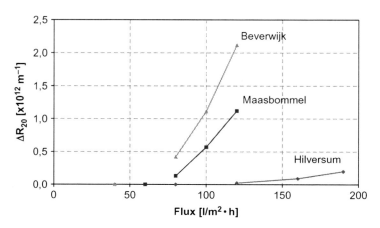

Figure 7.23 ΔR_{20} versus applied flux

For fluxes of 40 and 60 $l/m^2 \cdot h$ no fouling was recorded for all three pilots. Activated sludge from Beverwijk and Maasbommel show comparable behaviour with increasing flux, but with consistently lower ΔR_{20} values for Maasbommel sludge. The Hilversum sludge shows very different behaviour. Results at a flux of 80 $l/m^2 \cdot h$ already indicated a very good filterability of this sludge. This is confirmed by the experiments with higher fluxes: even at a flux of 190 $l/m^2 \cdot h$ the ΔR_{20} value is very low. In this research the filtration characterisation experiments were accompanied solely by SMP analyses. However, the filtration behaviour could not be correlated clearly to SMP concentrations.

7.3.4.2 Long term sludge quality monitoring

In the beginning of 2006 a full-scale MBR with a capacity of 100 m^3/h was started up at the WWTP of Heenvliet in the Netherlands. Activated sludge samples were collected on a weekly basis throughout the first year of operation of the MBR. Besides DFCm experiments several sludge quality parameters were monitored/determined: temperature, MLSS, SVI and SMP concentrations.

In Figure 7.24 the development of ΔR_{20} in the considered period is plotted. On the basis of the ΔR_{20} values a rough distinction can be made between four periods. Directly after the start-up of the installation (period I) ΔR_{20} is high; the filterability in this period can be qualified as "bad". From the beginning of March the filterability improves rapidly. During period II filterability is rather variable, but overall an improving trend continues. In the summer months (period III) the filterability is excellent, with ΔR_{20} values of practically 0. As from October (period IV) ΔR_{20} slightly increases but filterability can still be qualified as "good".

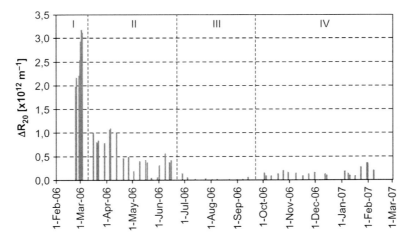

Figure 7.24 Development ΔR_{20} MBR Heenvliet in first year of operation

The excellent filterability that was measured in the summer months suggests a seasonal/temperature influence on the filtration characterisation results. In Figure 7.10a the ΔR_{20} values are plotted against the temperature of the samples. The overall results indeed show a lower ΔR_{20} at higher temperatures. On the other hand it can be noticed that in period I the ΔR_{20} differences are considerable while temperatures of all samples were similar and in period III and IV the differences in filterability are marginal while big differences in temperature occur.

Figure 7.25b presents the ΔR_{20} plotted against MLSS. The results are contradictory. In period I, when the biomass concentration was raised from 4.6 to 11.4 g/l, the results show a clear linear increase of ΔR_{20} with increasing MLSS concentrations. This trend is totally different from the situation in the other three periods: here the results suggest a better filterability at higher TSS concentrations.

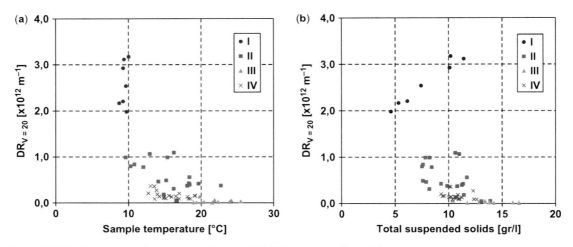

Figure 7.25 ΔR_{20} versus Temperature (a) and MLSS concentrations (b)

The conclusion of this research was that sludge filterability showed relation with mixed liquor suspended solids concentrations, sludge volume index and temperature in different periods of the year, but none of these parameters could be linked to filterability over the whole year. This suggests that different fouling mechanisms could have been dominant over the year. This research did again not demonstrate a clear link between sludge filterability and SMP concentrations. Another conclusion from this research might be that filterability depends on a combination of several sludge quality parameters. This implies that it is doubtful if relating only one sludge quality parameter to filterability can lead to useful/reliable conclusions.

7.3.4.3 Batch experiments

Three activated sludge samples of about 30 litres were collected simultaneously from the full-scale MBR of WWTP Heenvliet in May 2007. The samples were stressed in batch experiments over a period of 24 hours by imposing continuous aerated and anoxic circumstances and by a pulsed a addition of a high dose sodium acetate (high F/M-ratio, 300 mg COD/g MLSS).

Besides DFCm experiments, the SMP concentrations in several fractions of the activated sludge free water were analysed. As a first fractionation step the free water was separated from the sludge by filtration over a Schleicher and Schuell 589/2 filter paper (pore size 7–12 µm). Subsequently this free water sample was filtrated over three different cellulose acetate filters with pore sizes of respectively 1.2 µm, 0.45 µm and 0.2 µm.

The different circumstances opposed upon the three activated sludge samples lead to different filtration behaviour after 24 hours. Figure 7.26 presents the results of the four DFCm experiments. Continuous aeration of the sample appears to have no significant influence on the filterability; after 24 hours the curve is almost similar to the one of the start-sample. On the other hand, the continuous anoxic circumstances and the pulsed substrate addition have led to a strong increase of the filtration resistance, i.e. a severe deterioration of the filtration quality of the sludge.

The results of the fractionation tests and accompanying SMP analyses are graphically presented in Figure 7.27. Considering the fractions of the start- sample the results show that all fractions larger than 0.2 μm contain approximately the same protein concentrations. This implies that all proteins in the free water are smaller than 0.2 μm. The hypothesis that all proteins in the free water are very small is supported by the relatively high concentration that is measured in the permeate; over 50% of all protein constituents in the free water are smaller than the pore size of the membrane (0.03 μm).

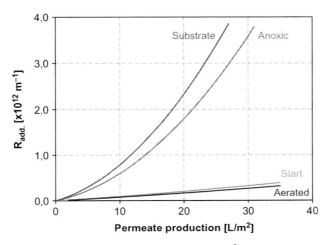

Figure 7.26 DFCm results batch-tests (CFV = 1.0 m/s, J = 80 l/m² · h)

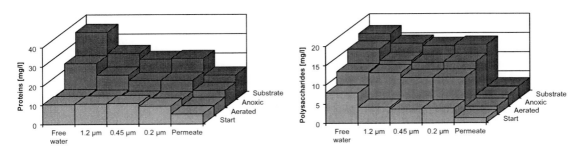

Figure 7.27 Protein- and polysaccharide concentrations per fraction for all batch-tests

Figure 7.26 shows that a 24 hour period of aeration had no significant effect on the sludge filterability. Besides this also the protein concentrations in the free water stay more or less unaltered. This is however not the case for the anoxic- and the substrate-sample. The deterioration of the filterability is accompanied by a considerable release of proteins in the free water. In the anoxic-sample the protein concentration doubles compared to the start- and the substrate-sample shows an increase of proteins by more than a factor three. Like in the start-sample also in the batch tests the protein concentrations for the fractions 1.2 μm, 0.45 μm and 0.2 μm are approximately similar.

The polysaccharide concentration in the free water of the start-sample is 7.9 mg/l. This is approximately twice the concentration that is measured in the filtrate of the three cellulose acetate filters. Considering the aerated-sample the behaviour of polysaccharides differs from proteins. While protein concentrations stay more or less similar, the polysaccharide concentrations increase by more than a factor 2. This increase of polysaccharides can however not be linked with the sludge filterability.

For the anoxic and the substrate batch tests the polysaccharides behaviour shows several similarities with proteins. For both experiments the concentrations in the free water approximately double. Like proteins, the polysaccharide concentrations in the 1.2 μm, 0.45 μm and 0.2 μm fractions are similar. This again indicates the absence of SMP particles in the size range 0.2–1.2 μm.

A major difference between proteins and polysaccharides is their extent of retention by the membrane. While protein breakthrough varies between 40% and 55%, the polysaccharide breakthrough only amounts to 20%. This indicates that the majority of the polysaccharide particles in the free water have a size ranging between 0.03 μm and 0.2 μm.

7.4 REFERENCES

Abdessemed, D., Nezzal, G. and Ben Aim, R. (2000). Coagulation-adsorption-ultra filtration for wastewater treatment and reuse. *Desalination*, **131**(1), 307–314.

Boerlage, S.F.E., Kennedy, M.D., Dickson, M.R., El-Hodali, D.E.Y. and Schippers, J.C. (2002). The modified fouling index using ultra filtration membranes (MFI-UF): characterisation, filtration mechanisms and proposed reference membrane. *Jour. Mem. Sci.*, **197**, 1–21.

Boerlage, S.F.E., Kennedy, M.D., Aniye, M.P., Abogrean, E., Tarawneh, Z.S. and Schippers, J.C. (2003). The MFI-UF as a water quality test and monitor. *Jour. Mem. Sci.*, **211**, 271–289.

Bourgeous, K.N., Darby, J.L. and Tchobanoglous, G. (2001). Ultra filtration of wastewater: effects of particles, mode of operation, and backwash effectiveness. *Wat. Res.*, **35**(1), 77–90.

Brauns, E., Faes, K., Hoof, E. van, Doyen, W., Dotremont, C. and Leysen, R. (2002). The measurement and presentation of the fouling potential method with a new method. In: *Proceedings 'Membranes in Drinking and Industrial Water Production'*, September 22–26, **37**, 381–388.

Brauns, E., Hoof, E. van, Molenberghs, B., Dotremont, C., Doyen, W. and Leysen, R. (2002a). A new method of measuring and presenting the membrane fouling potential. *Desalination*, **150**, 31–43.

Brahner, B. (2000). *Belebtschlammeigenschaffen in Membranbioreaktoren zur Abwasserreinigung* (Activated sludge properties in MBR for wastewater treatment). Diplomarbeit Institut für Verfahrenstechnik, November 2000, Berlin.

Brannock, M., Wang, Y., Leslie, G. (2010). Evaluation of full-scale membrane bioreactor mixing performance and the effect of membrane configuration. *Jour. Mem. Sci.*, **350**, (1–2), 15 March 2010, pp. 101–108.

Campbell, M.J., Walter, R.P., McLoughlin, R. and Knowles, C.J. (1993). Effect of temperature on protein conformation and activity during ultra filtration. *Jour. Mem. Sci.*, **78**, 35–43.

Chiemchaisri, C. and Yamamoto, K. (1994). Performance of membrane separation bioreactor at various temperatures for domestic wastewater treatment. *Jour. Mem. Sci.*, **87**, 119–129.

Cummings, G. and Frenkel, V. (2008). Membranes for Industrial Water Reuse - They're Not just for Municipal Applications Anymore. In: *Proceedings of the Water Environment Federation, Membrane Technology*, **15**, pp. 77–91.

Doyen, W., Baée, B., Lambrechts, F. and Leysen, R. (1998). Methodology for accelerated preselection of UF type of membranes for large scale applications. *Desalination*, **117**, 85–94.

Drewes, J.E. and Croue, J.-P. (2002). New approaches for structural characterisation of organic matter in drinking water and wastewater effluents. *Wat. Sci. Tech.: Water Supply*, **2**(2), 1–10.

Dubois, M., Gilles, K.A., Hamilton, J.K., Rebers, P.A., Smith, F. (1956). Colourimetric method for determination of sugars and related substances. *Analytical Chemistry*, **28**, 350–356.

Evenblij, H., Geilvoet, S.P., Van der Graaf, J.H.J.M., Van der Roest, H.F. (2005). Filtration characterisation for assessing MBR performance: three cases compared. *Desalination*, **178**, pp. 115–124.

Evenblij, H., (2006). *Filtration Characteristics in Membrane Bioreactors*, PhD thesis Delft University of Technology, The Netherlands.

Frechen, F., Schier, W., Linden, C. (2008). Pre-treatment of municipal MBR applications. *Desalination*, **231**, pp.108–114.

Frølund, B., Palmgren, R., Keiding, K. and Nielsen, P.H. (1996). Extraction of Extracellular polymers from activated sludge using cation exchange resin. *Wat. Res.*, **30**(8), pp. 1749–1758.

Galjaard, G., Schippers, J.C., Nederlof, M. and Oosterom, H.A. (1998). Quick-Scan: selection of micro- and ultra filtration membranes. *Desalination*, **117**, 79–84.

Geilvoet, S., van der Graaf, J. (2007). The Delft filtration characterisation method: description, assessment and an overview of research results. In: 2nd *Innovation of Membrane Technology for Water and Wastewater Treatment* (pp. 1–10). Sapporo: Hokkaido University.

Geilvoet, S. (2010). *The Delft Filtration Characterisation method – assessing membrane bioreactor activated sludge filterability*, PhD Thesis, Delft University of Technology, ISBN: 978–90-8957–010-9.

Ghosh, M., Amirtharajah, A. and Adin, A. (1994). Particle destabilization for tertiary treatment of municipal wastewater by filtration. *Wat.Sci.Tech.*, **30**(9), 209–218.

Graaf, J.H.J.M. van der, Kramer, J.F., Pluim, J., Koning, J. de and Weijs, M. (1999). Experiments on membrane filtration of effluent at wastewater treatment plants in the Netherlands. *Wat.Sci.Tech.*, **39**(5), 129–136.

Hermia, J. (1982). Constant pressure blocking filtration laws - application to power-law non-Newtonian fluids. *Transactions of the Institution of Chemical Engineers*, **60**, 183–187.

Huisman, I.H., Dutré, B., Persson, K.M. and Trägårdh, G. (1997). Water permeability in ultra filtration and microfiltration: viscous and electroviscous effects. *Desalination*, **113**, 95–103.

Jarusutthirak, C., Amy, G. and Croué, J.-P. (2002). Fouling characteristics of wastewater effluent organic matter (EfOM) isolates on NF and UF membranes. *Desalination*, **145**, 247–255.

Judd, S. (2002). Submerged membrane bioreactors: flat plate or hollow fibre? *Filtration and Separation* **39**(5), pp. 30–3.

Judd, S. (2006). *The MBR Book, Principles and Applications of Membrane Bioreactors in Wastewater treatment*, ISBN-10: 1–85-617481–6.

Kraume. (2007). Fouling in MBR – What use are lab investigations for full-scale operation. In: *Proceedings 6th IMSTEC*, Sydney 5–9 Nov 2007.

Lowry, O.H., Rosebrough, N.J., Farr, A.L. and Randall, R.J. (1951). Protein measurement with the Folin phenol reagent. *Jour. of Biological Chemistry*, **193**, pp. 265–275.

Le-Clech, P., Chen, V., Fane, T. (2006). Fouling in membrane bioreactors used in wastewater treatment, *Jour. Mem. Sci.*, **284**, p. 17–53.

Lee, S.A., Fane, A.G., Amal, R. and Waite, T.D. (2003). The effect of floc size and structure on specific cake resistance and compressibility in dead-end microfiltration. *Separation Sci.Tech.*, **38**(4), 869–887.

Lesjean, B., Huisjes, E.H., (2008). Survey of the European MBR market: trends and perspectives. *Desalination*, **231** (1–3), pp. 71–81.

Matsumoto, Y., Kawakatsu, T., Nakajima, M. and Kikuchi, Y. (1999). Visualization of filtration phenomena of a suspended solution including o/w emulsion or solid particle and membrane separation properties of the solution. *Wat.Res.*, **33**(4), 929–936.

Meng, F., Chae, S., Drews, A., Kraume, M., Shin, S., Yang, F. (2009). Recent advance in membrane bioreactors: membrane fouling and membrane material, *Wat.Res.*, **43**(6), pp. 1489–1512.

Moreau, A., N. Ratkovich, *et al.* (2009). The (in)significance of apparent viscosity in full-scale municipal membrane bioreactors. *Jour. Mem Sci.* **340**(1–2): 249–256.

Mulder, M. (1997). *Basic principles of membrane technology* (2nd edition, corrected), Kluwer Academic Publishers, Dordrecht.

Nakanishi, K., Tadokoro, T. and Matsuno, R. (1985). Separation of microorganism by membrane: utilization of cross-flow filtration (in Japanese). *Hakkokogku kaishi*, **63**, 457–480.

Persson, K.M., Gekas, V. and Trägårdh, G. (1995). Study of membrane compaction and its influence on ultra filtration water permeability. *Jour. Mem. Sci.*, **100**, 155–162.

Poele, S. te and Graaf, J.H.J.M. van der (2002). Physical and chemical conditioning of effluent for decreasing membrane fouling during ultra filtration. In: *Proceedings Membranes in Drinking and Industrial Water Production*, September 22–26, 2002, 37, 765–773.

Roorda, J.H. and Graaf, J.H.J.M. van der (2001). New parameter for monitoring fouing during ultra filtration of WWTP-effluent. *Wat. Sci. Tech.*, **43**(10), 241–248.

Stephenson, T., Judd, S., Jefferson, B., Brindle, K. 2000. *Membrane Bioreactors for Wastewater Treatment.* 1st Edn., IWA Publishing, London, ISBN: 1–900222-07-8.

Schippers, J.C. and Verdouw, J. (1980). The Modified Fouling Index, a method of determining the fouling characteristics of water. *Desalination*, **32**, 137–148.

Tiller, F.M. and Yeh, C.S. (1987). Compressibility of particulate structures in relation to thickening, filtration and expression — a review. *Separation Sci. Tech.*, **22**(2), 1037–1063.

van Bentem, A., Evenblij, H., Geraats, B., Kruit, J., van Voorthuizen, E. (2008). Ontwerp- en beheersaspecten van een MBR voor de behandeling van huishoudelijk afvalwater. (in Dutch) *STOWA report*, 2008-08, ISBN 978-90-5773-403-8.

Wiesner, M.R. and Aptel, P. (1996). Mass transport and permeate flux and fouling in pressure driven processes (Ch. 4). In: *Water Treatment Membrane Processes.* Mallevialle, J., Odendaal, P.E. and Wiesner, M.R. (eds.), McGraw-Hill, New York, 4.1–4.30.

Wright, S., Ranville, J. and Amy, G. (2001). Relating complex solute mixture characteristics to membrane fouling. *Wat. Sci. Tech.: Water Supply*, **1**(5), 31–38.

Yang, W., Cicek, N., Ilg, J., (2006). State-of-the-art of membrane bioreactors: Worldwide research and commercial applications in North America. *Jour. Mem. Sci.*, **270**(1–2), pp. 201–211.

Zhang, J., Chua, H.C., Zhou, J., Fane, A.G., (2006). Factors affecting the membrane performance in submerged membrane bioreactors. *Jour. Mem. Sci.*, **284**, pp. 54–66.

Chapter 8
Enhanced Flocculation/Sedimentation Process by a Jet-Mixed Separator

Y. Watanabe, S. Kasahara and Y. Iwasaki

8.1 INTRODUCTION

Mechanical flocculators with paddles followed by gravity settlers have been used to reduce the suspended solids loading on the sand filters. Tambo and Watanabe (1979) carried out a series of studies about flocculation kinetics, and formulated a collision-agglomeration function to express the effective collision rate resulting in the floc growth. Examining the flocculation kinetics, the following aspects of the flocculation process become clear: (a) flocculation time required for formation of settleable flocs is very short, compared with that required for reaching the ultimate floc size distribution, and (b) decreasing rate of concentration of micro-flocs is not significantly reduced if the larger flocs disappear in the flocculator. Based on the above tow aspects, Watanabe et al. (1990) invented a solid-liquid separator with porous plates inserted vertically in the channel perpendicular to the flow. In the separator, called a jet mixed separator (JMS), simultaneous flocculation and sedimentation occur. The JMS was applied to the rapid sand filtration system instead of the combination of mechanical flocculator and gravity clarifier (Kasahara et al., 1996; Hayashi et al., 1997a).

Since the major part of the contaminants in municipal wastewater is associated with particles, direct particle separation is an effective way of lowering the wastewater contaminants (Ødegaard, 1998). Watanabe et al. (1993, 1997c) used JMS as a physico-chemical pre-treatment instead of the primary clarifier. Because of the significant reduction of organic concentration by physicochemical pre-treatment, higher hydraulic loading can be applied to the post-biolocical treatment, resulting in a compact biological treatment process.

This chapter summarizes the previous authors research on the following points:

(1) Theoretical basis of simultaneous flocculation and sedimentation, and hydraulic characteristics of the JMS.
(2) Experimental results on the application of the JMS to the rapid sand filtration system.
(3) Performance of a hybrid municipal wastewater treatment system consisting of the JMS and rotating biological contactors.

8.2 FUNDAMENTAL STUDY OF JMS

8.2.1 Phenomenon of simultaneous flocculation and sedimentation

Tambo and Watanabe (1979) presented dimensionless flocculation kinetics (equation 8.1).

$$\frac{dN_R}{dm} = \frac{1}{2}\sum_{i=1}^{R-1} \alpha R\left\{i^{\frac{1}{3-K_p}} + (R-i)^{\frac{1}{3-k_p}}\right\}^3 N_1 N_{R-1} - N_R \sum_{i=1}^{S-R} \alpha_{R+1}\left(i^{\frac{1}{3-k_p}} + R^{\frac{1}{3-k_p}}\right)^3 N_1 \tag{8.1}$$

$$m = An_0 t \approx 1.22\sqrt{\frac{\varepsilon_0}{\mu}} d_1^3 n_0 t \tag{8.2}$$

$$N_1 = \frac{n_i}{n_0}, \quad \sum_{i=1}^{s} iN = 1 \tag{8.3}$$

where:

n_R and n_i = number of R-, and i-fold particles per unit volume (1/cm^3);
S = agglomeration number of micro-flocs in the maximum flocs;
K_p = a constant in the floc density function (equation 5.13);
α_R = collision-agglomeration coefficient (equation 5.14);
d_1 = diameter of micro-flocs (cm);
n_0 = initial number of micro-flocs per unit volume (1/cm^3);
ε_0 = effective energy dissipation rate in the fluid (erg/cm^3/s);
μ = dynamic viscosity of the fluid (g/cm/s);
t = flocculation time(s).

Equation 8.1 has been derived based on the following assumptions:

(a) floc particle can grow to S-fold particles without any break down;
(b) combination of an i-fold and a j-fold particle, which creates an R-fold particle larger than an S-fold particle, disintegrates into an i-fold and a j-fold at the moment of creation, i. e. these collisions are ineffective for floc growth;
(c) density of floc particles decrease with increasing floc size as expressed by equation 8.4

$$\rho_{ei} = \rho_i - \rho_w = \frac{a}{(d_i/1)^{k_p}} \tag{8.4}$$

where ρ_i and ρ_w = densities of i-fold particles and water (g/cm^3), ρ_{ei} = buoyant density of i-fold floc particle (g/m^3), d$_i$ = diameter of i-fold particle (cm). Constant a and K_p are the function of the ALT ratio which is defined as follows:

ALT ratio = aluminium concentration added/suspended particle concentration (d) among n_R collisions, α_n, n_R collisions are effective for the floc growth,

$$\alpha_R = \alpha_0\left(1 - \frac{R}{S+1}\right)^n \tag{8.5}$$

where α_0 =collision-agglomeration coefficient between micro-flocs ($R = 1$), having a value of around 1/3 for the optimum coagulation condition, and $n = a$ numerical constant with the value of approximately 6.

Watanabe *et al.* (1990) carried out research about simultaneous flocculation and sedimentation based on the flocculation, kinetics (Equation 5.10). In order to demonstrate the effect of disappearance of larger flocs on the flocculation process, numerical solutions of equation 8.1 were obtained assuming that flocs disappear when they grow to a limited size (S′). The S value was fixed at 500 but S′ value changed at 301, 201 and 151. Figure 8.1 shows the simulated results which make clear the following characteristics of the simultaneous flocculation and sedimentation process: the change in concentration of smaller flocs with an R value of less than 50 with the dimensionless flocculation time is almost the same independently of S′ value. The above evidence on the simultaneous flocculation and sedimentation was verified by the experiment using a batch flocculator 0–4 with rotating paddles on horizontal shaft. Figures 8.2 and 8.3 show the experimental data on the decreasing rate of concentration of micro and total flocs with and without simultaneous sedimentation, respectively constant with the value of approximately 6.

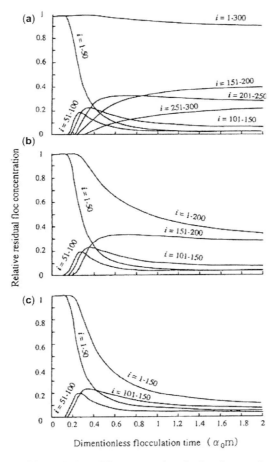

Figure 8.1 Numerical solution of flocculation difference exists in the decreasing rate of kinetics with simultaneous sedimentation (a) S′ = 301; (b) S = 201; (c) = 151

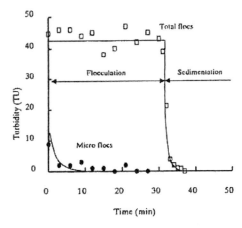

Figure 8.2 Reduction of micro-flocs in mechanical flocculator without settling of larger flocs

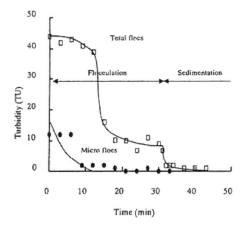

Figure 8.3 Reduction of micro-flocs in mechanical flocculator with settling of larger flocs

Comparing Figures 8.4 and 8.5, no significant difference exists in the decreasing rate of concentration of micro-flocs between the tow cases. Figure 8.6 shows the effect of paddle rotating speed on the simultaneous flocculation and sedimentation. At a paddle rotating speed of 4 rpm, the total floc concentration was lowest in any flocculation time. At paddle rotating speeds of 1 and 2 rpm, floc growth was not enough because of an insufficient mixing intensity. At paddle speeds of 6 and 8 rpm, floc growth was very good but sedimentation was negligible because of strong turbulence. Figure 8.6 demonstrates that an optimum strength and structure of the turbulence exists for the simultaneous flocculation and sedimentation process. In order to produce the optimum structure of turbulence for the simultaneous flocculation and sedimentation, the authors invented a simple solid-liquid separator called a jet mixed separator (JMS). It consists of a channel of porous plates inserted vertically in the channel perpendicular to the flow. On one-half of the porous plates, alternating right and left side, there are several holes with a diameter of 1 to 2 cm.

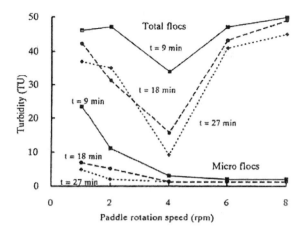

Figure 8.4 Relationship among residual floc with concentration, paddle rotation speed and flocculation time: Al/T ratio = 1/50

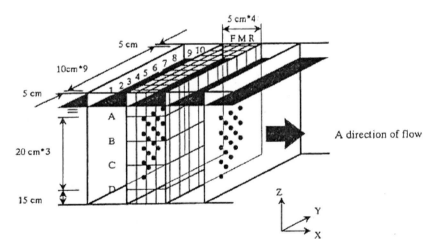

Figure 8.5 Measuring points of local flow velocity between porous plates

8.2.2 Hydrodynamic characteristics of JMS

In the mechanical flocculator, large-scale eddies in the vertical plane, that are produced by the rotating paddles fixed on the horizontal shaft, are present. In JMS, large-scale eddies in the vertical plane may not be present because water passes through the holes in the plates, thus creating jets which gently mix the water with itself. In order to evaluate hydraulic characteristics of JMS, a distribution of the local flow velocity between porous plates was measured (Hayashi *et al.*, 1997a). The effective depth and width of the channel were 84 cm and 100 cm, respectively. The distance of the plates was 20 cm. The G-value in JMS was 7.4 1/s, which is in the optimum range for the simultaneous flocculation and sedimentation as described later. The local velocity in 120 points between the plates, as shown in Figure 8.5, was measured using a three dimensional ultrasonic velocimeter.

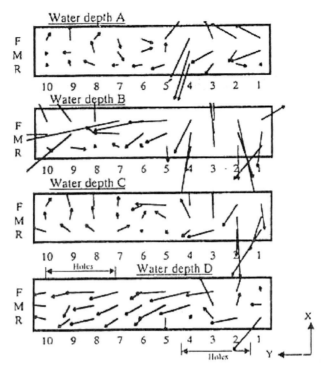

Figure 8.6 Vectors of flow velocity on horizontal plane

The local mean velocity and turbulent intensity were calculated. In addition, the local energy dissipation in the inertial subrange was determined by the MEM method. Figure 8.6 shows the vectors off low velocity on X-Y (horizontal) plane. The following hydraulic characteristics are observed from Figure 8.7: (a) water around the spout of a jet flows and is reflexed by the downstream plate with relatively high velocity, (b) water around the centre of the channel flows along the downstream plate, and (c) water around the suction of a jet is turned to pores sharply. Figure 8.7 shows the vectors off low velocity on X-Z RM (vertical) plane at a vertical section and 9. Figure 8.8 shows the distribution of dimensionless turbulent intensity.

Referring to these results described in Figures 8.6 and 8.7, the following hydraulic characteristics are obtained: (a) although strong mixing is produced around the spout of a jet, the local turbulent intensity is greater around the suction of a jet, and (b) large-scale eddies preventing flocs from settling are almost absent in the vertical plane, around the suction of a jet.

Figure 8.7 also demonstrates that local turbulent intensities on the Z direction are much smaller than that of other directions. Using the data on power spectrum obtained in the JMS, the effective energy dissipation rate (ϵ_0) was estimated and compared with the total energy dissipation rate (ϵ). The value of ϵ_0/ϵ was about 0.4 in the JMS. However, it was 0.1 to 0.2 in the mechanical and up/down flow flocculators (Funamizu and Tmbo, 1982; Tmbo and Hozumi, 1979; Watanabe and Tambo, 1983). Therefore, the JMS can give enough effective turbulent intensity for floc growth even in a lower G- value of around 5 l/s.

Enhanced Flocculation/Sedimentation Process by a Jet-Mixed Separator

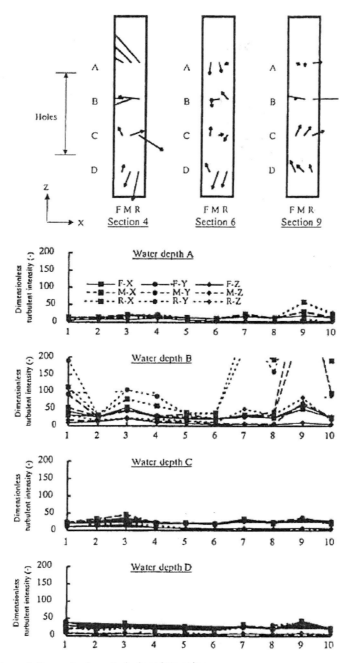

Figure 8.7 Distribution of dimensionless turbulent intensity

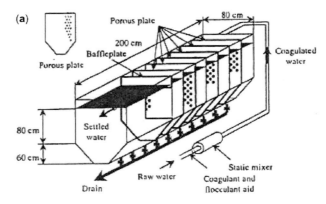

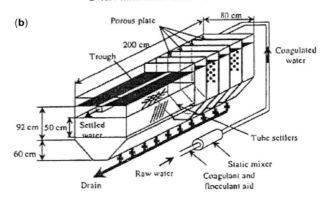

Figure 8.8 Jet-mixed separator with treatment capacity of 50 m^3/day

8.3 APPLICATION OF JMS TO WATER AND WASTEWATER TREATMENT

8.3.1 Pre-treatment for rapid sand filter

Tow types of JMS were used (Kasahara *et al.*, 1996; Hayashi *et al.*, 1997a). They are located at the Kamiebetsu water purification plant in Ebetsu city. The first JMS has the effective volume of 2 m^3 which is shown in Figure 8.8. Flow rate to the JMS was fixed at 50 m^3/day, corresponding to the hydraulic detention time of 49 min. and Jet velocity of 9.8 cm/s. The Chitose river water with relatively high humic substance concentration was fed into the JMS. Aluminium sulphide was added at the Al concentration of 5 to 10 mg/L with activated silicate of 1.5 mg/L. Figure 8.9 shows the turbidity profile in the JMS without inclined tube setters (Figure 8.8a). Effluent turbidity from JMS was about 5 TU because the latter part of JMS was not effective to remove smaller flocs. The effect of G-value on the JMS performance was examined by changing the hydraulic detention time in it and the number of holes on plates. The experimental results shown in Figure 8.10 demonstrate that the optimum G-value in the JMS is around 4 1/s. In order to increase the removal efficiency of smaller flocs, inclined tube settlers were incorporated in the latter part of the JMS (Figure 8.8b). Figure 8.11 shows the influent and effluent turbidities in the JMS with inclined tube settlers.

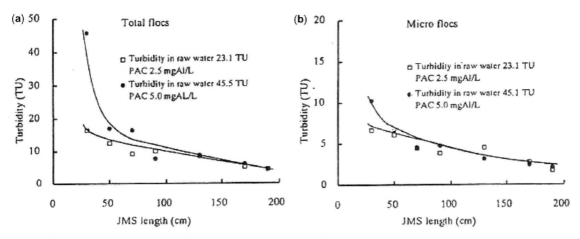

Figure 8.9 Turbidity profile in JMS without inclined tube settlers

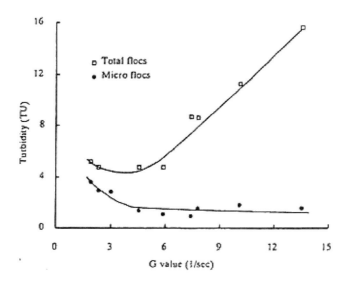

Figure 8.10 Effect of G-value on simultaneous flocculation and sedimentation

The second JMS was used in the water purification system described in Figure 8.12. The effective volume of JMS is 7.2 m^3. Flow rate into the JMS was fixed at 120 m^3/day, corresponding to the hydraulic detention time of 40 min. in porous plate part and 29 min. in inclined tube settlers part. Figure 8.13 shows the influent and effluent turbidity in the JMS with inclined tube settlers. The JMS effluent was fed into the triple media filter consisting of anthracite, sand and garnet. Figure 8.14 shows the changes of effluent turbidity and head loss in the filter with increasing filtration time. The number of particles with the size of 0.5 µm in the filter effluent was continuously measured by a newly developed particle counter (Yamaguchi *et al.*, 1997b). Figure 8.15 shows the relationship between the particle number per ml and turbidity with increasing filtrated water volume. Although the turbidity of the filter effluent was zero, particles number per ml was more than 10,000.

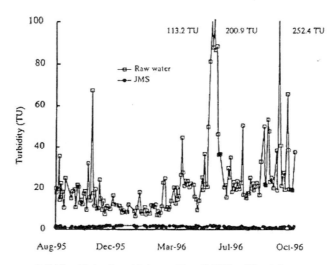

Figure 8.11 Performance of JMS with inclined tube settles (HRT = 49 min)

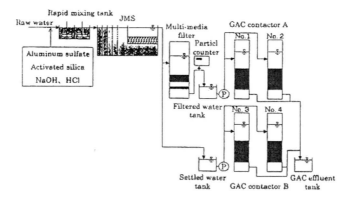

Figure 8.12 Water purification system with JMS and multi-media filter

8.3.2 Pre-treatment for biofilm reactor

Since the major part of the contaminants in municipal wastewater is associated with particles, direct particles separation is an effective way of lowering the wastewater contaminant level. An additional biological oxidation is usually required to remove the residual soluble contaminants. Figure 8.17 shows the

Enhanced Flocculation/Sedimentation Process by a Jet-Mixed Separator

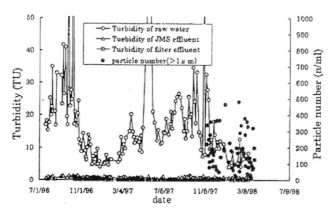

Figure 8.13 Performance of JMS inclined tube settlers (HRT 69 min)

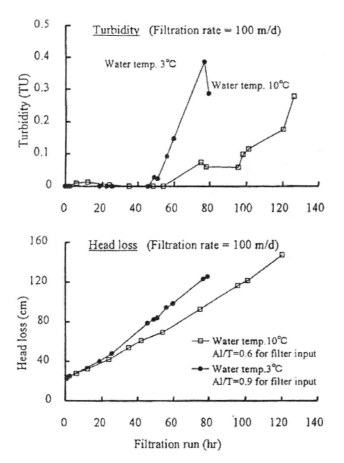

Figure 8.14 Change in JMS effluent turbidity and head loss in filter with operation time

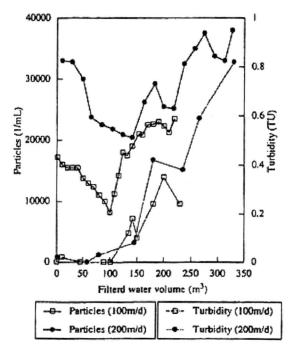

Figure 8.15 Relationship between particle numbers and turbidity in filtrate

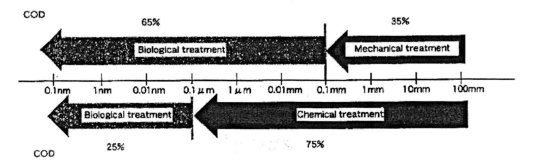

Figure 8.16 COD removal characteristics in hybrid wastewater treatment system

comparison of COD removal performance between the conventional activated sludge system and hybrid treatment system with the pr-coagulation and post biological processes (Karlsson, 1998). Watanabe *et al.* (1993, 1997c) have developed a hybrid municipal wastewater treatment system consisting of the JMS as physico-chemical pre-treatment process and upgraded rotating biological contactor (RBC) as biological post-treatment process. Figure 8.18 shows the schematic description of the hybrid system with a treatment capacity of about 100 m^3/day. The effective length, width and depth of the JMS are 200 cm,

Enhanced Flocculation/Sedimentation Process by a Jet-Mixed Separator

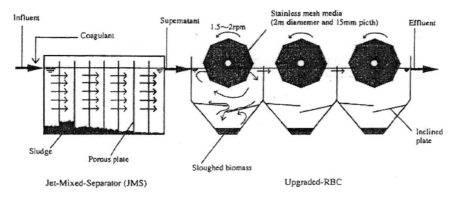

Figure 8.17 Hybrid municipal wastewater treatment system with JMS and RBC

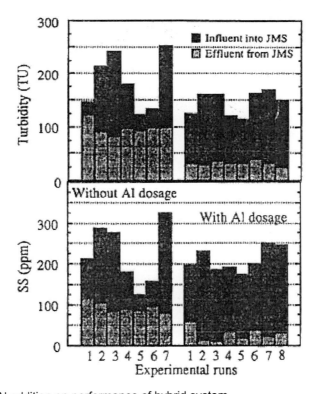

Figure 8.18 Effect of Al addition on performance of hybrid system

100 cm and 136 cm, respectively. The porous plates which have 77 holes with a diameter of 1cm on one-half of each plate are arranged at a distance of 20 cm between plates. The contactor rotating speed and flow rate at the RBC were fixed at 2rpm and 100 m³/day, respectively. In this case, hydraulic retention time in the JMS was 45 min, corresponding to jet velocity of 19.5 cm/sec.

178 Handbook on Particle Separation Processes

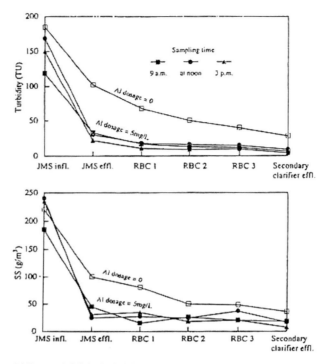

Figure 8.19 Profile of turbidity and SS in hybrid system

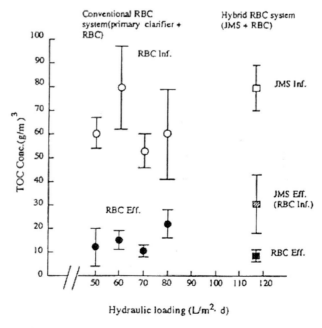

Figure 8.20 TOC removal efficiency of conventional and hybrid RBC

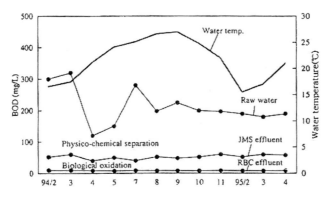

Figure 8.21 Annual trend of BOD removal in hybrid system

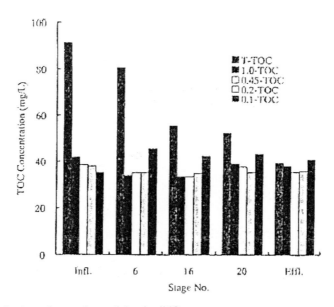

Figure 8.22 Size distribution of organic particles in JMS

The poly aluminium chloride (PCA) was added as the coagulant to the JMS influent which was the effluent from grid chamber in a municipal treatment plant treating the wastewater from a residential area. Coagulant dosage was fixed at 5 mg Al/L. Figure 8.18 shows the effect of the Al addition on the removal efficiency of turbidity and suspended solids. Without coagulant addition, the JMS worked as a sedimentation basin with low removal efficiency of the turbidity and suspended solids but it works as an effective solid-liquid separator with coagulant addition. Figure 8.19 shows the typical profile of turbidity and suspended solids in the hybrid system. Figure 8.20 shows a comparison of TOC removal efficiency between the RBC fed by the primary clarifier effluent and JMS effluent. As the TOC reduction in JMS was significant, much higher hydraulic loading was applicable to hybrid RBC. Figure 8.21 shows the annual trend of BOD removal in the hybrid system.

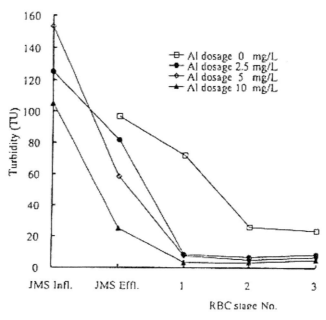

Figure 8.23 Profile of turbidity in hybrid system

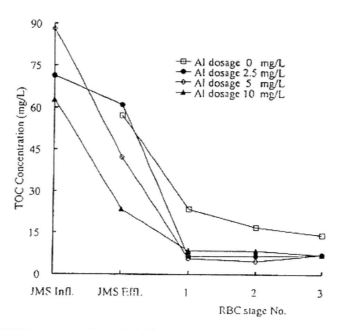

Figure 8.24 Profile of TOC concentration in hybrid system

Watanbe *et al.* (1993) carried out investigation of the effect of Al dosage on the performance of the hybrid system using s small experimental unit. The size distribution of the residual TOC was measured at the Al dosage of 10 mg/L. The result is shown in Figure 8.22. TOC concentrations in the filtrate through the membrane filters were identical to the pore 1.0, 0.45, 0.2 and 0.1 µm. As seen in Figure 8.22. organic materials with a size of more than 0.1 µm were almost removed in the JMS. Figures 8.23 and 8.24 show the profiles of turbidity and TOC concentration in the JMS and RBC. The lower the Al dosage the higher the turbidity and TOC concentration of JMS effluent. However, turbidity and TOC in the first stage of RBC were almost the same, independently of Al dosage. This means that unsettleable small flocs produced at the low Al dosage were adsorbed to the biofilm. The same effect of the Al dosage on the removal efficiency of phosphorous is shown in Figure 8.25. At a lower Al dosage, higher removal efficiency in total phosphorus is observed in the RBC.

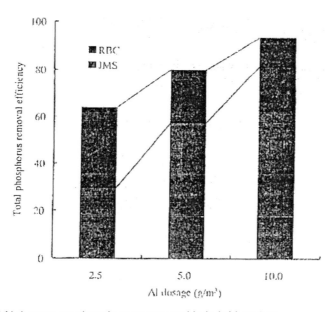

Figure 8.25 Effect of Al dosage on phosphorous removal in hybrid system

8.4 CONCLUSIONS

The JMS is an economical and effective solid-liquid separator with the phenomenon of simultaneous flocculation and sedimentation. It has porous plates inserted vertically in the channel perpendicular to the flow direction. The water passes through holes in the plates, thus creating jets which gently mix the water on itself resulting in the promotion of the flocculation of suspended particles. According to the local velocity measurement, it was demonstrated that large-scale eddies in the vertical plane are almost absent in the JMS. Therefore, larger flocs can settle in the JMS.

The JMS incorporated with inclined tube settlers was applied to the rapid sand filtration system instead of the combination of mechanical flocculator and sedimentation basin. In a hydraulic detention time of less than 1 hour, the effluent turbidity from the JMS was below 1 TU. The JMS without inclined tube settlers was applied to the municipal wastewater treatment where it was used as pre-treatment process to the RBC. The JMS produced an effluent with low concentration of suspended solids and TOC at a hydraulic detention time of less than 1 hour.

8.21 REFERENCES

Hayashi, M., Hamada, S., Kasaharaa, S., Watanabe, Y., Ozawa, G. and Funamizu, N. (1997a). Enhanced solid-liquid separation system consisting of JMS and multimedia filter (in Japanese). In: *Proceedings of the 48th Conference of Japan Water Works Association*, 72–73.

Kasahara, S., Watanabe. Y., Ozawa, G. and Tambo, N. (1996). Enhanced solid-liquid separation process with a jet mixed separator (in Japanese). *Jour. of Japan Water Works Association*, **65**(5), 22–31.

Karlsson, I. (1988). Pre-precipitation for improvement of nitrogen removal in biological wastewater treatment. In: *Proceedings of the 3rd Gothenburg Symposium*, 261–271.

Ødegaard, H. (1988). Coagulation as the first step in wastewater treatment. In: *Proceedings of the 3rd Gothenburg Symposium*, 249–260.

Tambo, N. and Watanabe, Y. (1979). Physical aspect of flocculation process-fundamental treatise. *Wat. Res.*, **13**, 429–439.

Watanabe, Y. and Iwasaki, Y. (1997c). Performance of hybrid small wastewater treatment system consisting of jet mixed separator and rotating biological contactor. *Wat. Sci. Tech.*, **35**(6), 63–70.

Watanabe, Y. and Tambo, N. (1983). Kinetics for the reduction of micro-floc concentration in the flocculation process (in Japanese). *Jour. of Japan Water Works Association*, **52**(10), 27–38.

Watanabe, Y., Fukui, M. and Miyanoshita, T. (1990). Theory and performance of a jet mixed separator. *Jour. of Water SRT Aqua*, **39**(6), 387–395.

Watanabe, Y., Kanemoto, Y., Takeda, K. and Ohono, H. (1993). Removal of soluble and particulate organic material in municipal wastewater by a chemical flocculation and biofilm processes. *Wat. Sci. Tech.* **27**(11), 201–109.

Yamaguchi, D., Watanabe Y., Ohto, T., Bian, R., Ikoma, M. and Ozawa, G. (1997b). Development of a new particle counter (in Japanese). In: *Proceedings of the 48th conference on Japan Water Works Association*, 490–491.

Chapter 9

Particle Behaviour and Removal in a Rainwater Storage Tank and Suggestions for Operation

J.S. Mun and M.Y. Han

9.1 INTRODUCTION

Recently, the necessity for decentralized rainwater management is becoming recognized for various purposes such as minimizing flooding and drought and securing a sustainable water resource. Several rainwater utilization facilities have been installed and stored water in a rainwater tank is used for toilet flushing, gardening and washing (Han et al., 2005). It is necessary to investigate the water quality in rainwater tanks for supplying stored rainwater (Han et al., 2004; Forster, 1996). Water quality in a rainwater tank is influenced by the rainfall pattern, atmospheric environment, catchment conditions, organization of the rainwater utilization system, conditions on rainwater use and the operation of the system (Lindberg and Lovett, 1985; Park, 1995; Tanner, 2000; Polkowska et al., 2002; Han, 2003).

A rainwater utilization facility consists of its catchment area, a treatment facility, storage tank, supply facility and pipes in general. The rainwater tank has the function of a settling tank as well as a storage tank (Kim, 2005). There is little information on water quality improvement by sedimentation, a low-cost and low-energy technique, in a rainwater tank under operation.

This study was performed to check the water quality of the first-flush runoff and stored rainwater flowing from the catchment area, which in this case consists of a concrete roof and marble terrace. We also examined the removal efficiency and behavior of particles under sedimentation in a storage tank with a fixed water level in the absence of inflow and outflow. The removal efficiency and PSD (Particle Size Distribution) were investigated according to retention time with regard to the quality of rainwater and the dimensions of the tank. The rainwater utilization facility was at Seoul National University, Seoul, Korea. Finally, based on these results, several considerations on designing a rainwater storage tank were suggested.

9.2 MATERIALS AND METHODS

9.2.1 Rainwater utilization facility

The rainwater utilization facility on the education research building (B/D 39) of Seoul National University was used for this study. A schematic diagram of this system is shown in Figure 9.1. The education research building was constructed in October 2005, about 1000 people work in the building and water consumption per day is about 120~150 ton (consumption for toilet flushing: 60~90 ton/day).

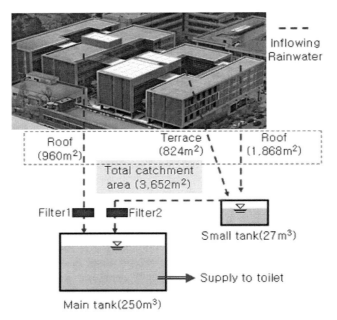

Figure 9.1 A schematic diagram of the rainwater utilization facility on the education research building (B/D 39) of Seoul National University, Seoul, Korea (*Photograph with permission of SNU*)

The rainwater utilization facility consists of a catchment area, a main storage tank, a small storage tank and supply facilities. The catchment area is 3,652 m^2 and the capacity of the main storage tank, small tank and supply tank are 250 m^3, 27 m^3 and 4 m^3, respectively. Rainwater collected from the roof area of 960 m^2 flows in the main tank. Rainwater collected from the roof area of 1868 m^2 and the terrace (824 m^2) flows to a small storage tank and then, when the water level in the small tank reached 1.2 m in depth, water is transported to the main tank by pumping.

The main tank consists of two rooms made of reinforced concrete and of effective water depth 4.25 m. The effective water depth of the small tank, which is made of reinforced concrete, is 1.8 m. Rainwater in the small tank has a high pH due to reaction of the rainwater with the terrace material, marble. Rainwater was supplied from the main tank to toilets through a supply tank of 4 m^3. The supply tank has both a rainwater pipe and a city water pipe, with rainwater supplied in preference to city water. However, if there is no rainwater in the main tank, city water was supplied instead of rainwater. A screen was established in the inlet of the small tank, and two filters, WFF100 (Rainharvesting Systems Ltd., Woodchester, UK) and

AFS200 (Wavin Co., Zwolle, Netherlands), were installed in the main tank. Rainwater from the roof area flows into the main tank through the two filters and when the small tank is full, rainwater from the small tank flows into the main tank through the AFS200 filter. The water level of the main tank, the small tank and the supply tank was monitored by a floating level transmitter (HT-100R, Hitrol Co., Ltd, Paju, Korea), and an amount of flowing water was checked by Magnetic flow meter (WTM1000, Wintec Co., Ltd. Korea). An automatic remote control operation was carried out by an HMI (Human Machine Interface) program (Wonderware In Touch v. 9.0, Maha net Co., Ltd., Sungnam, Korea).

9.2.2 Experimental conditions

This study was performed during June–August 2006 using three rainfall events, which showed: Case 1, long antecedent dry days and rainfall under 10 mm; Case 2, short antecedent dry days and rainfall about 10 mm; and Case 3, rainfall of over 300 mm, respectively. The order of degree of contamination of these three runoff events was Case 1, Case 2 and Case 3, in sequence. To examine the removal efficiency and behaviour of particles during sedimentation in the main tank, the main tank was operated under a fixed water level without inflow and outflow after stopping runoff from the catchment area to the tank. In Case 1, the water quality of the first-flush runoff was also investigated. Water quality was analyzed depending on retention time, depth of sampling point and the turbidity of the initial rainwater in the main tank (Table 9.1), and turbidity, pH, temperature and PSD were measured (Table 9.2).

Table 9.1 Experimental conditions

Case	Sampling period (Retention time)	Rainfall (Antecedent dry day)	Sampling points (level from bottom)	Initial rainwater turbidity (NTU)	Water level
1	9 Jun. 20:40 10 Jun. 9:40 (17 hrs)	6 mm (13 days)	F1, F2 T1(1) T2(1)	T1(1) 11.2 T2(1) 6.49	2.45 m
2	11 Jul. 11:00 15 Jul. 16:00 (100 hrs)	10 mm (3 days)	T1(1) T1(2)	T1(1) 6.28 T2(1) 4.18	3.32 m
3	31 Jul. 11:00 4 Aug 20:00 (105 hrs)	Over 300 mm	T1(3) T2(1) T2(2) T2(3)	T(1) 2.12 T2(1) 1.39	3.15 m

Table 9.2 Water quality measurements and devices

Items	Devices
Turbidity	Turbidimeter HACH 2100 (USA)
pH	pH meter HACH Sension 1 (USA)
Water temperature	pH meter HACH Sension 1 (USA)
PSD	Coluter Multisizer 2 (USA)

Water samples were taken from the nearby inlet (T1) and the outlet (T2), and also taken at the 1 m, 2 m and 3 m level (from the bottom) in the main tank (Figure 9.2). The distance between T1 and T2 was designed 15 m.

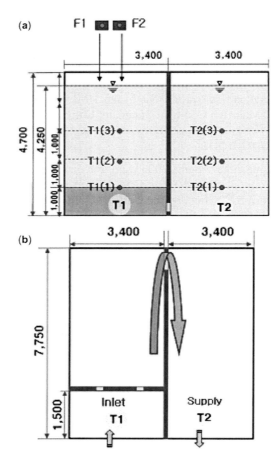

Figure 9.2 Sampling points (unit: mm). (**a**) Sampling points according to depth (Side); (**b**) Sampling points according to distance (Plane)

9.3 RESULTS AND DISCUSSION

9.3.1 Water quality of "first-flush" runoff and stored rainwater in the tank

The 'first-flush' runoff of Case 1 and stored rainwater in the main tank after three rainfall events were examined to find out the quality of rainwater from the concrete roof and marble terrace. The samples of first-flush runoff at Case 1 were taken before two filters (F1, F2) during a rainfall event of 50 minutes. Rainwater in the small tank was transported to the main tank for three hours after runoff ceased through the F2 filter. The samples were also taken before F2 filter during transportation of rainwater from the small tank to the main tank. In Case 1, the turbidity of the first-flush runoff was high (over 100 NTU) due to the long period of dry days (13 days) and small rainfall (6 mm) before the event (Figure 9.3).

As time passed, the turbidity declined sharply. In the late runoff at an elapsed time of around 50 min, the runoff turbidity was under 30 NTU. The pH of rainwater from the roof area was 6~8, but that of rainwater from the small tank was 10.5~11.5 due to contact with the marble terrace. The PSD of the first-flush runoff was analyzed to examine the variation of particle size according to elapsed time (Figure 9.4). As the elapsed time increased, particle numbers in first-flush runoff were decreased.

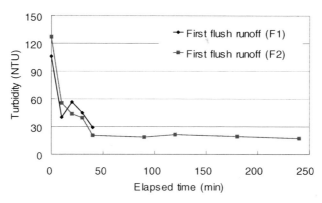

Figure 9.3 The turbidity of first-flush runoff (Case 1)

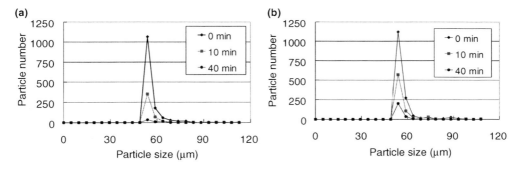

Figure 9.4 PSD of first-flush runoff for Case 1. (**a**) F1; (**b**) F2

Directly after the runoff ceased, the initial turbidity of stored rainwater in the tank after Case 1, Case 2, and Case 3 was 11.2 NTU, 6.4 NTU, and 2.1 NTU, respectively. This indicates that, as the number of antecedent dry days increased, the turbidity increased also. The pH was also high due to interaction with the marble terrace. The average particle size in all cases was 8~10 μm.

9.3.2 Particle behaviour and removal in a rainwater tank

Particle behaviour and the removal rate by sedimentation in the rainwater tank were examined for Case 1, where there had been a long period of dry days (13 days) and low rainfall (under 10 mm). The retention time was 12 hours without inflow and outflow. Samples were taken from the 1 m point (from the bottom) near the inlet (T1) and outlet (T2) of the tank. The initial turbidities of T1 and T2 were 11.5 and 6.5 NTU. The difference between T1 and T2 was two times. The removal rate increased rapidly during the first two hours, and increased gently thereafter. After a settlement time of 12 hours, the turbidity (removal rate) at T1 and T2 was 9.3 NTU (25.8%) and 4.1 NTU (36.5%), respectively (Figure 9.5).

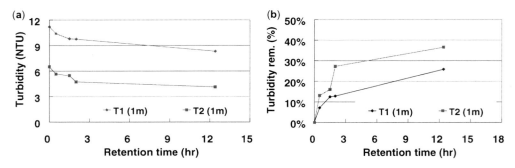

Figure 9.5 Turbidity and removal rate of Case 1. (a) Turbidity; (b) Turbidity removal rate (%)

The average particle sizes of the initial stored rainwater in the tanks were 9.3 and 10.0 µm in T1 and T2. The particle number classified by size in the PSD showed irregular patterns according to retention time. The particle number of T2 decreased to a half of T1 (Figure 9.6).

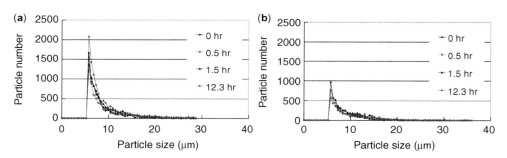

Figure 9.6 PSD of stored rainwater at T1 and T2 according to retention time (Case 1). (a) T1 (1m); (b) T2 (1m)

Particle behaviour and removal rate by sedimentation in the tank was examined under the condition of short antecedent dry days (3 days) and rainfall of about 10 mm (Case 2). The retention time was 100 hours without inflow and outflow. Samples were taken from points 1 m, 2 m and 3 m from the bottom near the inlet (T1) and outlet (T2) of the tank. The initial turbidity at T1 and T2 were 6.4 and 4.2 NTU. The difference of turbidity between T1 and T2 was smaller than that of Case 1. The removal rate according to retention time increased rapidly at the 2 m and 3 m points of T1 over the first eight hours, and increased gently afterwards. At the 1 m point of T1, the removal rate increased for up to 30 hours.

After 24 hours retention time, a disturbance occurred at T2. The retention time at 24 hours, therefore, was assumed to be 0 hours when we calculated the removal rate of T2. The removal rates at the 1 m, 2 m and 3 m points from the bottom were 30~40% after about 30 hours, and increased gently afterwards (Figure 9.7). A retention time of around 30 hours is recommended for efficient particle removal.

The average particle sizes of initial stored rainwater in the tanks were 9.6 and 9.7 µm in T1 and T2. PSDs were analyzed at each sampling points in T1, as shown in Figure 9.9. Initial PSDs at 1 m, 2 m and 3 m points were similar. As time passed, the particle of size 6.1~10 µm settled out preferentially at higher sampling position.

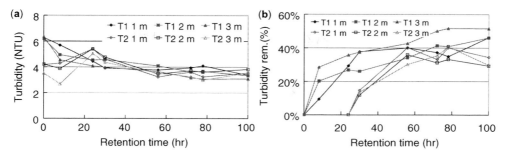

Figure 9.7 Turbidity and removal rate (Case 2). (**a**) Turbidity; (**b**) Turbidity removal rate (%)

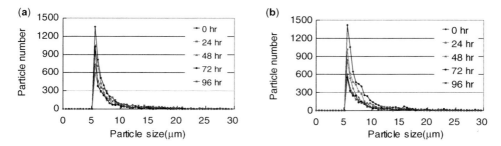

Figure 9.8 PSD of stored rainwater in T1 according to retention time (Case 2). (**a**) T1 (1m); (**b**) T1 (3m)

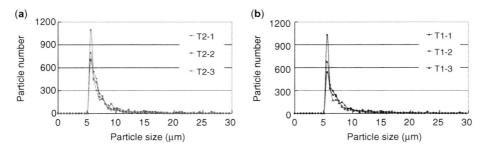

Figure 9.9 PSD of stored rainwater in T1 and T2 at retention time of 72 hours (Case 2). (**a**) Turbidity; (**b**) Turbidity removal rate (%)

After a retention time of 72 hours, the number of particles of size 5.6 μm, the channel with the greatest number of particles, was lower at the higher sampling position. As for particles of size greater than 6 μm, particle numbers were generally lower at the higher sampling position (Figure 9.9).

Lastly, particle behaviour and removal rate by sedimentation in the tank was examined following heavy rainfall, 300 mm (Case 3). The retention time was 105 hours without inflow and outflow. Sampling points were same as for Case 2. The initial turbidity of T1 and T2 were 2.12 and 1.39 NTU. Removals rate according to retention time had a tendency to increase regularly in T1 and T2. After 105 hours retention time, the turbidity (removal rate) of T1 was 1.12~1.33 (37~40%), and that of T2 was 0.85~1.01 (23~34%) (Figure 9.10).

The average particle sizes of the initial rainwater in the rainwater storage tank were 7.9 and 9.0 μm in T1 and T2. As retention time increased, particle numbers had a tendency to decrease in most cases (Figure 9.11). At a retention time of 8 hours, the particle numbers of the PSD according to sampling points had a tendency to be lower at higher sampling point (Figure 9.12).

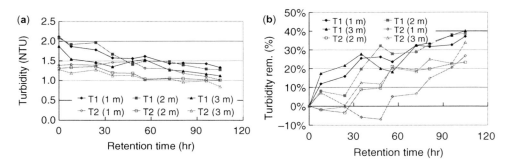

Figure 9.10 Turbidity and removal rate (Case 3). (**a**) Turbidity; (**b**) Turbidity removal rate (%)

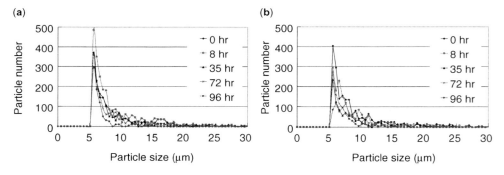

Figure 9.11 PSD of stored rainwater in T1 according to retention time (Case 3). (**a**) T1; (**b**) T2

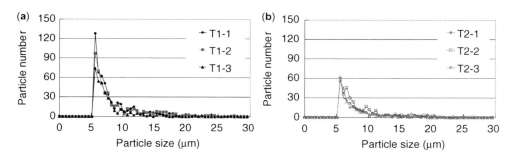

Figure 9.12 PSD of stored rainwater in T1 and T2 at retention time of 72 hours (Case 3). (**a**) T1; (**b**) T2

9.3.3 Design considerations for a rainwater tank

The turbidity of T1 and T2, which is 15 m from T1, was compared in Cases 1 and 3 to examine the removal efficiency of particles according to distance in the rainwater tank (Table 9.3).

In Case 1, T2/T1 ratios were 0.59 and 0.50 at retention times of 0 hour and 12 hours. The particle removal efficiency was increased by up to 50% with the greater distance. In Case 3, T2/T1 ratios were 0.66 and 0.77 at retention times of 0 hour and 105 hours. The particle removal efficiency was increased by 34% with the greater distance. As a result, for the condition of long antecedent dry days and small rainfall (i.e., high contamination) (Case 1), especially, the removal efficiency was high with the distance between inlet and outlet. We conclude that it is necessary to have an adequate distance between inlet and outlet.

Table 9.3 Turbidity of T1 (1 m) and T2 (1 m) in case 1 and case 3

	Case 1			Case3		
	Retention time 0 hr	Retention time 12 hr	Removal rate (%)	Retention time 0hr	Retention time 105 hr	Removal rate (%)
T1	11.2	9.31	25.8	2.12	1.33	37.1
T2	6.6	4.12	36.5	1.39	1.02	26.7
T2/T1	0.59	0.50		0.66	0.77	

The higher the turbidity was, the larger turbidity difference there was between points 3 m from the bottom and 1 m and 2 m from the bottom in Cases 2 and 3 (Table 9.4). So, if possible, it is better to design an effective water depth of over 3 m, and it is also better to supply rainwater near the water surface by using floating suction. It is recommended that the effective retention time in a rainwater tank be 30 hours, based on consideration of Case 2 (where there was an initial turbidity of 6 NTU in the rainwater tank). In Case 1 (initial turbidity of 11 NTU), besides retention time, distance difference should also be considered because it increases the removal efficiency.

Table 9.4 Comparison of turbidity according to water depth in case 2 and case 3

		Turbidity of T1			Turbidity of T2		
		1 m	2 m	3 m	1 m	2 m	3 m
Average turbidity of Case 2		4.44	4.37	3.99	4.01	4.11	3.61
Difference between 3 m and 1 and 2 m	Average	0.45	0.38		0.40	0.49	
	Max.	1.02	0.61		1.59	1.18	
Average turbidity of Case 3		1.61	1.60	1.40	1.30	1.15	1.09
Difference between 3 m and 1 and 2 m	Average	0.21	0.19		0.22	0.07	
	Max.	0.32	0.37		0.35	0.16	

9.4 CONCLUSIONS

In this study, the water quality of first-flush runoff and stored rainwater, as well as the efficiency of removal and behaviour of particles in a rainwater storage tank, was investigated using three rainfall events that had different histories of previous dry days and rainfall volume. Several considerations to be born in mind while designing a rainwater storage tank were suggested.

Turbidity of first-flush runoff was over 100 NTU in the case of long antecedent dry days (13 days) and slight rainfall (6 mm), but, within 1 hour, runoff turbidity decreased to under 30 NTU. Right after runoff stopped, the initial turbidity of stored rainwater in the tank was 2.1~11.2 NTU for the three rainfall events. As antecedent dry days increased and the amount of rainfall decreased, so turbidity increased. The pH was high due to contact with the marble terrace. The average particle size in all cases was 8~10 μm.

The main tank, which consists of 2 rooms of 125 m^3, was operated at a fixed water level, without inflow and outflow, after stopping the access of runoff to examine the removal efficiency and behaviour of particles during sedimentation. The removal rate increased regularly according to retention time for stored rainwater of around 2 NTU. However, the removal rate increased rapidly early on, but then increased gently, for stored rainwater of 6~11 NTU. The particle number and peak of PSD in stored rainwater decreased according to the retention time.

The removal efficiency was increased by having a considerable distance between inlet and outlet, even when there were long antecedent dry days and little rainfall. If possible, it is recommended to design the effective water depth to be over 3 m, and to supply rainwater near the water surface by using a floating suction.

9.5 REFERENCES

Han M. Y., Lee I. Y. and Park S. C. (2003). The effect of rooftop on the water quality of roof runoff. *Jour. of Korean Society of water and Wastewater,* **17**(3), 460–466.

Han M. Y., Han M. S. and Kim S. R. (2004). A Consideration in Determining the Tank Volume of Rainwater Harvesting System in Building. *Jour. of Korean Society of water and Wastewater,* **18**(2), 99–109.

Han M. Y. and Lee S. J. (2005). Evaluation of Stored Rainwater Qulity at Galmoe Middle School Rainwater Harvesting System. *Jour. of Korean Society of water and Wastewater,* **19**(1), 31–37.

Jurgen Forster (1996). Patterns of roof runoff contamination and their potential implications on practice and regulation of treatment and local infiltration. *Wat. Sci. Tech.,* **33**(6), 39–49.

Kim Y. W. (2005). *The design Plans considering Particle Characteristics and Behavior in Rainwater Storage Tank,* Master thesis, Environmental Engineering Research Group, Seoul National University, Korea.

Lindberg S.E. and Lovett G.M. (1985). Field measurement of partial dry deposition rates to foliage and inert surfaces in a forest canopy, *Envir. Sci. Tech.,* **19**, 238–244.

Park S. U. (1995). The effect of dry deposition on the ground level concentration. *Jour. of the Korea Meteorological Society,* **31**(2), 97–115.

Polkowska. Z, Georecki Z. and Namiesnik J. (2002). Quality of roof runoff waters from urban region, *Chemoshere,* **49**, 1275–1283.

Tanner P. A. (2002). Analysis of Hong Kong Daily bulk and wet deposition data from 1994 to 1995. *Atmospheric Environment,* **33**, 1757–1766.

Chapter 10
Direct Membrane Filtration of Wastewater

A. Ravazinni, A.F. van Nieuwenhuijzen and J.H.J.M. van der Graaf

10.1 INTRODUCTION

Water sources are depleting, both in quality and quantity, leading to stricter discharge policy and increasing number of wastewater reuse projects all around the world (Bixio *et al.*, 2004).

Because of its specific characteristics, membrane separation plays a significant role in water reuse: membranes provide both rejection of harmful pathogens and clear filtrate. As reported also by Wintgens *et al.* (2005), currently membranes are applied to the treatment of municipal wastewater mainly in MBR's and in MF/UF filtration of effluent, eventually followed by reverse osmosis (RO). In both cases, a biological treatment precedes the application of membranes, aiming to remove COD (chemical oxygen demand), BOD (biological oxygen demand), and nutrients (Nitrogen and Phosphorous).

However, membrane separation is a purely physical process that may be considered as a stand-alone process as well. The direct application of a membrane to wastewater would have the following characteristics:

(1) The typical limitations of biological processes (influence of temperature, feed stability and toxicity, start up period etc.) would be avoided;
(2) Wastewater constituents would be "separated" rather than "removed".

And in facts, this process has also been referred to as Direct Membrane Separation (DMS) (Ahn *et al.*, 2001).

10.2 REVIEW ON DIRECT MEMBRANE SEPARATION (DMS) OF WASTEWATER

During DMS the feed wastewater is filtrated directly on a membrane, after simple mechanical pre-treatments (see Figure 10.1, where the example of direct UF is presented).

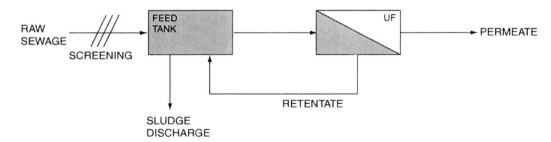

Figure 10.1 Schematic drawing of direct UF of raw sewage

High quality-water can be produced in one single treatment step. However, the quality of the permeate will depend on the feed water quality and the applied membranes. Strong fouling problems are likely to occur, as typically in membrane processes. Literature review shows that the concept has often been related to reuse purposes, and in most cases the target quality of the product-water has been achieved. Different wastewater sources have been used: graywater, blackwater, manure wastewater and finally municipal wastewater, either raw or after primary sedimentation. Microfiltration (MF), ultrafiltration (UF), nanofiltration (NF) and reverse osmosis (RO) have been applied. To the knowledge of the authors, the only full-scale application regards the treatment of pre-settled manure with MF or RO membrane, using VSEP (Vibratory Shear Enhanced Process) configuration. UF is used to concentrate the manure before digestion, and to produce a permeate that after chemical cleaning is recycled as irrigation, wash-down or cooling water; RO is used to produce drinking-water quality for the livestock and washwater for the barns (Johnson *et al.*, 2004).

All other researches have been limited to lab-scale or pilot scale for a duration up to one year. Ahn *et al.* (1998) and Ahn and Song (2000), treated pre-screened low loaded graywater from a resort and hotel complex with MF and UF tubular ceramic and hollow fibres membranes. They obtained an effluent satisfactory for Korean standard for secondary reuse (i.e. toilet flushing, landscape irrigation).

In California, on account of Orange County Water and Sanitation District, Sethi and Juby (2002) used a Memcor 6M10C pilot plant to test direct MF of primary clarifier effluent. The focus was on clarification and microbial removal, aiming to evaluate the suitability of the filtrate to direct ocean discharge (without chlorine disinfection) and further RO. The plant was steadily operated during one year and results were defined "promising" for both applications.

In China, high strength wastewater from university apartments was filtrated on UF and MF ceramic and organic membranes (Hao *et al.*, 2005). The effluent was used to irrigate winter wheat in small laboratory test field. The membranes were able to remove 3–4 log of bacterial counts and 4–5 of coliforms, increasing the wheat production of 7.5% in weight in comparison to tap water enriched with fertilisers.

Other researches merely focused on the evaluation of obtainable permeate quality in respect to the reuse application. Abdessemed and Nezzal (2002) treated primary effluent by applying combinations of coagulation, adsorption and UF in lab-scale experiments. Dosing 120 mg/l of $FeCl_3$ and 40 mg/l of PAC (Powdered Activated Carbon), they obtained a clarified filtrate with turbidity ~ 0 NTU and COD = 7 mg/l, which might be suitable for industrial applications. Ramon *et al.* (2004) tested UF and NF membranes for local reuse of graywater from a sport centre. They found that the permeate quality improves with the molecular weight cut-off (MWCO) of the membrane, and that only NF membranes would guarantee sufficient quality for the reuse applications, because of higher BOD removal.

In the Netherlands, several studies focused on the potential of crossflow ultrafiltration of municipal wastewater either as a tool for advanced particle removal or for irrigation purposes (van Nieuwenhuijzen et al., 2000, Evenblij et al., 2001). These studies were followed by the development of general wastewater treatment concepts based on complete chemical-physical treatment (Rulkens et al., 2005).

In Table 10.1 an overview of the permeate quality achieved when MF and UF membranes were applied is given.

Table 10.1 Permeate quality during MF and UF direct membrane separation of wastewater

Feed wastewater	Mem-type	COD mg/L	BOD$_5$ mg/L	TOC mg/L	TSS mg/L	Turb. NTU
Primary effluent	MF		64.8		1.5	0.52
Primary effluent	UF	78			ND	<0.15
Graywater (resort)	UF-MF	<15.6		<4.6		<0.7
Graywater (sport centre)	UF	<80				<1.4
Low-strength (hotel-shops)	MF	<20		<3.5	ND	0.2
Low-strength (dormitory)	MF	11	4.1	4.8	0.2	0.01
Low-strength (dormitory)	UF	67			ND	ND
Septic tank effluent*	MF	8.8	4.2	3.8	0.2	0.15
Municipal raw	UF	210			ND	0.2
Municipal raw	UF	138			ND	<0.3

* = biological removal in the tank
ND = not detected

10.3 DIRECT ULTRAFILTRATION OF MUNICIPAL WASTEATER

This chapter deals with the development of a particular DMS application: direct ultrafiltration of municipal wastewater. In Figure 10.2, a concept-diagram of the process is presented.

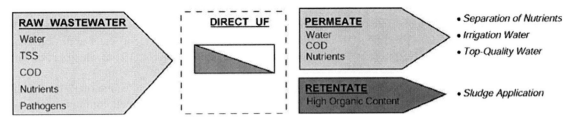

Figure 10.2 Direct ultrafiltration: separation of constituents and potential for reuse

The raw wastewater is regarded as a mixture of valuable compounds (water and nutrients) with undesired elements (summarised as suspended solids "SS" and potentially infectious microorganisms, bacteria and viruses). The UF membrane realises the separation of the desired-undesired components by constituting a barrier to particulate, colloids and bacteria.

The permeate is water free of particles, microorganisms and bacteria, but rich in soluble COD, phosphorous (P) and nitrogen (N). Nutrients content may be interesting in regard to irrigation reuse, while the low turbidity and the absence of particles may enable the production of high-quality water. The concentrate contains the removed organic-rich particulate, microorganisms and bacteria, and may be treated as sludge. Given the absence of chemical addition, it may be considered for soil application.

Great advantages are recognised with respect to reuse applications:

(1) municipal wastewater is already a widely available water source;
(2) the process is purely physical/chemical, therefore operation can be discontinuous;
(3) automation and remote control can be implemented.

10.4 APPLICATIONS AND REUSE POSSIBILITIES OF DIRECT UF

Direct UF can be regarded either as end-of-pipe treatment for of municipal wastewater or as technology to generate reusable water from existing sewers. In this case, the concept of "sewer mining", as reported in Butler *et al.* (1995), can be applied: water is extracted on demand and the process-wastes is returned to the sewer.

The quality of the product water greatly determines the type of application. The main characteristics of the filtrate are the following:

Positive: the permeate is clear (turbidity <1 NTU), particle-free, pathogens-free and rich in nutrients;
Negative: presence of unpleasant odours and organic components (eventually also undesirable micropollutants) which may affect stability during storage.

The following applications may be considered:

(1) *advanced pre-treatment:* in case of (temporarily) overloaded wastewater treatment plants (WWTPs), total particle removal and 60% COD removal can be achieved (van Nieuwenhuijen *et al.*, 2000); the reject stream can be treated as (anaerobic) sludge if the concentration factor is sufficient.
(2) *irrigation:* the presence of nutrients is valuable to increase crops productivity and realise saving on fertilizers. Blending with other water sources and confined agricultural practices can help to achieve water quality standards and protect water bodies from nutrients run-off. Evenblij *et al.* (2001) showed that a 5,000 PE direct UF installation can yearly supply sufficient water and more than enough nitrogen, phosphorous and potassium for the cultivation of 10 ha wheat, corn and sobeans in semi-arid countries.
(3) *ocean disposal:* the microbiological safety of the filtrate may enable a "sanitation" use of the process, where discharge of organic load is a secondary aspect (e.g. for small communities along the ocean coast, on ships, in emergency camps, etc.). Eventually, it can be considered also for the treatment of low loaded waters as in case of combined sewer overflow.
(4) *further membrane process:* direct UF permeate may represent a source for NF or RO; the dissolved organic content is high but the fraction of bacterial origin is lower than in membrane applications following biological treatment. Recovery of nutrients could be practiced, especially in the RO retentate, where ammonia and phosphates will be concentrated. An interesting proposal for a new wastewater treatment concept has been presented by Rulkens *et al.*, 2005 and is presented in Figure 10.3.

Direct Membrane Filtration of Wastewater

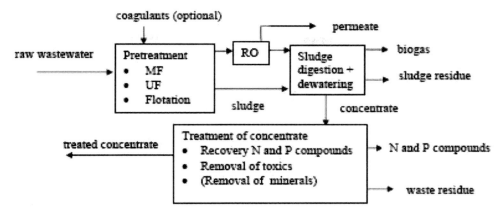

Figure 10.3 Innovative wastewater treatment concept possibly based on direct ultrafiltration (from Rulkens *et al.*, 2005)

10.5 RESEARCH STUDIES AT TU-DELFT

The research studies at TU-Delft focused on the filtration characteristics of crossflow ultrafiltration with tubular membranes, using untreated and pre-treated wastewater. The final aim was to develop sustainable operations.

Results were presented in Ravazzini *et al.* (2004, 2005, 2007) and are summarized in the following.

10.5.1 Background

10.5.1.1 Crossflow filtration

In crossflow filtration, the feed water flows parallel to the membrane surface. Because of the pressure gradient across the membrane (TMP), part of the flow is extracted from the bulk solution as permeate, but most of the flow just passes along the membrane and is recirculated to the feed tank. Such mode of operation prevents excessive concentration of the transported material on the membrane surface and allows taking advantage of the hydraulic turbulence created by the flow. In fact a shear stress tangential to the membrane surface is created (τ), which helps to reduce fouling phenomena.

Filtration through a porous mean can be described using an adaptation of the Darcy's law:

$$J = \frac{TMP}{\eta \cdot R} \tag{10.1}$$

where J is the Flux, TMP is the Trans Membrane Pressure, η is the dynamic viscosity of the filtrating liquid and R is the total resistance to filtration.

In particular R is a general parameter that complies for the resistance to filtration offered by the membrane and by all the different kind of fouling mechanism that may occur (i.e. concentration polarisation, gel layer formation, pore blocking and adsorption). It is the so-called "Resistance in Series" model:

$$R = R_{\text{mem}} + R_{\text{fouling}} \tag{10.2}$$

10.5.1.2 Fouling mechanisms

During the filtration process the retention of material operated by the membrane leads to accumulation on the membrane surface, resulting in concentration phenomena and eventually in the formation of a dense gel layer or a cake [16]. Material can depose and be adsorbed within the membrane pores as well. Such phenomena are known as *fouling* and result in decline of flux with time.

The entity of fouling depends upon three main issues: operating conditions (TMP, hydraulic) feed water characteristics and membrane characteristics [17]. Particle size distribution in the feed water is supposed to determine the major fouling mechanism: cake layer filtration would be predominant when particles are larger than the pore size, while pore narrowing and pore blocking would be caused by components dimensionally comparable with the pore size. It is suggested that higher TMP would induce the formation of a cake-layer of higher density, because of filter cake compressibility.

10.5.1.3 Filter cake compressibility

During micro- and ultrafiltration, the forming filter cakes are often found to be compressible.

The relationship between the resistance of a compressible filter media and the applied pressure is usually expressed by a power law (Belter *et al.*, 1988):

$$\alpha_{cake} = \alpha_0 \cdot \Delta P^s \tag{10.3}$$

where:

α_{cake} = the specific cake resistance (in $m \cdot kg^{-1}$)
α_0 = a constant related to size and shape of the particles within the deposit (usually a reference value of specific cake resistance at standard conditions).
ΔP = the pressure difference and "s" the compressibility factor, ranging between 0 (not-compressible cake) and 1 (maximum compressibility).

10.5.1.4 Filterability and reversibility

Fouling can be temporary or permanent. Permanent fouling is also known as "irreversible", and consequently temporary fouling as "reversible".

Because of fouling, during filtration, the resistance increases over time (and filtrate volume). The tendency to increase is known as "filterability" and depends on both the feed water characteristics. Filterability includes both reversible and irreversible fouling.

Sometimes the filtration is interrupted for a cleaning; afterwards a fraction of irreversible fouling can appear which can not be removed. To real applications, reversibility is eventually even more relevant than filterability.

10.5.1.5 Critical flux concept

The concept of critical flux, was introduced by Field *et al.* (1995). According to the "strong" formulation of this principle, a threshold value would exist, below which *at the start* no fouling would be produced. Therefore, a flux value as for clean water would be maintained. However, the more commonly accepted version is the "weak" formulation that recites that a little fouling is produced and a sustainable flux is attained.

10.5.2 Experimental set-up

A crossflow filtration unit was built (see Figure 10.4), using hydrophilic tubular PVDF membranes of 5.2 mm diameter. The membranes are included in a 1-m long module (X-flow F 4385) placed vertically. Clean water (tap water quality), wastewater and cleaning solutions are fed with a centrifugal pump. Chemical feed to the inner side of the tubes is also "statically" possible from the top of the membrane module, and backflush with demineralised water is provided with an independent pump. Process parameters are calculated as follows, on the basis of data automatically sampled every 10 seconds:

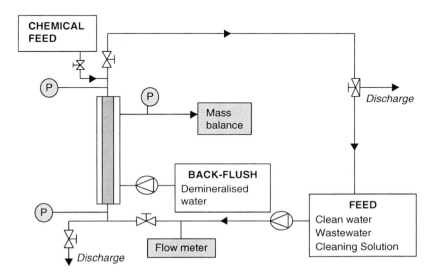

Figure 10.4 Schematic drawing of the installation rig

- TMP: pressure meters are placed at the inlet of the membrane module, at the concentrate outlet and at the permeate outlet; TMP is calculated as difference of the average pressure at the inner side and at the permeate side of the membrane.
- Flux (J): the extracted permeate is weighed on a balance, therefore the flux is calculated as mass increase with time per membrane surface;
- Resistance (R): according to Darcy's law, resistance is calculated from J and TMP assuming $\eta_{solution}$ equal to η_{water} at the measured temperature.

The crossflow u_{cr} is calculated from flow measurements.

10.5.3 Fundamental role of operating conditions

10.5.3.1 Experiments

A number of combinations of TMP and u_{cr} were tested during 30 minutes of continuous batch filtration at constant TMP. TMP values were 0.3, 0.5 and 1.0 bar; u_{cr} values 1.0, 1.5 and 2.0 m/s. During one day, 3 tests were performed on the same sample, where one parameter between TMP and u_{cr} was kept constant and the other was varied.

10.5.3.2 Results

The resistance increase during 30 minutes is strongly affected by the operating conditions, as shown by the filtration curves $R(t)$. Figure 10.5(ab) compares the effect of varying crossflow and TMP for "intermediate" operating conditions.

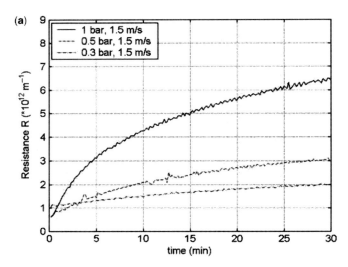

Figure 10.5a Effect of TMP on the resistance increase during 30 minutes of continuous filtration of raw sewage

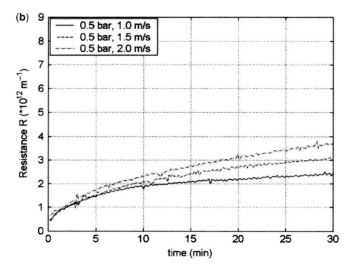

Figure 10.5b Effect of u_{cr} on the resistance increase during 30 minutes of continuous filtration of raw sewage

Direct Membrane Filtration of Wastewater

The effect of the operating conditions prevails also over the variation of feed water quality with days. When the experiments are repeated indeed results are reasonably reproducible (Figure 10.6).

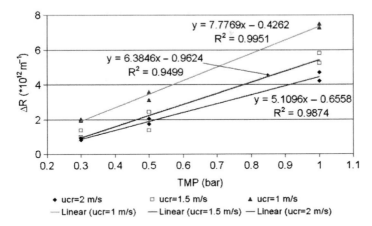

Figure 10.6 Total resistance increase during 30 minutes of continuous filtration at various TMP and u_{cr}: repeatability of results

It is important to note that the operating conditions really affect the fouling characteristics. When the resistance increase is plotted at equal filtration volume (R(vol)), it becomes visible that the same volume can be produced inducing different degrees of fouling (see Figs. 10.7a and b).

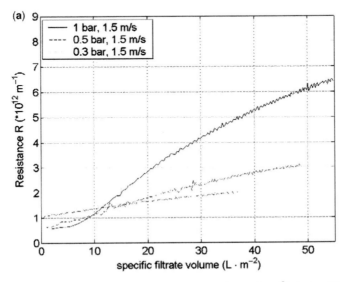

Figure 10.7a Resistance increase versus specific produced volume (L/m^2) during 30 min.: effect of TMP

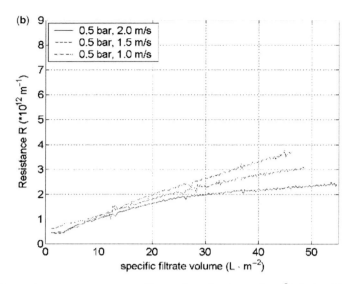

Figure 10.7b Resistance increase versus specific produced volume (L/m²) during 30 min.: effect of u_{cr}

Finally, the effect of operating conditions on fouling can be summarized in a short and very general form, that will allow (future) comparisons with systems of different geometry. Figure 10.8 shows the plot of resistance increase at fixed volume versus the shear stress at the wall (τ).

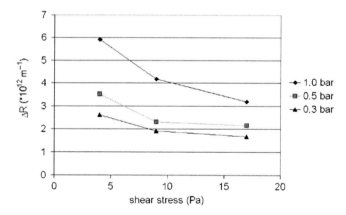

Figure 10.8 Resistance increase vs. shear stress for different applied TMP at equal filtrated volume (30 L/m²)

High TMP produces larger resistance increase. Through the shear stress, the crossflow velocity can positively counterbalance the effect of TMP. However:

(a) such positive effect becomes smaller at increasing values of τ: shifting from 4 Pa to 9 Pa, the reduction is at least two fold than shifting from 9 to 18 Pa.;
(b) the effect is bigger at higher fouling conditions, i.e. at higher applied TMP.

It can be concluded that fouling can never be completely avoided by means of crossflow velocity.

10.5.3.3 Conclusions

The observed behaviors are qualitatively in agreement with theory. The crossflow velocity helps to reduce the fouling phenomena, because:

- it increases the turbulence of the flow, enhancing back-transport phenomena;
- it produces a scouring effect on the wall of the membrane tubes (τ), thus changing the equilibrium in the deposition and removal of particles.

The effect of the applied TMP is more complex and can be explained as follows:

- from Darcy's law the flux is directly proportional to the applied TMP, therefore higher TMP results in higher starting flux J_{start};
- high starting flux enhances the transfer of material toward the membrane;
- both external and internal fouling can be increased. Higher permeation rate may enhance internal fouling because double layer rejection can be overcome, and small foulants can penetrate the membrane pores. The particles larger than the membrane pore size would instead deposit at the membrane surface, forming a superficial cake layer. Wastewater filter cakes are typically compressible, i.e. their porosity decreases with TMP and results in higher resistance to filtration. Therefore, in case of external fouling, increasing TMP has the double effect of increasing the mass of the deposit and its resistance.

From a quantitative point of view, it is surprising that the resistance increase at $\tau = 18$ Pa, at low TMP, is so close to the value at $\tau = 9$ Pa. Elmaleh and Abdelmoumni (1998) indeed advise an optimal shear stress between 20 and 30 Pa.

In contrast, the observation by Nieuwenhuijzen *et al.* (2000) appears to be confirmed, who suggested that 0.4 bar could be a limiting value for the TMP to avoid excessive cake density.

10.5.4 Compressibility of filter cake

Because of the rich solids content, it is easy to imagine that during filtration a conspicuous filter cake is formed on top of the membrane. Filter cake in wastewater filtration are rather compressible (Roorda, Boerlage), which could explain the relation between TMP and increase of resistance.

In the hypothesis that all the resistance increase is due to the cake:

$$\Delta R = \alpha_{cake} \cdot \delta_{cake} \tag{10.4}$$

where:

α_{cake} = specific cake resistance;
δ_{cake} = the thickness of the forming cake.

During dead-end filtration δ_{cake} can be easily calculated because the deposited mass of cake is proportional to the filtrated volume. In the case of crossflow filtration, it is more difficult to estimate the cake mass and calculate its thickness. However, considering the experiments at equal crossflow velocity using the same sample it is possible to formulate the hypothesis that the crossflow velocity is the dominant factor to determine the thickness of the filter cake. Therefore, in first approximation δ_{cake} is assumed to be more or less constant during those experiments.

The compressibility coefficient can be calculated as the slope of a log-log plot of ΔR vs. TMP. Results for the three tested crossfow velocities are presented in Figure 10.9. The observed slopes, however, are always above 1, which is the maximum theoretical value for the compressibility coefficient "s".

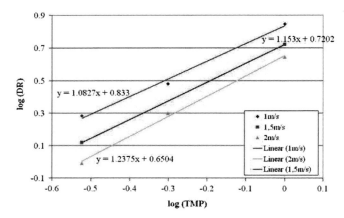

Figure 10.9 Compressibility of filter cake based on resistance increase

On one hand, this indicates that the cake is probably highly compressible. On the other hand, compressibility alone is not sufficient to explain the total increased resistance. In the absence of additional information, two explanations can be suggested:

(a) that the thickness of the filter cake δ_{cake} is not constant with u_{cr}, but increases with TMP;
(b) that fouling mechanisms other than cake filtration contribute to the total resistance increase (fouling).

10.5.5 Feasibility of constant TMP and constant flux operations

The main findings of the previous research steps can be summarized in 3 points:

(a) TMP has a very negative impact on filtration characteristics;
(b) At low TMP the resistance increase at 1.5 m/s and 2 m/s is almost equal;
(c) Not all the observed fouling can be ascribed to cake filtration.

When the aim is to extend the operations to longer filtration time, it is therefore compulsory to minimize the operating TMP. Obviously, this will reduce the permeate production, therefore a compromise should be found.

10.5.5.1 Experimental

Experiments are conducted at both constant TMP and constant flux. Constant flux operations indeed allow minimising the applied TMP at the start of filtration.

Constant TMP experiments are conducted in a cyclic way, i.e. 10 minutes filtration are alternated to 1 minute backflush. During the first tests, TMP is fixed to 0.3 bar and u_{cr} to 2 m/s; the duration is progressively extended from 1 to 7 hours. In the following experiments TMP and u_{cr} are varied in the range 0.2–0.4 bar and 1–2 m/s respectively. Also the filtration cycle is varied (see Ravazzini et al., 2005).

Constant flux tests are conducted at subcritical flux values. The flux to impose is selected on the basis of a quick critical flux (J_{cr}) measurement, effectuated extracting permeate at constant flux for minimum 20 minutes and observing the development of resistance and TMP. When they remain constant, the extracted flux is incremented of 10, 15, or 20 l/m²h and a new measurement takes place. The procedure is repeated until an increase in resistance and TMP shows that J_{cr} has been reached. Afterwards, the membrane is chemically cleaned (sometimes not) and the flux is set below J_{cr}, for a filtration test with duration between 2 and 4 hours.

10.5.5.2 Results

During few hours of operation direct ultrafiltration proved to be feasible (i.e. sustainable in time) at the applied conditions.

At constant TMP, stable operations can be maintained at $u_{cr} = 2$ and 1.5 m/s, at the cost of a limited resistance increase (R remains $<1 \times 10^{12}$ m^{-1}, see Figure 10.10a and b). In contrast, backflush appears strictly necessary.

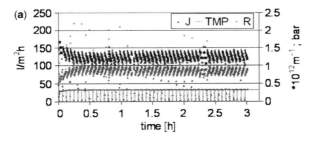

Figure 10.10a Filtration at 0.3 bar and 1.5 m/s with backflush (left, cycle 3'+18")

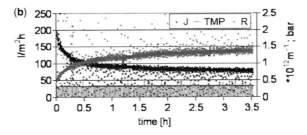

Figure 10.10b Filtration at 0.3 bar and 2 m/s without backflush (right, cycle 1'+5" idle)

The best gross-flux values are found at TMP = 0.3 bar, around 125 l/m²× h. This correspond to net-fluxes around 70 l/m²× h.

206 Handbook on Particle Separation Processes

At constant flux, it is found that operating at sub-critical flux effectively leads to stable operations. However, this is valid only when starting from a clean membrane (see Figure 10.11(a and b)). Fouling appear as "instable" process, in the sense that when "uncontrolled" fouling is started because $J > J_{cr}$ is imposed, reducing the imposed flux below J_{cr} is not sufficient to gain stable operations (as in Chen *et al.*, 1997).

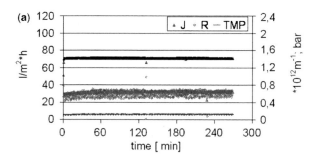

Figure 10.11a Direct ultrafiltration of raw sewage at sub-critical flux starting from a clean membrane

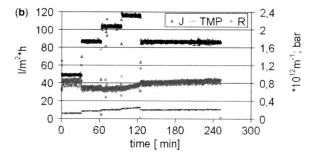

Figure 10.11b Direct ultrafiltration of raw sewage at sub-critical flux starting from a flouled membrane

Also during constant flux operations, sustainable fluxes are around 70 $l/m^2 h$.

10.5.6 Little effect of primary sedimentation

10.5.6.1 Experimental

The same constant TMP short-term tests as for raw sewage are done with primary effluent.

10.5.6.2 Results

Figure 10.12(a and b) reports the results of direct ultrafiltration of primary effluent by showing the same "summary" graphics as for raw sewage.

The resistance increase during 30 minutes of continuous filtration for primary effluent proved 20–30% smaller than for raw sewage. Nevertheless, the trends of resistance increase at equal filtrated volume show

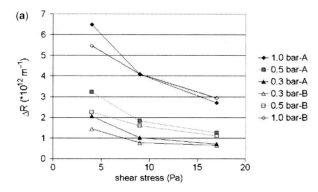

Figure 10.12a Primary effluent: increased resistance at 40 L/m² produced volume filtrating at various TMP

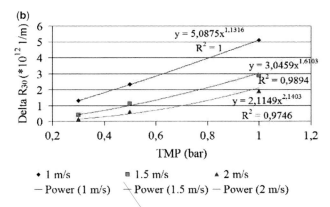

Figure 10.12b Primary effluent: corresponding calculation of cake compressibility factor

the same dependency on TMP and τ. Therefore, the same fouling mechanism seems to apply to both feed waters.

When the same calculation of the compressibility factor as for the raw sewage is done, again "s" is above 1, especially at high crossflow velocity. However, the increase is bigger for primary effluent than raw sewage. This means that the "unexplained" fraction, the one that cannot be explained with compressibility, is bigger for primary effluent and at high crossflow velocity. In other words, the lower the crossflow velocity and the higher fouling potential the feed water has, the more the compressibility of the cake layer can explain the development of Resistance with TMP.

From this observation it follows that the trend shown by "s" depends upon the efficiency of the crossflow velocity to prevent the accumulation of material on the membrane, which decreases for little filterable waters (raw sewage) and lower u_{cr}. When a low crossflow velocity is applied, similar amount of foulants reaches the membrane, independently from the applied TMP. Increasing the crossflow velocity, the quantity of material that can accumulate on the filter cake is reduced, or the kind of material is "selected". At increasingly high TMP and at low crossflow velocity the selectivity of the crossflow velocity decreases and more materials contribute to fouling, therefore the cake layer is thicker.

This hypothetical mechanism is visualized in Figure 10.13. The mechanism is based on the presence of large particles, which are more abundant in the raw sewage and are more easily removed at high crossflow. On the left, large particles shield the cake layer from the scouring effect of u_{cr}, favouring the accumulation of material. On the right, the smaller particle size distribution of the accumulated material result in a thinner and more dense cake, which is less compressible and even allows small foulants to reach the membrane pores.

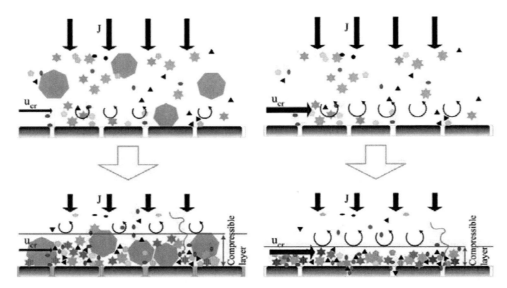

Figure 10.13 Hypothesis to explain the observed fouling dependency on TMP, u_{cr} and feed water characteristics

10.5.7 Little effect of coagulant dosage

The effect of metallic coagulants and high molecular weight cationic polymers are investigated. The batch tests simulate in-line dosing, in the sense that the entire coagulated suspension is conveyed to membrane filtration, and not the supernatant only. Coagulants are supposed to exert two mechanisms:

(a) floc formation should increase particle size and favour transport away from the membrane with crossflow velocity
(b) flocs should alter the amount and the characteristics of the cake layer, forming a kind of protective layer on the membrane and enhancing the reversibility of fouling.

10.5.7.1 Experimental

The effect of coagulants dosage is investigated with two kind of experiments executed at TMP = 0.3 bar, u_{cr} =2 m/s.

The first kind is batch filtration tests of 30 minutes similar to the ones of raw sewage and primary effluent, meant to evaluate filterability.

The second kind is a cyclic filtration test with duration of 2 hours. The cycle is 10' filtration, 30" backflush, which should be too short to attain stable operations. In this way, reversibility can be evaluated with the series of additional resistance increase after each backflush.

Chemical analyses of bulk parameters (COD and TOC) and potential foulants (proteins, polysaccharides, humic substances and colour) are used to support the interpretation of results.

The applied coagulants and dosages are reported in Table 10.2. The range is chosen comparable to the values applied in enhanced primary sedimentation.

Table 10.2 Coagulant dosages during ultrafiltration tests

Coagulant	FeCl3	PACl	C-592, cytec®	Mix
Dosage (mg/L)*	6–12	2–4	4–8	3 (PACl) + 0-0.5-1 (C-592)

*= for Metallic coagulants, concentration is in mg (Me^{3+})/L.

10.5.7.2 Results

From the analyses on the raw water and the supernatant, it is found that at the applied dosages the coagulants capacity to remove TOC and potential foulants is little. Nevertheless, filterability is increased substantially (see Figure 10.14).

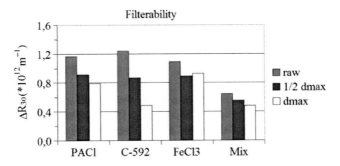

Figure 10.14 Resistance increase and coagulant dosages

When the reversibility is considered, surprisingly it is found that normally after 2 hours of filtration the coagulated and non coagulated feed water produce the same resistance increase (see Figure 10.15). Only coagulation with PACl seems to lead to a little increase in reversibility.

The explanation is found looking at the concentration of foulants in the permeate. Although in the supernatant prior to filtration coagulants addition produced little removal, the values in the permeate are more often the same. Sometimes the values in the permeate of the membrane (30 nm) are even found higher than in the 0.45 μm filtrate of the supernatant. One explanation is that during recirculation flocs break down and release the foulants that have previously entrapped.

In any case, the applied coagulant dosages did not enhance the reversibility, and therefore did not actively protected the membrane from fouling.

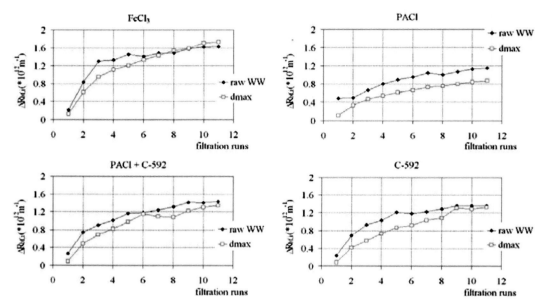

Figure 10.15 Reversibility of raw wastewater vs. coagulated water

10.6 COSTS

Given the little influence of pre-treatments the cost of water production with direct UF are calculated for the sustainable operating conditions obtained municipal wastewater. The scenario is the extraction of water from an existing sewer main for irrigation purposes, i.e. 75% of the total volume is extracted as permeate and the waste is returned to the sewer.

Assuming a chemical cleaning of the membranes every two weeks and the actual prices in the Dutch market, the overall cost of water production is found below 0.30 eurocent/m^3. This price is comparable with the cost of wastewater treatment and therefore it could be appealing in case of water scarcity.

10.7 CONCLUSIONS

In the frame of the worldwide interest for the development of novel applications for membrane processes, the concept of direct ultrafiltration of wastewater with crossflow tubular membrane has been explored.

The application has great potential with regard to water recycling and sanitation, especially because being a purely physical process it can produce water on demand starting from normal municipal wastewater. The main applications could be irrigation and advanced pre-treatments, especially for the production of high quality water with dense membranes and nutrients recovery.

The research at TU-Delft has shown that the process is technically feasible, with sustainable fluxes in the order 70-80 l/m^{2}h. This makes the application virtually economically reasonable. The cost of water extraction is indeed estimated below 0.30 eurocents/m^3.

The application should be evaluated further at larger pilot scale for continuous operation. Meanwhile, a deeper analyses of the permeate characteristics should be carried on, to evaluate in details treatment and reuse path.

It must be remarked that the application of simple pre-treatment, such as sedimentation and flocculation, does not affect significantly neither fouling formation nor permeate quality, and therefore appears useless.

10.8 REFERENCES

Abdessemed D., Nezzal G. (2002), Treatment of primary effluent by coagulation-adsorption-ultrafiltration for reuse, *Desalination*, **152**, pp. 367–373.

Ahn, K.H., K.-G. Song, I.T.-Yeom and K.Y. Park (2001), Performance comparison of direct membrane separation and membrane bioreactor for domestic wastewater treatment and reuse. *Wat. Sci. Tech.: Water Supply*, **1**(5-6), pp. 315–323

Ahn, K.H., Ji-Hyeon Song and Ho-Young Cha (1998), Application of tubular Ceramic Membranes for Reuse of Wastewater from Buildings, *Wat. Sci. Tech.*, **38**(4-5), pp. 373–382.

Ahn, K.H., Kyung-Guen Song (2000), Application of Microfiltration with a novel fouling control method for reuse of wastewater from a large-scale resort complex, *Desalination*, **129**, pp. 207–216.

Ahn, K.H., Kyung-Guen Song (1999), Treatment of domestic wastewater using microfiltration for reuse of wastewater, *Desalination*, **126**, pp. 7–14.

Bixio, D, B. De Heyder, H. Cikurel, M. Muston, V. Miska, D. Joksimovic, A.I. Schäfer, A.M. Ravazzini, A. Aharoni, D. Savic and C. Thoeye (2004), Municipal Wastewater Reclamation: where do we stand? An Overview of Treatment Technology and Management Practice, *Water Supply*, **5** (1), pp. 77–85.

Butler R., MacCormick T. (1995), Opportunities for decentralized treatment, sewer mining and effluent re-use, *Desalination*, **106**, pp. 273–283.

Johnson G., Culkin B., Stowell L. (2004), *Membrane Filtration of Manure Wastewater* www.vsep.com/downloads "Manure Slurry Filtration".

Nieuwenhuijzen, A.F., van H. Evenblij and J.H.J.M. van der Graaf (2000), Direct wastewater membrane filtration for advanced particle removal from raw wastewater. In: *Proceedings of the 9th Gothenburg Symposium*, October 2-4, Istanbul, Turkey.

Ramon G., Green M., Semiat R. and Dosoretz C. (2004), Low strength graywater characterization and treatment by direct membrane filtration. *Desalination*, **170**, pp. 241–250

Ravazzini, A.M., A.F. van Nieuwenhuijzen and J.H.M.J. van der Graaf (2004), Direct Ultrafiltration of Municipal Wastewater: comparison between filtration of Raw Sewage and Primary Clarifier Effluent, In: *Proceedings of Membranes in Drinking and Industrial Water Production (MDIW)*, 14–17 November 2004, L'Aquila, Italy

Ravazzini, A.M., A.F. van Nieuwenhuijzen and J.H.M.J. van der Graaf (2005), Towards sustainable operations via low fouling conditions. In: *Proceedings of Particle Separation*, 2–5 June 2005, Seoul, Korea.

Sethi S. and Juby G. (2002), Microfiltration of primary effluent for clarification and microbial removal, *Envir. Eng. Sci.*, **19**(6), pp. 467–475.

Wintgens, T., T. Melin, A. Schäfer, S. Khan, M. Muston, D. Bixio, C. Thoeye (2005), The role of membrane processes in municipal wastewater reclamation and reuse. In: *Proceedings of Integrated Concepts in Water Recycling (ICWR) 2005*, 14-17 February 2005, Wollongong, NSW, Australia.

X.-D. Hao, H.-H. Li and X.-Q. Cao (2005), Reuse of wastewater for irrigation after pathogens and viruses trapped with membranes, In: *Proceedings IWA conference Singapore*, July 200.